Diplomacy and Intelligence during the Second World War

F. H. HINSLEY

Portrait by Michael Noakes in
St John's College, Cambridge

Diplomacy and Intelligence during the Second World War

Essays in honour of
F. H. HINSLEY

Edited by

RICHARD LANGHORNE
Fellow of St John's College, Cambridge

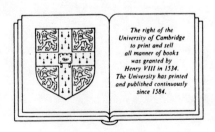

The right of the
University of Cambridge
to print and sell
all manner of books
was granted by
Henry VIII in 1534.
The University has printed
and published continuously
since 1584.

CAMBRIDGE UNIVERSITY PRESS

Cambridge
London   New York   New Rochelle
Melbourne   Sydney

PUBLISHED BY THE PRESS SYNDICATE OF THE UNIVERSITY OF CAMBRIDGE
The Pitt Building, Trumpington Street, Cambridge, United Kingdom

CAMBRIDGE UNIVERSITY PRESS
The Edinburgh Building, Cambridge CB2 2RU, UK
40 West 20th Street, New York NY 10011–4211, USA
477 Williamstown Road, Port Melbourne, VIC 3207, Australia
Ruiz de Alarcón 13, 28014 Madrid, Spain
Dock House, The Waterfront, Cape Town 8001, South Africa

http://www.cambridge.org

First published 1985
Reprinted 1987
First paperback edition 2003

A catalogue record for this book is available from the British Library

Library of Congress catalogue card number: 84-17040

ISBN 0 521 26840 0 hardback
ISBN 0 521 52197 1 paperback

Contents

v

Contributors

C. M. Andrew *Fellow of Corpus Christi College, Cambridge*

D. G. Boadle *Lecturer in History, Riverina College of Advanced Education, Wagga Wagga, New South Wales*

R. J. B. Bosworth *Assistant Professor of History, University of Sydney*

A. E. Campbell *Professor of History, University of Birmingham*

R. T. B. Langhorne *Fellow of St John's College, Cambridge*

S. Lawlor *Fellow of Churchill College, Cambridge*

B. A. Lee *Associate Professor of History, Harvard University*

D. Reynolds *Fellow of Christ's College, Cambridge*

P. Salmon *Lecturer in History, University of Newcastle upon Tyne*

D. Smyth *College Lecturer in History, University College, Cork*

J. Steinberg *Fellow of Trinity Hall, Cambridge*

M. C. Wheeler *Lecturer in History, School of Slavonic and East European Studies, University of London*

R. Zweig *Senior Lecturer in the Department of Jewish History, Tel Aviv University*

Abbreviations used in chapters 6, 10 and 11 are on pages 282, 303, 307.

Part I

1

Introduction

RICHARD LANGHORNE

(i)

Harry Hinsley is now the Master of St John's College, Cambridge, and in 1981–3 was Vice-Chancellor of the University of Cambridge. The circumstances in which his journey to the Vice-Chancellorship began marked the second occasion in his career when electors preferred to make sure of having him rather than follow the dictates of established custom. He was the first Vice-Chancellor of Cambridge in modern times to have been nominated before having actually entered office as the Head of a College. His election into a Fellowship of St John's College was similarly unusual, since he was at the time a third year undergraduate and had taken no degree. This event, which took place in 1944, was at least partly the result of wartime conditions. He had come up to St John's in 1937 as an Exhibitioner – he became a Scholar in 1939 – from Queen Mary's Grammar School, Walsall. His background was a poor one and the school helped him financially by supplementing his Exhibition from the College. Even so, his circumstances as an undergraduate were extremely difficult. His success, however, was marked by a First Class in Part One of the Historical Tripos in 1938, and neither this, nor his habit of working his way round Europe during the Long Vacations were lost on the Master and the Dean of his College. Both recommended him when particularly intelligent young men were being sought for war service. He returned to St John's in the autumn of 1939 to begin his third year, and, having written one essay, found himself recruited into the British Intelligence Service for the rest of the war. How this happened and what it was like at Bletchley Park is described in Christopher Andrew's contribution to this volume. His third year was thus never completed, and, having by then been elected into a Fellowship, he eventually took a degree under the special regulations introduced by the University for those called away on war service.

His Fellowship was for research, since the College was anxious to fill the gaps in academic work which the war was causing as quickly as possible, and a few others were elected into Fellowships in other subjects at the same time. Such was the pent up demand for teaching after the war, however, that when he returned in 1946, it was not to any ivory tower but to a punishing teaching load. In 1949, he was elected to a University Lectureship in History. He became Reader in the History of International Relations in 1967 and a personal chair followed in the same subject in 1969. Eminence in the Faculty was followed by elevation in the College. In 1977 he was elected President of St John's, and in 1979, was elected Master and moved, with perhaps a touch of resignation, from his family home of many years at The Grove in Newnham, and from the great chamber in the Shrewsbury Tower in St John's Second Court, into the Master's Lodge. There, a large part of the former kitchen wing having been turned into a library, the official history of British Intelligence during the Second World War is hammered out and steadily emerges volume by volume.

This collection of essays is a present from some of his former pupils to Harry Hinsley on the occasion of his retirement as Professor of the History of International Relations at Cambridge. The number of contributors and the fact that they are now to be found working in so many countries gives an indication of how significant a research school in the history of international relations has developed at Cambridge. It is, however, as the contributors to this volume would be the first to recognise, only the tip of the iceberg. From the early 1960s the number of research students attached to Harry Hinsley began to grow, until by the late 1960s he was carrying a load which few other men would have allowed to happen, let alone, as he gave every sign of doing, actually enjoyed. Only a few of the contributors to this volume worked with Harry Hinsley in those years, and it should be said at the outset that there already exists another tribute to him from his students of that generation, but which could not be so called because he himself was its editor. During the late 1950s and 1960s, because of the operation of the then fifty-year rule, there was a great concentration of work upon the papers which were gradually emerging on British foreign policy and the outbreak of the First World War. In the late 1970s that work was collected, revised and published by the Cambridge University Press under the title *British Foreign Policy under Sir Edward Grey* (1977), and has subsequently been widely accepted as a definitive work. All those who worked under his supervision and then under his editorship would wish to use the publication of the present volume as an opportunity to express their gratitude and admiration to him, even though many could not be invited to contribute to it.

It would have been impossible to include contributions from all who wished to make them simply on grounds of size. As it is, this is a long book. It would also have been impossible because of the need to give to collections of this character a unifying theme, and there was no doubt from the response which the initial enquiry received that the clearest unifying theme which emerged was that of British diplomacy and intelligence during the Second World War period. Inevitably and sadly that left out those who would have written on general and theoretical questions, themselves so much an interest of Harry Hinsley himself, those who would have written on earlier periods, particularly on the nineteenth and early twentieth centuries, and those who had an interest in the First World War and the Versailles settlement. The contributors to this volume therefore hope that they will only be the first to honour Harry Hinsley in this way.

(ii)

To be supervised by Harry Hinsley was a unique experience. A supervision with him was apt to be remarkable just as a physical fact. It was sometimes difficult to decide whether pupil and supervisor were more endangered from what appeared to be an imminent collapse of the surrounding piles of books – probably awaiting review in the *Historical Journal* – or from fire, arising from many matches inadequately dowsed in ashtrays full of spent tobacco. It was evident, too, that he had other commitments: to the administration of the University, for example, whose functionaries needed and were willingly given his time on the telephone, and to his College, both at an administrative and a tutorial level. Harry Hinsley did not share the craze for confidentiality which came to mark so much of 'student relations' in the 1970s, and many will remember with delight his refreshing habit of dealing with many wholly different problems, tutorial and academic, apparently almost simultaneously and certainly in front of what might have become a considerable audience. The Editor has never forgotten the tantalising glimpse given by a conversation never to be concluded when Hinsley the Tutor was interrupted before he could receive the answer to the question 'and what happened, my boy, *after* you set fire to the factory?' The point of this, however, is that no one in that situation was ever in any doubt that Harry Hinsley's whole attention was on them and their problem, whatever the surrounding distractions. And if this was so in the brief encounter in his crowded room when calling to make an appointment, how much more was it so when actually engaged in the discussion of draft chapters, or the quotidien problems of research. The combination of enthusiasm, quite extraordinary reserves of energy and a virtually faultless memory, all of which must have been stretched to the full during the years when he had over twenty research students, never failed to give inspiration. Whatever the problem, whatever the level of discussion, early stages or nearly completed final draft dissertation, no one left him without feeling reinspired, convinced of the importance of his work and certain of its having been given the most sympathetic, but also the most rigorous examination. The final admonition was and is delivered in that familiar, absolutely individual growl, 'keep cheerful, and don't let the work get you down'. At that moment being cast down never seemed remotely possible but the admonition told you that he understood how frighteningly lonely the essential independence of research could be. The essential independence of research was something not only sympathised with but also honoured. There was never pressure to come for frequent supervision, but instead the growing realisation on the part of the student that it was always possible to see him quickly and that any work handed in would be read with uncanny speed and commented on with great insight. And it should be said that these characteristics have remained with him despite the overwhelming obligations of the headship of a large College and the vice-chancellorship of the University of Cambridge.

The number of Harry Hinsley's research students increased greatly in the very late 1960s, and this enabled him to establish his own seminar in international history, held in his vast yet crowded room which occupied the whole first floor in the Shrewsbury Tower in the Second Court of St John's College, and subsequently in the Master's Lodge. Not only was the seminar practically useful once the number of students interested in international history had grown so large, it also found its place as part of a new atmosphere which that period generated in the University's attitude to graduate students in arts subjects. If there was a contemporary tendency to feel ignored and under helped – which no student of Harry Hinsley's could or did feel – this was the kind of enterprise which could meet the problem. The seminar became famous. Gently and often amusingly directed from behind clouds of pipe smoke, current research students could try out their latest interpretations of their material, describe what archives they had found, visitors from abroad – an increasingly common phenomenon – could be cajoled into presenting their own latest topics and existing teaching historians in Cambridge could from time to time be induced to talk to the seminar about their own research. The sessions could often be exhilarating and provided at once a sense of companionship and a sense of the broad scope which the history of international relations offers and which was represented by the wide range of subjects being studied under Harry Hinsley's direction. This breadth did not provide any apparent difficulties for Harry Hinsley himself, nor any constraints upon the life of the seminar. The reason is touched on by Jonathan Steinberg in his contribution to this volume. He comments on the fact that Harry Hinsley did not, because of the war, come into academic life possessing the usual research experience in terms of method, but he did come with a formidable experience in analysis. This was reflected in the way he reacted to the work of his pupils, or to the papers presented at the seminar. He did not primarily react to the archival problems, or to the methodological problems, though both could and did engage his careful attention, he reacted to the wider implications of what had been discovered or reassessed; and he would comment rapidly, almost electrically, on the true significance of what he had just heard or read. It was these flashes of illumination which made supervision by him or attendance at his seminar so memorable and so valuable.

(iii)

The contributions to this book divide into four sections. The first, including this introduction, is principally concerned with Harry Hinsley himself: his role as a supervisor of research, his published work, which is reviewed by Jonathan Steinberg and his recruitment into the wartime intelligence service. This last is discussed by Christopher Andrew in the context of an account which contrasts recruitment from Cambridge into both the Russian and British intelligence services. The second section includes three widely differing aspects of pre Second World War international politics. Bradford Lee reconsiders the relationship between strategy, available resources and the competence of commanders as applied to the collapse of France in 1940 and the defence policies which had dominated the ten years preceding it. He uses models drawn from the situation of NATO in more recent years to breathe new life into what has been a long running and sterile argument. He has also been able to make use of newly released archives in Paris which have served to underline the financial and political considerations affecting French policy. Only after stability was restored to the franc in 1938 could serious rearmament begin, and rapid as it then turned out to be, it was too late to sustain French strategy when the ultimate test came.

Donald Boadle looks at the reign of Sir Robert Vansittart at the Foreign Office. He notes that Vansittart has not been thought of as a notable administrator of the Foreign Office, and indeed was apt to slide away from awkward projects for innovations by pleading pressure of work created by the turbulent international politics of the period. But in the interests of spreading his gospel of the danger emanating from Germany, he did undertake significant internal reorganisation and redeployment, particularly designed to put policy towards Germany in the hands of officials who shared his views. The result was to create two poles of opinion within the Office, which by 1936 were so antagonistic as to make it easier for the Cabinet to follow the strong lead given by Chamberlain. At the inter-departmental level, and particularly perhaps in relation to the Services, Vansittart's unwillingness to follow a consistent path of reform and cooperation, and his attempt, insufficiently supported, to establish an economic relations section within the Foreign Office, led to jealousy and frustration, and to the emergence of a feeling among officials and ministers that he was erratic and unreliable. As his reputation suffered, so did that of the Foreign Office itself.

If Vansittart's attempts to maintain both the independence and the 'amateur' traditions of the Foreign Office represent the survival of one set of older ideas into new circumstances, Richard Bosworth's treatment of Italian fascism in historiography discusses it in another way. He shows how Italian historians responded to the highly traditional and expansion-ary elements in Italian policy while Mussolini was in power, rather than to the nature of the regime itself. Because of this, they were able to dismiss the regime and their role in it as easily as Mussolini was himself disposed of, and believed the slate to have been wiped clean. The consequence was that after the war there was no distinct break in the Italian historical tradition, nor any serious intellectual pressure upon the Republic to become a new kind of regime, stimulating new approaches to the problems of post-war Italy.

The third and largest section of this book contains contributions which all deal with aspects of the way Churchill and the War Cabinet handled the earlier stages of the Second World War. Ronald Zweig discusses the quixotic effects that misinterpreted military intelligence can have. The example is Palestine, where the local political administration tried to convince the Cabinet of the danger posed by semi-secret Jewish organisa-tions equipped with hidden supplies of arms. Their intelligence reports sent to London suggested alarmingly high quantities of arms – higher than was probable. The intended effect was to stimulate a policy of searches and confiscation, but the actual result was to convince the Cabinet that such a policy was too dangerous to pursue. Churchill's favourable stance towards the Jewish position in Palestine certainly helped, but it is plain that the decision of the Cabinet in 1943 to alter the anti-immigration policy laid down in a 1939 White Paper was affected by a particular interpretation given to military intelligence.

Even more difficult questions of interpretation, this time of a political kind, are discussed in Denis Smyth's account of the problem faced by the Cabinet in deciding how to deal with the conflicting embarrassments caused by the presence in Britain of the last Prime Minister of Republican

Spain, Juan Negrín. The Franco regime protested warmly and frequently about Negrín's presence in England, and alleged that he was engaged in political activities, which he equally warmly denied. This pressure gave great anxiety to both the Foreign Secretary, Halifax, and to the ambassador at Madrid, Hoare, who were engaged in trying to prevent Spain from joining the Axis, following the fall of France. They argued strongly for Negrín's preferably voluntary departure from Britain. To what extent Franco's attitude would actually be affected by ejecting Negrín was uncertain, and Attlee, supported by other Labour ministers, protested forcefully against putting any pressure on him to leave. They not only had a natural sympathy for Negrín's past and present position, but were also concerned that both at home and in occupied Europe Britain's resistance should be seen to arise from a profound, even revolutionary, vision of a new and more fairly organised society which would be created in Europe after the war. No such crusade was compatible with the voluntary or compulsory departure of Negrín, even for the sake of helping to keep Spain out of the war. The disagreement was sharp, and surfaced embarrassingly in Parliament despite the pressures of the war. The result was that Negrín's asylum was maintained for the comparatively short period which elapsed before the question was rendered largely irrelevant by Franco's neutralist policy and by Labour's acquiescence in the failure of Britain's stand to develop into a 'people's war'.

David Reynolds also deals with the agonising period following the defeat of France. He discusses the decision not to pursue peace negotiations but to fight on, describing it in practical rather than the romantic terms to be found in Churchill's own account. Churchill himself is shown to have had private doubts, and was in any case compelled to be sensitive to the views of Halifax and Chamberlain, both still powerful figures in the Cabinet. As time went on, the successful evacuation from Dunkirk seemed to give resistance a better chance, and by the end of 1940 both Halifax and Chamberlain had retired from the scene, thus removing potential opposition. Churchill's stance then became quite definite. But it is shown to have been based on wrong assessments of intelligence. He believed both that the Americans would join the war quickly when the Presidential election of November 1940 was over, and that, in any case, there was a strong likelihood of being able to defeat Germany by blockade and heavy bombing without embarking on a military campaign across continental Europe, which Britain alone could not have initiated or sustained. Far better but unexpected arguments were provided by Hitler himself when he decided to invade Russia in 1941.

It is British attitudes and strategic assessments in respect of the consequent Anglo-Russian alliance which are discussed by Sheila Lawlor.

Churchill's disposition, despite the emotional tone of his letters to Stalin, was to offer minimum help to the Russians despite their persistent demands for increased assistance. In this he was supported by the generals, who tended to regard their new ally with contempt. But, in the Cabinet, Eden immediately became the protagonist of the Russian cause, wanting more supplies sent to Russia and the opening of military operations in the West. He also wanted an early middle eastern offensive, as a means of boosting Russian morale, as well as being in support of British interests. Sheila Lawlor concludes from her discussion of these early British reactions to Russia's position as an ally that the problematic decisions which dominated the last years of the war had their origins in this very early stage.

Problems caused by the Russian alliance emerge, too, in Mark Wheeler's discussion of the process by which the British government secured recognition of each other by both Tito's partisan movement in Yugoslavia and King Peter's government in exile. The complications involved were enormous, but the stakes were high: the goal was to create the best possible chance that by adding the loyalty of the Serbs to Tito's movement, which the British believed the King could deliver, Tito might be prevented from falling into total reliance on the Russians. To achieve mutual recognition, pressure had to be brought upon the King and his ministers, as well as a very delicate handling of Tito himself. But the most striking achievement was the correct assessment which the British, particularly Churchill himself, made of the strength of Tito's movement and the certainty which they felt that in some form or other he would rule in post-war Yugoslavia. How to respond to that realisation, and, in particular, how to safeguard the future of the King, provoked disagreements between Churchill and Eden which had to be resolved. Mutual concessions by the Prime Minister and the Foreign Office, long and frustrating negotiations with Tito and the King, a German assault on Tito's Drvar headquarters, an unaccustomed American intervention and the inexorable advance of the Red Army finally brought forth a result: the Tito–Šubašič agreement of June 1944. It was not an agreement that was likely to last, and it did not. But there was no doubt that the British had done as much as they could both for King Peter and to relieve Russian pressure on Yugoslavia. Nor, in the end, was their belief that Tito would prefer to avoid complete dependence upon Russia wrong.

A. E. Campbell looks at one of the consequences of American entry into the war when it did come: the doctrine of unconditional surrender. There has been much controversy surrounding both the origins and effects of President Roosevelt's statement at Casablanca, but this discussion points to the conclusion that it was made principally to reassure American domestic opinion at a time when it was uncertain as to the wisdom of having dealings with men such as Admiral Darlan, or diverting military operations to North Africa at all. As to the consequences, A. E. Campbell's conclusions are radical. He thinks that closer investigation suggests that whether the idea had found expression at Casablanca or not, other attitudes and policies of the allied powers would in any case have compelled the total defeat of· Germany. Nor does it appear that the campaign in Italy could have been shortened by any retreat from the doctrine, since the Italians were not able to be genuine parties to negotiations had they been on offer. The true significance of the American position was the clear illustration that it gave of the difference between the United States and the other allies: only the Americans had no secondary war aims which might be forwarded by adopting one method of defeating Germany rather than another. Their only interest in Europe was the rapid and complete defeat of the Nazi regime.

The last section of this book concerns an aspect of the post-war period and is given to Patrick Salmon's discussion of the invasion of Norway, as it was dealt with at the Nuremberg Tribunal. The trials of Admiral Raeder and Alfred Rosenberg included the charge of waging aggressive war against Norway. The particular case of Norway suggested two possible defences, both of which were of great concern to the prosecution. One was that the German invasion was essentially defensive or preventive. This was a defence used by Raeder's not wholly effective defence counsel, and, although it was given little chance of success because the British government effectively resisted attempts to gain access to the relevant papers, Patrick Salmon concludes, after examining them, that such a defence could not have been successful. The second possible defence was that of *tu quoque*, and throughout the trials it was in general resisted by both prosecution and the Tribunal alike. It was, however, successful in the trial of Admiral Doenitz for naval war crimes. Had more British documents been available, the prosecution might have had more difficulty than it did in preventing the tribunal from considering the weight of the *tu quoque* defence in the particular case of Norway. Patrick Salmon concludes that the verdict of guilty was not unjust, but that aspects of the management of the Norway trial certainly were.

2

F. H. Hinsley and a rational world order: an essay in bibliography

JONATHAN STEINBERG

In November, 1947, F. H. Hinsley, then a recently appointed research fellow of St John's College, Cambridge, published his first historical writing. It was a review of Donald W. Mitchell, *History of the Modern American Navy* in the second number of the *Cambridge Journal*. Since that time he has written almost without interruption. He is the author of four substantial books, co-author of another, editor of two large collections of studies, one in the *New Cambridge Modern History* series and one on foreign policy under Sir Edward Grey, and has latterly been the principal author of the official history of British Intelligence during the Second World War. Throughout this span of time he has – with a brief interruption in the later years of his career – been a busy reviewer of the works of others. There is scarcely an important book on international relations, war, peace, armies, navies or diplomacy published in English in the last three and a half decades that Hinsley has not reviewed. He has also published several important articles and public lectures.

A review of this considerable body of written work must start by noting two unusual features. The first is that Hinsley has never done conventional research. He has not even produced the inevitable Ph.D., off which in subsequent years ordinary historians slice bits to make articles. Hinsley never did a Ph.D. for the same reason that he never took his B.A. because the Second World War occupied him from 1939 to 1947. Hinsley's undergraduate and graduate schools were corridors of power, places in which the silent war against Hitler was waged, a war fought by the use of intelligence in the narrow and broad senses of the word.

The second peculiarity of Hinsley's written work follows in part from the first: its extraordinary consistency of what the Italians call *impostazione*, that is, the location of his mind and interests. From first to last Hinsley has asked the same sort of question and dealt with the same issues. The scope of his work may be likened to a great loop. The loop begins and ends with intense and extremely meticulous reflection on Hitler's war, his strategy and the means used by the allies to defeat him. The arc of the loop took Hinsley into the questions of war and peace in more general terms, into the theoretical analysis of the international system and finally in 1966 to the publication of *Sovereignty*, in my view his most original and at the same time his most theoretical work. The casual reader of the Hinsley of the mid-1960s would not easily have discerned the author of *Hitler's Strategy* in discussions of Grotius and Kant.

Theoretician and practitioner were never, however, as far apart as our casual reader might think. Not only was the *impostazione* constant but certain features of Hinsley's thought remain constant too. The most important of these is Hinsley's rationalism. At no stage, not in his early work on Hitler nor in his most recent work on British intelligence, has he seen politics, even the politics of Adolf Hitler, as other than a rational pursuit, an activity in which governments and statesmen calculate advantage and disadvantage. They may get the sums wrong but they always try.

Even nationalism, says Hinsley, is more than mere romanticism. Nationalism is a conscious attachment, a form of loyalty which thinking persons adopt:

Nationalism has been defined as that state of mind in which the political loyalty is felt to be owed to the nation. This definition has its short-comings. Before we turn to them we should note that it has one great virtue.

It does not assume that, when nationalism comes to exist where it has not existed before, it does so because men have discovered a political loyalty which they previously lacked. On the contrary, it implies that men have then transferred to the nation the political loyalty which they previously gave to some other structure – that what has changed is not the quality of this loyalty but the object on which it is showered or the vehicle through which it is expressed. And all the evidence is in favour of this implication. (*Nationalism* (1973), p. 11)

Nationalism is, then, a conscious state of mind in which rational beings think about their world. Nor are they wrong to do so, for, as Hinsley shows in *Nationalism and The International System*, their ideas correspond to reality. There is a stage in the evolution of the modern state in which it is plausible to transfer loyalties from smaller or larger entities, the village, the tribe, the church or the empire, to the rising nation-state.

Hinsley's rationalism stands out most markedly in his treatment of Hitler. At no point from his first writings to his last has Hinsley seen Hitler as other than a fundamentally rational actor. In his brilliant demolition of A. J. P. Taylor's *The Origins of the Second World War* (1961) which first appeared in *The Historical Journal* and later in *Power and the Pursuit of Peace* as Chapter 15, he makes this point quite explicitly:

It is for these reasons that it must be regretted that Mr Taylor's analysis of these crises is insulated not only from all regard for the policy of the man who almost wholly caused them on one level but also, as was established earlier, from all recollection of the extreme international unbalance that was the chief cause for them on the other. It is only when the crises are studied in this, their proper, context that it emerges to what a large extent Hitler was responsible, and to what a small extent the conditions or the conduct of other men, for the outbreak of the second World War.

Both factors were involved. The unbalance was in a sense the cause of Hitler's policy. If it had not existed and if he had not known that it existed he would not have seen so continuously a 'chance of winning' so much. Because he knew it existed he remained confident until the summer of 1939 that he would achieve his aims without war and was thus content in each crisis, as Mr Taylor never tires of telling us, to wait for the opportunity of doing so. The unbalance was in a sense the cause of the war. Because Hitler's policy succeeded in the reoccupation of the Rhineland, in the Anschluss, in the Munich crisis, in the occupation of Prague, he could feel that it would go on succeeding. Because the unbalance was so great it was not easy for other Powers to convince him that it would not. The unbalance was so much the cause of Hitler's policy that anyone else in power in Germany might have had a policy similar to Hitler's at least in its objects. It was so much the cause of war that, while it was practically impossible for other Powers to resist Germany's revisionist attitude up to and including the Munich crisis, and equally impossible that they should not resist it if it were persisted in much beyond that point, it set up the danger that it would be so persisted in. (*Power and the Pursuit of Peace* (1963), p. 332)

It is essential to Hinsley's approach that Hitler be seen as rational for Hinsley argues in all of his work that until very recently war was not an irrational activity. There was always a balance of gain and loss to be considered. When that balance tilted towards gain, statesmen were not acting irrationally to go to war. In an essay in 1966, he summed up this point of view:

Now in such a situation we should not find it surprising that during the past hundred years, when the underlying developments have thus given rise to increasing incentives to the resort to war as well as to increasing deterrents against it, the incentives to war have continued to be stronger from time to time than the restraints – that the old belief in the profitability of war has continued to be more powerful, at least at intervals, than the new reluctance to unleash warfare's increasingly formidable and dangerous tools. ('Reflections on the History of International Relations' (1966), p. 27)

With rationalism goes a pervasive universalism. For Hinsley human nature has been a constant throughout history. Circumstances and problems have altered but the human mind and spirit have not. Hence he has no methodological or philosophical difficulty in talking about the ancient world as he talks about the modern. His prose is rich in universal statements, such as 'for all men at all times, there has been no choice but to belong to a political community' (*Nationalism*, p. 11) or 'Men will often in history have debated and quarrelled about who should rule, and by what right' (*Sovereignty* (1966), p. 27). The quarrel and the terms in which it was stated cause Hinsley no difficulty. His work has been unaffected by all the fashionable 'isms' of the last three decades. He writes of a past which he sees as unproblematically 'out there' and reads texts which yield unambiguous meanings.

Hinsley is also an optimist. Unlike Gibbon who saw history as no more than the 'register of the crimes, follies and misfortunes of mankind', Hinsley sees solid progress in spite of the horrors of our own age. His optimism is most marked where others despair, precisely in the area of war and peace. For Hinsley the most encouraging feature of what he calls the 'modern system of international relations' is the capacity to make peace. In the Arthur Yencken Memorial Lecture of 1980, he made the point this way:

The surest and the most telling guide to the character of an international system is to be found, I suppose, in its pattern of peace and war. If only by this test – though I shall later mention another which yields the same result – the modern international system came into existence at the end of the eighteenth century. Since that time the pattern of peace and war between the more advanced societies has exhibited two prominent features; it lacked them before that date. One of them has been a rigorous alternation between long periods of peace and briefer bouts of war. From the 1760s to the 1790s these societies were at peace; from the 1790s to 1815 they were at war; from 1815 to 1854, peace; from 1854 to 1871, war; from 1871 to 1914, peace; from 1914 to 1918, war; from 1918 to 1939, peace, from 1939 to 1946, war; and since 1945 they have again been at peace for 35 years already. The second modern feature has been no less pronounced. When war has occurred between the more advanced societies it has been fought on a greater scale at a higher level of violence, and it has carried with it a greater trail of destruction, than on every earlier occasion. (*The Fall and Rise of the Modern International System* (1980), p. 1)

It is, paradoxically, the second element which gives Hinsley the grounds for his optimism. In the conclusion of the Martin Wight Lecture delivered at the University of Sussex in May, 1981, he put it this way:

The modern international system collapsed on those occasions because states continued to hold the view that they had the legal right to go to war. It also collapsed because states holding this view were confronted with massive shifts in their relative power which persuaded them in the last resort that war was a reasonable means of defending or advancing their interests. States hold this view no longer, and in the wake of the great acceleration of scientific and technological development that has taken place in the last forty years and that has ensured that even conventional war between developed states would produce insupportable damage, they are unlikely ever again to make this judgment. Indeed, they are unlikely, such of them as have been caught up in this acceleration, to be confronted ever again with shifts in their relative power that will disturb the equilibrium between them. That shifts of power will continue to take place – this goes without saying, as does the fact that interests will continue to conflict. But these states have passed so far beyond a threshold of absolute power that changes in relative power can no longer erode their ability to uphold the equilibrium which resides in the ability of each to destroy all.

Such are the grounds for suggesting that we are now witnessing the formation of an international system which will be even more different from the modern system than that system was from all its precursors, and which will be so because its leading states will abstain from war with each other. ('The Rise and Fall of the Modern International System' (1982), p. 8)

Nothing could be less fashionable than Hinsley's rationalist optimism. The majority of his fellow students of international affairs take the opposite position. To them, and even to me, after many years of exposure to Hinsley's ideas, such optimism is startling. Yet it grows out of the same *impostazione* which gives Hinsley's work its characteristic unity. Rationalism, universalism, optimism and a belief in progress were, after all, the features of the enlightenment of the eighteenth century, and I do not think it is absurd to see Hinsley in the tradition he himself has so often expounded, the rational enquiries of men like Vattel and Hume. In the appendix to the Yencken Lecture, along with the charters of the League of Nations and the U.N., Hinsley published an essay by Hume on the balance of power written in 1752. Hume asks the same sort of question, and almost in the same tone of voice as Hinsley. For Hume it is why the ancients had not arrived at the modern idea of balance of power; for Hinsley in *Sovereignty* it is why they had not arrived at the full notion of sovereignty. For both, the universal application of reason to the affairs of mankind is so evident that it needs little emphasis. As Hume writes,

In short, the maxim of preserving the balance of power is founded so much on common sense and obvious reasoning, that it is impossible that it could altogether have escaped antiquity where we find, in other particulars, so many marks of deep penetration and discernment. If it was not so generally known and acknowledged as at present, it had at least an influence on the wiser and more experienced princes and politicians. And indeed, even at present, however generally known and acknowledged among speculative reasoners, it has not, in practice, an authority much more extensive among those who govern the world. (*The Fall and Rise* (1980), p. 76)

If Hinsley shocks us because he starts from premises more fashionable in the eighteenth century than in the present, he does so too because his style demands it. Hinsley's prose, both written and spoken, is dialectical. Causes and consequences come in antithetical pairs. Assertions meet and are contradicted by their negations, negatives cancelled by subsequent negatives. This style of writing has also been constant from the start. In one of his first substantial pieces of writing, *The Naval Side of British History*, in which Hinsley completed a work begun by Sir Geoffrey Callender, he writes of the Ten Year Rule,

This rule was perhaps the most successful system ever devised to hamstring the security of an Empire. Its effects were all pervading and they were cumulative. (*The Naval Side of British History* (1952), p. 293)

Or in *Hitler's Strategy* (1951);

Politics and diplomacy are apt to proceed by way of negative assumptions when these can profitably be made, and to shun positive assertions when these would be embarrassing . . . (*Hitler's Strategy* (1951), p. 8)

Or in *Sovereignty* (1966);

It was on this account, because circumstances were producing both the desire for greater powers on the part of the Crown and the possibility of more effective resistance on the part of the community, that there took place from the thirteenth century in the more developed societies a rapid development of constitutional procedures and ideas. (*Sovereignty*, p. 91.)

These are not mere tricks of style. Hinsley sees the clash of opposites as an essential causal element in the unfolding of historical processes. Societies move from simple to complex. Economic and technical change alters their structures and relations to other states. Statesmen react to such changes. There is a counterpoint of changed reality leading to changed activity.

The difficulty is to capture this ceaseless motion in prose. Take the following example from *Nationalism*:

We shall also be working with the definition which enables us to explain why it is that it is just when the national political loyalty is most extreme that it is ceasing to be national. That is the fact that, as we shall see later, it is then that it is moving from the national into another of the states – the tribal, the imperial – between which political loyalty may easily oscillate. (*Nationalism*, p. 23)

A close look at the passage shows that there are seven verbs 'to be' in a row and that four of them are attached to ideas of change or motion:

> 'is just when'
> 'is ceasing'
> 'is then'
> 'is moving'

This rather extreme example of Hinsley's technique tells us a good deal about what he is trying to do. The verb 'to be' functions in two ways at once. It marks the fact that one proposition equals another but, by attaching words of time or motion, Hinsley conveys the shifting realities of the real world.

All historical work contains statements about the past and statements which assert the existence of the past. The process might be likened to that of a geologist looking at a rock. He may be puzzled by the strange configurations on it and wonder at the possible causes, now remote and ultimately unrecoverable. The one thing he will not worry about is the reality of the rock. The historian, on the other hand, must first evoke a past which the reader cannot hold in his hand and then using the same tools – words – analyse a past reality also composed of words. Hinsley's technique is to use dialectical opposition and the verb 'to be' plus the participle or adverb of time. The two features give his prose a curiously wrought texture, as if the reader were undoing sets of complex Chinese boxes. The style, then, reinforces his general approach and is its reflection. History is manifestly a form of rational enquiry in which the historian deciphers the clues left by the unfolding of a past which, until it has become thought, is not yet history. In this respect too Hinsley's approach has been astonishingly consistent, whether in Bletchley as the master of decoding or as the historian who picks up the clues to the codes of thought or action left us by our ancestors.

Reality, then, requires deep thought to understand, but if we are tenacious enough, we shall in the end understand it. The sum of the actions and passions of human beings makes a pattern. As he writes of the international level of such actions, 'it is, after all, a system, and however unbalanced it may be it will respond to unbearable pressure in the end' (*Power and The Pursuit of Peace*, p. 333). Patterns and systems, actions and reactions, create a coherent flow of events, which must be seized, however contradictory they may seem, precisely in their contradictoriness.

Immanuel Kant becomes for Hinsley the intellectual model and inspiration, Kant's thought shines in all of Hinsley's theoretical work. As he puts it at the end of his Martin Wight lecture of 1981,

let me conclude by reminding you that Immanuel Kant, he who first foresaw that precisely such a system would one day materialize, allowed that it would remain subject to constant danger from 'the law-evading bellicose propensities in man' but judged that, once constructed, it would survive for that very reason.

In mentioning Kant, I am prompted to confess that Martin Wight might well have dissented from some of my conclusions; indeed, he might even have disagreed with me about Kant. Dividing into realists and idealists the men who have reflected to our great profit on the nature of international relations, he placed Kant among the idealists, whereas I regard Kant as having been a realist writing much in advance of his time. But he shared my admiration for Kant, and I feel sure that he would have approved of my suggestion that what we learn from the history of the modern international system bears some resemblance to what Kant expected it to teach us. ('The Rise and Fall', p. 8)

Kant functions in this way for Hinsley because Kant's subtle analysis of the state of nature among the states making up the international community depends on the dialectical or paradoxical way of looking at things which Hinsley finds congenial. In a fine chapter in *Power and The Pursuit of*

Peace, Hinsley works out the implications for our age of Kant's insight that the only way to overcome the existence of the sovereign state was by the very spread, multiplication and development of that sovereignty. The interaction of war and the situation of the sovereign state would, Kant believed, necessarily lead both to the evolution of more rational and freer institutions within each state and also to a gradual establishment of those grounds of common interest which alone could lead to lasting peace. At the end of his chapter on Kant, Hinsley quotes at length from Kant's *Perpetual Peace*:

It is the desire of every state (or of its ruler) to enter into a permanent state of peace by ruling if possible the entire world. But nature has decreed otherwise. Nature employs two means to keep people from being mixed and to differentiate them, the differences of *language* and of *religion*. These differences occasion the inclination towards mutual hatred and the excuse for war; yet at the same time they lead, as culture increases and men gradually come closer together, towards a greater agreement on principles of peace and understanding. Such peace and understanding is not brought about . . . by a weakening of all other forces (as it would under the aforementioned despotism and its graveyard of freedom) but by balancing these forces in lively competition . . . In this way nature guarantees perpetual peace by the mechanism of human inclinations. (*Power and the Pursuit of Peace*, pp. 78–9)

Kant and Hinsley urge upon us a view not unlike that of the 'invisible hand' of classical economics. Just as the market by its operations converts the selfish pursuit of individual advantage into the equation of supply and demand where the maximum is produced at the lowest price, so the competition of sovereign states leads in the end to a higher harmony in which competition limits itself.

This is an odd way of looking at the nuclear balance of terror but not unpersuasive. What Kant thought commerce and competition might achieve, Hinsley would argue, has been achieved by technology. Because we can destroy ourselves, we shall not do so. That is the message of Kantian optimism that emerges from a reading of Hinsley's theoretical works on the international system.

Rational actors remain the key to its operation. As in the classical model of perfect competition, so in the Hinsley model of the international system, the actors must be rational. If the buyers and sellers in the classical market model cease for one moment to maximise profit and to calculate gain and loss, the model seizes up. If the rulers of powerful states place ideological or religious purity above the risks of nuclear fall-out, our world seizes up.

Hinsley tells us that it won't happen but he does so as an act of faith, not reason. Because war no longer makes sense, states (or more accurately great powers) will no longer make them. It seems a flimsy barrier to keep us from Armageddon. Hinsley's view of international history neglects those manifest acts of barbarism and irrationality which do not fit the model. Hitler may have behaved rationally in the years of appeasement but he was not rational when he ignored Soviet dissidents like General Vlasov or wasted precious troops and material at the end of the war in the extermination of European Jews. There is a wisdom at least as old as rationalism which predicts that those whom the Gods wish to destroy they first make mad.

Hinsley's vision is an attractive one, for it requires of us no great flights of fancy. We need not imagine that human beings will suddenly become much better than we have reason to expect them to be, nor must we place any hope in the ramshackle structures of new federalisms of one sort or another. Hinsley teaches us that the sovereign state, in all its imperfection, indeed by the very nature of its imperfection, will in the end work out a system of rational relations with other sovereign states that will preserve the peace.

Paradox and irony are not just matters of taste or thought; they form part of an intractable reality in which, unlike most academics, Hinsley had a hard schooling. It is appropriate to close the loop by considering a passage in *British Intelligence in the Second World War*. In volume 1, Hinsley describes the way in which the *Bismarck* and several other German ships were located and sunk in June and July of 1941. An important part of these successes was the British ability to decode messages sent by the German Enigma cypher machine. The Admiralty had become nervous that its success might paradoxically force the Germans to the view that the Enigma was not completely secure and hence deprive Great Britain of one of its most important weapons. Here is how Hinsley concludes this section:

In the event, as we shall see, Germany's suspicions were, for a variety of reasons, deflected away from concern for the naval Enigma. Ironically, the reasons included the conviction that the Enigma was impregnable. No less ironically, this conviction was sustained by Germany's own intelligence sources. On 21 May, for example, the day after the British Naval Attaché in Stockholm had reported the *Bismarck*'s movement out of the Baltic, the head of the German Abwehr had informed the Naval High Command (OKM) that he had positive proof that the Admiralty had received such a report. Had OKM been more attentive, the opportunity to sink the *Bismarck* would not have arisen but, the more so since it knew that the *Bismarck* had been sighted at Bergen, it could account for her loss without resort to fears for the Enigma. Had the Admiralty known of these German tendencies it might have been somewhat relieved, but it would still have had to take every possible precaution to conceal a precious asset in the struggle against the U-boats – the fact that the Enigma was at last being read currently (*British Intelligence*, I, p. 346)

Few historians have been actors in the great events which they describe, but those that were – Tocqueville, Clausewitz, Clarendon – can give to their histories an authenticity which no mere observer, contemporary or not, can equal. Hinsley's work unites great event and observation in a unique combination. His peculiar graduate school taught him lessons about power, peace and reality which make his writing unusual among students of international relations and ensure him and his thought a special place in the affection and regard of all those who want to see a more peaceful world.

3

F. H. Hinsley and the Cambridge moles: two patterns of intelligence recruitment

CHRISTOPHER ANDREW

Cambridge University occupies a remarkable place in the modern history of both the British and the Russian intelligence communities. It has produced a long line of British intelligence officers from Christopher Marlowe, the first in a series of British secret agents who have achieved literary success, to Sir Colin Figures, the present head of the Secret Intelligence Service (SIS or MI6). That distinguished line includes Professor Harry Hinsley, who was recruited as a wartime cryptanalyst in Bletchley Park while still an undergraduate. But Cambridge has also provided a smaller number of able recruits to the KGB. When the KGB approached Kim Philby he 'did not hesitate'. 'One does not look twice', he writes snobbishly, 'at an offer of enrolment in an elite force.'[1] Remarkably, the KGB began its recruiting in inter-war Cambridge several years before British Intelligence.

I

Sympathy for the Soviet Union in Cambridge has always been limited. But it was much less restricted in the early 1930s than in the immediate aftermath of the Bolshevik Revolution. That greater sympathy had more to do with events in Britain than with events in Russia. What Philby considered 'the real turning-point' in his own political development came, as for many other left-wing intellectuals, with 'the demoralisation and rout of the Labour Party in 1931'. The great 'betrayal' of Ramsay MacDonald's National Government in August 1931 was followed by Labour's humiliation in the general election two months later. To Philby:

It seemed incredible that the party should be so helpless against the reserve strength which reaction could mobilise in time of crisis. More important still, the fact that a supposedly sophisticated electorate had been stampeded by the cynical propa-

22

ganda of the day threw serious doubt on the validity of the assumptions underlying parliamentary democracy as a whole.[2]

While Labour had lost its way in the Depression, Russia was in the middle of the great economic transformation of the first Five Year Plan. Even Fabian intellectuals were impressed. Hitherto the apostles of the 'inevitability of gradualness', they now began to have doubts about even the 'practicability of gradualness'. It would be 'an ironic development', wrote Beatrice Webb in December 1931, 'if the highly respectable Fabian Society – the Upper Chamber of the Labour and Socialist Movement – becomes the protagonist of Soviet Communism in Great Britain . . .' During 1932 that is what seemed to be happening. Beatrice Webb observed in March: 'What little intellect there is, be it noted, is in the Fabian Society and is swinging towards Soviet Communism – to the horror of continental Socialists.'[3]

The first undergraduate cells of Cambridge Communists were founded in the summer of 1931. By 1933 the Cambridge University Socialist Society was dominated by Communists, among them Philby, Burgess and Maclean. The *Granta* rightly saw little 'likelihood of Cambridge rivalling some of the continental Universities in political ardour and enthusiasm'.[4] A majority of Cambridge undergraduates remained Conservative or apolitical. But among the minority of activists the initiative had moved sharply to the Left. A writer in the *Cambridge Review* noted in January 1934:

Political activity in the older universities during the last few years has been largely confined to Socialists and, to an increasing degree, to Communists. Liberal clubs are defunct or moribund in both universities, and though there are numerically strong Conservative clubs, they are not politically very active, i.e., they are not keen propagandist bodies . . . The Russian experiment has roused very great interest within the universities. It is felt to be bold and constructive, and youth, which is always impatient of the cautious delays and obstruction of its elders, is disposed to regard sympathetically (often irrespective of political opinion) this attempt to found a new social and economic order.[5]

The Soviet sympathies of many British left-wing intellectuals offered Comintern new opportunities. Its Western European Bureau, revivified in the early thirties by the Bulgarian Georgi Dimitrov, aimed at expanding its intelligence network in Britain as well as winning public support. Comintern front organisations on the continent such as the League Against Imperialism already possessed a secret intelligence apparatus whose agents reported in code to cover addresses.[6] The majority of Comintern's member parties were forced to live a 'totally illegal' existence; Comintern encouraged the remainder to combine 'open and illegal work'.[7] Ernst Schneller, who recruited Arthur Koestler as a Comintern agent early in

1932 was one of a number of Comintern recruiters who engaged in both; he was simultaneously head of the KPD Agitprop section and head of an intelligence *apparat*.[8]

When the Cambridge moles took their first tentative steps in intelligence work they regarded themselves as working for Comintern rather than the KGB. When Guy Burgess set out to recruit others or boasted drunkenly to an unbelieving audience in the Reform Club about his undercover work he described himself as a Comintern rather than as a Soviet Agent.[9] Comintern had not yet visibly succumbed to the all-Russian blight which later deadened its appeal. Clever and attractive Central Europeans gave it a cosmopolitan identity far more alluring than the crude Stalinism which engulfed the KGB.

The centrepiece of both Comintern's public propaganda and its secret intelligence recruitment was anti-Fascism. During the anti-Communist witch-hunt which followed the Reichstag fire on 27 February 1933 Willi Münzenberg, Comintern's most successful organiser of Front organisations (or, as he called them, 'Innocents' Clubs'), was forced to move his headquarters from Berlin to Paris. There he founded in June 1933 the most influential of the 'Innocents' Clubs', the 'World Committee for the Relief of the Victims of German Fascism'. In August the Committee published in seventeen languages the *Brown Book of the Hitler Terror and the Burning of the Reichstag*. Koestler, who had been drafted by Comintern Intelligence to the Committee headquarters in Paris claimed, rather too enthusiastically, that because of its success in pinning the blame for the Reichstag fire on the Nazis, the *Brown Book* had 'probably the strongest political impact of any pamphlet since Tom Paine's *Common Sense*': 'It became the bible of the anti-Fascist crusade.' The evidence on which it was based – 'isolated scraps of information, deduction, guesswork, and brazen bluff' – was supplied by the Comintern Intelligence *apparat*.[10]

Münzenberg's most spectacular stunt took place in England. On 14 September 1933 a Committee of Inquiry into the Origins of the Reichstag Fire, composed of distinguished lawyers assembled by Münzenberg and his assistant Otto Katz, was opened in the London courtroom of the Law Society by Sir Stafford Cripps. On 20 September the Committee declared the Communists innocent and the Nazis guilty. When the real trial opened at Leipzig immediately afterwards, the German prosecution was forced to spend much of its time attempting to rebut the Committee's findings.[11]

While Münzenberg and Katz were organising a spectacular propaganda coup in London, other Comintern agents were prospecting for British members of the Intelligence *apparat*. The Comintern agent most interested in undergraduate recruits was probably Semyon Nikolayevich Rostovsky alias Ernst Henri, then operating under cover as a Soviet journalist in London. Henri remained convinced throughout his long and varied career of the need to 'stop underestimating the revolutionary moods and powers of the youth': 'For nearly two centuries bourgeois society has really feared only the working class. It now finds it has to fear another force – young people who until recently were ordered to listen and do as they are told.' Writing in 1982 Henri criticised 'both Right and Left extremists' for playing on the emotions of 'susceptible' students. In 1933 he himself played with some success on the same emotions.[12]

Henri's message to British anti-Fascist intellectuals was both simplistic and persuasive. After Hitler's conquest of power in 1933, he told them, they had a stark choice between Berlin and Moscow: 'In the modern world, torn between [these] gigantic opposing forces and on the verge of its final transformation, there is no such thing as political and social impartiality; nor can there be.'[13] It was sheer liberal escapism to look for a middle way. In private meetings with sympathisers, Henri put the same point more personally, 'You English', he would say, 'are such liberal do-gooders.'[14] The decent values of liberal democracy were thus plausibly portrayed as the private face of the public policy of appeasement.

The only hope for the future, Henri argued, was an anti-Fascist crusade under Communist leadership. Leading that crusade, he claimed, were the German *Fünfergruppen* – groups or rings of five. The phrase 'Ring (or 'Group') of Five' was to haunt MI5 for a generation. It was used by the Soviet *rezident* in the Netherlands, Walter Krivitsky, after his flight to the West on the eve of the Second World War, as well as by post-war Soviet defectors and in intercepted Soviet communications, to describe a dangerous group of Soviet moles at work in England.[15] The first step in the making of the Cambridge moles was probably Guy Burgess's decision in 1933 to join Comintern's secret war against the growth of Fascism and form a ring of five.

The idea of the group of five arrived in Cambridge quite openly – in a series of articles by Ernst Henri in the *New Statesman* on 'The Revolutionary Movement in Germany'. The first of these articles appeared on 5 August 1933 under the title 'The Groups of Five ("Fünfergruppen")':

There is perhaps no other example in history of a secret revolutionary movement with a completely equipped organisation and an effective influence extending over the whole country being able to develop in so short a time. Its core lies in the so-called *revolutionary groups of five*, a novel form of anti-Fascist organisation, which, under Communist leadership, has taken the place of the former party unions and associations . . . Together these persons form a small, compact, secret brotherhood, who in their hatred of the Hitler dictatorship and in defence against Nazi terror have become completely amalgamated, have buried all previous differences and pursue only one policy – anti-Fascism. Because each group of this kind is limited to just a few persons, it is almost invisible from outside and almost unseizable. . .

Henri's eulogy of the groups of five was wildly exaggerated. The *Fünfergruppen* offered little serious resistance to the Nazi dictatorship. The KPD, formerly the strongest Communist party outside Russia, was now, in Koestler's phrase, 'a castrated giant'.[16] But Henri's romantic account of groups of five engaged in a secret war against Fascism struck so deep a chord in the *New Statesman* staff and at least some of its readers, that they suspended their disbelief. The editor, Kingsley Martin, assured his readers that Henri's 'facts' were 'not open to question'.[17]

Henri's *New Statesman* articles reappeared, much expanded, in March 1934 as a book entitled *Hitler Over Europe?* twice reprinted over the next few months. There is little doubt about the influence of Henri's ideas on Guy Burgess and his friends. *Hitler Over Europe?* was reviewed in the *New Statesman* by Brian Howard, one of the closest and probably the most sinister, of all Burgess's friends.[18] Like Burgess, Howard was an Old Etonian Marxist homosexual with even more predatory instincts than Guy himself. Evelyn Waugh, who met Howard at Oxford, called him – quoting Lady Caroline Lamb on Byron – 'mad, bad and dangerous to know', and made him one of the models for the mincing figure of Ambrose Silk in *Put Out More Flags*. As a BBC producer, Burgess was later to arrange talks by Howard on the Home Service.[19]

Howard combined his 1934 review of Henri's book with a brief and abusive onslaught on Goering's *Germany Reborn*. 'Such enormous pots', he declared, 'cannot be allowed to call any kettle black.' Howard next paused briefly to defend the homosexual in public life: 'We do not agree with the common view that because a man's private life is of a kind usually frowned upon this necessarily unfits him for public service. History denies it.' He then launched on a eulogy of *Hitler Over Europe?* as 'probably the best work on the Third Reich that has appeared in English': 'Ernst Henri's book should be read at once by everyone who is seriously interested in understanding the real bases of Hitlerism . . . It discloses, for the first time, the dynamics of the Nazi movement.' Howard went on to endorse Henri's analysis of 'the celebrated Revolutionary Groups of Five' and ended with a rallying cry to English anti-Fascists to 'band themselves together' without delay.[20]

Burgess had already heeded the call. Inspired by Henri's romantic vision of the secret war against Fascism, he set out to form what one of those who knew him later called his own 'light blue ring of five'.[21] As a student of the Russian past and an able historian whom the Regius Professor, G. M. Trevelyan, thought to have the potential for a Cambridge Fellowship,

Burgess cannot fail to have been alive to the historical resonance of Henri's eulogy of the Group of Five. The first group of five had been founded in 1869 by the student revolutionary Sergei Nechaev whom Dostoyevsky made the model for Peter Verkhovensky in *The Devils*. While Dostoyevsky saw Nechaev as a psychopath, the conspirators of the People's Will regarded him with veneration as the embodiment of revolutionary courage and dedication.[22]

Philby, who graduated in the summer of 1933, spent the next year in Vienna where he married the Austrian Communist 'Litzi' Friedmann. It was probably in Vienna that he entered the Comintern Intelligence *apparat*. He wrote ominously to his father early in 1934, 'The ideal would be for people of extreme views to keep them dark from everyone, their own families included.'[23] But while Philby began his KGB career as a loner, Burgess set out to form a conspiracy of Cambridge friends. The 'light blue ring of five' into which Burgess drew Maclean and Blunt began as a curious mixture of undergraduate prank and heady idealism. None of the Cambridge moles had any idea at first of the seriousness of the secret world they had entered. All, in varying degrees, were influenced by the romantic vision of an underground anti-Fascist crusade suggested by words and images such as those of Auden: 'To hunger, work illegally and be anonymous.' To Burgess in particular there was the additional appeal of a hilarious undergraduate spree. For some time none of the Cambridge moles had any state secrets to betray, merely gossip to retail. Not until they were actually inside the 'bourgeois apparatus' did they discover the enormous tensions they would have to endure.

Though the KGB recruiting drive in Cambridge began with Burgess's 'light blue ring of five', subsequent patterns of Oxbridge recruitment varied. All the Soviet moles, however, began by becoming members of secret Communist cells rather than open members of the Communist party. Those, like Burgess, who were open Communists before being drawn into intelligence work had to go through the public charade of breaking off all contact with the party. By no means all the secret Oxbridge Communists became Soviet moles. One of those who refused to be drawn into the Comintern intelligence network was Jenifer Hart, now Fellow of St Anne's College, Oxford. She became a secret Communist on graduating from Oxford in 1935, 'quite excited by the idea of doing something secret,' but without any thought of 'working for Russia'. Her story, however, provides further evidence of the way in which Russian Intelligence sought (unsuccessfully in her case) to turn secret Communists in positions of influence into Soviet moles.

Mrs Hart applied to join the Communist Party in 1935 as an ordinary member. She was told that, since she hoped later to enter the civil service, she must become a secret member in order to be of most 'use' to the Party. She vaguely envisaged giving the Communist Party information about such matters as the bugging of its King Street headquarters, though in the event she did not do so. Her first controller was an Oxford friend. Her second was a British Communist. The third was a 'rather sinister' Central European who never revealed his name. There is little doubt (though it did not occur to Mrs Hart at the time) that he was also a Soviet control.

The Central European arranged his meetings with Mrs Hart with elaborate secrecy, changing taxis en route to destinations such as Kew Gardens. He explained that for ten years she 'wasn't to do anything' except progress up the civil service hierarchy, and he provided rather crude Stalinist briefings on international politics. After a few such meetings Mrs Hart 'felt rather uneasy about the whole thing and a faint sense of dishonesty'. Disillusioned by the Purges as well as by her control, she broke all contact with him in 1938.[24]

Like Jenifer Hart, the American Michael Straight – a secret Communist party member recruited by Blunt at Cambridge – was also disillusioned by the crudity of his Soviet control, 'Mr Green', who at each meeting after his return to the United States 'would raise some theoretical point and deliver a fifteen-minute monologue.' Mr Straight found the monologues 'very dull and very uninteresting': 'He very soon sank to asking me did I know where he could find a job, since he wanted a cover job, and did I know where he could buy a car cheap?'[25]

The leading Cambridge moles received much more sophisticated treatment. The resident Director of the Russian Intelligence Service in Britain and forwarding agent to Moscow Centre was Samuel Kahan, who worked under diplomatic cover at the Soviet embassy. According to a writer with extensive 'inside information' from MI5 sources, Kahan appointed first the Austrian Comintern agent Theodore Maly and then the Russian Yuri Modin as case-officer for both Burgess and Philby.[26] Ernst Henri was also an important member of Kahan's network. Though probably not a formal control or case-officer, he appears to have played a major role both in initiating Burgess and others into Comintern intelligence and in overcoming their ideological doubts as they found themselves gradually transformed from anti-Fascist conspirators into fully-fledged Soviet agents. Those doubts were considerable. Even to Philby, probably the most determined of the moles, 'it became clear that much was going badly wrong in the Soviet Union'. But he was persuaded 'to stick it out, in the confident faith that the principles of the Revolution would outlive the aberration of individuals, however enormous'.[27]

Ernst Henri was almost ideally equipped to provide such reassurance. He was the very antithesis of the crude Stalinists encountered by Jenifer

Hart and Michael Straight. Edith Cobbett, who worked with Henri on *Soviet News* at the end of the Second World War without realising he was an intelligence officer, found him exhilarating company and 'really a charismatic personality'. Indeed, he sometimes appeared to shock other Soviet officials in London by his disdain for their neo-Victorian morality, and the vulgar aesthetics of Socialist Realism. Though a deeply patriotic Russian and committed Communist, he was an ardent admirer of Matisse and other forbidden artists, dressed in well-made English suits, and was addicted to Westerns. He was, complained one Soviet journalist, 'not a Soviet man as I am'.[28]

It was typical of Henri's unconventional flair that on one occasion he even managed to broadcast a message of reassurance to the moles. Early in 1942, using his cover as a Soviet journalist in London, he broadcast over the BBC news from the Eastern Front. The Red Army would be victorious, he told his listeners, because 'they fight for the people, for their motherland and for the people's rule'. Then Henri had a special message for the moles. The Soviet Union, he told them over the air, had 'an intelligence service which is among the best in the world'. Even the Gestapo was powerless against it. (So, by implication, was MI5.)[29] It is no coincidence that one of the most influential members of the BBC's talks department at the time of Henri's remarkable broadcast was Guy Burgess. Though the BBC's records are incomplete, it is highly probable that Burgess arranged Henri's talk just as he commissioned talks by other Marxist friends like Brian Howard and Anthony Blunt.

When Burgess and Maclean fled to Moscow in 1951, Henri was recalled as well. But while the British moles received a hero's welcome, Henri was sent straight to a labour camp. His unorthodox views had been tolerated by the KGB as long as they helped to reassure Cambridge moles upset by Stalinist excesses. But in 1951 he suddenly became expendable.

Henri emerged from labour camp after Stalin's death in 1953 and resumed contact with Burgess and Maclean. For the next twenty years, as an influential member of the Soviet Writers Union, Henri was active in several campaigns against the revival of Stalinism which brought him into contact with leading dissidents. He collaborated for a time in writing on nuclear disarmament with the since persecuted Soviet physicist Andrei Sakharov. Though now in his late seventies, Henri still moves on the fringe of dissident circles today. But leading dissidents now realise that, despite his chequered past and unconventional tastes (still reflected in, for example, his large library of English detective stories), Henri remains a senior, if genial, KGB officer. His role among Soviet dissidents today is curiously similar to his role among Cambridge moles in the Thirties: to use his unconventional charm to try to contain dissidence within officially tolerable limits. With some dissidents Henri has succeeded. With others, like Sakharov, he has failed.[30]

The Cambridge and public school origins of the leading moles go some way to explaining their success as Soviet agents. Despite its diminutive size, MI5, with Special Branch assistance, kept some areas of Communist and Comintern activity during the 1930s under close surveillance. The Communist Party's King Street headquarters were bugged, and the Glading case in 1938 demonstrated MI5's efficiency in monitoring Soviet military espionage. But no watch at all was kept on Cambridge. Had Burgess, Philby and Maclean come from humbler backgrounds their doubtful early records would scarcely have been so easily dismissed as youthful indiscretions. At his interview before joining the Foreign Office Maclean was asked, 'We understand that you, like other young men, held strong Communist views while you were at Cambridge. Do you still hold those views?' Maclean replied, 'Yes, I did have such views – and I haven't entirely shaken them off.' Instead of causing apprehension, Maclean's reply seems to have been admired for its honesty.[31] Once in the Foreign Office his intelligence and social assurance quickly disarmed his colleagues. The personnel department wrote to Sir Eric Phipps, the ambassador in France, in March 1938 warmly recommending Maclean for the post of third secretary:

Maclean, who is the son of the late Sir Donald Maclean, whom you may remember as a Liberal Member of Parliament, has done extremely well during his first two years here and is one of the mainstays of the Western Department. He is a very nice individual indeed and has plenty of brains and keenness. He is, too, nice-looking and ought, we think, to be a success in Paris from the social as well as the work point of view.[32]

Burgess's background at Eton and Trinity, combined with his considerable though less conventional charm, was also felt by many to compensate for his undergraduate Communism and frequently outrageous behaviour. Less than a year after joining the BBC as a producer, Burgess successfully persuaded the deputy head of political intelligence (Section I) in SIS, David Footman, to give a broadcast talk on Albania.[33] Footman was blithely unaware that his producer was a Soviet agent. He was later probably partly instrumental in arranging Burgess's entry into Section D of SIS where he served from 1938 to 1940. Though Philby's Communism had been better concealed at Cambridge than that of Burgess and Maclean, his background was quite sufficient in itself to establish him as a potential security risk. In 1932 the Foreign Office received evidence that Philby's father, to whom Kim was greatly attached, had stolen secret documents while serving as Chief British Representative in Transjordan and given them to King Ibn Saud. That evidence seems never to have been properly investigated.[34] The evidence of Blunt's past Communist associations was likewise treated remarkably casually. Late in 1939 Blunt was expelled from a military intelligence training course after those associations were discovered. A few months later, however, he was accepted by MI5.[35] But Blunt's Communist past remained such common knowledge even after he joined MI5 that Burgess, when suggesting broadcasts by Blunt on Soviet Art in 1941, felt obliged to circulate a memorandum within the BBC denying that Blunt was now a Communist. No doubt seeking to divert attention away from Blunt, he added mischievously: 'Christopher Hill (a Fellow of All Souls) is a Communist . . .'[36]

Ironically, one of Burgess's friends, the writer Cyril Connolly, wrote to the *New Statesman* in 1940, to complain that, despite widespread 'spy-mania', a public school and Oxbridge background were widely and quite improperly regarded as a sufficient evidence in themselves of reliable patriotism. He had, he said, been briefly detained on suspicion of eaves-dropping on the conversation of a group of army officers in an Oxford hotel. Their suspicions deepened when he was discovered to be a writer with a Irish name and a British passport issued in Vienna, but were rapidly defused as soon as he mentioned his education: 'It then transpired I had been at Oxford – and at Eton. "Eton", the officer was incredulous. "What house?" The atmosphere became more cordial, and soon after the Forces left.' Connolly had been considerably put out to be detained on suspicion of espionage but was even more indignant at the reasons for his release: 'The most sinister point was the importance attached to my having been at Eton . . . The Old School Tie should count for nothing.'[37]

II

During the 1930s Cambridge aroused less interest from SIS than from the KGB. SIS was small and underfinanced with only about twenty officers at its headquarters in Broadway Buildings opposite St James' Park tube station. It depended for its occasional recruits on personal contacts and recommendations. The retired SIS 'master-spy', Sir Paul Dukes, wrote an article in 1938 entitled 'The Secret Service: Can It Be Called A Career?'[38] The answer, he explained, was in the negative:

. . . that this form of service should ever be regarded in the light of a separate 'career' indicates a misapprehension about it at the outset . . . In whatever way a young man may envisage his activities as a possible member of the secret service, he must not imagine it as a 'career' and must not look upon this service as a 'department'.

Dukes poured scorn on the idea that 'some particular course of study' was relevant to a career in SIS, or that Britain possessed – or needed – a secret service training school like that of the KGB. New entrants to SIS during the thirties did indeed discover that, after basic instruction in communication and accounts, they were left to their own devices. When Leslie Nicholson joined SIS in 1930 he was assured that 'there was no need for expert knowledge'. When he asked a senior SIS station chief for 'tips on *how* to be a spy', he was told 'you'll just have to work it out for yourself'.[39]

Like most officers in the inter-war SIS, Sir Paul Dukes was a convinced supporter of the amateur tradition. The qualities required for secret service work were, he declared, 'judgement, discretion, tact, ingenuity and daring':

But these qualities are not acquired in any secret service training establishment. They are bred first in school and university life, in form room and lecture room, on cricket and football grounds, in the boxing ring, at the chess table, in debating clubs, in a thoughtful approach to the problems of the day that beset mankind, in studious observation of your fellows, and above all in your study of yourself.

Job opportunities in SIS, wrote Dukes, came 'fortuitously without preparation', and often 'without anticipation', and were usually filled by officers or ex-officers from the armed services. But Dukes was wrong to suggest that SIS saw 'university life', as opposed to public school life, as valuable experience for its recruits. According to Lord Dacre, a wartime recruit to SIS, its pre-war leadership preferred its officers to have minds 'untainted by the solvent force of a university education'. Colonel (later Sir) Claude Dansey, who became Assistant Chief of the wartime SIS, let it be known before the war that he 'would never knowingly recruit a university man'.[40] His experience of wartime graduate recruits did little to change his mind. Dansey wrote in 1945: 'I have less fear of Bolshies and Fascists than I have of some pedantic but vocal University Professor.'[41]

Like SIS, MI5 was badly run down during the inter-war period and filled most of its occasional vacancies with men from a military background. Major-General Sir Vernon Kell, head of MI5 from 1909 to 1940, recruited his first recent graduate, DickWhite, the future head of both MI5 and SIS, in 1935. After graduating from Christ Church, Oxford, White had gone on to the Universities of Michigan and California, and thence briefly to schoolteaching. Kell recruited White specifically to build up German contacts and sent him to spend a year in Germany before he officially joined MI5 in 1936.[42] White was later to take perhaps the leading part in tracking down Kim Philby and other moles. Had SIS and MI5 not allowed the KGB a head start in their Oxbridge recruitment, the moles would surely have found the penetration of the Foreign Office and the intelligence community more difficult than they did.

Unlike SIS and MI5, the Government Code and Cypher School (GC & CS), Britain's communications intelligence agency, already had a well-established tradition of university recruitment at the outbreak of the Second World War. Oxbridge dons had figured prominently among the official 'decypherers' of the seventeenth and eighteenth centuries. But the tradition was interrupted when the Decyphering Branch at the Foreign Office was closed after parliamentary protests in 1844. For the next seventy years the British government abandoned code-breaking altogether. The revival of the Cambridge connection with communications intelligence was an almost accidental by-product of the outbreak of the First World War.

At the beginning of the war Admiral Henry 'Dummy' Oliver, the Director of Naval Intelligence, received a series of intercepted, coded German wireless messages. At first he had little idea what to do with them. Then, one day in mid-August 1914, while walking to lunch at the United Services Club with the Director of Naval Education, Sir Alfred Ewing, it suddenly struck him that Ewing was 'the very man I wanted'. Ewing was a former Professor of Engineering at Cambridge University and Fellow of King's, whom Oliver considered to have 'great brainpower'.[43] With Ewing the Cambridge connection in the history of British sigint (signals intelligence) properly begins. For among those recruited by Ewing to Room 40, the newly established cryptanalytic unit in the Admiralty, during 1915 were three young Fellows of his old College: the classicist 'Dilly' Knox, the modern historian Frank Birch, and the ancient historian Frank Adcock (later knighted).[44] Knox became Room 40's most successful code-breaker and stayed on after the war in the newly founded GC & CS, where he worked until his death in 1943. Adcock and Birch returned to King's in 1919. Adcock became Professor of Ancient History in 1925; Birch left Cambridge for the stage in 1934. Both, however, reappeared at Bletchley Park at the beginning of the Second World War.

GC & CS remained too small between the wars to develop a regular recruitment programme. It began in 1919 with only twenty-five 'pensionable officers', drawn mostly from Room 40 and its smaller military counterpart MI1b. When the establishment was raised to thirty-one in 1925, GC & CS immediately took the opportunity to recruit 'young staff direct from the University'. There were scarcely any opportunities for further university recruits over the next decade: the GC & CS civil establishment remained static and the naval, military and air sections (added in, respectively, 1924, 1930 and 1936), were staffed mainly by men from the services. GC & CS suffered from the general rundown of interwar intelligence. From 1921 it was placed under Foreign Office control. In 1923 the newly appointed head of SIS, Admiral (later Sir) Hugh 'Quex' Sinclair, was also given responsibility for GC & CS by the Foreign Office. As Commander Alastair Denniston, the operational head of GC & CS from 1919 to 1942, complained: '. . . Beyond a salary and accommodation vote GC & CS had no financial status; it became in fact an adopted child of the Foreign Office with no family rights, and the poor relation of the SIS, whose peacetime activities left little cash to spare'.[45]

Even a very modest expansion of GC & CS did not begin until two years before the outbreak of war. During 1937 and 1938 Denniston was authorised to recruit eight additional recruits, chiefly to deal with the growing Italian signals traffic generated by the Spanish Civil War and increasing Japanese traffic in the Far East. In 1937 'Quex' Sinclair told Denniston that he was now 'convinced of the inevitability of war' and 'gave instructions for the earmarking of the right type of recruit to reinforce GC & CS *immediately* on the outbreak of war'. Treasury approval was gained for an additional wartime establishment of eighty-six: '56 seniors, men or women, with the right background and training (salary £600 a year) and 30 girls with a graduate's knowledge of at least two of the languages required (£3 a week)'. Denniston immediately began recruiting in the universities but quickly ran into difficulty:

It was naturally at that time impossible to give details of the work, nor was it always advisable to insist too much in these circles on the imminence of war. At certain universities, however, there were men now in senior positions who had worked in our ranks during 1914–18. These men knew the type required.[46]

The most active recruiter among those former members of Room 40 who 'knew the type required' was Frank Adcock, now Professor of Ancient History at Cambridge. Adcock went about his work with great enthusiasm and even greater secrecy. Among those recruited by Adcock and Birch to Bletchley Park were ten other Fellows of King's. Probably Adcock's first recruit, however, was a Fellow of Corpus Christi, E. R. P. 'Vinca' Vincent, the 43-year-old Professor of Italian who had perfected his German also while interned in Germany during the First World War. Vincent's unpublished memoirs record an invitation to dinner with Adcock in the spring of 1937:

We dined very well, for he was something of an epicure, and the meal was very suitably concluded by a bottle of 1928 port. It was then that he did something which seemed to me most extraordinary; he went quickly to the door, looked outside and came back to his seat. As a reader of spy fiction I recognised the procedure, but I never expected to witness it. He then told me that he was authorised to offer me a post in an organisation working under the Foreign Office, but which was so secret that he couldn't tell me anything about it. I thought that if that was the case he need not have been so cautious about eavesdropping, but I didn't say so. He told me war with Germany was inevitable and that it would be an advantage for one of my qualifications to prepare to have something useful to do.

Soon afterwards Vincent was summoned by telephone to Broadway

Buildings near St James' Park tube station in London, the joint inter-war headquarters of SIS and GC & CS. At intervals over the next two years he returned to practise work on some of the cryptographic problems which he was expected to encounter when war came. Vincent found little of his training much use in wartime, but he 'picked up the jargon and got to know some of the people'.[47]

GC & CS also arranged several short courses designed to give potential wartime recruits 'a dim idea of what would be required of them'. Thus partially enlightened, the recruits were able to 'earmark, if only mentally, further suitable candidates'.[48] Following the traditions of Room 40, the pre-war university recruiting drive was centred on arts faculties. Despite Sir Alfred Ewing's own background in mathematics, Room 40 had been suspicious of mathematicians, viewing their personalities with the traditional prejudices of the arts graduate. Wartime experience was held to show that 'the right kind of brain to do the work' was 'not mathematical but classical'.[49] It was not until late 1938 that GC & CS, prompted perhaps by the problems posed by the German Enigma cipher machine, set out to recruit its first mathematician. The new recruit, Peter Twinn, who had graduated from Oxford a few months earlier, was told after his recruitment:

that there had been some doubts about the wisdom of recruiting a mathematician as they were regarded as strange fellows notoriously unpractical. It had been discussed whether, if some scientific training were regretfully to be accepted as an unavoidable necessity, it might not be better to look for a physicist on the grounds that they might be expected to have at least some appreciation of the real world.

Twinn's postgraduate work in physics since his graduation may have lessened apprehension in GC & CS at the prospect of recruiting a mathematician. In the event he found his new job 'fascinating' and his colleagues congenial.[50]

The first sixteen men on the list of what Denniston called 'professor types' from the universities arrived at Bletchley Park, the wartime home of GC & CS, on the eve of or in the first fortnight of the war. Of these, six (W. H. Bruford, L. W. Forster, A. H. Hatto, F. Norman, E. R. P. Vincent and G. Waterhouse) were German linguists (though Vincent's primary expertise was in Italian). The other 'professor types' comprised four classicists and ancient historians (Adcock, R. J. H. Jenkins, H. M. Last and L. P. Wilkinson; Jenkins' interests also included modern Greek), two modern historians (Frank Birch and E. J. Passant), one art historian (T. S. R. Boase), one lawyer (A. H. Campbell) and two mathematicians (A. M. Turing and J. R. F. Welchman).[51]

The inclusion of two mathematicians among the first 'professor types' to arrive at Bletchley Park was of crucial importance. During the first year of the war it was Turing and Welchman, building on the earlier work of the

Poles and the French, who made the crucial breakthroughs in the solving of Enigma. Turing and Welchman were recruited, however, not because of their distinction as mathematicians but because of their skill at chess. 'Someone', wrote Vincent later, 'had had the excellent idea that of all people who might be good at an art that needs the patient consideration of endless permutations, chess-players filled the bill.' Among other chess players who arrived at Bletchley Park in the winter of 1939–40 were Dennis Babbage, Stuart Milner-Barry and Hugh Alexander.[52] The mathematicians at Bletchley Park so quickly established themselves as indispensable, however, that during the first weeks of the war the recruiting drive was extended to mathematicians without a reputation for chess.[53]

The 'emergency list' prepared by GC & CS before the war included clever undergraduates (again mostly from arts faculties) as well as more senior 'professor types'. During the summer vacation of 1939 Denniston wrote to the heads of about ten Cambridge and Oxford Colleges, asking to interview half a dozen of the ablest men in each for war work. Harry Hinsley was not yet twenty-one, at the end of his second year at St John's College, and had just taken first-class honours in Part I of the Cambridge Historical Tripos. He remembers being interviewed at 10.45 a.m. one morning in the second week of the Michaelmas term at St John's by Denniston, Colonel (later Brigadier) J. H. Tiltman (head of the military section at GC & CS), and 'one other shadowy figure' whose identity he can no longer recall: 'The kind of questions they asked me were: "You've travelled a bit, we understand. You've done quite well in your Tripos. What do you think of government service? Would you rather have that than be conscripted? Does it appeal to you?"' The only government service mentioned, however, was the Foreign Office. Harry Hinsley was, he believes, one of about twenty Oxbridge undergraduates earmarked in this way for wartime work at Bletchley Park. Unlike the 'professor types' they were given no inkling of the secret world which awaited them. Initially Harry Hinsley was simply told to present himself at Euston Station where he would receive further instructions. Over breakfast on the day of his departure he repeated his instructions to 'Hugo' Gatty, the John's medieval history don. Gatty, who had also been recruited by GC & CS, quickly realised that Hinsley was bound for the same destination and drove him to Bletchley later that day. Not till they arrived did Harry Hinsley finally discover the nature of the organisation which had recruited him.[54]

The success of the pre-war undergraduate recruiting drive which brought Harry Hinsley to Bletchley Park encouraged others during the war itself. One of the most remarkable resulted from the urgent need for Japanese-speaking intelligence officers after the attack on Pearl Harbor in

December 1941. From his own experience in gaining a working knowledge of written Japanese, Colonel Tiltman was convinced that carefully selected undergraduates could be taught to translate decrypted Japanese telegrams in six months. His efforts to persuade the London School of Oriental and African Studies, then the only English university department teaching Japanese, to put on six-month crash courses were, however, unsuccessful. Though SOAS was later to put on Japanese courses of its own for intelligence personnel, its initial response to Tiltman was to remind him that it took five years to make British diplomats reasonably proficient in Japanese and to argue that a three-year course would be the shortest practicable. Tiltman was undeterred. He turned instead to Oswald Tuck, a retired 64-year-old naval captain working in press censorship. Tuck had left school at fifteen, taught himself Japanese while serving on the China station before the First World War, and had no experience either of teaching or of universities. When Tiltman asked him to teach bright young men to read Japanese cables within six months, Tuck noted in his diary that though the idea 'sounded impossible', it was 'worth trying'. He agreed to try.[55]

Tiltman had firmly traditional views about the kind of boys most capable of mastering Japanese in six months. They were, he believed, boys who had won classics scholarships to Cambridge and Oxford Colleges. For advice on how to recruit such scholars, Tiltman turned to L. Patrick Wilkinson, a classics don from King's College, Cambridge, who had arrived at Bletchley with the first batch of professor types at the outbreak of war. At Wilkinson's suggestion, S. W. Grose, Senior Tutor of Christ's, M. P. Charlesworth, Dean of St John's College, Cambridge, and Lord Lindsay of Birker, Master of Balliol – all prominent classicists – were asked to look out for suitable classics scholars either already at university or waiting to go up. Tiltman was also convinced that some schools were more likely than others to mould the character of good intelligence officers. Both he and Wilkinson had been to Charterhouse. Tiltman began by striking it off his list. 'Carthusians never grow up', he told Wilkinson.[56]

Twenty-two men and one woman assembled for Captain Tuck's first Japanese crash course, begun somewhat improbably in the Bedford gas showrooms on 2 February 1942. All but three were classics scholars from Oxbridge, most of them aged nineteen or twenty. Three went on to become Fellows of the British Academy: Hugh Lloyd-Jones, now Regius Professor of Greek at Oxford, Maurice Wiles, Regius Professor of Divinity at Oxford, and Laurence Cohen, Praelector in Philosophy at Queen's College, Oxford. Among others on the course who later achieved academic distinctions were R. H. Robins, now Professor of Linguistics at SOAS, M. A. N. Loewe, Lecturer in Chinese Studies at Cambridge, and

Eric Ceadel, successively Senior Tutor at Corpus Christi College, Cambridge, and University Librarian until his death in 1979. Another of the classics scholars was the subsequently celebrated mountaineer, Wilfred Noyce. The improbable combination of pupils chosen for their proficiency in languages utterly remote from Japanese and a 64 year-old novice teacher with no experience of higher education using untried teaching methods is striking evidence of how Bletchley Park's faith in the potential of intelligent, creative amateurs remained undiminished half-way through the war. The improbable combination worked. After only five months' teaching Tuck was able to send five of his students to translate the recently captured Japanese airforce code. He wrote in his diary on 27 June 1942 after saying good-bye to his first course: 'As I quite honestly told them, I think my work with them has been the happiest of my life.' Although no subsequent group quite equalled the first in ability, only nine of Tuck's 225 pupils failed to pass his six-month courses.

The remarkable successes of Captain Tuck's improvised courses, like the even more remarkable successes of Bletchley Park, provide at least a partial vindication of the now unfashionable virtues of British amateurism in general and Oxbridge amateurism in particular. The amateurs could not, however, have succeeded in isolation. Had Bletchley Park been forced to start truly from scratch, like Room 40 in 1914, Ultra intelligence would scarcely have been possible. Bletchley depended on the expertise painstakingly built up between the wars on minimal resources by A. G. Denniston, himself a 'professor type' recruited from the Royal Naval College, Osborne, in 1914. Nor would the German airforce Enigma (still feared by Denniston to be possibly unbreakable at the outbreak of war) have been regularly broken as early as May 1940 without the help supplied by Polish and French intelligence. In certain respects, too, GC & CS would have benefited from less amateurism and greater professionalism. It was slow to overcome its suspicions of mathematicians. Administratively, it lacked the expertise to cope with a four-fold expansion in the first sixteen months of the war. Harry Hinsley concludes that 'At the beginning of 1941 it was by Whitehall standards poorly organised.'[57]

Despite its organisational problems, however, Bletchley was already providing probably the most valuable intelligence in the history of warfare. The amateurism of the early Bletchley Park was central to its success in at least two ways. First, the belief of Denniston, Tiltman and others in the ability of the highly intelligent and well educated to grapple successfully even in their late teens with unfamiliar problems of great complexity enabled GC & CS to assemble with great speed perhaps the ablest team of cryptographers and intelligence analysts in British history. A more 'professional' service or civil service department would have been unlikely to show quite such faith in such raw recruits. When Winston Churchill arrived to inspect Bletchley Park as Prime Minister, he is said to have told Denniston: 'I told you to leave no stone unturned to get staff, but I had no idea you had taken me literally.'[58]

Bletchley's early amateurism was also crucial to the 'creative anarchy' of its working methods which took little account of rank and hierarchy. Since few of the wartime recruits thought of a post-war career in GC & CS there was remarkably little jockeying for position.[59] As Harry Hinsley later recalled:

It was a delightful amateur place which gradually became an enormous hive of professional activity. It never lost what I think was the key to its success – that as in University, which was very much what it was like, there was no discipline, no hierarchy, in terms of what anyone got on with. You were all left free to get on with your own work and it had that atmosphere of real academic preoccupation.[60]

Recognising no bureaucratic demarcation lines in intelligence analysis, by early 1941 the staff of GC & CS had already begun to move on from their intended roles as cryptanalysts and translators to offer their own appreciations.[61]

Some post-war intelligence communities have tried to recreate Bletchley Park's freedom from hierarchy in order to improve their own efficiency. Since the Yom Kippur War Israeli military intelligence officers have been invited to approach the Director of Military Intelligence directly if they disagree substantially with their superiors' views – and assured that their careers will not suffer if they do so. Officially at least, the rank of the Israeli intelligence analyst is disregarded when divergent views are assessed.[62]

The informality of Bletchley Park meant that it was able to exploit the talents of unconventional and sometimes eccentric personalities who would have found it difficult to conform to military discipline or civil service routines. Alan Turing, possibly Bletchley's most gifted code-breaker, is a case in point. He kept his mug chained to a radiator to prevent theft, sometimes cycled to work wearing a gas mask to guard against pollen, and converted his life savings into silver ingots which he buried under a bridge and in the Bletchley Woods.[63] Such eccentricity was enjoyed rather than reproved. Even the young Harry Hinsley had at the beginning of the war a slightly unconventional appearance. Admirals were sometimes taken aback to be briefed by a long-haired undergraduate who had completed only two years of his Cambridge degree course. The mop of long fair Hinsley hair is affectionately remembered in Patrick Wilkinson's epic wartime poem 'The Other Side', composed during a blackout on the train to Cambridge. In it the staff of Bletchley Park are transformed into the heavenly host:

Wings of all colours from their shoulders grew
From ADCOCK-pink to heavenly LUCAS-blue,
A dazzling sight. On Mrs EDWARDS' head
There beamed a halo of unearthly red;
STPACHEY's was black and of stupendous size,
But for extension HINSLEY's took the prize.[64]

No Cambridge undergraduate since has spent his third year in such
remarkable company.[65]

Part II

4

Strategy, arms and the collapse of France 1930–40

BRADFORD A. LEE

As momentous events like the fall of France in 1940 recede ever further into the past, they may lose their power to stir up passions, and even their capacity to provoke wonder, but all the while the scope for intellectual rigour in explaining what happened ought to be expanding in three dimensions. First of all, one comes to see how the basic elements of the historical situation in question developed in succeeding years (and perhaps to see more clearly how they had developed in the preceding eras as well); this, of course, represents the proverbial advantage of hindsight. Beyond that, new analytical approaches – in many cases worked out by those trying to come to grips with more recent phenomena – may be turned to the purposes of historical understanding; the historian is then in a position to transcend the terms in which participants and observers in the past thought. And, not least, the evidence that one can bring to bear on the events becomes much more copious as the relevant archives open up.

In all three of these respects, historians have today reached an especially propitious point from which to reconstruct the French military road to defeat in 1940. Certain basic elements in France's strategic situation then have analogues in NATO's position now, and increasingly since the mid-1970s there has flared up an important debate among experts over the dilemmas of pursuing a conventional strategy of forward defence, in an era of rapid technological change in weaponry, against the threat of a blitzkrieg. There have also been some re-examinations of past warfare in search of 'lessons' or 'models' that might be useful in the present. An historian should be able, with all due circumspection, to make some inferences from both types of recent work and shape them into a context against which to clarify aspects of the French predicament that have hitherto been indistinct. From a different angle, one can also now extend approaches developed by economists in order to analyse the maximisation of 'output' of military power from 'inputs' of resources devoted to defence.

43

In terms of alternative uses for potential sources of military strength, what logic – and what limits to it – might there have been in France's military posture, and how well did that posture fit the constraints of French resources? Then, having exploited hindsight and novel approaches for whatever they may be worth, the historian can work on more familiar ground, the archives, to fill in the analytical points with empirical substance. It is, indeed, only in the last several years that a broad range of archival material for France in the 1930s has become generally available to researchers.

Though from our current vantage point we are in a much better position than before to see the military collapse of France in deep perspective, we still face the problem of having to look back over a tangled historiographical terrain. One nasty thicket developed early on in the form of a debate over whether the French defeat was due to inadequate rearmament or inappropriate strategy. The Riom trial under the Vichy regime was designed to demonstrate the former and preclude consideration of the latter, though in the event the former ministers being tried were able to make a powerful case against their military counterparts. The post-war parliamentary inquiry under the Fourth Republic, if less skewed in conception, was still primarily motivated by a desire to affix responsibilities, and it came back again and again to the question of inadequate rearmament or inappropriate strategy.[1] Even where subsequent historical work on military issues has not been merely the continuation of such politics by other means, it has failed effectively to transcend the terms of debate set by political figures of the bygone era itself. Whenever there develops such a tangle around a major historical question, one should ponder anew the question itself, to see if it has been *mal posée*. In this case, it seems indeed to have been misconceived. For one can judge a certain level of armament sufficient or insufficient only in relation to a certain strategy. Equally, one can judge a strategy appropriate or inappropriate only in relation to the resources available to execute it.

Defensive posture, rules of thumb, and the illusion of parity

For over a decade before 1940, the principal preoccupation of French strategists was not how to restrict the growth of German power or contribute to collective security in Europe, nor even how ultimately to win a war if one should develop, but rather how to keep Germany from overwhelming France at its outset. There was a further preoccupation that crucially affected the prospects for achieving this primary objective: the Germans had to be kept even from penetrating French territory to any significant depth. Once France's industrial base in the north and northeast

was overrun, the prospects for sustaining a long war would be bleak, even
if the initial German thrust was not decisive by itself. Beyond this
pragmatic calculation loomed a more elemental consideration. Never
again should France have to bear the appalling human costs of serving as a
battlefield as she had in the First World War.

The upshot of such considerations was a commitment, virtually unquestioned in France by the 1930s, to a forward defence along a continuous
front. In the east, along the only French–German border, there were to be
the formidable concrete strong points of the Maginot Line. In the north,
the continuous front was to be projected into Belgium, if circumstances
permitted. This would leave the region facing the Ardennes as the hinge of
the front. It was to be much more thinly defended than either the front in
Belgium or the Maginot Line; the assumption was that the forests of the
Ardennes and the water of the Meuse would render any rapid German
armoured attack on this hinge either unlikely or unsuccessful.

All three elements of this tripartite forward defence came under withering critical attack once the stunning German attack succeeded in 1940.
Yet, as historians further from the event have begun to appreciate, each of
the three elements had a certain logic of its own.[2] The Maginot Line was
supposed to allow the most efficient use of manpower, which the French
regarded as the resource in which their inferiority was greatest. If after the
construction of the Maginot Line France could not be strong everywhere
else in her forward defence, the Ardennes region was no doubt the best
place to risk being thin (up to a point). It is worth noting that American
commanders in late 1944 chose to leave the same region thinly protected
(and also were jolted by a German surprise). As for the move into Belgium,
it held out the advantages of displacing a major area of battle from French
territory, of shortening the front to defend, of permitting the incorpora-
tion into the Allied war effort of the Belgian army, and of giving the Allies
an avenue for attack into Germany, away from the Siegfried Line, when
they ultimately attained the material superiority deemed necessary for
taking the offensive.

Even if a reasonable case can be made for each of the three elements
constituting France's forward defence, one cannot jump to the conclusion
that the strategy as a whole was logical or appropriate. After all, there may
have been not only offsetting disadvantages within each element, but also
perverse interactions among the different elements. Strategy is a realm in
which there is considerable intellectual vitality left in the old saw that the
whole is not necessarily equal to the sum of its parts. The technical
problem facing the historian is precisely how, even with the advantage of
hindsight, to evaluate French strategy as a whole in order to determine the
level of armament appropriate to it.

We shall address this problem by moving back and forth between past and present while working in upward steps from the tactical domain of battle. In that initial domain, our point of departure is a prominent rule of thumb: attacking forces require a superiority in aggregate power of at least 3:1 if they are to have a reasonable prospect of overcoming defending forces in prepared positions along a given sector. The general basis of the convention is that defenders in fixed, protected, and concealed positions should see the attackers earlier and more clearly than vice versa, less of their weapons should be exposed as a target, and their fire should be more accurate.[3] One can trace the quantitative formulation of the rule of thumb as far back as the First World War; and one can find Marshal Philippe Pétain endorsing a similar notion in France on the eve of the Second World War, Allied commanders (including the Soviets) subsequently planning offensives against the Wehrmacht on such a basis, and the American army today still affirming its validity.[4]

For our purposes, the critical issue in the tactical domain is whether or not historical evidence would support use of the rule of thumb. Military historians, as distinct from military planners, are wont to see a long-term cyclical pattern in the relative advantages of offensive and defensive forces. The story along these lines for the past century is that new infantry weapons, above all the machine gun, gave the defence an edge that was revealed most dramatically on the western front in the First World War; then the development of tanks and aircraft gave the offence an advantage that emerged with stark clarity in 1939–41; and now the application of microelectronic technology to anti-tank and anti-aircraft weaponry seems to be restoring the defence to dominance. There is, however, an altogether different story, laid out by B. H. Liddell Hart. Having made his reputation in the 1920s by virtue of his studies of the offensive potential of tanks, he culminated a long process of turning his original work on its head by declaring in 1960 that since the Napoleonic wars, the defence had been gaining 'a growing material ascendancy over the offence' and that even mechanised warfare had 'brought no radical change in this basic trend.'[5] According to Liddell Hart, the trend expressed itself in a steady decline in the number of troops required to defend a front of any given extent, a decline due to technological improvements in mobility and especially firepower. He explained away as aberrations the successful German attacks in 1939–41. Yet another story could be offered by an historical gadfly with a perverse thrust equal and opposite to that of Liddell Hart: had it not been for France's 'miracle' at the Marne in 1914 and Hitler's delay in attacking the Soviet Union in 1941, the pattern for over a century would show a growing ascendancy for the offence.

Among this welter of historical patterns, only Liddell Hart's story is compatible with the 3:1 ratio as a general rule of thumb. But the pattern put forward by Liddell Hart rests, like the others, on a crude technological determinism, namely the assumption that an innovation inherently favours either the offence or the defence. The current debate over who will gain from terminally guided munitions illustrates how problematic such a determinism is.[6] If what really matters is which side adapts an innovation to its own purposes in the most timely and effective way, any pattern or rule of thumb that pretends to cross-national or long-term validity must be suspect. In this connection, note that in the cases selected by Liddell Hart to sustain his pattern in the twentieth century, those who held out in defensive postures against heavy numerical odds were, by and large, Germans.

Thus, it appears that historians, no less than military planners, have allowed their generalisations to outrun their empirical base. This is particularly easy to do in the tactical domain because the quantitative data necessary to test theories are fragmentary and scattered, and many possible determinants of success in battle do not lend themselves to numerical expression. The best collection of combat data now in print is that of T. N. Dupuy and other retired American military officers in the Historical Evaluation and Research Organization (HERO). One of their published tables gives manpower ratios for the offence and defence in forty-two major battles from 1805 to 1967.[7] The shortcomings of such a compilation notwithstanding, it does yield two propositions upon close examination. The first is that whatever may be the mean value over time of a ratio giving a likelihood of success for defensive forces, the deviations from that mean are both frequent and large.[8] The other is that if an historical pattern in the relationship between offence and defence can be found, that pattern will not unfold, in either cyclical or monotonic fashion, across different wars, but rather will cover developments within wars. In the initial stages of a war, the offence's prospects for decisive success without highly favourable numerical odds are at their greatest; evidently, if the defenders survive with sufficient forces to remain viable, they will have been able to begin learning how to anticipate and counter the attackers' moves, and the conflict will be likely to end up as a war of attrition. The primordial force behind this pattern is surprise. It is the possibility of surprise at all levels – tactical, operational, and strategic – that makes the initial stages of a war quite unpredictable and therefore makes conventional rules of thumb quite unreliable for the defence until, perhaps, the scope for surprise diminishes (without ever disappearing) as the war goes on.[9]

To keep our empirical base not too far removed from even this modest generalisation, one can refer to another set of numbers put together by

Dupuy and his associates on eighty-one battles in 1943–4. Dupuy's group assembled data on weapons and manpower and estimated values for seventy-three variables relevant to the outcomes of the engagements. The goal was to construct a quantitative model that would account for success or failure, which Dupuy also expressed numerically. If the procedures by which the statistics were aggregated and manipulated are open to challenge, we can nevertheless draw from the exercise some points of interest for our purposes. The first is that the model represents the advantage of being on the defence in the Second World War as no greater than 1.3:1 (though it seems that some favourable repercussions of a defensive position may enter into the model in indirect ways not captured by that figure).[10] Another is that if one confines one's use of Dupuy's estimates to an index of only those factors whose magnitude can be calculated *ex ante* with a reasonable degree of certainty – numbers of troops, quantity and quality of various weapons, effectiveness of the firepower under different environmental circumstances – one finds significant deviations in outcomes of one-third of the battles in 1943–4 from what one would expect simply from the balance of manpower and firepower between the two sides, even with the advantages (indirect as well as direct) factored in for the defence.[11] The deviations are accounted for by residual variables that can be as decisive as they are elusive – the impact of air power in varying circumstances, the relative combat effectiveness of soldiers of different armies, and the effects of surprise. If surprise retained such importance even in the penultimate stage of the war, that strongly suggests how much more it could vitiate rules of thumb in the earlier stages, when it was easier to achieve on a broader scale.

The power of surprise provides us with the key link from the tactical domain to the next level of military action and analysis – the operational domain. The significance of this domain lies in the potential that it holds for the translation of gains at the tactical level into success for the front as a whole.[12] Clausewitz suggested that where surprise is most likely to have efficacy – the strategic level – it is least likely to be feasible, and that where its feasibility is greatest – the tactical level – its efficacy tends to be more limited; but he missed the opening at the operational level for a potentially fruitful convergence of feasibility and efficacy.[13] It was this opening that proved crucial in 1940. Though the Germans were remarkably successful in springing surprises even at the strategic level early in the Second World War, that was not their most significant achievement on the western front. Indeed, one could argue that the Allies would have been in a better military position if the Germans had achieved greater strategic surprise. For if Germany had got one jump ahead of France and Britain in moving into Belgium, the Allies might have limited their own plunge beyond the French border and then have found it easier to shift forces to counter the main point of the German attack further south. At that point of attack, the German forces attained great tactical success with the shock effect of their coordinated use of armour and air power. Yet it was German application at the operational level of new ideas (above all, those of Liddell Hart) that not only conditioned the tactics but also converted an initial breakthrough into the collapse of France.

As an operational concept, blitzkrieg in its 1940 manifestation can be analysed in terms of two related elements.[14] The first is the criteria by which forces were concentrated for attack at a particular point along a front. For Hitler and the more audacious of the German generals in 1940, the decisive point was defined neither by the proximity of important concrete political objectives nor by the existence of inviting àggregations of enemy forces. Rather they concentrated their attack on the weakest spot in France's defensive posture and thereby gained the largest possible local superiority of power that could be achieved anywhere along the front. Since that spot was the weakest in French manpower and firepower precisely because it was the point at which the French High Command least expected an attack to come, the Germans were thus able to maximise the element of operational surprise as well. The second conceptual element of the blitzkrieg facilitated the use of these criteria for selecting a main point of attack by allowing the Germans to avoid the horn of Clausewitz's dilemma that pointed to the limited efficacy of tactical surprise. The breakthrough at the spot of maximum local superiority was to be exploited by rapid, radical manoeuvre to disrupt the French structure of command and control rather than by slow, incremental attrition to wear down French forces or by a direct, predictable campaign to take Paris. Accordingly, as Edward Luttwak has noted, initial points of attack could be selected 'freely' or 'opportunistically' because 'the immediate areas behind the breakthrough points were of no particular significance in themselves'.[15] Once armoured columns had broken through, they cut across lines of communications and passed by centres of resistance in such a way that the initial surprise at the front was compounded by perpetual surprise in the rear.

This double-edged surprise in the first two weeks of the blitzkrieg made it impossible for the French to rely not only on standard operating procedures but also on conventional rules of thumb. We have already seen that the 3:1 rule of thumb for defensive planning is likely to be an unreliable one, in the sense that the historical record shows frequent and large deviations from such a ratio. We have also suggested that the deviations tend to be especially pronounced in the initial stage of a war, when the scope for surprise is at its greatest. And we have just seen that in the particular instance of May 1940 Hitler stretched this scope nearly to its limit. Since he could choose the time and place to concentrate his powerful forces along the front, the French had at all times and every place to be strong enough to prevent him from achieving overpowering superiority at his chosen spot. Failing that, the French needed general reserves agile enough to cut off deep penetration and powerful enough to prevail in encounter battles in which the defensive side had no inherent advantage.

We have now advanced the argument to the strategic domain, where we can finally arrive at a conclusion about what level of armament was appropriate to France's defensive posture. It is common for strategists to suppose that 'parity' with the adversary should suffice for the defence of a front. This is the reflex that one can see at work among military planners in France as they weighed the changing balance of French and German rearmament in the 1930s and as they charted the front-wide order of battle on the two sides during the war. It is, furthermore, the assumption behind efforts by historians ever since to retrieve data on the arms possessed by France and Germany in May 1940: if France can be shown to have achieved parity in weaponry, then her rearmament can presumably be pronounced adequate and the causes of her collapse must be sought elsewhere.[16] But along with the 3:1 rule of thumb in the tactical domain, the assumption about the significance of parity at the strategic level needs scrutiny. Parity may be important politically or psychologically; it may even serve to deter an adversary. When war breaks out, however, it does not necessarily have strategic significance.

In an examination of this issue for the case of France in 1940, an indirect approach may well yield (as in military strategy itself) the optimal results from the available means. For such an approach, we require another point of reference from which to draw inferences based on a structured comparison of roughly analogous situations. It is for this purpose that we can make our most explicit use of recent work on NATO's military position. Within the analogical structure we shall set up as a foil the most cogent presentation of the optimists' view that as of the late 1970s NATO was not far from having sufficient forces on or near the central front successfully to carry out a non-nuclear forward defence against a Soviet blitzkrieg conducted in the fashion of the Nazi invasion in 1940.[17] That view rests on an array of assumptions and considerations – the bounds imposed by geography and topography on the number and width of potential avenues of invasion, the putative 3:1 guideline for defensive planning and associated rules of thumb for force-to-space ratios, the number of first-line armoured divisions that can be concentrated in a given avenue of invasion and the speed with which second-echelon forces can follow them up, the ability of defensive forces to shift quickly along the front to fill gaps that may open, the relative sequence of mobilisation and reinforcement on the two sides, and the capability of intelligence to provide early warning of an attack and unambiguous information on the operational distribution of enemy forces – all of which may be important mediating factors in determining whether a certain front-wide level of relative defensive strength translates into sufficient forces in successive tactical zones for the defence to have a solid chance of containing an armoured thrust concentrated at a particular point along the front. If one knows the overall balance of forces on NATO's central front, if one considers the extent to which the mediating factors might shape outcomes in vulnerable tactical domains, and if one finds a reasonably consistent pattern of differences in a comparison of those factors along the western front in 1940 and the central front in the late 1970s, then one can infer what level of rearmament was appropriate in relation to French strategy.

The optimists' calculation of relative force levels of NATO's central front shows the Warsaw Pact with an overall advantage of 1.2:1 in the late 1970s; this ratio holds for both manpower and firepower, and takes into account quality as well as quantity of weaponry.[18] The optimists assume that technologically sophisticated means of surveillance would give sufficient advance warning of a Soviet attack that NATO could begin mobilising within a few days after the Warsaw Pact did. Even the optimists concede that if NATO lags behind in mobilisation by more than four days, or if it does not reinforce the front rapidly enough to keep relative force levels close to the initial ratio, there would be little prospect of withstanding a blitzkrieg.

Having fixed the strategic conditions in this manner, the optimists then must show that the Warsaw Pact's overall advantage in force levels cannot be translated into an overpowering local superiority at any spot along the front. One argument in this part of their case is that so long as the Warsaw Pact falls short of a 2:1 overall advantage after mobilisation, the Soviets will not be able at the outset to achieve significantly greater than a 3:1 local superiority on more than three axes of advance.[19] The next point is that even though NATO's central front is nearly 500 miles long, there are arguably no more than four axes of advance where the topography is conducive to the penetration of large armoured forces and where tempting strategic objectives are located in the contiguous rear.[20] Even in these four axes, it is said, the terrain would to some extent help channel the offensive thrusts and make them easier to contain. In addition, the optimists stress that there are physical limits to how many armoured divisions can be concentrated at a point of attack, and they doubt that the Soviets' second-echelon forces could be introduced into the battle before NATO could make countermoves to bolster soft spots. Even if the Warsaw Pact has the ability to achieve greater concentration in space or time than the optimists anticipate, it might hesitate actually to do so, lest its closely concentrated forces present an inviting target for NATO's tactical nuclear weapons.

Thus, at the operational level, the optimists play down the scope for surprise. Then, at the tactical level, they rely heavily both on the rule of thumb – familiar to us by now – according to which the defence in a given zone can hold out in the face of a 3:1 material superiority on the offensive side, and on the calculation – derived ultimately from Liddell Hart's ruminations on force-to-space ratios – that a brigade with modern weaponry can defend up to fifteen kilometres along a front.[21] If the threat of a breakthrough develops nevertheless, there still remains the possibility for NATO to reinforce the vulnerable spot with reserves drawn from the rear – to the limited degree that they will be available in the early stages of a war – or with forces drawn from contiguous sectors on the front – to the extent that there will be an extra margin of units not tied down at the point of their initial disposition. Of course, such reinforcement would require considerable mobility and would presuppose the ability of NATO intelligence to discern very quickly the main operational thrust of the Soviet attack.

When the case of the optimists is dissected in this manner, with its tissue of assumptions laid bare, one scarcely has to expatiate on why it represents a minority view among contemporary experts on conventional war.[22] Historians, for their part, can see much to discount in some of its major premises.[23] The exercise can nonetheless be of heuristic value for our purposes. Indeed, to the not insignificant extent that at least some of the mediating factors or mitigating assumptions are valid, the overall weakness of the optimists' case about NATO in the late 1970s will make our conclusions about France in 1940 stronger. Even with an array of partially mitigating factors, NATO cannot have much confidence that its inferiority of 1:1.2 in relative force levels is narrow enough for a successful forward defence. If one examines the same factors for the comparable case of France in 1940, one finds that their applicability or potency is in no respect greater than for NATO and in most respects is much less. The minimal inference to draw is that France could not rest secure even with the narrow inferiority which NATO (under the broken American nuclear umbrella) was later willing to accept.

For the sake of comparison, consider first the vital factor of intelligence. Given that cryptology was not yet producing much immediately useful output by May 1940, the French in the critical early stages of the campaign suffered from a shortage of intelligence on German operations; today, whatever the difficulties likely to be posed by electronic countermeasures on the part of the adversary and by 'information overload' at data-

processing centres, high-technology airborne sensors should certainly
provide NATO with much more solid information near to 'real time' than
the French command had from its traditional sources of intelligence.
Consider also another important point where there has been major
technological change since 1940 – the ability to attack concentrations of
forces after they have been detected. In 1940, France suffered from a
pronounced inferiority in the air; today, though the major edge that
NATO once had in tactical air power seems to have been blunted by the
development of sophisticated ground-based air defence systems, there
remains the potential threat presented by tactical nuclear weapons to any
concentration of forces (not to speak of the new non-nuclear threat posed
by the emerging generation of sub-munitions).

Next consider more down-to-earth points. Because French strategists
feared the possibility of a German attack through Switzerland, they had to
worry about covering a front that was 600 miles long even after the move
into Belgium and even leaving aside the Italian menace on France's
southeastern front; NATO's central front is over 100 miles shorter.[24] And
whereas by the optimists' reckoning there are four axes of advance into
West Germany (or six, in a more pessimistic evaluation), France had to
contend with eight invasion routes north of the French–Swiss border: the
unexpected one that Germany took in May 1940, plus the others that had
hitherto preoccupied French planners – through the Belfort gap northwest
of Basle; across the Lauter tributary of the Rhine; from the Saar towards
Metz; down the Moselle valley towards Metz, Longwy, or Montmédy;
along the Sambre from Belgium in the general direction of Saint Quentin;
across the Escaut in Belgium and past Lille; and along the Flanders coast.[25]
Of the four most likely avenues of attack into West Germany, only in the
northernmost one would an armoured thrust not tend to be canalised by
the topography; in the French case, the two northernmost invasion routes,
and to some degree the third as well, were relatively unconstrained by the
terrain, and none of the northern four was protected by the Maginot Line.
More important still, once the invader penetrated the forward defences,
the topography of the rear area in northeastern France was much more
hospitable to free-flowing armoured manoeuvre than would be the case in
most of the interior of West Germany.

Finally, in the technical realm, there are two points of comparison to
register. The first is that if there is some validity to Liddell Hart's view that
technological advances in firepower and mobility have made it possible for
forces of a given size to defend longer fronts, this would operate more to
the advantage of NATO than for France in 1940. The other technical point
– and the only element for which a comparison seems at first glance to
show France in a favourable position relative to that of NATO – concerns

the question of the attacker's second-echelon forces. Lacking an adequate complement of motor vehicles, the German infantry formations that followed the Panzer divisions in 1940 were slow. They not only were quickly outrun by the armoured columns, but also got in the way of the logistic effort to resupply those spearheads.[26] The French, however, were not able to move units along the front and decapitate the German army as it stretched its thin neck. Conversely, the optimists with respect to NATO argue that the Warsaw Pact's second-echelon forces, though highly mechanised and motorised, will not play a decisive role because NATO units have the mobility to cut them off.

Thus, a structured comparison of the western front in 1940 and the central front in the late 1970s suggests that even if NATO may rest somewhat secure with a modest inferiority in firepower and manpower, France would not have been reasonably safe without a much more favourable ratio of forces. One can push one's conclusion further still: to the extent that the 3:1 rule of thumb is unreliable for defensive forces in the tactical domain, NATO's overall inferiority of 1:1.2 cannot be regarded as sufficient. If one takes into account how surprise can undercut that rule of thumb at the outset of a war, one can conclude that NATO requires at least parity with the Warsaw Pact, in effective fighting power, in order to have a reasonable expectation of a successful non-nuclear forward defence against a blitzkrieg. And if that is indeed so for NATO, the strong inference to draw for the French in 1940 is that they needed considerably more than parity to have a solid chance of withstanding Hitler's Germany.

Quantity, quality, and force multipliers

The conclusion that even parity would not have sufficed for a France committed to forward defence against a Germany bent on surprise might seem to foreclose the case for any closer look at the French collapse in 1940. After all, Germany had substantially superior industrial and demographic potential to develop military power, and the Nazi regime was determined to capitalise on these assets. How, then, could the French have possibly compensated for their inherent inferiority in material terms? An obvious answer was to gain strong allies, and the diplomatic history of France for much of the 1930s centres on her unhappy quest for other Great Powers to share her security burden. But in an investigation focused on France's military posture, one should not discount the possible scope for a state in her unenviable position to enhance its own power by intelligent use of limited resources. It is an important counterpart to our analysis so far to determine whether the French made choices that gave them the most force for the franc.

To help us organise our thoughts and tease out points that might otherwise elude us, we may turn to our purposes the intellectual investment that economists have made in the business of evaluating alternative uses of available resources. One return that economists have sought on this investment has been in making calculations for defence departments of which weapon among several would be most cost-effective for a given military mission. The practical success of this type of systems analysis has been modest. As one early practitioner conceded, 'it applies best to small variations of choice within a given framework . . .'[27] Since our purpose here is to evaluate the military 'framework' as a whole in France, we need a broader vision, though one inspired by the same reasoning that is at the heart of microeconomic systems analysis.

When economists seek to understand the growth of an economy as a whole, one of their standard constructs is the 'aggregate production function', which relates output to inputs primarily of capital and labour. An economy grows with quantitative increments to units of the inputs or qualitative improvement in the productivity per unit of the inputs. By analogy, one can conceive of a 'military-power function', in which weapons play the part of capital and troops assume the role of labour. Such an analogy, crude though it may be, is suggestive in two ways for an assessment of whether choices made by French strategists were optimal in relation to the resource constraints under which they operated. The first way arises from a premise underlying the conventional version of the aggregate production function: there may be substitution among the inputs. Accordingly, shortages of one input can be compensated for by reliance on others; alternatively, resources can be shifted away from an input with relatively low marginal productivity. A second way in which the analogy may be instructive emerges from empirical applications of the aggregate production function. In using it as a framework in which to account for economic growth in recent decades, economists have found that increases in output over time were substantially greater than measurable increases in the primary inputs. There was a large residual factor whose elements were difficult to specify but that mainly involved advances in knowledge, not least of which seemed to be new strategies for organising and deploying labour and capital.[28]

If the implications of the production function pertain to military power, one would thus be led to seek out three potential methods for maximising effective strength from limited resources: making 'substitutions' (of an input that is cost-effective or abundant, for an input whose marginal productivity is relatively low or whose supply is restricted); enhancing quality (to make individual units of inputs more productive); and devising 'force multipliers' (that is to say, concepts for organising or deploying combinations of men and material in much more cost-effective ways). And indeed promising military applications of these ideas are not far to seek. An example of substitution would be an increase in an army's 'teeth-to-tail' ratio – that is the proportion of combat forces to its overall size. Quality can be enhanced by technological improvement in weapons or better training for troops. We have already identified a force multiplier in our discussion of the conceptual thrust behind the German blitzkrieg. It is also worth recalling that in Dupuy's accounting for battle outcomes in 1943–4, as in economists' accounting for growth, 'number-crunching' brings out – ironically enough – the pivotal importance of residual factors that cannot be directly measured, of force multipliers such as surprise, air power, and combat effectiveness of different groups of soldiers (which should be considered as a force multiplier to the extent that superior leadership, organisation, or deployment, rather than simply better training, is involved). Air power, though costly to produce, may nevertheless be cost-effective; the other major force multipliers need not cost much at all in a direct financial sense. None of these methods, to be sure, offers any certainty of net gains in the maximisation of power from limited resources. They may involve off-setting costs, great risks, or perverse consequences. Hence, both sides of the ledger must be opened to view as one evaluates the choices made by France before the Second World War.

Even if French military planners did not think in such abstract terms, in some ways they felt compelled to act upon the logic of our military-power function. When they laid the foundations of a forward defence in the second half of the 1920s, the resource constraint that weighed most on their minds was a lack of manpower. In the 'hollow years' (années creuses) of 1936–40, this constraint would largely be set by a hard demographic fact: the drastic diminution of annual contingents of conscripts as a result of low birthrates in 1915–19. Until the mid-1930s, however, the shortage of manpower was primarily a result of politics: Parliament in 1928 passed legislation that by the autumn of 1930 brought down the length of active service for conscripts to one year. This reduction had important implications for the quality as well as the quantity of manpower, as the average level of training of conscripts declined along with their number.[29] Not until 1935, on the verge of the hollow years, was a French government willing to take the domestic political risks of raising the length of service to two years; but since Germany proceeded at once to reintroduce conscription, France's relative position in manpower by no means improved even then.

The French High Command sought to compensate for the effects of one-year service – and, more generally, for France's demographic inferiority – by all three methods that we have identified for maximising power against resource constraints. There was a modest effort to enhance the quality of manpower by increasing the number of professional soldiers. Extracted from the government by the military leaders as their price for accepting a reduction in conscripted service, this measure required extra expenditure (in 1934 prices) of ten million francs per year for every increment of one thousand professionals. That was over three times more than the outlay required for an equal number of conscripts, and was equivalent to the cost of approximately fifty modern light tanks.[30]

The French military leadership made a more significant effort to maximise strength through the substitution of firepower for manpower.[31] There was not only an attempt from 1930 to increase the quantity of powerful weapons in the army; there was also an intense concern with enhancing their quality. This concern reflected both the image that the French had of themselves as craftsmen uniquely able to produce items of high quality and the view in the High Command in the early 1930s that the opportunity for technological advance at that point was great.[32] It was mobile armoured weaponry that attracted the most sustained interest. However deficient virtually all French generals were in comprehending the full range of operational possibilities opened up by the tank, few needed to be convinced of its potential for putting new force behind old tactical conceptions.[33]

There are dangerous pitfalls in the pursuit of technical perfection. It may lead to weapons unsuited in a crucial way to the mission for which they were originally conceived. It may lead to some weapons whose advantages at the margin over others do not justify the extra cost of producing them. It may take up so much money and time, or result in such complicated processes of production, that few of the superior weapons will be procured in the end. In developing tanks, France's army fell into all of these traps.

Though French military leaders valued speed and firepower in tanks, the quality that they sought most ardently was strong armoured protection, especially after tests of a new 25 mm anti-tank gun in the early 1930s demonstrated that such weapons had more perforating power than expected. Tanks with stronger armour required more powerful motors, and since cost was primarily a function of weight, the French ended up with expensive machines. The D type of tank was initially designed to accompany infantry, replacing in that role the Renault F.T. tanks, which dated back to the First World War. Because the infantry wanted large numbers of tanks, it was highly desirable that their unit cost be low. By the time that a D2 model with stronger armour was ready for mass production in 1934, it was much too expensive to suit the infantry's needs, and French planners turned their attention to new types of lighter tanks.[34]

Even as the D series was rejected by the infantry, it was also shunned by strategists who were contemplating armoured units less closely bound to foot soldiers. For more extensive missions, the powerful B type of tank was preferred. The B1 model, also ready for production by 1934, and its even more thickly armoured successor, B1 bis, were in many respects the best tanks of their time anywhere; they were heavily armed and quite fast as well as strongly protected. But they had two defects that arose with their virtues. One was that as the power of their motors was augmented to carry more armour, their range of action between refuellings declined precipitously – a shortcoming that was to prove fatal in May 1940.[35] The other major defect was the price of B tanks. In 1934, their projected unit cost was 1.3 to 1.6 million francs, at a time when the French army was allotted less than 500 million francs for all weaponry. The B1 model was three times more expensive than the D2 tank, but it had no greater thickness of armour and was only 25 per cent faster (25 kilometres per hour to 20) in good terrain; though it did carry a 75 mm cannon in addition to the 47 mm cannon and machine gun of the D2 tank, it turned out in 1940 that a 47 mm cannon was sufficient to pierce all German armour. In 1936, the unit cost of the new B1 bis model was seven times higher than that of the new light Renault and Hotchkiss tanks, which had been adopted the previous year to accompany the infantry.[36] Faced with such trade-offs, the French retreated from their quest for quality, and opted for a higher proportion of the cheaper light tanks than had been originally planned.[37] Thus, for the most vital type of weapon, the pursuit of technical perfection did not give France more force for the franc.

Much the same can be said of the most important French project to maximise power from limited resources – the Maginot Line. Such permanent fortifications can be a substantial force multiplier. In principle, they not only permit fewer troops to hold a given front, but also – once the framework of forward defence is set – may economise on firepower by the protection that they provide for weapons.[38] An experienced defence economist has recently suggested that a system of prepared barriers along NATO's central front with a projected cost over ten years of $7 billion would be the defensive equivalent of seventeen new area-specialised divisions (or eight and one-half existing mobile armoured divisions) with a cost of nearly $60 billion.[39] Even if these figures are accurate, and even if fortifications could stand up to a massive attack by modern weaponry, what may be cost-effective for NATO might nevertheless have been ruinous for France in the 1930s. For a country whose economy is as large as that of West Germany today, and even more for an alliance whose collective wealth is as great as that of NATO, such an outlay would be much less burdensome than the corresponding sum for the French during the Great Depression. Fortifications may save on combat soldiers and perhaps on weaponry, but the concrete and mechanical infrastructure may consume a disproportionate share of scarce financial resources.

From the end of 1927 to the middle of 1936, France spent 5,000 million francs on fortifications and only 3,400 million francs on weaponry.[40] The expense of the Maginot Line thus cut across the simultaneous effort to substitute firepower for manpower. Indeed, as cost overruns developed in the course of construction, plans for arming the fortifications themselves were scaled down or put off. The drain of resources into concrete did not stop even as the primary works of Alsace and Lorraine neared completion, for political pressures had arisen for the extension of the system elsewhere. France could not afford to replicate the type of elaborate fortifications that had already cost 5,000 million francs for roughly the first thirty per cent of the front north of Switzerland. Hence she had to carry on with a considerably less formidable array of concrete. Small well-armed defensive works, arranged in depth in a checkerboard configuration, can be effective against attack by tanks (though not particularly economical in their requirements of manpower); but France's prepared defences to the north of the Maginot Line were too linear and, especially at the hinge of the front in the Sedan area, too weakly armed for anti-tank warfare.[41]

There were two other potential force multipliers that the French High Command regarded with much less favour. The first was uses of air power that went beyond narrow subordination to ground forces. The most expansive claims for the new air arm as a force multiplier were those of the Italian strategist Douhet, who argued that massive bombing of an enemy's air bases, cities, and industries could bring a war to an early end and that such overwhelming effectiveness could be achieved at a relatively modest cost in terms of the personnel, material, and financial resources required to build up a bomber force. His conclusion was not simply that a nation's air force should have operational autonomy, but also that the sole rational course was to concentrate resources on bombers and make only minimal provision for all other military arms.[42]

Advocates of air power in France shared Douhet's enthusiasm for strategic bombing, if not his more audacious notions about severely limiting outlays on ground forces. But the French air force had difficulty in attaining even a measure of operational independence. Though an Air Ministry was finally established in 1928, it did not wrest from the army and navy an autonomous military arm under its own jurisdiction until 1933. Its ensuing bureaucratic drive to create a powerful bomber force met with stiff resistance from the army. Records now open in the archives at Vincennes indicate that this opposition rested less on doctrinal considerations than on budgetary calculations. To be sure, the leaders of the army by no means accepted the Douhetian vision that strategic bombing would be decisive in the next war; but they did agree in principle that France should have a bomber force sufficient to deter a German air attack. What they feared in practice was that the budget of the air force would grow at the expense of the army and that emphasis on strategic bombing would mean neglect of reconnaissance, observation, and fighter planes whose support was vital for ground forces.[43]

With hindsight, we know that for most of the Second World War strategic bombing was considerably less effective than its advocates had predicted. We also know that in May 1940 close air support of the German tank offensive had a major impact on the morale of French ground forces, which lacked adequate fighter protection and anti-aircraft guns. But Dupuy's calculations suggest that interdiction – that is, bombing of an adversary's supply effort, lines of communication, and movements of troops well behind the front – was from two to six times more effective than close air support in shaping outcomes of battles later in the war.[44] Since logistics and the lack of mobility of second-echelon formations were the main weaknesses in the German campaign in 1940, it would seem that interdiction could have been a substantial force multiplier for France. One should also have thought that such a use of air power, falling between the extremes of independent strategic bombing and narrow subordination to ground forces, would have represented an obvious middle ground for compromise between the army and the air force. As it was, no such meeting of minds took place and, until 1938, the air force by and large wasted what modest resources it was able to obtain.

Another potential force multiplier, proposed in 1934 by a hitherto obscure colonel named Charles de Gaulle, was the formation of an elite corps consisting of powerful tank units manned by professional soldiers. The most striking formulation in the case put forward by de Gaulle and his political *porte-parole*, Paul Reynaud, was that France did not have 'the army of her policy'. That policy was not only the integral defence of French territory, but also the provision of military assistance to France's allies in the event of German aggression; and yet the French army was not organised in a manner that would permit offensive action, or even a major counterattack, until large numbers of reserves had been mobilised. According to de Gaulle and Reynaud, this deficiency could be rectified by a shock force of six armoured divisions (and a seventh lighter division), which had to be composed of career soldiers because the tanks would require skilled handling and because the corps had to be ready at all times to intervene.[45]

We have already seen that the French High Command, in order to compensate for limits on available manpower, wanted to recruit more professional soldiers and produce as many new tanks of high quality as possible. In 1933, moreover, the military leadership had established a light mechanised division in which half of the combat troops were to be professionals. Nevertheless, de Gaulle's superiors did not look with favour upon his scheme. One reason for their negative attitude had to do with the mission of the elite corps as it was envisioned by de Gaulle and Reynaud. The High Command, and civilian policymakers at the War Ministry as well, shied away from the risk of sending such a force into Germany before the rest of the French army had been brought up to full strength. Summoning up memories of what had happened as a result of the cavalry offensive of August 1914, they thought it foolhardy to thrust eastward while, further north, a large German force might be coming westward into France. They claimed that even if Germany was concentrating on an offensive in Eastern Europe, a French armoured corps would by itself gain only local successes, at best, on the western front against defensive forces equipped with modern anti-tank guns.[46]

Such qualms over an offensive mission were not, however, the fundamental reason for the resistance of the High Command in the mid-1930s. After all, quite apart from the issue of intervention in Germany, de Gaulle had pointed out that armoured divisions would complement the Maginot Line in defending against a German surprise attack – the eventuality that French military leaders feared the most. This dimension of his scheme might have opened up more eyes if he had worked out ideas for mobile defence at an operational level. There was a serious incongruity in the outlook of virtually all French generals. While committed to the strategic defensive in the early stages of a war, they devoted the bulk of their attention to offensive tactics. For all their fear that Germany might achieve surprise and penetrate into France, they gave little thought to what operational manoeuvres, with what types of forces, would be necessary to rescue the situation in that case.[47] Still, even if there had been keener appreciation of the defensive potential of an armoured corps, de Gaulle's proposal would no doubt have been regarded as premature at best. As was the case in the debate over air power, more than simply doctrinal considerations were at stake: the scheme raised profound issues about the allocation of scarce resources.

Both de Gaulle and Reynaud realised that an elite corps had no chance of acceptance if it was seen to require a substantial commitment of additional money and manpower. Both, therefore, were at pains to demonstrate that all but 25,000 of the 100,000 men under contract needed for the new divisions could in effect be found by a gradual shift of professional soldiers from other units in the army. And they claimed that the tanks and much of the other equipment for the corps would have to be procured in any case if the French were to be adequately prepared for war with Germany. De Gaulle's private estimate was that an expenditure of 3,000 million francs over five years should suffice for the necessary material.[48]

The War Ministry and the High Command discounted the calculation that no more than 25,000 extra professional soldiers would be required, and they argued that, in any case, with the diminution in the pool of young men of military age during the hollow years, it would be difficult to get even 25,000 additional enlistments, except perhaps by offering very costly financial inducements. As for material, the figure of 3,000 million francs was more than the War Ministry had spent on all weaponry in the five years from 1930 through 1934. It seemed clear to de Gaulle's superiors, therefore, that an elite corps would absorb so many of the army's professional soldiers and new weapons that the rest of the army would become little more than a militia.[49]

If the High Command had been willing to concentrate its best manpower and its mobile firepower in such a fashion from the mid-1930s, if it had then been able to devise ways to achieve operational surprise with such a shock force on the defensive, and if it was lucky and skilful when the German attack came, the effectiveness of an armoured corps might have greatly outweighed its cost both in financial terms and in other forces foregone. But there would have been major risks involved in counting on such a potential force multiplier. With the relatively neglected non-elite component of the French army stretched out even more thinly along the front than would otherwise have been the case, the threat of a German breakthrough would have been especially great. And the dilemma of how to position the armoured divisions in the rear would have been especially acute, because so much would depend on delivering the right type of counter-attack at the right place at the right time. To concentrate these reserve divisions would be to risk having them end up too far from the main axis of attack; to disperse them would be to risk having them chewed up piecemeal by concentrations of offensive armoured power.

French planners opted instead to mix professional soldiers with conscripts and reservists, to give higher priority to cheap light tanks than to the expensive B tanks, and to disperse the light tanks among infantry divisions. Most of the leading generals were ultimately not opposed in principle to armoured divisions with a high proportion of professional soldiers. In the late 1930s, when other needs were on their way to being met and when enough B tanks were finally coming to hand, they began to form such divisions; by May 1940, they had three and could improvise a fourth.[50] Indeed, one can discern a certain methodical pattern in the shaping of France's defence posture. First came the basic elements of a forward defence in the form of the Maginot Line along the French–

German border and of motorised infantry divisions and a partly mechanised cavalry to establish the projected line in Belgium. Next came an effort to provide the units along the front with modern armament, especially tanks. Only later was a serious start made on adding depth to the long front and building up a mobile reserve of armoured divisions. The major risk in following this course was that, unless France had enough money available from year to year to compress all three elements of this incremental process into a short period, an attack would come while she was still thin on the front and deficient in the rear.

This observation dovetails with the other main points that have emerged from our analysis of French choices within the framework of the military-power function. Accordingly, to our first conclusion that a forward defence required more than parity with Germany to have a reasonable chance of success, we may now add the further conclusion that the particular ways in which French strategists prepared the forward defence were appropriate only for a state with an abundance of financial resources. The basic logic of France's defence posture was that manpower represented the input most in need of economising; but to compensate for limits on the quantity of men, French strategists took measures that absorbed substantial amounts of money. Then as the financial constraint grew tighter, it stiffened their stance against diverting resources to force multipliers that, though costly, might have proved to be cost-effective. In the end, even if France succeeded in generating more force for each Frenchman, she by no means got the most force for each franc.

The force of finance

Our anatomy of France's defence posture has now exposed its soft underbelly: finance. To uncover the structure of the financial predicament in which the French military effort became entangled, one should start from the late 1920s. At that time the French industrial sector was at the peak of an upsurge in which the rate of growth, over the course of the 1920s, had exceeded that of any other major country in Europe and of the United States, surpassed that of any earlier ten-year period in French history, and matched the rate later achieved in the first decade (1947–56) of France's celebrated economic boom after the Second World War.[51] With increased tax revenue being generated by this upsurge, and with capital flowing back into the country after the Poincaré government's stabilisation of the franc in 1926–8, France had the means to finance a substantial expansion in military power. But given the increased cost of manpower in the transition to one-year service, the outlays that would be needed for fortifications, and the requirements of a modernisation of

French weaponry, the High Command doubted even then that it would have sufficient financial resources at its disposal to do all that it wished.[52]

Archival evidence now available suggests that though a consensus had been reached by the late 1920s among the leading generals on the need for a forward defensive line, most of them wanted to give top priority to weaponry rather than concrete. It was political leaders, Premier Raymond Poincaré above all, who insisted that the primary commitment of new resources should be for fortifications.[53] To be sure, after Parliament passed the major legislation for the Maginot Line in 1930, War Minister Maginot was able to get the approval of Poincaré's successor, André Tardieu, for a programme to spend over 600 million francs annually for eight years on modern weapons and other new equipment. But whereas the bulk of the financing for the Maginot Line was to come from extra-budgetary sources, Maginot was unable to secure the same measure of insulation for the armaments programme from the forays of budget-cutters.[54]

This budgetary vulnerability was to become a matter of great moment when the full force of the Great Depression hit the French economy from 1931. As the flow of revenues into the Treasury diminished, successive governments went on a quixotic budget-balancing crusade, and the military establishment bore a major burden in the efforts to restrict expenditure. First came a ceiling imposed on defence spending in late 1931 by Pierre Laval. Then, after the elections of the spring of 1932, a series of centre-left governments made major cuts in the military budget. Finally, in 1934, even though a government oriented more to the right of centre had assumed power, and even though the scope of German rearmament under Hitler had become quite apparent, still more reductions were made at the expense of the army. Not until 1935 was the downward trend of budgetary allocations reversed, and not until September 1936 did a French government decide to launch a major new rearmament programme.

Except for the Maginot Line, all the elements that might have contributed to an expansion of military power were casualties of this prolonged budget-cutting campaign. The arms programme of 1930 had fallen far behind schedule by 1935. Orders for weapons were not only small, but were also made piecemeal, because of the pervasive uncertainty about levels of funding in both the near and the long term. As a result, unit costs rose, and firms making arms had no incentive to expand their productive capacity and achieve economies of scale. Since relatively few weapons could be produced, there was a distinct tendency for the army's quest for quality to degenerate into an excess of technical perfectionism. As for the element of manpower, the search for economies led to a reduction both in the number of men drafted into service each year and in the length of training of those who did serve. In addition, at the very time that the army was prepared to experiment with how tanks should be used, credits for large-scale manoeuvres (outside of camps) were suppressed. And, not least, the onslaught against the army's budget helped to produce a beleaguered state of mind among the leading generals and, consequently, made them less willing to consider the merits of new ideas offered from outside their ranks.[55]

If the records of the War Ministry suggest that budget-cutting, with all its manifold repercussions, had reduced the army to a structure without substance by 1935, the records of the Finance Ministry reveal how narrow was the financial room for manoeuvre that political leaders had. For all the devotion of premiers and finance ministers to orthodox budgetary conventions in principle, most of them were quite ready in practice to resort to the expedient of trying to balance the budget by shifting major items of expenditure 'off budget' – such as was done for the Maginot Line. But even extra-budgetary outlays have to be financed, and there are only two methods of doing so: have the central bank print money or have the Treasury borrow from the public. The Bank of France was unwilling (until 1935) to re-discount government bonds or (until 1936) to advance funds directly to the state or even (until 1938) to engage in open-market operations. And especially as anxiety over the stability of the franc arose after mid-1933, capital flight and hoarding drained the pool of funds from which the Treasury could borrow. It was these constraints that limited the number of francs available for generating military power.[56] Short of reforming the Bank of France, the easiest way around the constraints was devaluation. But opposition to devaluation was the one and only point upon which all segments of the French political spectrum, from the Communist Party to the right-wing leagues, could agree.

Not until September 1936 was a French government prepared to accept the domestic political risks of devaluing the currency. It was no mere coincidence that major rearmament and devaluation were decided upon at the same time by the Popular Front ministry of Léon Blum. The announcement of heavy expenditure on rearmament both made devaluation inevitable and provided a political justification for it.[57] In turn, the economic and financial ramifications of devaluation – along with changes in the Bank of France – made it easier to mobilise more resources for defence, though the financing of rearmament ceased to be a major problem only when large amounts of capital flowed back into France from 1938.

Pressed onward by Edouard Daladier, first as Minister of National Defence from 1936 and then also as Premier from 1938, the rearmament programme launched in September 1936 proved to be a remarkable effort to make up lost ground after the French had allowed Germany to outpace them in the arms race from 1933 to 1936. Measured in constant 1938 francs, French expenditure on weapons and other equipment for the army was nearly two and one-half times greater in 1937 than in 1935 and over three and one-half times greater in 1939 than in 1937; outlays by the Air Ministry for material were more than six times greater in 1939 than in 1937.[58] The results of the effort would have been more remarkable still, if the army had not called to military service in September 1939 an excessive proportion of industrial workers making arms. This move, which ran counter to the logic of substituting firepower for manpower, disrupted the production of various war materials, in some cases until March 1940.[59]

When the German attack came in May 1940, France was still deficient in critical types of weapons. The most glaring deficiencies were in air power and anti-aircraft artillery, but the French also did not yet have sufficient medium and heavy tanks for a powerful mobile reserve or enough anti-tank weapons to saturate the entire front. The weakness of the French reserve forces was exacerbated by the decision to send two light mechanised divisions into Belgium to cover the Gembloux gap and the third one toward Breda in Holland to link up with the Dutch.[60] The thinness of the French presence along the centre of the front, where the greatly overextended divisions were of poor quality and were appallingly short of anti-tank guns, was exacerbated by the overcommitment of infantry divisions and tank battalions in the region of the Maginot Line. This allocation of forces undercut the logic behind the decision to build the fortifications in the first place.[61]

Yet even if the French had distributed their strength more evenly along the front and had kept in reserve the excellent medium SOMUA tanks of the light mechanised divisions, their chances of withstanding a blitzkrieg in May 1940 would not have been great. Against an adversary willing and able to concentrate more than eight hundred tanks along eight to ten kilometres at a sector of its choosing, France required twenty anti-tank cannons for each kilometre and, therefore, over 13,500 for the entire front north of Switzerland. As of May 1940, however, she had little more than 6,000, plus another 1,000 old and not very powerful 37 mm cannons in the light Renault and Hotchkiss tanks that were used to accompany infantry units.[62] In these circumstances, a breakthrough was far from unlikely. Then, if the French had kept their light mechanised divisions in reserve, if they had not hastily thrown their armoured divisions piecemeal into battle, and if they could safely have concentrated only on the seven of ten Panzer divisions that came through the centre of the front, they could have counter-attacked with a force approximately equal to that of the German armoured spearhead. But the German tank units, with their much more extensive training and more adaptive leadership, would have been superior in any encounter battle of equal forces. Thus, France's hopes would have rested with the ability of her commanders to improvise and execute a manoeuvre to achieve massive surprise. One can find little indication in the campaign of 1940 that they possessed such skill.

The concluding point, then, in this extended argument is that financial constraints, by delaying the onset of French rearmament in the first half of the 1930s, left France short of what she needed to have in 1940 against an adversary as resourceful as Germany. But this conclusion is by no means simply a reaffirmation of the self-justifying claim made by many French generals at the time. For France's rearmament was not inadequate in some abstract or disembodied sense; rather it was insufficient in relation to a specific strategy implemented through a succession of particular decisions on how to use scarce resources. Both strategy and arms must stand together in analysis, just as they collapsed together in defeat.

5

Vansittart's administration of the Foreign Office in the 1930s

DONALD BOADLE

The way Sir Robert Vansittart administered the Foreign Office during his eight years as permanent under secretary has received no close study. Rather it is assumed that his overwhelming preoccupation with alerting ministers to the dangers of German resurgence led him to neglect both administration and reform.[1] Admittedly most of his effort was devoted to discharging his responsibilities as an adviser on policy, and this effectively precluded him from initiating any far-reaching reform. But his preoccupation with policy itself led him to make significant administrative adjustments involving the Foreign Office's departmental structure and its deployment of senior personnel, so as to keep closer watch on foreign developments, and facilitate appropriate responses to perceived changes.

These adjustments clearly fulfilled Vansittart's formal administrative obligations, for in practice a permanent under secretary in the Foreign Office took no responsibility for routine administration, but concentrated on supervising the efficient distribution and handling of work, and making recommendations on senior appointments. This was the outcome of an arrangement introduced after the First World War, and maintained until 1938, whereby the permanent under secretary's functions as chief accounting officer were delegated to a principal finance officer, who oversaw the spending of monies voted by parliament, justified that expenditure before the public accounts committee, and shared day-to-day control over the Foreign Office establishment with a chief clerk.[2] On several occasions during the latter part of his term Vansittart was criticized by the public accounts committee for not taking a greater share in financial administration, but he repeatedly – and not unreasonably – insisted that the unsettled international situation made it impossible for him to assume additional responsibilities.

Although Vansittart himself initiated no major reform, he gave his support to an ambitious proposal, conceived by the deputy under secretary, Sir Victor Wellesley, for an economic department within the Foreign Office. Originally intended to provide economic expertise, Wellesley's proposal encountered fierce opposition from the permanent under secretary of the Treasury and head of the Civil Service, Sir Warren Fisher, who compelled Vansittart to create a more limited economic section, charged among its other functions with facilitating exchanges of information between the Foreign Office and the financial and economic departments. Fisher's intervention was much resented in the Foreign Office; and while Vansittart in this instance was careful to distance himself from his colleague's more extreme manifestations of particularism, he strongly resisted subsequent attempts to bring the Foreign Office into line with reformed Treasury administrative practice.

Vansittart's readiness to embrace Foreign Office particularism, with its inbred exclusiveness and self-assured disdain for outside expertise, is frequently identified as his major administrative shortcoming.[3] This is by no means unfounded criticism since he was undoubtedly less ready than Fisher to recognize that the growing complexity of international affairs demanded better liaison between the Foreign Office and the specialist departments dealing with finance, economics, and defence. Yet it is perhaps too easily forgotten that Fisher was in his own way as much a particularist as Vansittart, and correspondingly determined to force inter-departmental liaison on Treasury terms. In the case of the Foreign Office such an approach was bound to arouse resentment which served to defeat the very purpose Fisher aimed to achieve.[4]

An understanding of this clash between Foreign Office particularism and Treasury-inspired reform is fundamental to the administrative history of the period; so before considering Vansittart's own administrative achievement in more detail, it is necessary to review Fisher's ideas, and consider his attempts to impose them on the Foreign Office.

The extent of Fisher's influence over the workings of other departments owed much to his dual role as head of both the Civil Service and the Treasury. On the one hand his Treasury post gave him scrutiny over all departmental spending proposals; and while this permitted substantially less influence over foreign policy than over domestic policy, he could, through the Treasury's control over the size and composition of the total Foreign Office establishment, directly affect its administration. On the other hand his Civil Service post offered enormous scope to advise the government on senior appointments, and to interfere in the most minute procedural questions in individual departments. The extent to which he was able to do so, however, usually depended on his success in asserting jurisdiction. A man of formidable energy and determination, he relied on hammering away at recalcitrant officials and their ministerial chiefs. Invitations to tea, accompanied by wide-ranging talks that exposed listeners to the full force of his personality, gradually wore down their opposition in most cases.

That this was not mere purposeless meddling needs to be emphasized. Since 1919 Fisher had waged a campaign for a reformed and fully integrated Civil Service, staffed from a central Treasury pool, itself filled with the most gifted men in Whitehall. His ultimate objective was

to make the Treasury a 'general staff' with the recognized right to recruit at any grade from other Departments; in this way a 'corps d'élite' might be formed ... Such a 'corps d'élite' would be able to carry out the proper functions of the Office [i.e. the Treasury] which include the forming of independent and constructive views on policy questions, not merely negative criticism. The Treasury should not attempt to replace the specialist Departments but should not hesitate to concern itself with policy as necessary in exercising the power of the purse. In particular it must concern itself with foreign ... affairs (which are nowadays largely economics, finance, and armaments).[5]

By 1930 he had already taken some steps toward this goal by persuading the majority of departments to model their administrative procedures and career structures on reformed Treasury practice. He had also succeeded in securing the appointment of their permanent under secretaries by transfer from other departments. But the Foreign Office, almost alone among departments, had declined to make any modifications. Nor had Fisher overcome Foreign Office particularism and secured the appointment of an outsider to the permanent under secretaryship.[6]

There is no first-hand evidence of the part Fisher played in securing Vansittart's appointment at the beginning of January 1930. Some observers believed Vansittart was Fisher's own choice; others insisted that he continued to lament his failure to appoint an outsider.[7] Whatever the truth of the matter, similar ambiguities surround most dealings between the two men: a fact underlined by Vansittart's description of Fisher as 'the best friend that I ever had in adversity, less good in better days'.[8] This characteristically obscure remark takes on some significance when it is considered how Fisher, during 1934 and 1935, was able to conduct an all-out drive aimed at compelling Vansittart to countenance the extension of Treasury influence over both the Foreign Office and foreign policy; while in April 1936 – perceiving that Vansittart was worn out by anxiety and overwork – was ready to offer the public accounts committee an infinitely tactful and considerate defence of his administrative shortcomings. Fisher's compassion, and willingness to stand by his friends, is ignored by his Foreign Office critics like Sir Walford Selby and Lord Avon, whose depictions of a vindictive, petty intriguer verge on caricature.[9] Even so, his disconcertingly impetuous behaviour – his tendency to express his views on 'the demerits of those – quite a large number – whom he held in no high repute', and his regrettable readiness to act upon his 'quick enthusiasms both for people and for causes' – was frequently misinterpreted by friends as much as by enemies.[10]

If Fisher was often an uncertain friend, he was always a difficult colleague; and never more, so far as Vansittart was concerned, than at the beginning of 1934, when he returned from a long convalescence, following an illness which, according to a by no means friendly colleague, involved 'some mysterious nerve disorder'.[11] Possessed of abundant reserves of energy, he moved quickly to regain his influence. An immediate outcome was that he persuaded his minister, Neville Chamberlain, to pressure the government into establishing a Defence Requirements Committee, on which he soon established a close working partnership with Vansittart, based on their shared perceptions of the dangers posed by Germany. Towards the end of January 1934, he decided to exploit this opportunity to raise the question of inter-departmental liaison.

The pretext was his discovery of what he chose to regard as the 'unauthorized' existence of an economic section within the Office's League of Nations and Western department. This 'good and useful measure of reform', as Vansittart described it, was originally conceived by Wellesley, and presented to the Treasury in March 1931, as a fully-fledged department, headed by a professional economist. But it had failed to win approval: no doubt because Fisher took exception to its evident intention of reducing, rather than increasing, dependence on Treasury expertise. Such an objection applied even more strongly to the economic section which finally had been introduced in February 1932, since it was staffed entirely by non-specialists, drawn from the Foreign Office's own ranks.[12] Confronted by this blatant assertion of self-assured amateurism, Fisher responded with an attack on Foreign Office particularism. He accordingly called Vansittart's attention to the way 'the higher mysteries of [foreign] "politics"' had 'been downgraded, alas, into common bread and butter problems' of 'finance, economics, and defence'. The fact that modern developments had 'forced the Treasury, the Board of Trade and the Ministry of Agriculture to become international Offices' could not 'be evaded by amateurish attempts on the part of the Foreign Office to play the role of "Poohbah" in the "Mikado"'. Instead, this 'urge to absorb and manage' the functions of other departments should be channelled into a standing inter-departmental committee on economic information, chaired by Sir Frederick Leith-Ross, the government's chief economic adviser. In return for Foreign Office participation on the new committee, Fisher offered Treasury recognition of the 'Economic Relations Section', as the existing section was now to be known.[13]

This compromise was very much on Treasury terms, since the duties of the Economic Relations Section were to be determined by the standing inter-departmental committee. And on that committee, it was Treasury representatives like Leith-Ross and the government's chief industrial adviser, Sir Horace Wilson, who appeared to dominate proceedings. The ability of other departments 'to encroach on F.O. preserves' was almost universally deplored by counsellors in charge of Foreign Office departments. Their deeply ingrained particularism emerged in minutes regretting a departure that 'might easily prove another stage on the road to abdication by the Foreign Office of control of negotiations in which it hitherto had a deciding voice'; or summoning up the ghost of Eyre Crowe, who, it was alleged, had experienced so much difficulty in stamping out similar practices after the First World War.[14] But as the economic section's principal sponsors recognized, the 'dice are so heavily loaded in favour of the Treasury' that Vansittart had no alternative to accepting Fisher's offer. Without Treasury approval it would be impossible to make a substantial increase in the section's staff, or diversify its functions, so the committee had to be tolerated, if only to provide 'the necessary maternity for our own system'.[15]

By contrast, Fisher's singularly provocative attempts to assert Treasury jurisdiction over foreign policy could be opposed without fear of damaging consequences; and Vansittart did not hesitate to respond to the outraged particularism of his Foreign Office colleagues. His readiness to take a firm stand was increased by the brazen fashion in which Fisher overplayed his hand. Elated by his victory over the Economic Relations Section, Fisher was eager to consolidate his advantage. Already he had used the Defence Requirements Committee to win recognition for the Treasury's right to influence Imperial defence policy; now he sought to stake out a related claim to act as a 'general staff', formulating similarly 'independent and constructive views' on foreign policy.[16]

With assistance and backing from his like-minded minister, Neville Chamberlain, Fisher launched a two-pronged assault between July and November 1934, in the hope of harassing the Foreign Office and Cabinet into safeguarding Britain's Far-Eastern interests through the conclusion of an Anglo-Japanese agreement.[17] These efforts reached their peak during October 1934, while Vansittart – who had persistently obstructed them – was holidaying in Rome. Chamberlain thereupon urged Fisher 'to be extremely indiscreet' and negotiate directly with the Japanese ambassador. The Japanese response was 'very encouraging', but Treasury diplomacy foundered on fears among senior ministers that any attempt to draw closer to Japan would inevitably alienate the United States.[18] Their opposition did not prevent Fisher and Chamberlain from taking a new initiative in May 1935, when the Treasury announced – without consulting the Foreign Office – that Leith-Ross would lead a financial mission to the Far East. Despite the foreign secretary's plea that they not adopt a 'negative or over-critical attitude', Vansittart and his deputy, Wellesley, determined to bring Leith-Ross' meddling to an end. 'After all', wrote Wellesley, 'it is we and not the Treasury who are responsible for our Far-Eastern policy, though I confess at times I wonder whether the roles have not become reversed.' The same thought apparently struck the Far Eastern department's adviser, who objected to Leith-Ross behaving in China as if he were a second ambassador – albeit one at odds with official British policy. Yet a formal Foreign Office protest that Leith-Ross' attempts to stabilize the region through a Sino-Japanese rapprochement were in fact worsening Anglo-Japanese relations did not persuade the Treasury to recall the mission until July 1936; by which time Leith-Ross had made a second visit to Japan. 'I think and always thought', minuted Vansittart, 'that it was a pity he went.'[19]

Throughout this confrontation Vansittart appeared to remain aloof from the more extreme particularism of his colleagues: a stance he had also taken up quite emphatically during the dispute over the Economic Relations Section, when he checked more extreme reactions by warning that he was 'out for efficiency, not for our own hand'.[20] Most likely he was concerned to preserve the understanding he had evolved with Fisher, based on their shared determination to prepare British defence against a possible German challenge. Nevertheless, between February and May 1934, he was drawn into an acrimonious dispute with the Treasury and the Civil Service commissioners, over the Foreign Office entry examination, which led him to associate himself fully with these particularist sentiments.

At his own suggestion the Foreign Office had requested that written and spoken Russian should attract increased marks, in the hope of overcoming an acute shortage of Russian speakers. The commissioners, however, had increased the marks for the written component only. When the matter was taken up with the Treasury it was suggested that the Foreign Office should walk hand-in-hand with the Civil Service as a whole, and bring its recruitment procedures into line with those of other departments. In particular, it should give less attention to examinations and more emphasis to assessing 'personality'. Vansittart responded furiously: 'Rubbish', he wrote. 'I strongly and naturally object to Sir J. Rae [of the Treasury] running our exam for us, when he does not even know how the Selection Board works.'[21] Much of Vansittart's anger seems to have arisen over this stupid slight on the uniqueness of the Selection Board – made up of Foreign Office officials, members of Parliament, a Civil Service commissioner, and a representative of the defence departments – which assessed the personal qualities or 'character' of candidates after they sat for the entry examination. Although the 1930 Royal Commission on the Civil Service had endorsed the Board 'as a reasonable and proper arrangement to which no objection can rightly be taken', its usefulness was questioned by left-wing critics, who believed it tended not so much to reject good men as to stop them from ever applying.[22] Vansittart understandably was reluctant to revive this controversy, having avoided testifying on it to the 1930 Royal Commission by – somewhat implausibly – pleading his preoccupation with 'the many important problems of foreign politics which are to the fore at the moment'.[23] And when the question of bringing the Foreign Office entry examination into conformity with its Civil Service equivalent was again raised in February 1936, he once more was adamant, insisting that the compulsory economics paper – introduced with his backing in 1932 – should 'certainly' be retained.[24] As on the earlier occasion, his attitude was clear-cut: 'Our branch of the Civil Service is different from any other, and it is of course the principle . . . that I care for.'[25]

Even though Vansittart's public utterances were usually more cautious, it is doubtful whether Fisher had been deceived for long by his reasons for refusing to undertake reform. (Might there not, for example, be a touch of irony in Fisher's January 1934 minute on the Economic Relations Section, where he castigates the particularism of Foreign Office officials, 'with the exception always of Sir Robert Vansittart'?) However, at the April 1936 hearings of the public accounts committee, he chose to support the convenient excuse that Vansittart was too preoccupied with foreign affairs, in order to explain his refusal to assume the responsibilities of chief accounting officer. This was a matter to which Fisher attached the greatest importance, since he believed the best way of alleviating the impression of old-style heavy-handed Treasury control was through informal collaboration between heads of departments with joint responsibility for finance and policy.[26] Yet, in spite of criticism in the committee's 1935 report, Vansittart had continued to insist that the unsettled international situation made it imperative not to disturb the existing arrangement, evolved after the First World War, whereby the responsibilities of chief accounting officer were delegated to Sir Frederick Butler, the principal finance officer.[27] When the committee again raised objections at its 1936 hearings, Fisher himself responded that the 'only reason . . . why I should prefer it if the present situation were left undisturbed for the time being, is that beyond all doubt the present Permanent Head of the Foreign Office is really overwhelmed. I do not think that is an exaggeration at all.'[28] From conversations Fisher had with Sir John Reith of the B.B.C. at this time it is apparent that he was not referring merely to Vansittart's preoccupation with the recent German reoccupation of the Rhineland, but also to his deteriorating health: his 'high-strung state' and appearance of being 'in a flat spin about everything'.[29] Such a considerate defence of Vansittart's administrative deficiencies was almost certainly made easier by the expectation that the prime minister would soon give way to mounting pressure, and post him to the Washington or the Paris embassy. When this transfer occurred, Fisher hoped to ensure he was not succeeded by Sir Alexander Cadogan, the deputy under secretary. Fisher therefore devoted much of the summer to lobbying ministers about the desirability of appointing an outsider, who could be relied upon to undertake thorough-going reform. If there was no more suitable candidate than Cadogan, he wrote to Neville Chamberlain in September 1936, 'I shall have to ask the Government to put me there, though that would mean a step down in rank and a loss of £500 a year.'[30] Needless to say this self-sacrifice was not demanded, so in May 1937 Fisher turned his attention to championing the claims of Sir Findlater Stewart from the India Office. But the foreign secretary, Anthony Eden, was not to be persuaded. In January 1938 he secured the appointment of Cadogan, his own candidate, following Vansittart's elevation to the specially created, but powerless, post of chief diplomatic adviser.[31]

Although particularism made Vansittart hostile to Treasury-inspired reform, he was ready to back initiatives from within the Foreign Office which promised to increase expertise and efficiency in handling work. These were not conceived as part of a comprehensive programme of reform, akin to Fisher's, but were prompted by the need to cope with new demands and pressures generated by external events. Thus Wellesley's proposal for an economic department reflected awareness of the growing importance of tariffs, and various forms of trade and investment, as instruments of foreign policy;[32] while a major reorganization of the Office's political departments was undertaken because of an upsurge in German work, and the need to keep closer watch on developments in Germany itself.

At the outset the attempt to increase economic expertise was gravely prejudiced by Fisher's refusal to sanction the appointment of a professional economist to head a new department. In order to circumvent him, Wellesley persuaded Vansittart, in mid-November 1931, to make an experimental redistribution of work in the Western department, so that Frank Ashton-Gwatkin – a first secretary with Consular experience – could concentrate on tariff work.[33] From this arrangement the Economic Relations Section haphazardly evolved, without any real attempt to define its scope or functions. In particular little thought was given to whether the new section was to have the executive responsibilities of a regular Office department, or a merely advisory role; though this question was raised in January 1932 by the head of the American department, who protested that the section would deprive his department of virtually all dealings with central and south America, since their relations with Britain were purely commercial. He therefore proposed confining the economic section to a co-ordinating role, and returning day-to-day dealings to the political departments. There is no evidence that Vansittart ever gave an unequivocal ruling; but an unsigned typescript memorandum, dated 18 February, approved the continuance of the section on an interim basis, in order that a foundation would be laid against the time when it could assist the Office and Diplomatic 'sides' in their work. If this meant the section was to be advisory only, neither Wellesley nor Gwatkin was inclined to accept such a limitation. They realized that the existence and expansion of their embryonic section depended on its visibility and indispensability, so in practice they took every opportunity to assume an executive, as well as an advisory role. In addition they sought to fulfil many of the functions envisaged for the more extensive economic department, including the preparation of guidelines intended to assist overseas posts in improving the standard of their economic reporting.[34]

The maintenance of all these functions meant that Gwatkin was hard-pressed. Yet without official status the section could only increase its staff through transfers from other Office departments; and while Vansittart assigned a third secretary and a shorthand typist in January 1933, they were not actually moved until June. Even then it was difficult to deal adequately with fundamental tariff work, despite the fact that tariffs were originally intended as the section's staple.[35] With Treasury recognition in January 1934 the situation was slightly eased. But while Vansittart was emphatic that the section 'will have to be, and will be expanded', he was 'not going to force the pace in any provocative manner'. He consequently sought a modest increase in the Foreign Office's total establishment in June, to allow the allocation of a new first secretary, and Gwatkin's promotion to counsellor.[36]

If anxiety about lingering Treasury resentment dictated a cautious approach to the augmentation of the economic section, so too did the need to find extra staff for the political departments. Already, in autumn 1933, Vansittart had reorganized the Central department to enable it to give precedence to the increasingly heavy volume of German work. He simultaneously had transferred French and Belgian work from the Western department, so that the Central department could also concert a common Anglo-French approach to Germany. And finally, he had created a new Southern department with responsibility for Italy, Austria, Czechoslovakia and the small states of south-eastern Europe. Almost immediately a procedural difficulty arose over the assignment of Austrian work to the Southern department. The trouble was that files 'relating to Germany often had relevance for Austria and Austro-German relations were of importance to the department responsible for the general strategy of Anglo-German relations'. This was partly overcome by exchanging files, circulating relevant telegrams, and relying on the assistant under secretary who supervised both the Central and Southern departments to co-ordinate action. But the head of the Central department became notorious for his attempts to get all German-related questions entered on his files, while his Southern department colleague acquired a reputation for obduracy in repulsing his onslaughts. Although Vansittart made no further procedural adjustments, he tried on two occasions to persuade the head of the Southern department to take an overseas posting.[37] Meanwhile, in June 1934, he proceeded to seek Treasury approval for an additional counsellor, and four extra second and third secretaries, to regularize interim staffing arrangements made in the previous autumn.[38] In December 1935 he again gave priority to staffing a political department; personally intervening with Fisher to secure an additional counsellor on a temporary basis to head the recently formed Abyssinian department – split-off from the Egyptian department for the duration of the conflict between Italy and Abyssinia.[39]

By this time the economic section was very much in need of augmentation. The best solution, as Gwatkin pointed out towards the end of February 1936, was to redistribute the few remaining political duties of the Western department, so that it could be converted into a general department, with full responsibility for economic work. This would overcome the staffing problem, and put an end to the confusion and wrangling which continued to arise because the section was still 'in a transition[al] state between a purely advisory and an executive department'. The desirability of finally clarifying the section's precise role was highlighted three weeks later, when Owen O'Malley, the head of the Southern department, complained that Gwatkin had again taken executive action without prior consultation. Vansittart thereupon called a meeting of senior officials, who agreed to deal with the staffing problem separately, by appointing a French-speaking clerical officer. The reorganization of the Western department meanwhile was deferred until the Abyssinian department could be liquidated, and the overall level of staffing in the Office assessed. Before this was achieved, the outbreak of civil war in Spain burdened the Western department with a heavy load of political work, which once more led to the shelving of Gwatkin's proposal.[40]

In retrospect the sponsors of the economic department maintained that Vansittart ought to have given it more robust support. Yet it is difficult to see how he could have done so, in view of continuing Treasury hostility, and the competing demands of the political departments. Had crises not erupted in Abyssinia and Spain, it is probable that the long-hoped-for executive department would have been created. But there was never any chance of achieving this earlier. So, in 1934, when Vansittart decided to give priority to staffing the political departments responsible for central and southern Europe, he unquestionably showed both realism and foresight; especially since many of his most senior colleagues – including Wellesley, the economic department's chief advocate – still regarded Japan, rather than Germany, as the immediate threat to peace.

Hand-in-hand with the reorganisation of the political departments went changes in the deployment of senior personnel. Some of these changes led to murmurings about Vansittart's favouritism; though more persistent and general criticism fastened on the intensely personal and unsystematic way in which the Foreign Office made appointments.

Strictly speaking, appointments to the rank of counsellor and above were made by the foreign secretary on the basis of recommendations from a senior promotions board. But the way the system operated gave the permanent under secretary a singularly influential role. As chairman of a committee comprising the parliamentary under secretary, the deputy under secretary, the assistant under secretaries, and the private secretary to the secretary of state, the permanent under secretary initially was responsible for securing agreement on recommendations. This was done in a largely unstructured way, since the Foreign Office kept no personnel records beyond the rudimentary 'individual' files, casually maintained by the foreign secretary's private office. Even these were not consulted as a matter of course. Instead recommendations were made with reference to the seniority list; though the 'weight attached' to 'merit and suitability for particular posts' supposedly increased 'in relation to the importance of the post'. In practice evaluation of these elements was simply a matter of opinion, and here a forceful and persuasive permanent under secretary, competent in managing meetings, was at a real advantage. His advantage was increased by virtue of his responsibility for carrying recommendations to the foreign secretary, and advising him on them.[41] The only serious rival in terms of access was the private secretary; but following the departure of Sir Walford Selby in 1932, the private office offered Vansittart no real challenge. Only after Eden's arrival as foreign secretary in 1936 did the private office again emerge as a source of opposition: in this case based on personal antipathy, as well as differences over policy. Until then Vansittart's contemporaries never doubted his ability to manipulate, if not actually dominate, the promotions board, and utilize his access to the foreign secretary to uphold its recommendations. The counsellor in charge of the Abyssinian department put it bluntly when he observed how Vansittart liked to keep appointments in his own hands, and was able to do so because he was 'the only strong man among the senior officials in the Foreign Office. . . . Unfortunately Van is a fanatic on the subject of Germany. . . . To get on in the Foreign Office you have to be one of Van's men.'[42]

Certainly it can hardly be fortuitous that the redeployment which preceded and accompanied the reorganization of the political departments in 1933 placed control and supervision over most aspects of relations with Germany in the hands of men who shared Vansittart's uncompromising views on the dangers of German resurgence and expansion. Thus the always sympathetic head of the Central department, Orme Sargent, became supervising assistant under secretary of both the Central and Southern departments. His place was taken by Vansittart's closest associate, the fiercely anti-German Ralph Wigram. Another 'very good friend', Allen Leeper, was given charge of the League of Nations and Western department, and with it responsibility for disarmament negotiations, which Vansittart rather forlornly hoped might provide the foundation for a comprehensive settlement with Germany. Leeper's brother, Rex, who generally was considered one of Vansittart's most loyal supporters, was promoted counsellor in charge of the News department, so he could oversee the 'education' of the public. And Vansittart's brother-in-law, Sir Eric Phipps, was translated from Vienna to his first embassy in Berlin, where he appeared to glory in his 'chronically anti-Nazi' reputation – epitomized in malicious stories, like the one which related how 'Goering apologized . . . that he had been shooting, whereupon I remarked "Animals I hope?" '[43]

The importance Vansittart attached to surrounding himself with close associates is nowhere better illustrated than in his relationship with his brother-in-law in Berlin. Immediately Phipps took up his post, Vansittart began to shower him with private letters which urged him to 'collaborate in the fullest sense' in the campaign to alert 'this sleepy and complacent country of ours' to the German menace. Such collaboration would have been inconceivable with Phipps' distinguished predecessor, Sir Horace Rumbold. He was just as pessimistic about developments in Germany, but saw himself in the traditional role of an independent observer offering disinterested advice. Accustomed to dealing with his London-based colleagues on a somewhat formal basis, he freely admitted his perplexity when Vansittart, Sargent and Wigram persisted in consulting him about 'the highest aspects of foreign policy' through exchanges of 'semi-official letters'. Yet contact of this kind was absolutely fundamental to Phipps, so long as Vansittart expected him to be his personal spokesman, imbued with crusading spirit, and ready, when asked for an opinion, to provide 'exactly the answer I felt should come'.[44]

It cannot have been an easy relationship, but Phipps' ability and willingness to maintain it made him so indispensable that Vansittart determined to keep him in Berlin. Unhappily Phipps had set his heart on the Paris embassy – not merely because it was the highest prize the Diplomatic service had to offer, but also because of his life-long sympathy for France – and when he learned it was soon to be vacant, he wrote to the foreign secretary, Sir John Simon, pleading to be transferred. At the time he had spent scarcely three months in Berlin. Understandably angered at his churlishness, Vansittart reminded Simon how Phipps had previously spent nineteen years in Paris, precisely because he had asked to do so. To grant his latest request would, he warned him, arouse fresh resentment in the Diplomatic service, and expose them to charges of favouritism![45] Coming from Vansittart this was a monstrous argument. Nevertheless it would probably have been sufficient to win Simon's endorsement for the promotions board's recommendation that Sir George Clerk go to Paris, had Phipps' close friend, Warren Fisher, not taken the unprecedented step of writing Vansittart a long letter accusing the board of indulging in 'personal predilections'.

Since our last talk the Paris succession continually recurs to my mind, and the more I think of your idea of George Clerk, the less I like it. I would agree at once that no one could possibly be such an ass as he looks; but I am prepared to exercise my imagination to the point of accepting for him a rating of B+. But this is by the standards of his own branch of our Service, for by those of the rest of our Service he would not be more than a B–.

It must be common ground to all that our Paris embassy is and will continue to be of the first importance; . . .

It follows that we should have in Paris a man well-known to and thoroughly trusted by the French – conditions which are fulfilled in the person of Phipps . . .

The general situation is far too serious in my opinion for us to allow personal predilections to influence us; and it really is imperative to apply selection pure and simple in the filling of a key post such as Paris.[46]

Fisher's uncomfortable reminder of how Clerk owed his selection to the refusal of Sir Ronald Lindsay to leave Washington led a by now desperate Vansittart to sacrifice 'a Saturday's leisure' to preparing Simon a list of overseas postings, based on unanimous recommendations from the promotions board, and contingent on Clerk's appointment.[47] This proved sufficient to clinch the matter, and ensure that Phipps continued as 'Van's man' in Berlin until 1937, when he at last realized his ambition to preside over the Paris embassy.[48] But the episode had left scars, for Vansittart valued personal loyalty, and while he outwardly maintained his close and cordial relationship with Phipps, the hectoring note in some of his private letters betrayed his lack of confidence in a colleague from whom he still needed loyalty as well as wholehearted support: '. . . these are not only my own feelings;' he admonished him, 'they are the frame of mind and attitude which I expect from those who work with me in the Foreign Office . . . and there is no-one on whom I count more in this direction than yourself'.[49]

The fragility of these arrangements, which Phipps' narrowly averted defection had so painfully demonstrated, was again emphasized with the emergence of Owen O'Malley, the head of the new Southern department, as Vansittart's most outspoken and obstructive critic. In O'Malley's view, Vansittart exaggerated the consequences of German territorial expansion, and so was driven into the regrettable expedient of seeking Italian support to maintain Austria against German pressure. Instead of aligning them-selves with the contemptible Italian regime, O'Malley proposed making a settlement with Germany, by trading recognition of Austro-German *anschluss*. Under different circumstances his forceful advocacy could have proved helpful in ensuring that all available options were constructively examined within the Foreign Office, and presented to policy makers for consideration. But his contemptuous, not to say antagonistic, attitude towards Italy and Austria, his dogmatic certainty of the correctness of his views, and his belief in speaking the truth, as he saw it, regardless of the consequences put him at loggerheads with the equally implacable head of the Central department, Ralph Wigram.[50] Since O'Malley's department actually was responsible for relations with Austria, and close co-operation was needed with the Central department if Austrian policy was to be kept in step with policy towards Germany, this irreconcilable clash of tempera-ment and opinion was bound to militate against the efficient dispatch of business. In particular, it seriously handicapped initiatives aimed at using British commercial concessions to buttress Austria against German economic pressure. These initiatives invariably originated with Sargent and Vansittart, while O'Malley and his first secretary, E. H. Carr, found reasons for doing nothing. Thus, in November 1933, and again in February 1934, O'Malley and Carr argued against propping up an illiberal Austrian regime through either economic concessions, or political action in collaboration with an unreliable Italian government. According to Carr, *anschluss* was inevitable and ought to be anticipated by a spheres of influence agreement allowing Germany continental hegemony, and Britain maritime supremacy. Such 'realism' was altogether too much for Vansittart. His immediate response was to refuse to sanction the circulation of Carr's papers, on the grounds that he wished to leave the foreign secretary and other ministers with the impression of 'some measure of general agreement between us *en famille*'. But about this time he also attempted to persuade O'Malley to take an overseas posting as counsellor in Brussels or minister in Bogota. O'Malley declined both offers, and Vansittart did not press him further.[51] Consequently he remained in charge of the Southern department until October 1937; providing a rallying point for those who shared his disgust at Vansittart's efforts to buy continued Italian support through the recognition of her Abyssinian conquests – whether in the still-born Hoare–Laval pact of December 1935, or in fitful and finally inconclusive bilateral negotiations during 1937.[52]

Despite their subsequent disagreements, it is fairly certain Vansittart concurred in O'Malley's appointment; as he did in the choice of Sir Nevile Henderson to succeed Phipps in Berlin. This more notorious, but otherwise comparable, appointment is commonly seen as the result of an unavoidable lapse of judgement. Yet enough was known about the shortcomings of both Henderson and O'Malley for a little careful thought to have revealed how ill-suited they were to the posts for which they were being considered. That such thought was not given is a telling comment on the promotions board's unsystematic procedures, and a clear vindication of contemporary critics like Harold Nicolson, Hugh Dalton and Robert Bruce Lockhart. Admittedly, in O'Malley's case, the root of the problem was far from obvious, based as it was on his temperamental incompatibility with Wigram, in a situation where the division of German work made a cordial working relationship essential.[53] But in Henderson's case, the problem was far more clear-cut, and evidence was at hand in his 'individual' file, in a letter from Rumbold to Selby, written ten years previously, which asked 'to modify what I said about Nevile Henderson in the following sense: I said that, in my view, he was not what I would call a "strong man". I would rather express myself differently. I think he is a man who might, in certain circumstances take the line of least resistance.' Even without consulting this file, Vansittart ought to have forseen the danger of sending Henderson to Berlin, after all the trouble he had created in 1935, during his term at Belgrade. There his complete, and indiscreetly public, identification with the Yugoslavian cause had so 'disconcerted' the Foreign Office that Vansittart had twice found it necessary to caution him.[54] Within three months of his arrival in Berlin, Henderson was publicly expressing support for the policy of the government to which he was accredited; and, encouraged by O'Malley, was working directly with Foreign Office critics like Neville Chamberlain.[55]

The advent of the pro-German Henderson in the wake of Phipps' defection, and the sudden deaths of Allen Leeper and Ralph Wigram, put an end to Vansittart's hopes of keeping close personal control over relations with Germany. Inside the Office, Sargent remained sympathetic, but he showed no sign of following Wigram's example, and supplying Winston Churchill with information critical of government policy. 'He was,' Vansittart realized, 'a philospher strayed into Whitehall. He knew all the answers; when politicians did not want them he went out to lunch.'[56] Rex Leeper also remained friendly, and Vansittart counted him an influential ally. But Vansittart established no comparable bond with William Strang, the former League adviser, who took Wigram's place as head of the Central department. This is not to say that Strang was actively hostile in the way O'Malley could be; though he and O'Malley were friends of long standing, united in the belief that it would be preferable to abandon attempts to detach Italy from Germany, and instead aim for an agreement with Germany which allowed peaceful changes in the territorial status quo in central and eastern Europe. Similar views were held by Cadogan, whom Eden brought back from China in October 1936, and appointed deputy under secretary. His subsequent appointment as Vansittart's successor, at the beginning of January 1938, was itself significant, for his personality and style were more in accord with the traditional model of Civil Service anonymity to which Vansittart and his now diminished band of crusading associates had never conformed.[57]

By surrounding himself with crusading associates, and waging his campaign to 'educate' ministers, Vansittart adopted a radical approach to the permanent under secretary's advisory functions. 'The proper official', he admitted in his memoirs, 'should give his advice and then efface himself. I was ready to do so in all save matters of public safety. "You should not have been a public servant", [the Russian ambassador, Ivan] Maisky once said to me.'[58] In part this was a matter of temperament. Self-assertive and ferociously single-minded, he was a 'relentless, not to say ruthless, worker' for his own views, with little taste for the obscurity of officialdom. Unlike the self-effacing Cadogan, he saw himself as a public figure who could consider resignation over the Hoare–Laval affair; contemplate 'the effect abroad of my retirement'; and not scruple to sue *Time* magazine for libel when it misrepresented his opinions 'as the *diametrical opposite* of everything I have ever stood for': behaviour which led Eden to conclude, far from approvingly, that he was 'much more a Secretary of State in mentality than a permanent official'.[59]

In comparison his approach to administration was more conventional. Steeped in the Foreign Office amateur and particularist tradition, he followed his immediate predecessors in narrowly construing his duties – confining himself mainly to the distribution of work and the deployment of personnel – and evading Treasury demands for innovation which threatened to create additional burdens. Within these limits his achievement in adapting the Foreign Office to meet the needs of an unusually crisis-ridden period was far from negligible; though the consequences of giving priority to German work were not uniformly beneficial. Thus, his ruthless use of patronage to keep German work in the hands of like-minded friends and supporters undoubtedly hastened the development of antagonistic opinion groups, whose differences over policy options were sharpened by personal antipathy and resentment; while his reluctance to divert manpower away from the reorganized political departments seriously qualified his support for attempts to increase the Office's economic expertise. In other respects, however, his limited conception of his administrative functions proved a serious handicap. When dealing with the scheme for an economic department, he never resolutely challenged the particularist assumptions on which it was founded. Yet a meaningful attempt to concert financial, economic and foreign policy was only possible on an inter-departmental basis, and his reluctance to acknowledge this fact could not fail to create jealousies. Similarly, his efforts to concert defence and foreign policy, though punctuated by bouts of expedient co-operation through existing institutional channels, ultimately foundered on his deeply-ingrained traditionalism: strikingly illustrated by his preference for the advice of a Central department third secretary – 'himself a very competent aviator'[60] – to the expertise of the Air Ministry.

6

Italy's historians and the myth of Fascism

RICHARD BOSWORTH

In September 1955, some 2,200 delegates from thirty-five countries assembled in Rome for the Tenth International Congress of Historical Sciences. Commentary on the meeting was benign. A group of Russian scholars had attended for the first time, and if their papers were criticised as too uniform, their 'urgent' representations ensured, at least, that Russian was acknowledged as the sixth official congress language. The Vatican, too, had sent an official delegation. Indeed, despite the hot weather and the presence of the Soviet scholars, Pope Pius XII had come down from Castel Gandolfo in order to welcome guests with full pomp and ceremony.

Lay Italians had also worked hard to make the Congress a success. One of their number, Federico Chabod, was elected President of the central committee, whose task it would be to organise the next meeting set down for Stockholm (despite a campaign to persuade the delegates that Moscow was more appropriate) in 1960.[1]

The Italians were praised not only for their hospitality but also for their scholarship. Chabod himself was acclaimed the 'outstanding ... historian' among Italy's new generation, rugged and incisive in his non-determinist, intellectual independence. His colleagues, similarly, had their merits affirmed. In Italy, 'complete intellectual freedom' now prevailed; the most plain characteristic of contemporary Italian historiography was evident in its 'repudiation of fascism'. For Italian historians (and perhaps also for West Germans since Gerhard Ritter had won a place on Chabod's committee), it seemed that the Second World War was over. The historical profession in Republican Italy had broken with its immediate past. Mussolini's regime could be forgotten as a parenthesis in the course of Italian history.

Or, perhaps better, by 1955 it could be understood that Fascism had 'seldom corrupted the minds of Italy's best historians' anyway. At the moment in which the *fuoruscito*, Gaetano Salvemini, was accorded the International Prize for Moral Sciences by the Accademia nazionale dei Lincei, it could appear that Italy's historians, even that overwhelming majority which had remained at home, and sought and found employment in Fascist Italy, had really been Anti-Fascists at heart and, thus privily, had participated in the Resistance.[2] The tyrant Mussolini, as, after all, Winston Churchill had declared, had lorded over a system based on 'one man alone'.

In 1955, there were many reasons to believe and to broadcast this pleasing message. Pleasing it may have been, but true it was not.

It is commonplace that modern war offers historians two alternatives of employment: they can be propagandists or spies. That special relationship between history and nationality which, until very recently, has characterised so much historiography, has justified the first vocation. The intellectuality of historians, the generality of their subject and the sense that history could be improved by an acquaintance with foreign languages or cultures explains the latter. Or perhaps intelligence work of one kind or another perfected those academic and social skills which were required after 1945 to progress in the historical profession.

Whatever the case, the post-war historiography of contemporary Europe has been deeply influenced by those who defended the national cause in the Second World War. Harry Hinsley, the ex-Bletchley student of Hitler's strategy and the British intelligence service, F. W. Deakin, M. R. D. Foot, E. P. Thompson (eternally avenging his betrayed brother Frank) and many others, despite their spread of political commitment or cultural expertise, nonetheless indicate how the Second World War has intruded into 'modern memory' and remained there.

In Anglo-Saxon historiography, great debates about certain countries or themes can replenish the passion and commitment of war. Modern Greece is discussed around the interpretative poles erected by the ex-S.O.E. agent, C. M. Woodhouse, and the ex-O.S.S. agent, W. H. McNeill.[3] The growing sophistication of the interpretative model of totalitarianism by C. J. Friedrich, Z. Brzezinski and their successors can be linked both to the Cold War and to intellectual baggage originally picked up in the period of social crisis known as the 'prelude to World War Two'.[4]

Nor is continental Europe any different. The 'Fischer affair' in West Germany (like the controversy over A. J. P. Taylor's *The Origins of the Second World War* in Britain)[5] or the conflict over Marc Ophuls' 'documentary', *Le Chagrin et la pitié* (1968) in France[6] all demonstrate how difficult and professionally perilous it is to attack fundamental national myths about the Second World War, and how entrenched in the historical profession are such conservative and national myths. On the other hand, in Britain, France and West Germany, the result of each 'affair' was at least a partial demolition of the national myth and an acceptance of responsibility in causing the war or condoning genocide. The Fischer, Taylor and Ophuls debates extracted even from many conservative historians a recognition of a sort of historiographical Oder-Neisse line for the future.

If the historical profession in the United States, Britain, France and West Germany can readily be shown to have preserved many equivocal legacies from the Second World War, so, too, can that of Italy. Indeed, for all sorts of reasons, Republican Italy since 1946 offers ideal terrain on which to study the complex relationship between past and present.

In one sense, Italy provides an excellent array of control factors. A Fascist dictatorship ruled the country from 1922 to 1945 and imposed a blanket of consensus. Pronouncedly Anti-Fascist historians, of whom the most renowned was Gaetano Salvemini, fled abroad.[7] Those who remained at home either had to acknowledge Fascism directly or retreat mentally into internal exile. Under a system in which the Director-General of Historical Research was Cesare Maria De Vecchi di Val Cismon[8], sometime quadrumvir, Governor of the Somaliland, the Dodecanese islands, Minister of National Education and Ambassador to the Holy See, dissent was difficult. Historians could either be outright Fascists, 'conformists' or those who passively endured 'a time of indifference'.

The reality of the historical profession however, as of other areas of culture[9] in the Fascist years, is more complicated and ambiguous than it might seem. At a formal level, the Fascist regime was a rigidly totalitarian one, which aimed to bind all minds into a single *fascio*. The creation of a Fascist Academy, the imposition of an oath of loyalty to Mussolini, and even, by 1933, the design of compulsory professorial uniforms, all implied a dictatorial (if somewhat Ruritanian) intrusion into intellectual life.

However, in other ways Fascism did, intermittently and erratically, permit and even stimulate intellectual debate. The role of the ex-Nationalist, Giuseppe Bottai, is well-known in this regard, although the effort still continues to discover whether he aimed further to free or to 'fascistise' the intellectuals.[10] One of the keys to Mussolini's own complex personality seems to have lain in his grudging respect for intellectuals. Certainly, he was always at pains to emphasise his acquaintance with the most up-to-date developments in many areas of the arts. His conversion to interventionism in 1914 had owed much to his fear of being left behind the current intellectual trend,[11] and he never quite lost that uneasy provincial sense that his own mind might be neither the quickest nor the most profound among his contemporaries. Even as his regime rigidified (and ossified) in the 1930s, still Mussolini turned a blind eye to the negative implications for a totalitarian state of the existence of a sort of court intelligentsia, many of whose members, at some time or another, were beginning their 'long journey out of Fascism'.[12]

Just as the motives of Bottai or Mussolini can be questioned, so, too, can those whose 'Resistance' was nurtured at *Cinecittà* or the Villa Torlonia. The culture of Fascist Italy awaits full-scale sociological and philosophical analysis. What is plain however is that, in the restricted domain of historiography, Fascism did not represent an enormous break with the Italian past. Under Mussolini, the historical profession was not in any sense purged. Nor, very likely, was it in any profound fashion fascistised.

Emblematic in this regard is the career of Gioacchino Volpe, a man who was in many senses the 'boss' of Italian history throughout the inter-war period. Consistently defended thereafter by the conservative, Rosario Romeo,[13] Volpe has been more recently praised by moderate and even by some Marxist historians for his alleged soundness and methodological breadth.[14] It has been suggested that he understood both the '*Annales* revolution' and the coming triumph of the concept of the 'primacy of internal politics' in diplomatic history.[15] In the last years, a family publishing concern has busily re-issued many of his works.[16]

Well before 1914, Volpe had earned a distinguished place in Italian historiography, being particularly notable for his research in medieval history and for his administrative zeal in organising conferences and publications.[17] He had become sufficiently well-known and powerful for Giustino Fortunato, with the natural comradeship of one southern intellectual for another, to imply that his special responsibility as the New Historian was to lead the next generation of Italian intellectuals into purer realms than those of Giolittian Italy.[18]

With war, Volpe became a fervent interventionist and a volunteer. He did not, however, renounce his professional skills and, by 1918, was employed as an assistant to General Caviglia in crafting propaganda for Italy's VIIIth Army Corps, of which he also published a history. War, he had remarked in 1916, in phrases typical of his class and generation, was having a useful effect on 'the rather dreamy [Italian] people'; it meant 'death, but also life'.[19] His enthusiasm for politically inspired contemporary history quickly diminished his interest in the middle ages.

Given his interventionism and his conservatism, Volpe was a natural fellow-traveller with the new Fascist movement. By November 1920, he was famous and committed enough to have a letter to the *Duce* publicly acknowledged by Mussolini as 'squisitamente fascista'.[20] Cautiously, he refrained at first from taking out a party ticket but, after the March on Rome, he was elected as a Fascist deputy to the Chamber. In that capacity, from 1923 to 1928, he served on the *Consiglio superiore della Educazione*

Nazionale. Academic preferment accompanied political success. In 1924, he won the chair in Political Science at the University of Rome. On 18 March 1929 he was received into the new Fascist Academy, of which he would act as Secretary-General until 1934.

Despite these many official labours, Volpe found plenty of time to write history, though much of it had something of an official air. Foreign policy became the natural object of his attentions and an appropriate vehicle by which past history could be utilised to justify present politics. Thus, he explained that Italy, precisely because she was the 'smallest and last arrived' of the Powers, could renounce neither war nor diplomacy if they worked to her advantage. Whatever the peacemakers had done to it, Dalmatia was a naturally united and Italian area. Those facts should be remembered when Italy overcame the 'diplomatic Caporetto' of Versailles. Egypt, where British power was fading, was an 'absolutely vital' interest for Italy. Britain should realise that, if the sort of attitude displayed during the Corfu incident continued, her relationship with Italy might be irreparably severed.[21]

In these circumstances, it was natural for Volpe in 1935–6 to applaud the Ethiopian War. Though he was delighted by the military triumph, and by the evidence which it provided of the progress achieved by the nation under the stern guidance of the *Duce*, Volpe was also characteristically anxious to connect this success with the 'precursors', those 'best men' of Liberal Italy who, particularly before the First Battle of Adowa, had sown the seeds of imperial greatness.[22] For Volpe, it seemed, Mussolini's foreign policy was not so much new or 'fascist' as traditionalist and nationalist. The *Duce* was merely pursuing Italian interests in the way that any leader of proper moral fortitude would pursue them.

In this regard, Volpe had continued to favour a mobilisation of public opinion at home and abroad in words which recalled the nationalist strain in Italian foreign policy before 1914.[23] Emigration, he had warned in the 1920s, would bleed Italy like an open wound. The government therefore should marshal its powers in order to defend *italianità* and to spread Italian culture: 'We must ascertain whether Italy wishes to pursue a great policy. If the answer is yes, then this preparatory work [of cultural imperialism] is necessary, and indeed is an indispensable basis for greatness.'[24] History, at least of the Volpe variety, could and should be harnessed to drive the nationalist dynamo of Fascist foreign policy.

Even before 1922, Volpe had advocated dangerously oppressive themes in this regard. Teachers, he had noted in 1916, could never be internationalists: 'A non-Italian or non-German or non-French teacher is in Italy or Germany or France a non-teacher.'[25] The pronounced nationalism of these phrases could readily be adjusted to Fascist reaction. For, explained Volpe as he looked back on the origins of *Squadrismo*, the Fascism of 1920 expressed 'the will to exist by that part of the population which still feels itself to have the capacity and justification for living'.[26] Open dictatorship after January 1925 also met with Volpe's approval. Writing in the P.N.F.'s theoretical journal, *Gerarchia*, Volpe did deplore the 'excesses' of dictatorship within the regime but, he added, in the event, they had been necessary to overcome a 'journalistic uproar'.[27] Thereafter, there were occasional moments at which Volpe detected that Fascism was retreating from its best aims but, on such occasions, he could always comfort himself with the knowledge that nationalists remained within the system. The old A.N.I. 'had been organisationally absorbed into the Fascist Party', but therein, 'through the world of ideas', nationalists could act as an ignition point for what was good and wise.[28]

One natural corollary of his opinions and abilities was that Volpe became the historian to which Fascism first turned when an Italian delegate was needed on the various international educational and professional institutions which were being fostered by the League of Nations. In 1934, Volpe wrote, under the title *Pacifismo e Storia*, a brief account of his experiences as an historical ambassador of Fascism.

His tone was ironical. Pacifism was the special plaything of groups such as the 'International Alliance of Women for Suffrage and Equal Suffrage', or of more sinister figures – Anatole France was one – who preached 'the hatred of hatred'. History, he feared, had become the favourite target of such people. 'International text-books' were being produced 'in millions of copies for people of every race.' 'Commissions, committees, bureaus and councils' multiplied. 'Congresses, conferences and seminars' assembled at 'Geneva, Paris, Stockholm and Prague', 'places where a solicitude for the good of human kind is at its most vibrant'.

In skyscrapers of glass, cement, aluminium or cardboard, a new breed of teachers, instructors, history lecturers, professional pacifists, specialists in the 'organisational sciences' or 'scientific historians' labour to give birth to international conferences; to launch investigations or to compile and examine reports or reports on reports; to receive commissions, committees or sub-committees arrived from the most far-off countries; and from all this to find final and definite answers, the real truth, the 'scientific truth' . . . [and thus create] one single history . . . [which, by implication,] would annul our own modern history, seeing in it little more than echoes or reflections from the history of other nations.[29]

Despite his stated distaste for international junkets, Volpe kept showing up for meetings at Oslo, Geneva or Budapest (and had the duty of presiding over one himself at Venice in 1929). By his own account, Volpe's purpose in attending such conferences was to preach an iron realism which could stop any wishy-washy internationalist in his (or, more likely and more deplorably, her) tracks. His other task was to demonstrate that, whatever the situation among foreigners, historiography in Italy had never given itself over to 'narrow nationalism'. Rather, he concluded, Italian historians, like Italians generally, had been labouring 'for peace, a real peace . . . The whole decade of Fascist rule in Italy, the decade of the foreign policy of Mussolini [who has presided over] a genuinely European policy, has been the proof of this fact.'[30]

Ethiopia, Spain, Albania and the Second World War soon made the peacefulness of Fascist foreign policy (and its 'realism') less than obvious. Volpe, however, did not break from the regime. Rather he chose January 1939 as a suitable moment to launch his *Storia della Corsica Italiana* and thus, for all his protestations of historicist objectivity, Volpe acted as a sort of ignoble second to those Fascist deputies and journalists who were chanting 'Tunis, Djibouti and Corsica.'[31] Indeed, given that Volpe had presided over the *Archivio Storico di Corsica* since its foundation in 1925, it could be argued that it was his 'preparatory work' which provided the 'indispensable basis' for Italy's quite unhistoric claims to Corsica.[32]

In 1940, Volpe left 'political science' in order to return to his earlier interests and acceded to the chair of medieval history at the University of Rome. During the war, he distanced himself to a certain extent from extreme Fascism and emphasised rather his nationalism and his monarchism (he had published a laudatory biography of Victor Emmanuel III in 1939).[33] After the war, he retired from his various offices, but he kept writing, finishing, for example, his three volume general *Italia moderna*, a book which Romeo regards as the best of its type.[34]

From this and other post-war works, overt Fascist ideologising had disappeared, but nationalism certainly had not. Thus, already in 1946, a study of the Libyan war was, he noted in a preface, 'conceived in the fullness of pain and memory' and was 'dedicated to those soldiers and workers of all kinds, alive and dead, who, from 1885 to 1943, conquered, made fertile and defended our African territories by [the spilling of] their blood and their sweat. May their recollection help us to the new Risorgimento.'[35]

Volpe's nostalgia extended to Europe as well as to Africa. In 1959, his biography of D'Annunzio eulogised one who had 'an unshakeable faith in the destiny of the *patria*' and who had understood that the new Italy needed 'a military victory . . . as the full legitimisation, the necessary proof of [her] right to exist'. Volpe's rhetoric grew especially ornate as he contemplated D'Annunzio's heroism in the First World War. The leaflet bombing of Vienna expressed the soul of 'a poet, an Italian poet' at that happy time in which 'the greatest liberators, the ultraliberators, the highest champions of "European and Christian civilisation", with their total bombing of defenceless cities even after the signing of an armistice, had not been born'. Volpe similarly justified D'Annunzio's objections to the Versailles Treaty. Then 'a Victor saw herself degraded almost to one of the defeated' through the machinations of the Allies with their 'Wilsonian ideological simplicity and their Puritan or professorial disparagement of Italians, the continuous and congenital malevolence and jealousy of France, the astute and far-seeing (or was it short-sighted?) calculation of Britain'.[36]

Volpe, then, was plainly one old man who did not forget, but despite his manifestly unreconstructed nationalist sentiments, he rapidly re-emerged as a major influence on post-war, anti-Marxist, historiography. By 1958, when he was honoured with a two volume *Festschrift* to which thirty-two historians contributed,[37] Volpe had regained the sort of stature then possessed by Gerhard Ritter in West Germany (though he lacked Ritter's honourable claims eventually to have actively resisted Nazi-fascism). Indeed, before his death, Volpe was closely associated with Federico Chabod (who himself died in 1960) and Rosario Romeo, perhaps technically the best and most innovative historians then working in Italy, in defending the Risorgimento against the Gramscian thesis of the *rivoluzione mancata*. Today, the Volpe revival continues. Commentators remember that Salvemini defined him as 'the greatest historian of his generation' and forget that Salvemini viewed this not as a matter of celebration but one for regret.[38]

What was it about Volpe that made him such an influence at least on the non-Marxist strand of Italian historiography? No doubt, he did have major abilities. He could write very well, and the extent and the breadth of his publications are impressive. Though the structure behind his writing remained both fundamentally idealist and fundamentally 'political', he was more alive than were some of his contemporaries to social issues and forces. In his research on international relations for example, he did stress the possible role of 'public opinion' on foreign policy[39] (though he scarcely prefigured some of the more sophisticated modern methods of probing the 'structure of decision-making' or of measuring 'unspoken assumptions').

Research skills aside, two other factors played a part in enhancing his role in both inter-war and post-war culture. In his period of academic power, Volpe was an assiduous, solicitous and reasonably open-minded patron. At a time in which the number of university posts remained static while the student population grew rapidly, and in which the regime's determination to fascistise the universities hardened,[40] Volpe was able both to place his students and to keep them in their posts. Many a young historian who was his client at the University of Rome, on the *Comitato Nazionale per la Storia del Risorgimento*, the *Reale Istituto per la Storia moderna*, the *Giunta centrale per gli studi storici*, the *Accademia dei Lincei*, the *Enciclopedia Italiana*, the *Dizionario politico* of the P.N.F., the *Rivista Storica Italiana*, *Nuova Antologia*, or the rest, remembered him as 'warmhearted, generous and loyal to his friends'.[41] He was also recalled as the intellectual leader to whom a young man turned if he wanted to be inducted into stimulating debate. A. M. Ghisalberti, Franco Valsecchi, Mario Toscano and many others were later willing to stand up for Volpe's decency and analytical zest.

The fact that Volpe was a good patron explains much but not everything about his reputation among the next generation of Italian historians. These younger historians, whose careers commenced under Fascism and then blossomed under the Republic, also generally did not have much need to quarrel ideologically with Volpe. The conservative fellow-travelling with Fascism in which their master had engaged was difficult to distinguish from nationalism, an ideology to which they almost all subscribed.

Typical was A. M. Ghisalberti who, after a period of schoolteaching, gained his first university job in 1931 with the help of a recommendation from Volpe. The fact that he was married to a Jewess shook Ghisalberti's allegiance to the regime after 1938, but Volpe was also known to have criticised the racial laws, and he (and Chabod) seem to have helped Ghisalberti win promotion from a chair at Perugia to one at Rome in 1941. When, very recently, Ghisalberti published his memoirs, he was anxious to condemn Italy's role in the Second World War[42] and to endorse the 'one man alone' thesis about Mussolini's responsibility for it.[43] At the same time, Ghisalberti piously defended Italy's policies leading to the First World War and, for example, justified the seizure of Libya in 1911–12. The image of Rome, the 'Eternal City', the 'sanctuary of the Nation', he said, had remained graven on his heart since a youthful visit. In turn, this generic nationalism blended easily with professional conservatism. As far as Ghisalberti could see, no reason existed seriously to criticise the baronial, patron–client, side of the Italian academic system.[44] Its tutelary gods had guided him through a time of troubles and, as he grew older, he remarked somewhat innocently, every time that one of his students found an academic job he felt himself rejuvenated.[45]

Ghisalberti's own special area of expertise, like that of his even more distinguished and durable colleague, Franco Valsecchi, was the Risorgimento, a subject which produced bitter debate in the 1950s as non-Marxists strove to defend the thesis of the *rivoluzione nazionale* from Gramscian or radical attack.[46] Ghisalberti had been made secretary of the *Società nazionale per la Storia del Risorgimento* back in 1935 when, inevitably, Volpe was a leading light in that body.

During the second decade of Fascism, the organisation which expanded almost to the extent of becoming the umbrella under which all Italian contemporary historians, especially those expert in foreign affairs, could shelter, was the *Istituto per gli studi di politica internazionale* (I.S.P.I.).[47] In retrospect, I.S.P.I. appears one of the most characteristic creations of the historical profession in inter-war Italy. Originally founded in Milan by elements near G.U.F. (and headed by Pierfranco Gaslini), I.S.P.I. soon acquired a guardian angel in the tyre magnate, Alberto Pirelli, who became President on 14 March 1935. Apart from his career as an industrialist, Pirelli had experience in financial diplomacy both before and after the March on Rome. From 1927–9, he had been President of the International Chamber of Commerce and he preserved excellent contacts with the English and French speaking business worlds. Pirelli had the head office of its international affiliate at Brussels.

After the event, I.S.P.I. has sometimes been regarded as a centre of Anti-Fascism, a haven for young historians who opposed the regime.[48] Perhaps the caution of I.S.P.I., or, better its professionalism (most of its publications did attempt to get 'the facts' straight) does amount to Anti-Fascism. Ruggero Zangrandi, whose book is the source of so much information and so many myths about the Resistance, cites I.S.P.I. and its journals as the place to which dissidents turned for 'information which the daily press ignored or distorted'.[49]

It is clear that I.S.P.I. publications were less given to Fascist excess than were those of a rival body such as the *Istituto nazionale fascista di cultura*. Yet, again ideological divisions are hard to map out precisely. In I.S.P.I., though criticism of Staracean or Hitlerian Fascism may have been possible and even *de mode*, there were few signs of any deviation from that brand of conservatism which Volpe represented so well, or from that nationalist continuity which united so many aspects of expert 'public opinion' in Fascist and Liberal Italy.

Typical was the handbook on Russia published by Lino Cappuccio in October 1940. There, amid much useful and accurate detail, Cappuccio explained that the Russians were not naturally hard-working owing to their 'overwhelmingly Eastern tendency to mysticism and fatalism'. Bouts of lassitude could be followed by bouts of (ill-directed) energy: 'Every action and every idea ... [would then be] conducted to its logical conclusion'. Demonstrably, argued Cappuccio, the Russian people had not wanted the Revolution but 'they resigned themselves to it' as, similarly, they resigned themselves to the 'iron yoke of Bolshevism'.

Given the publication date of his book, Cappuccio was not surprisingly a little ambiguous about that 'typical peasant', Stalin, whose 'totalitarian regime' he said, manifested a natural drift to 'an integral national communism'. Though the time when the Russians would don black shirts might still be far off, Cappuccio was comforted by his prediction that Russia and Britain were geopolitically at opposite poles and therefore doomed to inevitable conflict. It was also pleasing that, by contrast, geopolitics and tradition gave Italy the chance to pursue a realistic foreign policy in the East. Although Marxism remained 'the greatest existing danger for the civilization of the white race and especially that which is Roman and Catholic', Italy could cope with Stalin's Russia by the sensible mechanism of merely pursuing her own 'vital interests'.

In any case, the Future belonged to Rome. 'The Marxist tradition is dead . . . The twentieth century is undoubtedly destined to be the century of fascism.' Even in Russia, the 'Asiatic darkness' of the purges might eventually be lit up by the bright light of Fascism.[50]

In a different key, but of similar overall ideology were the various handbooks which I.S.P.I. published from time to time on regions nearer to Italy's natural sphere of interest. Both before and after the sad coup of Good Friday 1939, I.S.P.I. publications stressed the civilising mission being conducted by Italy in Albania.[51] Volpe implied that such a mission might not be out of place in Corsica, while a younger author deplored the manner in which 'the long and rapacious claw' of Britain had penetrated into the 'living flesh' of Malta.[52]

Similarly, I.S.P.I. addressed paternal attention to the *quarte* (and *quinte*) *sponde*. The old nationalist historian and politician, Arrigo Solmi (whose student Gaslini had been),[53] argued, for example, that Italo-Egyptian friendship had sprung from 'a profound and spontaneous popular senti-ment', and that the Italo-British war in North Africa was by no means the responsibility of Italy. Other commentators agreed that archaeology, emigration and commerce together made it obvious that the 'African continent' was the 'natural and necessary field for the political and the economic expansion of Italy'.[54] Renzo Sertoli Salis, an historian of more overt Fascism, reminded I.S.P.I. members that Italy should not forget her old interests in Arabia and the Yemen. British ownership of Aden need not be permanent and all Italians should comprehend that 'the freedom of . . . the Red Sea – no less than that of the Mediterranean of which it is only a continuation – is indispensable for whomever is called by history and by destiny to live and to grow'.[55]

Nor did I.S.P.I. forbear from publishing works of more immediate propagandist significance. The nationalist and Fascist journalist, Concetto Pettinato, brought out his *La Francia vinta* in 1941. Though not refraining from criticism of Germany, Pettinato mocked that France which had so passively accepted its defeat. He went on to warn against the 'chivalrous spirit' which he discerned as being displayed by both the victors, but especially by Italy. France should be pressed harder to purge the Jews,

Masons and others who had caused her defeat. In particular, Pettinato gloated over the fashion in which 'the catastrophe had surprised [France's] intellectuals while they were all at table, all fat, all rich, all famous'. It was rubbish, added Pettinato ingenuously, to think that Italians had any sense of inferiority towards France, when the manifest achievements of Italian intellectuals (which he listed at length) were so clearly equal to those of their French rivals.[56]

Rather similar was the writing of Amedeo Giannini, a journalist, diplomat and historian who, by 1940, could boast the authorship of over three hundred books. That year, he added to his total by publishing for I.S.P.I. a brief survey of Anglo-Italian relations. He had a plain message to relate. 'Perfidious and ruthless' England was always a destined opponent of passionate, poetic, idealistic and romantic Italy. England had never been a loyal friend and her long trail of ruthless betrayals of Italy had been finally exposed during the Ethiopian War. By 1940, that Italy which had become 'by itself and for itself a living force in Europe and in the world' could embark on war joyfully because England had left her with no alternative.[57]

Given the volume of I.S.P.I.'s productions, this list of works, and these sentiments, can be repeated almost endlessly. But perhaps the most interesting of I.S.P.I.'s publications was a lengthy study by Pirelli himself on war economy, *Economia e guerra*. Volume I was published in May 1940; volume II in July.

As befitted I.S.P.I.'s purposes, much of the book is devoted to information. The second volume in particular gives detailed lists of the provisions for war being made by various combatant and non-combatant states. Pirelli also firmly underlined the need for a thoroughgoing economic and social preparation for modern war. At times, this might have seemed to have hinted at a criticism of Mussolini's Italy which, it would soon be plain, would run by far the least modernised war effort of any of the major belligerents.

Yet, if criticism was intended, it was certainly very muted and often outweighed by praise of Mussolini and by endorsement of some of the more non-materialist and silly aspects of Fascist ideology. Rationalisation, mechanisation and standardisation may appear the answers for a modern war economy. But, Pirelli opined, qualitative factors such as military or political leadership, in which Italy was so well equipped, could always outweigh quantitative ones. In any case, noted Pirelli, 'in respect of war production, especially in some fields, [Fascist Italy has already] reached . . . a technical perfection of the highest kind'.

There were other ways in which Pirelli strayed from 'objective' analysis. The first volume of *Economia e guerra* concluded with some hortatory remarks addressed to those old Powers which were seeking to deny to 'the younger Nations' the chance of 'growth and a sufficient level of economic independence'. Recoiling from too stark a conjuncture of Fascist Italy and Nazi Germany, Pirelli wistfully recalled the Four Power Pact of 1933. This agreement could have opened the ideal pathway along which 'the proletarian Nations' could have been admitted into that spiritually united Europe of which Mussolini was the special prophet.[58]

In his second volume, Pirelli cast aside the image of Mussolini as a sort of Fascist Common Marketeer. Rather, he declared, the solution to the Mediterranean question presently being attempted in war was for Italy 'a necessity of life, an essential pre-condition' for further economic growth. In this instance, as in so many 'the Italian people have another motive of gratitude to the *Duce* for his anticipatory vision and for his indomitable will'.[59]

Despite the difference in emphasis between his comments before and after June 1940, Pirelli, throughout his book, expressed a world view which had been repeatedly endorsed by other members of I.S.P.I. and which can be regarded as standard among those historians who fellow-travelled with Fascist Italy. Mario Toscano,[60] Pietro Silva,[61] Augusto Torre,[62] Francesco Cataluccio,[63] Volpe, and even Luigi Salvatorelli[64] and Federico Chabod[65] did not object to this curiously idealist kind of 'realism'. In relation to foreign affairs, this Italian version of *realpolitik* had three aspects. Italy may have been the least of the Great Powers, but she was a Great Power and therefore should and indeed must pursue the policy of a Great Power. The world of diplomacy, however, was harsh and cruel, a place of Darwinian struggle in which might created right. Wars, explained Augusto Torre, an I.S.P.I. historian whose career had begun before Fascism and would continue well beyond it, were 'natural phenomena'. Historians should not waste their time trying to determine a Power's responsibility in causing a war, since each dispute was prompted simply 'by a conflict of interests . . . and ambitions'.[66]

The third piece of data regarded as basic by most I.S.P.I. historians was that Mussolini's regime represented a continuity and not a parenthesis in Italian diplomacy. Though figures like Mussolini or Crispi normally received the most praise, all Italian diplomatists from Cavour onwards were assumed to have recognised the 'cardinal points' of Italy's special international position. Moments of stasis and moments of expansion alternated largely because the opportunities offered within the international constellation did also.[67]

Very similar to I.S.P.I. in their expression of an overt if at times critical loyalty to Mussolinian Fascism and a continuing and uncritical conservative nationalism were the articles contained in the *Dizionario di Politica*.

This four volume work was published in 1940, but is of special interest because almost all of its contents had been prepared in the hiatus period of 'non-belligerency'.

Just as I.S.P.I. received both praise and finance from Mussolini himself,[68] so the Dizionario was formally blessed by the Partito Nazionale Fascista. Fernando Mezzasoma, in his capacity as Deputy Secretary of the Party, wrote the preface, with the assistance of the Fascist academics, Guido Mancini, Antonio Pagliaro and Giuseppe Martini. Such Fascist luminaries as Roberto Farinacci (he was the expert on squadrismo)[69], Alessandro Pavolini, Carlo Curciò or Francesco Repaci contributed their skills.

Amid these more notorious Fascists was once again Gioacchino Volpe. Though he contributed only one article in his own name (inevitably it was the entry on Corsica, 'isola italiana, dipartimento francese'),[70] Volpe played a major organising role for the Dizionario. Working through the Istituto dell'Enciclopedia italiana, a body which Mezzasoma had declared to have 'created in its circle, a nucleus of fervent Fascist activity',[71] Volpe was able to assemble many young historians of promise who had already participated in I.S.P.I. and who were destined to have distinguished careers after 1945.

Rodolfo Mosca was one pertinacious contributor whose expertise could extend from Denmark to Mexico. For the most part, Mosca wrote with that scrupulous accuracy which, as it had done in I.S.P.I., typified much of the Dizionario. But, every now and again, Mosca's objectivity wavered. What he said was not surprising but it was characteristic.

Thus, Mosca averred, Italian entry into the Spanish Civil War had been provoked by 'Russian interference in the Mediterranean'. Thereafter, Spain had been duly and consistently appreciative of the generosity of Italian aid. Fascism had also done well by its emigrants. The simple fact of its existence brought 'example and comfort' to Italians in Argentina and thus both stimulated their nationalism and enhanced their prestige.[72]

Another very frequent contributor to the Dizionario was A. C. Jemolo, a man who, under the Republic, would become perhaps the best known of Christian Democratic historians.[73] Appropriately enough, Jemolo generally wrote about clerical themes – Catholic Action, canonical law, Modernism – in a reasonably pious vein. But piety could extend to Fascist State as well as to Papal Church. 'No press censorship currently exists in Italy', Jemolo noted in the entry 'Censura'. Rather there were 'controls as required' to assist the periodical press especially towards ideal 'cultural roles', such as that expressed in the formation of a 'national consciousness'. In close agreement with Volpe, Jemolo saw Crispi as the last statesman of Liberal Italy, the genuine precursor of Fascism, who, 'like few of his generation, possessed an ardent love for the *patria* combined with an adequate vision of what a Great Power must be'. Even Crispi was no real competitor for Mussolini. One telling piece of evidence was that Mussolini in the Lateran Pacts had found the ideal answer to that tiresomely ancient conflict between Church and State. As a result, he presided over 'a very strong regime which possessed enormous [domestic and international] prestige'.[74]

Other clichés of the Right echo through the pages of the *Dizionario*. 'History', explained the military historian, Piero Pieri, in his entry on Napoleon, 'is not a mechanistic process: rather it is the Great Man who gives form and life to what is otherwise developing naturally.'[75] When the Risorgimento was mentioned by historians such as Valsecchi or Walter Maturi, it was naturally defined as the *rivoluzione nazionale*. This *rivoluzione*'s best sentiments were in turn bequeathed to Crispi and from him passed to the A.N.I. and on to Mussolini.[76] International affairs offered only a sombre tale of struggle, in which the best policy was always realism. The Triple Alliance, noted Augusto Torre, had permitted Italy no chance of realising her aspirations towards the Alps, in the Adriatic or Mediterranean. 'Therefore, the moment at which the chance of satisfying these aspirations could be perceived, [the Alliance][77] was destined to collapse. And so it did.' The Great Powers, underlined Federico Chabod, had been and remained the major engines of international affairs.[78] Any 'balance of power' was, according to Carlo Morandi, no more than a temporary expedient. Peace could 'not be based on a utopian equality of the nations'; rather, to be effective and lasting, it must accept an 'inevitable hierarchy among the Powers'.[79]

As has already been noted, most of these ideas were scarcely controversial to that generation of historians over which Volpe presided. Rather more interesting and idiosyncratic were the entries composed by Delio Cantimori, a young intellectual historian who would become a Marxist and teach Renzo De Felice who is currently Italy's major historian of Fascism.

Cantimori wrote many articles for the *Dizionario*. Most were restricted to his special area of expertise, intellectual history – the Anglican Church, Calvinism or Kant. But he also wrote about more recent political events. Crispi was 'the last great exponent of the traditional liberal movement'. Bismarck was an admirable figure who had diagnosed the weakness and the threat of that 'mastadonic organisation', the S.P.D., but who nonetheless, by contrast with more modern figures, lacked 'a new political or social idea'.

These views may have been trite, but Cantimori could be more intellectually ambitious than were some of the more circumspectly historicist writers. In a number of entries, Cantimori began an exploration of the meaning of the Fascist and totalitarian state. The P.N.F., he declared, had taken over the 'function of *the* party of State' and thus had absorbed those sections which might previously have found a resting place in a party of the Centre. 'In any case', he explained, 'in a totalitarian philosophy such as the Fascist one, the terms, "right", "centre" or "left" no longer have any present value and instead merely preserve an historical significance.'

But perhaps Cantimori's most interesting pieces were those on Germany and on National Socialism. There, as in some other entries (for example, that by Amedeo Tosti on Poland)[80] and as in some I.S.P.I. publications, appeared discreet criticism of Nazi practice and theory. Nazi foreign policy, it was remarked, had pursued the laudable 'national principle' until March 1939. But, after that, Germany had switched to a programme of *Mitteleuropa* and more, which in turn, had brought on a war with Britain and France, the result of which none could foretell. Nazi racism (a rigid anti-Semitism was defined as the staunchest of all Nazi beliefs) was not 'an historic and cultural concept but rather an ethico-racial one'.[81]

In this last regard, Cantimori was patently differentiating Fascism and National Socialism. It was true that the segment on National Socialism contained no explicit parallels with Fascism. But this omission became all the more eloquent given the alleged comparisons with Fascism which were elsewhere dragged into the most diverse subjects. By his silence, Cantimori was stressing both the virtue of the Fascist State, and his belief in its myth, while denying that such virtue should be wasted in a necessary alliance with that Nazism which might well be both diplomatically dangerous and intellectually dubious.

In 1937, Giorgio Pini, full of Fascist zeal, remarked that Massimo D'Azeglio's famous comment needed up-dating: 'oggi, fatto l'impero, bisogna fare gli imperialisti'.[82] By contrast, a couple of years later, Pierfranco Gaslini praised a new I.S.P.I. publication (to be edited by Morandi and Chabod) for assembling 'in the most totalitarian fashion possible all those involved in historical or geographical study'.[83] These two statements sum up the debate which has continued over the contribution of historians to the Fascist 'consensus'.[84] Was an institution like I.S.P.I. or a publication like the *Dizionario* 'the most characteristic cultural fruit of the imperial policy of Fascism'? [85] Was a figure like Volpe one of the 'foremost managers of the regime's culture'?[86] Or were such organisations and individuals healthy elements which did their best to resist Fascism?

Or perhaps is the question wrong? For, in fact, what a study of the Italian historical profession, particularly that element expert in foreign affairs, in the period between the wars seems to indicate is a marked continuity both in personnel and in world view. Volpe, Solmi, Ciasca,[87] Silva and the rest, for all their individual differences, were fundamentally united in their cherishing of an anti-Giolittian, authoritarian and nationalist tradition originally sprung from the A.N.I. These ideas were then passed on to the new generation which won its spurs under Fascism, yet remained sufficiently detached from Mussolini's regime not to lose too many of their positions or too much of their intellectual prestige after 1945. In turn, these *curricula vitae* imply that fellow-travelling with Fascism was not so difficult either to succeed in before 1943 (if an individual possessed certain skills needed in the academic game) or to disavow in the ostensibly changed world of the Republic. Before 1941–2, these mainstream historians deplored a certain crudeness, especially a populist anti-intellectualism, which they saw in Fascism; they may well more actively have disliked the racial laws and the German alliance, but their real quarrel with Mussolini originated most plainly in the fact that his Italy lost the war and thereafter again made it perilously evident that 'if we want things to stay as they are, things will have to change'.

Although it has rarely been remarked on, this contamination of Italian historiography by Fascism (and the accompanying and more extensive conservative watering down of Fascism through so many conservative survivals) should not cause much astonishment. After all, the German historical and teaching professions before 1944, were not a source of much resistance to Nazism, though figures such as Ritter doubtless objected to the 'beast from the abyss' aspect of Nazism.[88] Indeed, as has already been noted, everywhere mainstream history, especially mainstream diplomatic history, has had a special relationship with nationalism in which the historian's chief task has been to watch over the national myth.

In Italy, this background in moderate, 'fellow-travelling' Fascism has had an interesting effect on the historical profession since 1945. Many historians who had worked with the regime undoubtedly detached themselves from it genuinely as it became clear that Italy had lost the Second World War and as the enormity of German war crimes and the Fascist complicity in those crimes became apparent. Alberto Moravia, for example, has recalled how, in the aftermath of Fascism, he 'observed pathetic scenes of self-criticism, almost of self-flagellation'. He saw a nameless historian 'burst into tears' when he contemplated his previous political role.[89] A genuine revulsion from Fascism thus could occur, though it is fair to add that, for historians as for other members of the Italian cultural elite, opportunism must also often have played a part. Moreover, perhaps the abjuring of Fascism did not always need to be too traumatic. In many instances, post-war 'Anti-Fascism' did not require abandonment of ideas which had been endorsed or praised by Fascism but which now did not seem necessarily part of it.

One striking feature of post-war Italian historiography has been until recently its almost total repudiation of the Mussolinian regime. In the area of foreign policy, for example, only such die-hards as Luigi Villari, the erstwhile semi-official propagandist to the Anglo-Saxon world, and Attilio Tamaro, in the special tones of a 'border Fascist', sought to defend the regime à l'outrance.[90] Rather, the 'one man alone' thesis that Mussolini had personally and capriciously taken Italy into the Second World War and then paid the inevitable penalty received almost universal endorsement.

Yet, the men who now made their careers writing Italian diplomatic history were precisely those who had worked with Volpe before 1943. By the 1960s, for example, the Commission whose job it was to publish the *Documenti diplomatici italiani* contained a galaxy of pre-war talent. Mario Toscano who, as a Jew, had not collaborated openly in the *Dizionario,* but who had written nationalist and conservative history in the 1930s, was the President. Members of his committee included Rodolfo Mosca, Giacomo Perticone, Ernesto Sestan, Augusto Torre, Luigi Salvatorelli, Franco Valsecchi and Giuseppe Vedovato of I.S.P.I. or *Dizionario* days. The most prominent figure from the next generation was the Marxist, Giampiero Carocci, who, as Vice-Secretary, marked out for the P.C.I. its own plot in this small academic example of *lottizzazione.*

This sort of sociological analysis could probably be taken much further. But what is perhaps more interesting is what Italy's post-war historians generally said about Fascism and why they said it.

In one sense, Italian historians split into two opposing camps as they surveyed Fascism. The liberal school, in one form or another, agreed with Benedetto Croce (a figure whose resistance to Fascism from the aristocratic redoubt of his Neapolitan *palazzo* has already been subjected to withering fire from Denis Mack Smith).[91] Fascism was a 'parenthesis' in Italian history. The 'moral sickness' which swept Europe as a result of the First World War took root in Italy almost by accident. Fascism had broken from all Italy's best traditions. The individual, Mussolini, was overwhelmingly responsible for these ills (in the same way that conservative German historians sought to blame Hitler, British historians Neville Chamberlain and French historians Pétain or Laval).

In Italy, as elsewhere, the thesis of the parenthesis had one unstated but very plain implication. The bracket was closed at the end as well as at the beginning. The political revolution which created the Italian Republic need not be accompanied by a social one. And, intellectually, the academic world could proceed unpurged and with its ideas unmodified, since it had shared none of the negative aspects of Fascism.

Liberal historiography was of course contested by Marxism whose practitioners usually owed some sort of allegiance to the P.C.I. For such historians, Fascism was not a moral sickness but 'the open terrorist dictatorship of the most reactionary, most chauvinist and most imperialist elements of finance capital'. Rather than being a parenthesis, Fascism expressed the natural movement of Italian history into an imperialist phase. This movement became threatening during the Giolittian period and was symbolised by the *svolta imperialistica* into the Libyan war. This colonial campaign merely opened a phase of general war which itself further pushed Italian industry towards monopolisation. In the *dopo-guerra*, Fascism came to power in a conspiracy between certain industrialists and financiers and their 'legal representatives' (the King, Pope, Parliament, Army, Judiciary and Bureaucracy). The foot-soldiers of such forces were the members of that petit-bourgeoisie which economic change was rendering redundant. Fascism was not a 'revolution' in the sense that it did not win the genuine 'consensus' of the Italian people. It was, however, very wicked and far more blatantly so than anything which had occurred in the Italian past.

Opposing this Evil, Marxist historians emphasised, there had always been a Good – the Resistance which had never given up the fight against Fascism. This Resistance had attracted some Catholics, liberals or radicals, but they had only played out again that part which Marx and Engels had assigned to the intelligentsia in the *Communist Manifesto*:

In times when the class struggle nears the decisive hour, the process of dissolution going on within the ruling class, in fact within the whole range of old society, assumes such a violent glaring character, that a small section of the ruling class cuts itself adrift, and joins the revolutionary class. . . . In particular, a portion of the bourgeois ideologists, who have raised themselves to the level of comprehending the historical movement as a whole [join the Revolution].[92]

However, the real centre of the Resistance always remained the working class and that P.C.I. which was its natural vanguard.

Despite their drastically different interpretations both of past and of present, the Marxist and liberal Crocean factions did possess ground for compromise in much the same way that the D.C. as the 'party of government' could co-exist politically with the P.C.I. as the 'party of opposition'. Indeed, for an outsider, it almost tempting to detect a tacit, *de facto* alliance.

Since Catholic historiography was so weak as to be almost non-existent, non-Marxist Italian historians found sanctuary under the generic label of 'liberalism'. Their political support was directed to the minor 'lay', 'centre' parties of the Italian system (P.L.I., P.S.D.I., P.R.I., and after 1961, P.S.I.). They could also rely on international recognition from the 'West', especially the United States, in events such as that Tenth International Congress of Historical Sciences with which this paper began.

Non-Marxist historians did not write much about Fascism, though they usually stressed the despicable nature of Mussolini and his entourage and the absurdity and unpopularity of the Fascist decision to enter the Second World War. But, rather than Fascism, the Risorgimento or Liberal Italy proffered more worthy and more illuminating areas of study.

Given the slow but steady withdrawal of the P.C.I. from Moscow's tutelage, it might be expected that Italian Marxism, in contrast to Italian liberalism, would stimulate a luxuriant and innovative historiography on Fascism. Yet, despite some achievement, for a long time this was largely not so. Rather than engaging in general analysis, Marxist historiography turned in on itself to produce often very able local histories, accounts of the pre-Fascist origins of Italian socialism or studies of the Resistance. With the exception notably of Giorgio Rochat, the pro-P.C.I. Left preferred to write the history of its friends rather than its enemies.

This decision was reinforced by another factor. From the 1950s, the theories of Gramsci gradually ousted more straightforward, 'Stalinist' Marxism. And, as far as historians were concerned, Gramsci could be read in a markedly idealist fashion. His theory of hegemony appeared to indicate that ideas mattered and so did intellectuals. Intellectually, Crocean and even Gentilean idealism could resurface in Italian Marxism.

Politically, the message was more precise. It might be that 'the wind from the North' had not swept Italy into Revolution from 1943 to 1948. But a revolution could still be in the making in the minds of the citizens of Republican Italy. To this purpose, historians should make plain the longevity and the nobility of the socialist tradition, the goodness of which had triumphed over wicked Fascism and must be destined to go on triumphing. 'Society' and the powerless, which were the source of this tradition, should be studied; 'politics' and the powerful could be left to await their imminent end.

For, once it was plain that Fascism was wicked, nothing much more need be said. Again, in retrospect, another strange, *de facto* alliance can be perceived. Leftist historiography would largely leave Fascism alone; but Leftist 'national popular' literature and 'neo-realist' film would endlessly portray to the masses the vileness of the Fascist period and the urgency of the requirement to keep struggling against a Fascism whose position in past or present became increasingly ill-defined. It was this constellation of ideas which created the 'myth of the Resistance' which soon fundamentally underpinned much of both the politics and culture of the Italian Republic.

Rather as in the historical professions of Britain, France and West Germany, in Italian historiography both of Left and Right the Second World War lived on beyond 1945. Indeed in Italy, precisely because the myths of the war were so interwoven into the perhaps fragile political and social system, the chanting of old refrains has been hardest to silence. In the 1970s, the 'De Felice affair' did begin to expose some of the frailties of myths on the Left. By contrast, the myths of the 'parenthesis' and of the 'one man alone' thesis, the myths of the Right, remain only very feebly contested.

Politically, the elections of June 1983, with the severe weakening of the D.C. and the modest stengthening of the P.S.I., P.R.I. (and M.S.I.), have left Italy at the cross-roads. The historiography of Fascism has a similar Janus face. Until liberal and conservative Italian historians are willing to be more frank about the size of their Fascist inheritance and the extent to which Nationalism dominated Fascism rather than vice versa, Italy, for all its current freedom and diversity, will remain a country which has only partially experienced what K. D. Bracher has termed the 'emancipation from yesterday'.[93]

Part III

7

The political uses of military intelligence: evaluating the threat of a Jewish revolt against Britain during the Second World War

RONALD ZWEIG

The White Paper on Palestine of May 1939 represented a major turning point in Britain's pre-war policy in the Middle East. In an attempt to meet Arab demands (and hopefully thereby ensure the support of the Moslem world should war break out against Germany) Britain agreed to limit Jewish immigration into Palestine and to terminate it completely after five years; to limit drastically the sale of land to Jews by Arabs and move towards responsible self-government with a promise of a constitutional conference after five years leading to independence for a Palestinian state. However when the British Government released the White Paper in May 1939, neither Arabs nor Jews endorsed the new policy. The Jews rejected the basic premises of the policy – that the Jewish National Home in Palestine had already been established and that Britain had thus fulfilled its obligations to the Jewish people under the Balfour Declaration. The Arabs of Palestine (as represented by the Arab Higher Committee) rejected the new policy because they felt that in a number of matters the new policy did not go far enough to meet their demands, while the leading independent Arab states (Egypt, Iraq and Saudi Arabia) refused to endorse the new policy until it had first been accepted by the Palestinians. While the rejection of the new policy by the Jews was anticipated, the response of the Arab world to the wide concessions made to them over Palestine disappointed British officialdom in Whitehall. But there was a limit to the concessions which the British Government felt it could make to Arab opinion. As one Colonial Office official pointed out, 'The objections of the extremist Arabs and of the Jews to the White Paper policy are so fundamental that in neither case will [their] objections be dispelled by

109

tinkering with that document. We must now go straight ahead with a firm front and let both sides know we have said our last word.'[1]

Just as Britain felt that it could live with the lack of Arab endorsement of its new Palestine policy so it also knew that Jewish opposition to the policy could, in 1939, be overcome. Physical opposition by the Jewish community in Palestine (the *Yishuv* as it was called in Hebrew) to the British was discounted at the very beginning. As General R. H. Haining (ex-General Officer Commanding, Palestine Forces) pointed out to the Colonial Office when he returned to London, the Jews were 'hysterical, and not, by nature, very brave or determined'.[2] Despite isolated acts of Jewish terrorism, no general Jewish revolt against Britain was seriously considered. In the course of the next two years this assessment underwent a radical change. Parallel with the growing difficulties which Britain faced in implementing the White Paper policy, the ability of the Jews to physically obstruct Britain's freedom of movement in Palestine after the war came under discussion in London and amongst the various British authorities in the Middle East. Eventually this topic came to be the major preoccupation of all British officials dealing with the Palestine problem. How and why this came about is the subject of this article.

During 1941, when it became apparent that the White Paper's prescriptions for the constitutional advance of the Mandate towards independence could not be implemented,[3] British official circles began to debate various other solutions to the Palestine conundrum in unofficial, informal debate and correspondence. From Palestine itself the High Commissioner, Sir Harold MacMichael, who had strongly supported the pro-Arab redirection of policy embodied in the 1939 White Paper but had equally strongly opposed its constitutional provisions, argued that any new policy would have to be based first and foremost on the abolition of the Mandate and the conversion of Palestine into a Crown Colony.[4] The aim of this proposal was to allow the disestablishment of the Jewish Agency, the political and organizational heart of the Jewish community in Palestine, whose official role had been enshrined in the terms of the League of Nations Mandate by which Britain was bound. In September 1941 MacMichael repeated this proposal in a lengthy despatch to London, in which he argued that only after prolonged British tutelage unrestricted by the obligations of the Mandate towards the *Yishuv*, and only by disestablishing the Jewish Agency (which 'with its palatial offices, its network of Departments, and its powerful international affiliations, tends to overshadow the local Government') would it be possible to foster the sort of Jewish–Arab cooperation which would permit eventual independence.[5] In subsequent correspondence with the Colonial Secretary, MacMichael gave additional reasons for the measures he proposed:

If we are not very careful His Majesty's Government will be faced with the dilemma of either having to give way to the exaggerated demands of the Jews and so provoking rebellion in the Middle East . . . or of having to suppress the Jews *vi et armis* (which I do not see them doing). It will be difficult enough, in any case, to avoid bloodshed here at the end of the war and the best way of minimizing the risk is to put the brake on the Jews betimes.[6]

In his earliest proposal in 1941, and in all subsequent versions of it, MacMichael had consistently argued that the Jewish Agency must be disestablished if the Jewish community in Palestine was to be prevented from imposing its own solution to the Palestine problem. Despite the official dismissal of MacMichael's proposals generally, and the impossibility of taking up this specific suggestion, by late 1941 both the Foreign and the Colonial Office had come to share the concern of the British authorities in the Middle East at the growing radicalization of the *Yishuv*. The crystallization of a Zionist political programme during 1942, the growth of Jewish illegal military organizations and the opening of a pro-Zionist propaganda campaign in the United States all confronted Britain with a new challenge to its authority in Palestine at a time of great uncertainty concerning its own policy there. As a result of the interviews which the Colonial Secretary at the time, Lord Moyne, had held with Chaim Weizmann and David Ben Gurion in August 1941, the Colonial Office realized that authoritative Zionist circles were looking to the creation of a Jewish state in Palestine as a solution to the inevitable post-war Jewish refugee problem. This awareness prompted the Colonial Office to circulate a Cabinet paper in September 1941 advocating that the Government formulate a policy designed to cope with the Jewish refugee problem, and at the same time issue a statement of its commitment to the White Paper of 1939 in order to deflate the Zionists' rising expectations concerning Palestine. However consideration of the paper was delayed indefinitely and the matter progressed no further at Cabinet level. Shortly afterwards the question of the post-war Jewish refugee problem came under consideration in the Foreign Office when it was learnt that even non-Zionist Jewish circles were beginning to consider that Palestine would have to absorb large numbers of Jewish refugees after the war, contrary to the specific provisions of the White Paper of 1939 and to the policy it embodied.[7] In December 1941 both the Foreign and the Colonial Offices came into possession of a number of documents which confirmed the earlier indication of the lines on which both Zionist and non-Zionist Jews were thinking. The most significant of these documents was a lengthy memorandum by Ben Gurion entitled 'Outlines of Zionist Policy', in which the Chairman of the Jewish Agency Executive argued (as he had already done in his interview with Lord Moyne in August) that the Jewish refugee problem could be solved only by large-scale Jewish immigration into Palestine, and that this could be achieved only by a sovereign Jewish government.[8]

Weizmann's and Ben Gurion's candid comments to Moyne in August 1941, and Ben Gurion's political programme, had not been formally endorsed by any authoritative Zionist body. In fact, during 1941–2 the question of Zionism's final objectives, and the means to be employed to obtain them, were the subject of considerable controversy in Zionist circles in Palestine and elsewhere. Before Ben Gurion left Palestine in July 1941 for London and subsequently America, he had failed to obtain authority from the Jewish Agency Executive or any other body to raise the demand for a Jewish state publicly.[9] Nevertheless, by late 1941 both the Foreign and the Colonial Offices were convinced that, regardless of whether Ben Gurion's programme had been endorsed or not (a question they did not ask), the views it contained did represent the demands which the Zionists would eventually articulate. Thus, when Weizmann published an article in January 1942 in the journal *Foreign Affairs*, arguing that: 'The Arabs must . . . be told that the Jews will be encouraged to settle in Palestine, and will control their own immigration; that here Jews who so desire will be able to achieve their freedom and self-government by establishing a state of their own . . .'[10] it occasioned no comment from either of the Departments concerned. Similarly, when Ben Gurion succeeded in having the establishment of a Jewish 'Commonwealth' in Palestine after the war adopted as a plank in the formal policy of the Zionist Organisation of America at the Biltmore Conference of May 1942, it was not considered by the British Government as being a particularly significant development.[11]

The Foreign Office considered that Ben Gurion's political programme, which it had discussed six months prior to the Biltmore Conference, was the definitive indicator of Zionist thinking, and the Eastern, Refugee, American and Central Departments minuted on it at length. The Eastern Department expressed the most obvious British anxiety – that Ben Gurion's programme 'could only be achieved by bloodshed, i.e. not the shedding of Arab and Jewish blood alone, but inevitably British blood'.[12]

The problem posed by the illegal Jewish military organizations (primarily the *Hagana* and the *Irgun Zvai Leumi*),[13] together with the existence of large numbers of Jews in the various para-military Police formations (formed by the Government of Palestine during the Arab revolt to protect Jewish settlements), had been raised tentatively in Whitehall shortly before the release of the White Paper in May 1939.[14] British officials were concerned that despite the general record of self-restraint on the part of the *Yishuv* in the inter-communal violence of the Arab revolt, the isolated incidents of Jewish terrorism during the negotiations which had preceded the release of the White Paper and immediately afterwards might presage a more serious attempt by the *Yishuv* to prevent Britain from imposing the immigration or land sales restrictions of the White Paper, or from implementing its constitutional provisions.[15] Consequently during 1939 the functional cooperation between the *Hagana* and the British Army in Palestine, which had developed in the course of the Arab revolt, was terminated.

The outbreak of war saw the cessation of incidents of Jewish terrorism, and in September 1939 over one hundred and thirty six thousand Jews registered in a campaign organized by the Jewish Agency as a demonstration of the size of the *Yishuv*'s potential contribution to the British Imperial war effort.[16] Ironically, the size of the response alarmed rather than impressed the Palestine authorities, who saw it as a measure of the resources which the Agency might be able to mobilize against Britain should it choose to oppose the White Paper by force. In early October, shortly after the registration, forty-three members of the *Hagana* were arrested during an illegal para-military training exercise, and the General Officer Commanding in Palestine, Lt-General M. Barker used the occasion to request authority for an energetic campaign designed to reduce the numbers of arms available legally to the Jewish settlements,[17] to reduce the number of Jewish Settlement Police (the best armed and trained of the various Jewish Police formations) and to demand the disbanding of all Jewish illegal organizations and the surrender of illegal arms (to be followed by 'a thorough search for Jewish arms' if the demand was not complied with).[18]

Commenting on the size of the Jewish illegal arsenal, Barker stated that 'Reports vary widely as to the number of illegal arms held. A fair estimate is 1,500–2,000 rifles and 8,000–10,000 pistols of all types, and a considerable but incalculable stock of handgrenades.'[19] This was not a particularly large arsenal given the disturbances of the previous three years, when the Palestine authorities had effectively lost control of the countryside to rebel Arab groups. Nevertheless, Barker argued that the continued existence of the illegal arms, and of the *Hagana*, after the Army had restored law and order, was 'based on the belief that [the Jews] cannot trust the British Empire to produce the necessary forces for the defence of Palestine, and, secondly, a firm determination that sooner or later the Jewish community will occupy Palestine by force of arms and hold it against any aggression from any power whomsoever.'[20] However both the High Commissioner and the Commander-in-Chief, Middle East Forces, General Wavell, were opposed to the policy of active disarming and wholesale arms searches which Barker advocated, proposing instead that searches be conducted only in cases where definite information on the location of hidden arms caches in individual Jewish settlements had been received.[21] The Colonial Secretary at that time, Malcolm MacDonald, brought the question to the Cabinet in February 1940, warning (in a Cabinet paper) that the Jewish illegal military organizations 'though primarily designed for use against the Arabs, might even be used in certain circumstances against the British forces in Palestine'.[22] MacDonald added that the cautious policy advocated by the High Commissioner and by General Wavell might stop the growth of the *Hagana* but would not force it to disband. Nevertheless the Colonial Office shared their concern that more radical measures of forcible disarmament might cause serious unrest in Palestine, and the Cabinet endorsed the restricted policy of acting only on specific information.[23] (The Cabinet also endorsed the accompanying recommendation that the various Jewish Police formations be reduced 'to the limits compatible with the effective protection of the Jewish settlements'.)

Between the trial of the forty-three members of the *Hagana* who had been arrested in October 1939, and the receipt in Palestine of the Cabinet's instructions on arms search policy, there had been further arrests of small groups of Jews engaged in para-military exercises and more arms searches. The last of these searches, on 22 January 1940, uncovered an arms cache and was followed by a controversial trial (in April 1940) during which the Jewish Agency and other representative institutions of the *Yishuv* issued a public manifesto stating that the arms concerned had been held for self-defence and claiming the right of Jewish settlements to hold arms for that purpose. As a result of these events, and presumably also of the Cabinet decision not to allow a campaign of active disarmament, the Government and the military authorities in Palestine attempted to persuade the *Yishuv* to surrender its arms voluntarily. In a series of talks between the General Officer Commanding (Lt-General G. J. Giffard, Barker's successor), the Jewish Agency and other Jewish bodies, the authorities offered not to reduce the number of Jewish Settlement Police and to allow a proportion of the arms surrendered to be registered and returned to the settlements. The alternative, it was stated, was a continuation of the arms searches and the imposition of lengthy prison sentences if arms were found.[24]

Although Giffard's real concern, as he made clear in a report to General Headquarters, Middle East Forces in Cairo, was that 'the Jewish leaders may not be able in all circumstances to control their followers',[25] Giffard told the Agency that he was concerned that 'fifth-columnists' might obtain control of the illegal Jewish arms. The Agency replied that the war situation only increased the risk of Arab attacks on Jewish settlements, especially if the front was to approach Palestine, and that any degree of disarming of the Jews would only encourage such attacks. Giffard then made a compromise proposal: 'Would the Jews be prepared to give him the numbers of arms in their possession, without prejudice to anything else? He would make no promise as to the use he would make of the information, but at least it would tell him where he stood.'[26]

This modified proposal was debated at length both by the Jewish Agency and within the *Hagana*. While there was a consensus against any voluntary surrender of arms, serious disagreements arose as to whether details of the illegal arms held should be given to the authorities.[27] The Agency finally resolved that it would offer to canvas the settlements as to their holdings of arms on condition that an assurance be given that no arms would be confiscated.[28] However when this proposal was put to Giffard (at the third and final meeting in mid-June 1940), he insisted that a proportion of the arms would have to be surrendered ('especially machine guns and bombs') and that he would 'adjust the distribution of arms [as] he saw fit'. The talks were thus deadlocked and Giffard refused to discuss the matter any further, concluding with a threat that he would greatly intensify the arms searches.[29]

The talks had ended acrimoniously, and the Jewish community anticipated the active resumption of arms searches and a full effort at enforced disarmament. However Chamberlain's Government had already resolved against such a policy, and a new General Officer Commanding (Lt-General A. R. Godwin-Austin replaced Giffard shortly after the talks) decided that 'with regard to hidden Jewish arms, he wanted at the moment to let sleeping dogs lie, and searches for these would not be carried out'.[30]

Although the Colonial Office wanted to maintain the pressure on the illegal organizations by persisting with the policy of limited arms searches,[31] and Godwin-Austin's successor (Lt-General P. Neame) did revert to a more active policy,[32] the military crisis in the Middle East of 1941 and 1942, together with Winston Churchill's sympathy with the *Yishuv*'s desire to be able to defend itself, combined to delay any confrontation on the question of Jewish illegal arms until 1943, after the threat of a German invasion of Palestine had passed. Occasional arms searches were conducted in 1941 and 1942, but in view of Churchill's attitude the Colonial Office resolved not to bring them to the Cabinet's attention.[33] The searches were conducted only on the receipt of definite information and care was taken to avoid any unnecessary untoward incidents. However the Colonial Office wanted to pursue the question of disarmament more actively, and it resented the constraints that Churchill's attitude placed on it in this matter. In a revealing minute (written in 1941 in response to the Jewish Agency's continued refusal to reveal details of the size of the Jewish illegal arsenal), Sir John Shuckburgh, the senior Colonial Office official dealing with Palestine affairs, expressed something of the frustration that the Colonial Office felt on this, and on all other Palestine-related matters:

One cannot help being conscious all the time that [the Zionists] consider themselves strong enough owing to their influence in high places, to defy the High Commissioner and the C.O. with impunity. That is a factor which becomes more and more evident as time goes on. No-one can regard such a state of affairs as satisfactory; but there it is, and I suppose that we have got to make the best of it.[34]

Rommel's successes in North Africa during March and April 1941, and again from March until October 1942, meant that the threat of a German invasion of Palestine had to be taken seriously. On both occasions the Agency and its sympathizers in London demanded that steps be taken to increase the opportunities available to Palestinian Jews to participate in the war effort through enlistment in the British Army, and to increase the arms and training available to the Jewish settlements so as to improve the *Yishuv*'s capacity for self-defence in the event of a British withdrawal.[35] Clearly these demands conflicted with the desire of the British authorities in the Middle East to prevent the *Yishuv* from acquiring the sort of military capacity which might eventually allow it to oppose British policy in Palestine by force, and during both crises the British military and political authorities in Jerusalem and Cairo successfully opposed almost all the proposals to strengthen the *Yishuv*'s ability to defend itself which were put forward.[36]

Shortly after the crisis of 1941 had passed, MacMichael delivered his first attack on the Jewish Agency, calling for its disestablishment. Above and beyond the Agency's formal rejection of the White Paper policy, the increasingly frequent expressions of the demand for a Jewish state, which had so alarmed Lord Moyne in his talks with Weizmann and Ben Gurion in August and September 1941, similarly alarmed the Palestine Government. The British authorities there were well informed of the confidential deliberations of the Agency Executive and had a generally accurate estimate of the alignment of political opinion in the other institutions of the *Yishuv* as well.[37] By September 1941 Military Intelligence in Palestine observed of the state of Jewish opinion that 'The Jews as a whole seem to be working up for a great drive for some sort of recognized nationalism, and in the present frame of mind of the Agency leaders this might easily lead to trouble in the Zionist ranks.'[38] At the same time, concern at the strength of the Jewish illegal military organizations was revived when, in the wake of the Syrian campaign, the authorities observed an increase of the traffic in illegal arms.[39] The crystallization of the Zionist political programme around the objective of Jewish statehood, the increase in the Jewish illegal arsenal, and the apparent passing of the threat of an Arab revolt against Britain, encouraged MacMichael to take up the question of the military threat which the *Yishuv* would eventually pose for Britain.

In October 1941 the High Commissioner forwarded to London a lengthy and revealing despatch entitled 'Note on Jewish Illegal Organizations, Their Activities and Finances.' The 'Note' was prepared by the Secretariat of the Palestine Government in collaboration with the Criminal Investigations Departments of the Palestine Police (the C.I.D.) and Military Intelligence, and MacMichael considered that it brought 'into the full limelight the fact that the Mandatory is faced potentially with as grave a danger in Palestine from Jewish violence as it has ever faced from Arab violence, a danger infinitely less easy to meet by the methods of repression which have been employed against Arabs'.[40]

The 'Note' did indeed present an alarming picture, giving the first official estimate of the size and strength of the *Hagana*, as some one hundred thousand members of both sexes, about half of whom could be provided with firearms. In addition, the 'Note' assessed the strength of the right-wing *Irgun Zvai Leumi* as being between five and eight thousand. However, the concrete information on the strength of both the *Hagana* and the *Irgun* was cautiously worded, and occupied only a small part of the sixteen closely typed pages of the 'Note'. The burden of the despatch was an examination of the close ties between the various institutions of the *Yishuv* – political, economic, agricultural and military – and the discipline which the leaders of the Zionist movement could command. The despatch was intended to reinforce the message which MacMichael was at the same time repeating to London at every possible occasion: that the Jewish Agency would have to be disbanded if Britain wished to be able to impose the White Paper or any other policy which did not allow for the creation of a Jewish state or the continuation of Jewish immigration. In a separate introduction to the 'Note', MacMichael argued that any attempt to disarm the *Yishuv* and disband the *Hagana* would be converted into a confrontation with Jewish Palestine as a whole by the Agency, the *Histadrut* [the Jewish Trades Union Federation], the *Va'ad Leumi* [the *Yishuv*'s 'National Council'] and *Mapai* [the Labour Party], all of which were controlled by a closely interlocking leadership which exercised 'almost Nazi control' over the Jewish community. The aim of this leadership, MacMichael argued, was no longer the creation of a 'National Home' but rather the creation of a 'national socialist state' [*sic*]. He concluded by noting: 'As matters stand now it seems to me inevitable that the Zionist Juggernaut which has been created with such an intensity of zeal for a Jewish national state will be the cause of very serious trouble in the Near East'.[41]

MacMichael anticipated by over a year the formal adoption of the objective of statehood by the Zionist bodies in Palestine. The objective of a Jewish state which Ben Gurion had set out in his 'Outlines' in 1941, to which Weizmann had also committed himself in his article of January 1942, and which had been adopted by the American Zionists in May 1942, was only adopted by the Jewish Agency Executive in November 1942. Nevertheless, like the Foreign and Colonial Offices in London at the same time, MacMichael had correctly identified the trend of Zionist thinking. What was distinctive in his despatch was the emphasis on the alleged capabilities of the illegal Jewish military organizations and the intention to employ them in order to achieve the objective of statehood.[42]

However, the facts which the High Commissioner wished to impress on London were guesses given the mantle of authority by the ambiguous wording of the 'Note'. Separate reports prepared by Military Intelligence in Palestine and Security Intelligence Middle East in Cairo (S.I.M.E.) made frequent reference to the great difficulties the authorities had in obtaining any accurate information on the military organizations of the *Yishuv* (as opposed to the political bodies).[43] Estimates of the size of the *Hagana* and the *Irgun* were purely conjectural. MacMichael's 'Note' referred to one hundred thousand members of the *Hagana* and five to eight thousand members of the *Irgun*, excluding the Palestinian Jews serving with the British Forces outside of Palestine. If this latter group were to be included, the total military strength of the *Yishuv* would be suspiciously close to one hundred and thirty six thousand – the number of people who had registered in the Agency's registration in September 1939. MacMichael clearly did not want to deprive anyone of the possibility of claiming *Hagana* or *Irgun* membership, as the figures he gave represented almost the total Jewish population of males between the ages eighteen to thirty-five and half the female Jewish population of the same age-group.

Estimates of the strength of the illegal Jewish military groups prepared during 1940 (which were, incidentally, fairly accurate) did not justify the alarming figures which MacMichael presented in late 1941.[44] By mid-1942 the sources of information on the *Hagana* and the *Irgun* available to British intelligence improved considerably, and more accurate estimates were circulated in intelligence bulletins. These show that even on the basis of the information available to the British authorities, the image of a force over one hundred thousand strong – half of which was purported to be armed – was a threefold exaggeration.[45] (In fact it was an even larger exaggeration.[46] However the question here is the relationship between the information available to the British authorities in the Middle East and the information which the Palestine Government chose to transmit to London.) Nevertheless subsequent reports which were despatched to the War Office as well as to the Foreign and Colonial Offices and were prepared after more accurate information was available to British intelligence in the Middle East not only failed to revise the impression which the October 'Note' created, but actually increased the official assessment of the military strength of the *Yishuv*.

Whatever official credence was given to the details of MacMichael's alarming account,[47] by early 1942 both the Foreign and Colonial Offices had agreed that 'There seems little doubt that the conclusions to be drawn from the secret material is that the Jews intend to resort to direct action if they fail to secure a post-war settlement compatible with their present aspirations.'[48] The Foreign Office seized upon the 'Note' as a valuable contribution to its anti-Zionist public relations efforts in America, and the document was passed on to the Embassy in Washington for discreet communication to American officials. (Parenthetically, it is interesting to note that American intelligence was also interested in the strength of the *Yishuv*, and in summer 1943 the O.S.S. (Office of Strategic Services) prepared its own estimate. Although the O.S.S. did not have the resources available to the various British intelligence organizations by virtue of Britain's position as the Mandatory authority, the Americans prepared an accurate and sober assessment of Jewish (and Arab) armed strength, which gave quite a different picture than the alarmist reports which the British Embassy was circulating.)[49] However in the months which followed the receipt of MacMichael's 'Note', while Palestine faced the threat of a German invasion in 1942, no reconsideration of the policy of disarming the *Yishuv* was possible (although the policy in February 1940 remained in force and arms searches were occasionally conducted). Lord Cranborne, Moyne's successor as Colonial Secretary, referred generally to the radicalization of the *Yishuv* in a Cabinet paper of March 1942 (relating to immigration policy), and he mentioned the inevitability of either a 'showdown' with the Jews, or else meeting their demands and facing a confrontation with the Arabs instead.[50] Although Cranborne made only passing reference to the armed strength which MacMichael attributed to the *Yishuv*, the previous Minister of State in the Middle East, Oliver Lyttelton, examined the question in detail in a draft Cabinet paper on Palestine which he prepared on his return from Cairo in April 1942.[51] Churchill, however, dissuaded Lyttelton from circulating it and the question was not discussed by the Cabinet for a further fifteen months.[52]

When the victory at El Alamein had removed the German military threat to Palestine, MacMichael returned to the question of Jewish illegal arms, forwarding to the Colonial Office a lengthy document which gave an even more inflated estimate of the total armed strength which the *Yishuv* could mobilize.[53] By passing these reports on to London, and in his increasingly polemical descriptions of the Jewish Agency ('Zionist Juggernaut', 'Todt

Organisation', pursuing the objective of a 'nationalist socialist state') MacMichael continued to impress upon the authorities in London that the Agency would have to be suppressed if any policy which embodied the principles of the White Paper was ever to be implemented.

The increasingly strident terms which MacMichael used to describe political Zionism, and the Jewish Agency in particular, were matched only by the efforts of the Minister of State's advisers in Cairo. Their perjorative references to Zionism, the Jewish Agency and the *Yishuv* were no doubt a reflection of their inability to do anything to counter the radicalization of Palestine Jewry and to defend the White Paper policy.[54] Ironically, however, the inflated reports which were received in London had quite a different effect. As all the authorities concerned agreed that nothing could be done during the war to disarm the *Yishuv*, and as the Colonial Office had dismissed the idea of disestablishing the Jewish Agency, the fear that the Jews would attempt to implement their own solution to the Palestine problem, by force if necessary, undermined any residual faith in the specific provisions of the White Paper policy. Since its inception in May 1939 this policy had been under severe pressure because of the wave of Jewish illegal immigration which flaunted the immigration restrictions, which were central to the provisions of the White Paper. The apparent threat of a Jewish revolt further undermined a policy which was proving almost impossible to implement, and by the beginning of 1943 both the Foreign and Colonial Offices accepted that the White Paper of 1939 would have to be replaced. As the head of the American Department of the Foreign Office observed, 'White Papers, like Treaties, are sacred but not immortal.'[55] Henceforth their concern was not to defend the specific provisions of the 1939 White Paper but to uphold the principles it embodied – that the growth of the Jewish National Home would end and Jewish immigration into Palestine be terminated.

These were essentially departmental deliberations, and the disillusionment with the White Paper was expressed only at departmental level. At the political level a *modus vivendi* on Palestine policy remained in force – that is, the White Paper was considered the definitive statement on Palestine until Churchill's Government had had an opportunity of taking the question up at a later date, presumably after the war. Following the removal of the German threat to the Middle East, it appeared possible that such an opportunity had arrived, and Nuri Said, the Foreign Minister of Iraq, renewed the call for a declaration of the British Government on its general Arab policy and on the future of the Middle East.[56] Similarly the Zionists in America intensified their lobbying of the United States Government in the hope that Roosevelt's Administration might endorse a Jewish state as a contribution to solving the Jewish refugee problem. Nevertheless, both the Foreign and Colonial Offices wished to avoid a Cabinet debate during 1943 on Middle East policy and on the future of Palestine. The official acknowledgement in December 1942 of the Nazi extermination of the Jews did not create an atmosphere conducive to a debate which, they hoped, would reaffirm the principles embodied in the White Paper. Furthermore, following El Alamein, it was no longer possible to use the argument of the need to appease Arab opinion over Palestine. The Foreign Secretary, Anthony Eden, now wished to delay any reconsideration of Palestine policy until after the war, in the hope that the Peace Conference would resolve the Jewish refugee problem within the borders of Europe.[57] However a series of developments in Spring 1943 brought the question to the Cabinet's attention, and the fate of the White Paper policy had to be confronted directly.

In February 1943 the British Ambassador to Washington, Lord Halifax, reported from Washington that the State Department was considering a joint Anglo-American declaration on the Jewish question, designed to dampen the growing Zionist agitation in America.[58] The Eastern Department in the Foreign Office welcomed the willingness of the State Department to make such a declaration, but pointed out that Britain was not able to participate because of the constraints which Churchill had imposed on references to the White Paper as fixed British policy.[59] Thus the Foreign Office could only reply that while it could not support the idea of a joint statement, it would welcome any independent efforts by the Americans to counter Zionist lobbying.[60] However, almost immediately afterwards, Halifax informed London that in a series of talks with the State Department, Weizmann had spoken of 'the Prime Minister's plan' to work with Ibn Saud of Saudi Arabia to bring about a pro-Zionist solution of the Palestine problem through Arab Federation.[61] This alarmed the Foreign Office. Any hint that Churchill favoured a pro-Zionist solution in Palestine would have hindered the State Department in its efforts to have the Administration issue a declaration rejecting such a solution. Eden wrote to Churchill pointing out that while he knew the Prime Minister's views on the White Paper, 'there has, I think, been no discussion suggesting that the United States Government should be approached as regards the possibility of modifying it' and he invited Churchill to refute Weizmann's claim to speak in his name.[62] Churchill did so, but at the same time he added: 'As you know, I am irrevocably opposed to the White Paper which, as I have testified in the House, I regard as a breach of a solemn undertaking to which I was a party.'[63]

The Foreign Office recognized that this reply prevented it from informing the American Government that Weizmann had misled it, and from issuing a *démenti* which would have countered the impression (created by

Weizmann) that Britain favoured a Zionist solution in Palestine. As a result, in lieu of any *démenti*, the Eastern Department argued that some form of statement either reaffirming the White Paper or at least making it clear that Britain did not endorse a Jewish state would now be necessary, even if it required obtaining Cabinet approval to overcome the ban on references to the White Paper.[64] However, after further deliberation and the intervention of the Colonial Secretary,[65] it was decided that 'it would be injudicious to insist on the [White] Paper in the teeth of a formidable opposition to it in high places',[66] and a more moderate Cabinet paper was drawn up which made no reference to the White Paper, simply explaining why it was considered necessary to get the United States Government to counter Zionist agitation. As a Foreign Office official subsequently explained, 'In accordance with an agreement between Mr Law [the deputy Foreign Secretary] and the Colonial Secretary, it is intended mainly as a warning note and purposely does not raise the general question of the future of Palestine.'[67]

The draft paper explaining the dangers of Zionist agitation in America took some weeks to prepare, and was further delayed when Oliver Stanley (who replaced Cranborne as Colonial Secretary in November 1942) was hesitant about giving the Colonial Office's concurrence to its circulation to the Cabinet in case it did, unintentionally, prompt the very debate on future policy concerning Palestine which he and Anthony Eden were anxious to avoid.[68] However another minute by the Prime Minister brought the question of future policy to the attention of the Cabinet.

While the Foreign Office Cabinet paper was under consideration, Churchill received a letter from Weizmann in which the latter claimed that both Stanley and his predecessor, Lord Cranborne, had referred to the White Paper as 'firmly established policy'. Weizmann went on to argue that 'Instead of keeping the way open for a revision of policy, the road to it is being further and further blocked.'[69] In effect Weizmann was saying that the *modus vivendi* on Palestine policy had been progressively flaunted by Churchill's Colonial Secretaries, and this prompted Churchill to send both Cranborne and Stanley a strongly worded statement of his own views on the White Paper and on the understanding which governed the continuation of that policy during the war:

I have always regarded [the White Paper] as a gross breach of faith committed by the Chamberlain Government in respect of obligations to which I was personally a party.... I am sure the majority of the present War Cabinet would never agree to any positive endorsement of the White Paper. It runs until it is superseded.[70]

Churchill's description of the White Paper as a 'gross breach of faith' offended Stanley, who had been a member of Chamberlain's Government, and in his reply he asked that if Churchill circulated Weizmann's letter (as Churchill said he would) then Stanley be allowed to circulate a paper of his own setting out the details of the 'potential dangers' which were developing in Palestine and which threatened 'a serious outbreak of disorder throughout the Middle East'.[71]

Churchill eventually decided not to circulate Weizmann's letter, but to circulate instead to the Cabinet his own speech in the House of Commons in May 1939 attacking the White Paper. He prefaced the Cabinet-paper-reprint of his speech with a suggestion that some of the difficulties inherent in the Palestine problem concerning Jewish immigration might be overcome by the conversion of Eritrea and Tripolitania into 'Jewish colonies, affiliated, if desired, to the National Home in Palestine',[72] concluding with a general attack on the Arab world.[73] In a separate minute he invited both Cranborne and Stanley to submit papers of their own to the Cabinet on the Palestine question.[74]

In a cautiously worded paper prepared by the Colonial Office, Stanley described the growing military strength of the *Yishuv* and the crystallization of Zionist policy around the demand for a Jewish state. The paper also pointed out that the Arabs of Palestine, although not as well organized as the Jews, also held 'considerable number arms and stocks of ammunition'. Stanley concluded by arguing that while there was no likelihood of a conflict in the immediate future,

there is obviously much combustible material in Palestine and every effort must be exerted to avoid an explosion. Even if we cannot prevent an ultimate outbreak between the two races in Palestine, I feel we must be extremely careful while the war lasts to avoid any action which is likely to exacerbate either race.[75]

These last comments were intended to discourage the adoption of a new policy towards Palestine, and in the Foreign Office paper, circulated afterwards, Eden observed that he also had 'no wish to press my colleagues to take any major decision on our Palestine policy at this moment'. Accordingly, he limited his remarks to a request for Cabinet authorization to make a representation to the United States Government appealing to them to take steps to dampen Zionist agitation in America.[76]

Despite their clearly-stated desire to avoid a debate on future policy, the papers circulated by Eden and Stanley prompted other ministers who wished to comment on the Palestine problem. Lyttelton took the opportunity of circulating the paper which he had prepared in April 1942 giving details of the growth of the *Hagana* and the *Irgun* and warning of the dangers which the demand for a Jewish state created for British interests in the Middle East.[77] Richard Casey, Lyttelton's successor as Minister of State Resident in the Middle East, was in London and he circulated a paper making the same point in much more emphatic terms, claiming that Britain faced the risk of a *coup de main* by the Zionists at the end of the war, or even before then.[78] At the same time he circulated the resolutions of the Middle East War Council (on which Casey, MacMichael, the British Ambassadors to the Arab capitals and the various Commanders-in-Chief in the Middle East theatre all sat) calling for a reaffirmation of the White Paper policy.[79] Eden had hoped to avoid this demand being raised, and both he and Stanley had eschewed it in their own Cabinet papers.[80] However, once the recommendation had been put forward, it became increasingly clear that the whole question of future Palestine policy would have to be considered.

The various accounts of the growing military capabilities of the Zionists repeated the inflated estimates which MacMichael had sent to the Colonial Office in October 1941 and in December 1942. The danger that the *Yishuv* would oppose by force any British policy which did not allow for continued Jewish immigration was certainly a real one, and the experience of the early years in dealing with illegal immigration had shown that there was ample scope for confrontation. However, as discussed above, the strength of the *Yishuv* had been seriously exaggerated. The danger that the Zionists would attempt a *coup* against the Mandate and the British Army in the Middle East and impose its own solution existed,[81] but it was more a reflection of Britain's vulnerability to pressure on Palestine policy (from the Zionists and their sympathizers) than a measure of the real strength of the *Yishuv*. The officials who participated in the Middle East War Council particularly wanted to challenge Churchill's sympathy for Zionism (the 'influence in high places' which was frequently referred to as the reason why stronger measures could not be taken against the Jewish Agency and the illegal military organizations) and his support for a Jewish state.[82] At the very least, they hoped to be able to reduce the number of his supporters in the Cabinet. Thus, whereas previously Zionism was presented only as a political embarrassment to Britain's position in the Middle East, by 1943 it was depicted as a potential military threat to Britain.

The Cabinet met on 2 July 1943 to consider the various papers on Palestine (ten in all) which had been circulated in the preceding two months. The question of a joint declaration with the United States Government was considered and approved in principle. It was also decided to permit Jewish immigration beyond the 31 March 1944 deadline set out in the White Paper, to make a number of concessions concerning immigration from enemy controlled territory and to continue the policy on arms searches (i.e. acting only on specific information – Churchill insisted that there be no change on this policy without specific reference to the Cabinet). The central issue, however, was that of future policy in general.

All the members of the Cabinet agreed that nothing should be done to re-open public controversy on the Palestine question at that moment in the war, but a majority agreed that, nevertheless, steps should be taken to consider long term policy (i.e. a policy to replace the 1939 White Paper) without delay.[83] Leo Amery, the Secretary of State for India and a strong sympathizer with the Zionists, suggested that partition should be reconsidered, and Churchill, contrary to his position in 1937 when partition had been proposed by the Peel Commission, supported him.[84] Partition was not discussed at any length, and the Cabinet decided instead to appoint a Cabinet Committee 'to consider the long term policy for Palestine', leaving the task of appointing its members to Churchill.[85]

The Cabinet Committee on Palestine commenced its deliberations in August 1943, and in December of that year it was able to submit to the Cabinet detailed proposals for the partition of Palestine.[86] These proposals were adopted by the Cabinet as a whole on 25 January 1944,[87] although a public announcement on the demise of the White Paper policy and the adoption of partition in its place was not to be made until after the war. The sudden collapse in mid-1943 of the *modus vivendi* which had governed the Cabinet's position on Palestine since 1940 afforded Churchill the opportunity of revising the policy on Palestine which the Chamberlain Government had adopted in 1939. The partition decision brought British policy full circle, back to the recommendation of the Peel Commission of 1937.

The inflated reports sent by the Palestine Administration and the British authorities in Cairo to London on the nature and size of the military threat which the *Yishuv* posed to Britain and to Britain's freedom of manoeuvre in Palestine and the Middle East had exactly the opposite effect from that intended. Rather than discredit the Zionists and weaken Churchill's support for them in the Cabinet, these reports proved to the Cabinet the urgency of the Palestine question and the inadvisability of delaying consideration of the fate of the White Paper until after the war. In all, here was a clear case where the political manipulation of the intelligence input into the policy making process had unintended, and from the perspective of the British establishment in the Middle East, thoroughly undesirable consequences.

8

The politics of asylum, Juan Negrín and the British Government in 1940

DENIS SMYTH

On 1 November 1940 the British war cabinet debated an aspect of their country's relations with Franco's Spain, but the discussion proved heated enough to puzzle two of the more politically dispassionate figures present.[1] Britain's foreign secretary, Lord Halifax, was moved to comment in his diary on the fact that only talk of Spain seemed capable of upsetting the cosy consensus among members of the British Conservative, Labour and Liberal parties on the constraints governing political debate. Halifax noted that once a Spanish topic obtruded into a British political argument the exchanges rapidly reached fever pitch.[2] Sir Alexander Cadogan, the permanent under-secretary of state at the Foreign Office, had also been present at the cabinet session. His private reaction to what he termed that 'frightful discussion' was similar to his minister's: 'Any Spanish topic makes the politicians go all hay-wire and Attlee (the Labour party leader and lord privy seal), otherwise a dormouse, becomes like a rabid rabbit. Why?'[3] The purpose of this essay is to answer Cadogan's question, and to do so by concentrating on the particular Spanish problem that had been the subject of the British war cabinet's deliberations on 1 November 1940: namely, whether Dr Juan Negrín López should be allowed to continue enjoying political asylum in Britain when his presence there caused its government such 'great embarrassment.'[4]

Britain has traditionally afforded sanctuary to refugees of diverse political denomination and ideological persuasion, fleeing from peril or persecution in their native lands. At no other time, perhaps, did Britain shelter more political exiles from continental Europe than during the Second World War, when opponents and victims of Hitler's 'New Order' sought haven or a base from which to continue the fight against German Nazism. A distinctive grouping among those European refugees were the various national political elites who had escaped invading German forces. Many of these were gathered together as governments-in-exile symbolizing the national sovereignties grossly violated by Hitler and, sometimes, deploying substantial resources in support of the allied cause.

There was one group of prominent political refugees in wartime Britain, however, that was not granted any official recognition in London: the Spanish Republican personalities forced into exile by Franco's victory in the Civil War. The exodus from the continent of European politicians, caused by Hitler's western offensive of May to June 1940, had brought Juan Negrín López to Britain on board a royal naval warship, on 25 June. But the president of the council of ministers of the Spanish Republic was allowed to land in Britain only on a 'provisional visa', on the understanding that his stay would not exceed a few weeks' duration. Moreover, permission to stay in Britain was granted to Negrín solely on condition that he abstain from all political activities during his sojourn there.[5]

In fact, the absolute British priority in the period following the fall of France was survival. To those immediately concerned with the management of Britain's relations with Spain, there seemed no advantage in aggravating their country's already dangerous strategic situation by antagonizing the Franco regime. Advised by Sir Samuel Hoare, ambassador to Spain from May 1940, the British government decided to try to consolidate Spanish neutrality or 'non-belligerency' (declared by Franco on 12 June 1940) by economic and political blandishment.[6] Although Hoare's pro-Nationalist stance during the Spanish Civil War was well known, he argued that he was not advocating British support for Franco, merely championing 'the most effective way of keeping Spain out of the war altogether if possible, and if that is not possible, for as long a period as we can'.[7] Lord Halifax (who, despite being one of the 'men of Munich', retained the foreign secretaryship under Churchill's premiership until December 1940) fully agreed with Hoare that every week gained in Spain was of value to Britain.[8] The British Chiefs of Staff, too, endorsed on 7 August 1940 this formula as official policy towards Spain: even if it proved impossible to keep Franco out of the war, Britain should try to delay his entry into it for as long as possible.[9] Any British governmental involvement with anti-Franco Spaniards would have undermined this effort to court the *Caudillo*, or at least to avoid alienating him. Thus, Hoare rebuffed an approach in August 1940 from a Spaniard whom he described as 'the leader of the Left Wing malcontents'. Despite being assured by the latter that the Spanish dissidents were 'both numerous and well organised', the British ambassador emphasized his unwillingness 'to have relations with any organisation whose object was to upset a Government that seemed bent upon keeping Spain out of the war'. Hoare regarded this attitude as the 'only safe and honest' one that he could adopt. His action was approved in London.[10]

It appears that the Nationalist regime hardly deserved this British act of faith in its alleged intention to keep Spain non-belligerent. Only Hitler's refusal to meet Franco's asking price of territorial aggrandizement, especially at the expense of French North Africa, kept the Spanish ruler from leading his country into active participation in the Axis war effort.[11] Nevertheless, the British government, unaware of the extent of Franco's attempts to barter his belligerency for territorial expansion, maintained its decision to gamble on his *bona fides*.

Hoare, however, pointed out, early on, that the presence of prominent Spanish Republican refugees in Britain might undermine his government's endeavours to win Franco's goodwill. Halifax was soon impressed by Hoare's complaints that British hospitality towards 'Negrín and other anti-Franco leaders' was seriously impairing the effectiveness of the ambassador's holding-action in Madrid.[12] The foreign secretary, therefore, called the attention of the war cabinet, on 2 July 1940, to the 'most embarrassing' presence of the anti-Francoist Spanish politicians in England, but was made aware immediately that the Republican exiles, too, could count on a measure of sympathy and support inside the British government. For Churchill's wartime coalition executive contained enough representatives of the labour movement who felt sufficient regret and, perhaps, guilt over the Republican defeat in the Civil War to be concerned with the fate of the Spanish exiles in Britain. It was, doubtless, a Labour member of the cabinet who argued that the expulsion of the Spanish political refugees would be bad in principle and in practice: 'It was our traditional practice to admit and to give sanctuary to refugees, and it would be undesirable to turn out this party to please the Government of a not too friendly state.' However, Labour leader, Clement Attlee, was persuaded to consider, along with Lord Halifax, 'what steps could be taken to induce . . . Negrín and other anti-Franco leaders to leave England voluntarily as soon as possible . . .'[13] Hoare clearly believed that the matter was worthy of such high-level attention. Only a few days after the cabinet meeting he again urged Halifax to pursue the issue in London:

may I renew my warnings about the presence of Negrín and his friends in England. It is these things that loom much larger in the eyes of Spaniards than the great events that are happening in the world . . . I do really rely upon you to help me . . . I know your difficulties with the Left and I would not go on bothering you about it. It is, however, in the eyes of Franco's Government, a test case and as in my view the only hope of keeping Spain out of the war is to keep in with Franco and his friends, it is essential to give them no chance of breaking with us.[14]

Halifax did, indeed, have difficulty convincing some Labour members of the cabinet, notably Attlee and the minister without portfolio, Arthur Greenwood, that Negrín should be encouraged to leave England.

However, Halifax managed to talk Attlee into approaching Negrín in an endeavour to persuade the Spaniard to quit Britain.[15] Juan Negrín agreed to leave but only for the United States, where the presence of some of the Republican leader's family would make his departure appear to be a private affair. This latter aspect of the trip would belie any suspicion that the president of the council of ministers of Republican Spain was fleeing Britain because that country was now about to bear the brunt of German military onslaught.[16] Nevertheless, Negrín apparently soon had misgivings about leaving even for the United States and he informed the Soviet ambassador in London, Ivan Maisky, about the pressure being exerted upon him to abandon Britain. Maisky, who was a confidant of Negrín, and who became a regular visitor to the Spaniard's country retreat for much of the Second World War, hastened to exercise his good offices on his friend's behalf.[17] In an interview with R. A. Butler, parliamentary under-secretary of state at the Foreign Office, on 25 July 1940, Maisky expressed his hope that 'Dr. Negrín would not have to leave for America – he thought that this would be deplorable . . . speaking unofficially.' The Soviet ambassador added that he had 'very strong personal feelings for the Spanish Republicans'.[18] Lunching with Hugh Dalton, minister for economic warfare and another Labour member of the government on the following day, Maisky used the opportunity to denounce Attlee's attempt to induce Negrín to leave Britain. Moreover, the Soviet diplomat argued that this effort to push Negrín off to the United States proved that the instinct towards appeasement of the fascist dictators was still alive among Britain's rulers.[19] Although Dalton was non-committal during his conversation with Maisky, the Labour minister proceeded, along with other Leftists alerted by the Soviet ambassador, to protest to Attlee about their leader's involvement in the effort to get rid of Negrín.[20]

Circumstances beyond British control combined with this developing political intervention on Negrín's behalf, to frustrate this particular attempt to end his stay in Britain. For, in spite of a personal request from Lord Halifax to the American ambassador in Britain, Joseph Kennedy, that Negrín be granted a visa to enter the United States, the application was rejected as early as 20 July. Moreover, the refusal to permit Negrín to enter the United States came from the highest authority in that land, the president himself.[21] Franklin D. Roosevelt was standing for re-election in November 1940 and his aversion to admitting the Spanish Republican leader into U.S. territory probably stemmed from his anxiety to avoid alienating conservative catholic voters in the contest. Halifax was still disposed to try to get Negrín out of Britain by inducing him to go to Mexico.[22] However, Attlee refused, on 27 July, to participate further in the enterprise, maintaining that 'to suggest' that Negrín should go 'elsewhere would, I think, savour too much of expulsion, a course of action which I would not like to give even an appearance of following'.[23] Halifax did obtain the cabinet's sanction on 30 July 1940 for an attempt to persuade Negrín to leave Britain for Mexico, but only on condition that if the Spaniard proved 'unwilling to go, the matter should not be pressed'. Indeed, the war cabinet realized that Negrín was unlikely to respond positively to pleas, unsupported by British Labour politicans, that he should depart England's shores. They, therefore, decided on the appropriate arguments to advance in case the Franco regime renewed its protests at the Republican leader's presence in Britain: '. . . if the Spanish government returned to the charge, we should say that we had suggested that Dr Negrín should go to another country, but that the country in question had not been willing to receive him; and we should remind the Spanish government that Dr Negrín was not allowed to engage in any political activity while in this country'.[24]

The Franco government did continue to complain about the British reluctance to expel Negrín from their country. Moreover, the Spanish regime voiced its protests not only through Sir Samuel Hoare in Madrid, but also employed its own ambassador in London, the seventeenth duke of Alba, in this campaign. Alba was not only a Spanish grandee but also held a British Jacobite title as duke of Berwick. With his many contacts inside the British establishment, he seemed ideally placed to urge Francoist complaints against Negrín's presence in England.[25] As a fervent monarchist, Alba had no great affection for Franco and would resign his ambassadorship in 1945 as part of the royalists' efforts to pressurize the *Caudillo* into relinquishing the headship of the Spanish state to the then legitimist candidate, Juan de Borbón.[26] However, an intense anti-republicanism had prompted Alba to support the Nationalist rebels during the Civil War, by acting as their diplomatic agent in London, and also to accept appointment as Spain's official ambassador to Britain in March 1939. His antagonism towards the 'red ringleaders', as he described them, caused the duke of Alba to apply himself with diligence to implement Madrid's instructions to press for the Republican exiles' ejection from the country to which he was accredited.[27]

The Spanish ambassador personally presented his government's request that Dr Negrín be expelled from Britain, in an interview with Lord Halifax in early August 1940. The British foreign secretary replied that 'in spite of the difficulties presented by the heterogeneous composition of the (British) government to the adoption of such measures, it had been decided to request of Negrín that he should leave this country as soon as possible'. Halifax explained, however, that the United States government's unwillingness to grant Negrín an entry visa had frustrated the British resolve to rid themselves of the Republican leader. Alba was not discouraged by this official response, for he discerned Britain's vested interest in supporting the Franco regime which appeared intent on keeping Spain neutral. The Spanish ambassador, thus, fully accepted Halifax's assurance that the British government did not have 'the slightest contact, understanding or relationship of a political character with the Spanish refugees'. Alba also realized that the foreign secretary's assertion that 'England would not tolerate intrigues against our government' still gave him the chance to secure Negrín's expulsion from Britain if it could be shown that the Republican leader was engaging in anti-Francoist political activities on British soil.[28]

Alba certainly did his utmost to acquire evidence against Negrín which could be used to prove that the latter was in breach of his pledge to abstain from political activity while resident in England. The duke had managed to place a spy in the office of Pablo de Azcárate, ex-Republican ambassador to Britain, who acted in Negrín's interest. This Francoist agent supplied Alba with information and stolen documents.[29] Again, in order to ensure that surveillance of Negrín would be as complete as possible, Alba also employed a former Scotland Yard detective, F. Price, to trail the Republican leader and report regularly on his behaviour.[30] Armed with information from these sources, Alba wrote to Halifax on 12 August 1940 to claim that Negrín was 'contemplating opening an office' in London, under the pseudonym, Jaime Benjamin Viliesid. The ambassador contended that Negrín's apparent intention constituted 'a definite proof' that the latter was going 'to remain in England and to indulge in activities that require the use of an office'.[31] This was hardly a gravely prejudicial charge, but it did evoke the reply from Lord Halifax that the British government would set its own home security service into operation to ascertain if Negrín was reneging on his promise to refrain from political action.[32]

However, a protracted inquiry by M.I.5 failed to yield any incriminating evidence, as Halifax reported back to Alba on 8 October:

A close watch has in fact been kept on Dr Negrín in recent weeks and no political activity has been traced of him. In these circumstances, perhaps you will be good enough to let me have the evidence on which your letter to me was based. I should be very glad to consider it and to have the matter further investigated. You will appreciate that Dr Negrín was only permitted to enter this country on condition that he did not concern himself with politics.[33]

Halifax's request placed the Spanish ambassador in an awkward position, as he explained to the ministry of foreign affairs in Madrid, on 15 October: '. . . I do not have documentary evidence, and on the other hand neither do I want to confess that we have a spy in Azcárate's offices and a person who follows Negrín in his adventures through London. . . .' However, Alba resolved to reiterate his protest against Negrín's alleged political involvements, in a future conversation with Halifax. Moreover, the Anglophile ambassador welcomed the British government's investigation of the official Spanish complaint as a 'good indication' of its desire 'to have nothing to do with Negrín and Company'.[34]

If Alba was relatively satisfied, by mid-October 1940, with the British government's attitude towards the problem of the Republican politicians resident within its jurisdiction, Sir Samuel Hoare, on the contrary, was making an all-out effort, at that time, to hound the Spanish refugees out of his country. The British ambassador in Madrid had already supported Alba's late-August accusation that Negrín was indulging in political machinations in London. Hoare had written to Halifax in early September to express his full agreement with Alba's assessment of the Republican leader's behaviour, asserting that beyond 'a shadow of doubt' Negrín was 'being very active politically in London'. He had warned the foreign secretary of the dangers inherent in such a state of affairs: '. . . it seems evident that Negrín is busy making himself a sort of Spanish de Gaulle and I foresee that if this is allowed to continue a situation may develop which will wreck all that we have so far done here and everything that we are trying to do'. Hoare had denied that he entertained any personal ill-will towards Negrín, but claimed that the latter's 'presence in England and his steadily increasing activities' greatly helped the German cause in Spain. He had concluded his communication by urgently calling, once more, for the Spanish politician's removal from Britain.[35]

Hoare, subsequently, maintained the momentum of his campaign against Negrín. He persuaded his government to contradict the German-instigated rumour that Britain, if victorious over the Nazis, would reinstall a Republican regime in Spain. On several occasions in late September 1940, at Hoare's prompting, the B.B.C. broadcast the following message to Spain:

German propaganda is assiduously spreading the idea that (the) British Government propose to return Negrín to power in Spain when the war is over. There is, of course, no truth whatever in this. The Government have no negotiations of any kind with Negrín and have no official relationship with him. He is in England as a political refugee in the same way as any other refugee of whatever political leaning. He has no other standing at all.[36]

The British ambassador remained convinced, however, that the most effective counter to Francoist suspicions of British collusion with Negrín would be the latter's departure from the United Kingdom.[37] He relayed to London on 10 October the advice of 'friendly Spaniards' that the British could not really counteract German-inspired propaganda that they were intent on 'fomenting a "red" upheaval in Spain, and restoring the republican regime' while Negrín and other exiled Spanish politicians were allowed to remain. Hoare contended that the continued presence of the Republican refugees in England prevented a rapprochement in Anglo-Spanish relations and even jeopardized the possibility of keeping Spain out of the Axis camp. Yet again, he exhorted British policy-makers to consider ways and means of ridding themselves of Negrín's presence.[38]

As was normal with important telegrams from His Majesty's ambassadors abroad, Hoare's communication of 10 October was circulated amongst the members of the war cabinet. It caused one of them to react in a manner that suggests an answer to the question that was posed at the beginning of this essay: namely, why did Spanish issues provoke such divisive passions within Britain's wartime political elite?

Clement Attlee wrote to Lord Halifax, on 30 October 1940, to challenge the arguments contained in Hoare's 10 October telegram. The Labour leader questioned whether Britain had 'a large body of well-wishers in Spain', and asserted that the Spaniards' war-weariness and their economic plight were the only factors that could prevent them from joining the Axis war effort. It was these harsh facts of Spain's economic and social life, not gestures like the expulsion of the Republican refugees from Britain, which would determine the Franco regime's final choice for war or peace. More fundamentally, Attlee argued that such a concession to please Britain's potential enemies might well antagonize her actual friends: 'those who are in sympathy with our aims and who really believe in freedom and democracy'. The lord privy seal even suggested that Britain should consciously cultivate such progressive and democratic elements in Europe, as the general principle of her international political strategy in the war against Nazism: 'I think we must realise that the active forces to be mobilised against Hitlerism must be those people who are devoted to the ideals for which we stand, and must, therefore, include a stronger Left Wing element.'[39]

It was not, therefore, merely vestigial Spanish Civil War loyalties that moved Attlee to oppose Hoare's attempts to have Negrín expelled from Britain. Certainly, the British left remained sympathetic to their defeated Spanish comrades whose struggle in the years 1936–9 they had seen as 'the class war played out on an international scale'.[40] The Spanish Civil War split Britain's public opinion precisely because the Spaniards were coming to blows over the same issues, the pursuit of social justice and economic reform or the defence of privilege and wealth, that were the essential stuff of British political controversy. British hearts and minds were inevitably engaged in an open fight over the problems that they sought to settle by peaceful, constitutional means. Indeed, R. A. Butler had reminded Sir Samuel Hoare, on 20 July 1940, that Spain remained a potent symbol to

Britain's politicians, even at a time when they had declared a truce on party conflict: 'The feeling about Spain remains extremely acute, since it is all bound up with the division which all sections here feel is inevitable in English society and politics.'[41] Regret over the defeat of democracy in Spain could easily flare into politically divisive resentment if the British right appeared to be consorting with the victorious Francoists or persecuting the defeated Republicans. Lord Halifax cautioned Hoare about this point on 24 September 1940: 'There are large sections of (British) opinion in Parliament and elsewhere who do not accept, or only accept most grudgingly, our present policy towards Spain. I have, for example, had very serious difficulties in dealing with the Negrín affair.'[42]

However, it was not only sorrow over the fate of the Spanish Republic that induced Attlee to object to the proposed ejection of Negrín from Britain. For, the Labour leader had maintained, in his 30 October letter to Halifax, that such action would vitiate the very political strategy that the British should adopt in their life-and-death struggle against Nazism. Attlee had defined the rationale behind this claim in July 1940, within government circles:

... we should put before the country a definite pronouncement on Government policy for the future. The Germans are fighting a revolutionary war for very definite objectives. We are fighting a conservative war and our objects are purely negative. We must put forward a positive and revolutionary aim admitting that the old order has collapsed and asking people to fight for the new order.[43]

Attlee was no creative intellectual. If he had come to this conclusion in the summer of 1940, then it was because the conviction that Britain should fight a revolutionary war, thenceforward, was widespread.

Taking Churchill's dictum that this was 'a war of peoples and of causes' literally, many socialists, radicals and those simply appalled at the dreadful danger that Conservative appeasement had brought on their country, began to argue that British resistance to Nazi Germany must assume a new form. Believing, along with George Orwell, that Hitler was 'the leader of a tremendous counter-attack of the capitalist class', they concluded that 'any real struggle means revolution'.[44] The author, J. B. Priestley, in a series of immensely popular radio talks, became the most powerful propagandist for the notion that the conflict with Hitler's Germany should be regarded 'as one chapter in a tremendous history, the history of a changing world, the breakdown of one vast system, and the building up of another and better one'.[45] Every Sunday evening from 9 June until 20 October 1940, Priestley's resonant Yorkshire tones and anecdotal style celebrated the decency and the vitality of the British people at work and play under aerial bombardment and the threat of invasion. Priestley, however, preached as often as he praised. His recurring message was 'the merest and mildest sermon': 'that free men could combine, without losing what's essential to their free development, to see that each gives according to his ability, and receives according to his need'.[46] Hailing Priestley as 'a leader second only in importance to Mr Churchill', another English author, Graham Greene, said of him that 'he gave us what our other leaders have always failed to give us – an ideology'.[47] Priestley elaborated that progressive ideology on the B.B.C., on 21 July 1940:

... we must stop thinking in terms of property and power and begin thinking in terms of community and creation ... we want a world that offers people not the dubious pleasures of power, but the maximum opportunities for creation ... the war, because it demands a huge collective effort, is compelling us to change not only our ordinary, social and economic habits, but also our habits of thought. We're actually changing from the property view to the sense of community, which simply means that we realise we're all in the same boat. But, and this is the point, that boat can serve not only as our defence against Nazi aggression, but as an ark in which we can all finally land in a better world ... I tell you, there is stirring in us now, a desire which could soon become a controlled but passionate determination to remodel and recreate this life of ours, to make it the glorious beginning of a new world order.[48]

Priestley suggested later in 1940 that his generous vision should be given practical expression. In his radio 'Postscript' on 6 October he declared

that now was the time for our leaders to use a little imagination, to light beacons in this gathering darkness, to warm our hearts and set fire to our minds, by proclaiming noble and universal aims; by so ordering affairs in this country that we might serve as an example to the world, not merely in courage and endurance, but in bold and hopeful planning for the future, releasing in us great creative forces.[49]

In a written 'Postscript' for the liberal paper, the *News Chronicle*, on 25 November 1940, Priestley advised that the time must be seized:

Now it is certain that we shall have to announce our aims and policy very soon. . . The Government will have to come into the open and choose ... the road of peoples really on their way to a genuine freedom, a freedom not merely from aggressive dictatorships, but also from privilege, brigand interests, economic insecurity, and all the deadening sterility of plutocracy.

Many other influential voices were also raised, at this time, exhorting the British government to adopt a set of radical war aims that could act as the charter for 'a definite democratic crusade' against fascist oppression.[50] There was an effort to translate Priestley's idealistic prospect into a comprehensive programme for a British-led people's war against Nazism, an offensive design embodying revolutionary means and ends.

To the advocates of a people's war, the appropriate methods for waging such a struggle seemed obvious. The *Daily Express* succinctly defined the means, and the rationale for their employment, on 23 July 1940: 'Our allies are ordinary people, not Fascist dictators. And since the ordinary people of Europe are now ruled by Fascists we must organise revolutions.' A campaign was conducted by the left-wing publisher, Victor Gollancz, and leftist members of the ministry of economic warfare, like R. H. S. Crossman, in support of a British instigated revolutionary movement against Nazi tyranny.[51] Moreover the champions of this people's war of national and social liberation perceived the inherent connexion between means and ends in its development. One of the Labour party's leading socialist intellectuals, Harold Laski, linked the call for a British declaration of war aims to the need to foment popular rebellion in Europe, in an 'Open Letter to the Labour Movement' published in the *Daily Herald* (Labour's official newspaper), on 21 October 1940: '. . . men and women all over the world must be given the vision of a new social order. . . To win, we need a revolution upon the European Continent; we have to persuade the masses to throw off their chains. But we must tell them, if they are to act, the great purposes for which they must throw away their chains.' The *Daily Herald* had described the socialist-style statement of war aims that it wanted Britain to adopt, in an editorial of 5 October 1940, as 'the code of those revolutionary movements in the enemy and occupied countries which might so dramatically hasten the end of the war'.

The proponents of a people's war were quick to recognize its implications for British policy towards Spain. The journalist, William Forrest, singled out the Spanish Republicans in the *News Chronicle* of 18 July 1940: 'These are our allies in this war of peoples and of causes. They have fought and suffered in a cause which we now realise to have been OUR cause – the cause of OUR people.' He demanded that 'the restoration of the democratic Spanish Republic' be included in Britain's war aims. The same newspaper editorialized in a similar vein on 30 September 1940:

Our proper policy in Spain is surely clear. . . . Our diplomatic activities should aim not at hobnobbing with reactionary generals whose views and actions the British people loathe, but at organising the tattered shreds of the Spanish Republican movement by overt and covert action into a force which will effectively hamper Hitler if the Spanish clash comes. It is a great misfortune for Britain that the British Government still fails to recognise the essentially revolutionary nature of the present struggle.

Charles Duff, in his book, *A Key to Victory: Spain*, published by Victor Gollancz in late 1940, suggested a similar course of action: 'In her foreign policy and in her propaganda, Great Britain must do everything possible to disintegrate totalitarian influence everywhere – including Spain – if necessary by "revolutionary" methods . . . the first step is propaganda – a propaganda which must explain what are our war aims, and that these aims coincide with the general ambition of the Spanish people to achieve its freedom.'[52]

It was in the context of this political campaign in Britain for the official adoption of a people's war strategy that the attempt to eject Negrín provoked such righteous indignation on the part of British leftists and progressives. As Attlee emphasized in his letter of 30 October 1940 to Lord Halifax, cited above, a move to expel the Spanish Republican leader would rob Britain of any legitimate title to the leadership of a pan-European, democratic crusade against Hitlerism: 'There is a danger of our being misunderstood and appearing hypocrites if we appear to be playing up all the time to reactionary elements.'[53] What supplied particular intensity to the British government's debate in late 1940 over Negrín's presence in England was the coincidence of the affair with the ideological demand for a people's war. Spain, in the person of Negrín, had become the touchstone of Britain's claim to be espousing human liberation in opposition to Nazi enslavement. If Halifax and Cadogan were surprised at the passions unleashed during the British cabinet wrangle over Negrín on 1 November 1940, then it was because they had not fully understood, or entirely accepted, the extent of the questions that the Spaniard's fate raised: namely, what kind of war Britain should be fighting, and what positive goals – economic, political and social – it should be struggling to secure.

It was the renewal of Sir Samuel Hoare's complaints to Lord Halifax about Negrín's continued residence in England that persuaded the foreign secretary to bring the matter before the war cabinet, once more, on 1 November. Moreover, the British ambassador was able to reinforce his case against Britain's sheltering Negrín any longer with a telling argument in later October 1940. For, events inside Franco's Spain developed in such a way as to lend substance and urgency to Hoare's campaign against Negrín's being allowed to stay on in England. On 17 October 1940, Colonel Juan Beigbeder Atienza, with whom the British ambassador had established an apparently excellent relationship, was dismissed from his position as Spain's minister for foreign affairs and replaced by the reputedly pro-Axis Ramón Serrano Suñer. The British knew that the latter had led a diplomatic mission to Berlin, the previous month, to negotiate a possible Spanish entry into the war on the Axis side. Moreover, within a week of Serrano Suñer's appointment as Spanish foreign minister, Franco, himself, was conferring with Hitler at Hendaye – on 23 October.[54]

These developments might have seemed to vitiate Hoare's advice that Britain should gamble on Franco's upholding his stance of non-belligerency, and thereby removed the need to harry Negrín out of that country in order to appease right-wing Spaniards. However, the British ambassador was able to report home a startling encounter with Beigbeder on 18 October which, again, placed Britain's relations with Spain in a more promising light. Meeting the dismissed foreign minister for a farewell interview on that day, Hoare found him in a very candid mood. Beigbeder expressed his conviction that Germany would demand a right of passage through Spain (to get at Gibraltar), within a few months, and advised that Britain should have plans ready for such a situation in which Franco would vacillate. Beigbeder argued that the Spanish army was the only hope for an effective opposition, and that in the groundswell of anti-German feeling following upon their entry into Spain other groups, such as the Basque and Catalan separatists, would join the national resistance movement. Although he strongly recommended that London should be ready to support such a movement once it had begun, Beigbeder warned Hoare that the British government would have to observe certain 'basic conditions without which (it would) merely play the German game'. Primary among the conditions Beigbeder defined was the following one:

. . . we (the British) must realise the fact that the Spanish army is the hope to which we must tie our interests. Most of the Generals and even more of the men will be against the Germans. If we are to have their support, we must rely upon them. A fatal course for us to take would be to come out with a policy of backing the Reds or the Separatists with the object of stirring up internal disorder. It is upon the army that we must base our policy.[55]

Subsequent to this interview, Colonel Beigbeder maintained clandestine contact with Hoare and declared himself ready to proclaim a regency on behalf of the Spanish monarchy, if and when the Germans entered Spain.[56] Of course, that eventuality was never realized, but Beigbeder's dramatic 18 October *démarche* indicated that even if Franco had sold himself to the Nazis, the power-base of the Nationalist regime, the army, might still be worth courting by Britain. Hoare saw one obvious way in which to impress Spanish military opinion favourably, as he informed the Foreign Office on 22 October:

If we are to stimulate a national movement of resistance in the (Spanish) army it is essential to get Negrín out of England. As long as he is there even our best friends will distrust our intentions. I do hope therefore that you will reconsider the question as now one of high politics upon the settlement of which may depend very big issues.[57]

Important figures in the British government were certainly influenced by Hoare's advocacy. The prime minister, Winston Churchill, regarded Hoare's report of his secret conversation with Beigbeder as 'most important', while Halifax was persuaded that an army-based 'national movement of resistance to German domination' in Spain was 'the firmest patch' upon which Britain could build its diplomacy amid the shifting international terrain of later 1940.[58] He, therefore, brought the problem of Negrín's position before the cabinet for further review on 1 November.

Halifax, in his presentation of the case to the war cabinet for Negrín's removal from Britain, concentrated first on the specific points at issue. Commenting that 'Dr Negrín had behaved badly in that, although he had been given permission to come here for three weeks, he had stayed for over four months', the foreign secretary proceeded to detail his argument:

. . . Dr Negrín's continued presence in this country lent support to the view that we were intriguing in Spanish politics and plotting the overthrow of the existing regime. This provided admirable material for German propaganda. Sir Samuel Hoare was constantly being asked by our well-wishers in Spain why we permitted Dr Negrín to stay here. The Spanish Government represented that he was indulging in political activities, but there was no evidence that this was so.

If the Germans marched into Spain, the real hope of Spanish resistance turned on the attitude of the army. The army leaders were unlikely to fight the Germans if they thought that we were intriguing with the revolutionaries in Spain.

Halifax, however, showed some awareness, too, of the more general implications of the Negrín affair, for he added this explanation:

Our object in this matter had nothing to do with internal Spanish affairs, but turned on the best way to win the war. For this purpose we wanted to keep Spain out of the war and to keep the leaders of the Spanish Government friendly to us. The Left Wing in Spain were in any case likely to be more friendly to us than to the Germans.[59]

Attlee immediately contested the foreign secretary's argument with a vigour that even the bland minute-taking style of the cabinet secretariat could not conceal:

The *Lord Privy Seal* thought that the question whether Spain came into the war would be decided by Spanish interests, and Spanish xenophobia. He did not believe that Dr Negrín's departure from this country would have any material effect on those of the present leaders in Spain who professed to be our friends. On the other hand, the action suggested would have a most discouraging effect on the people, the world over, who believed that we were fighting for democracy, and on those who might otherwise carry on disruptive activities in the occupied territories.

He understood that Dr Negrín would regard leaving this country at the present moment as the equivalent of running away.[60]

This sharp and overt division of opinion between senior members of the war cabinet, not only over the fate of Negrín himself, but over the proper practices and purposes of Britain's war effort, which the Spaniard's case had raised, posed quite a problem for the prime minister. Churchill's overriding domestic political priority was to maintain a governing consensus among the members of the Conservative, Labour and Liberal parties who constituted his wartime coalition executive. The national unity so crucial to Britain's fight for survival against Nazi Germany could only be sustained by a cohesive political elite. Churchill was acutely aware that any recrudescence of party hostilities within Britain's political system, while she was exposed to the full blast of war, could have fatal consequences. He revealed his concern in a letter to a Labour minister around this time: '. . . we are all working together, in the full stress of this dire war . . . this is not the time to emphasize points of difference. We cannot afford to indulge in Party strife at the present time, and it would be disastrous if it broke out. . . . I have to try to keep all together till the Hun is beat.'[61] Anxious, therefore, to restore unity to his fractious war cabinet, Churchill intervened in its 1 November discussion to urge moderation. Although conciliatory, the prime minister was also careful to ignore the more fundamental questions, pertaining to the means and ends of Britain's war effort, that had obtruded into the cabinet's deliberations as a result of the controversy over Negrín:

The *Prime Minister* wished it to be on record that, in his view, by keeping Dr Negrín here in this country we imposed a further strain on this country. Nevertheless, having regard to the conflicting views put forward, and since it was not clearly established that Dr Negrín's continued residence here involved us in any mortal hurt, he thought that a compromise solution should be reached.[62]

The Liberal party leader and secretary of state for air, Sir Archibald Sinclair, had already suggested compromise, wondering 'whether the matter could not be settled by, for example, arranging for an invitation to be extended to Dr Negrín to visit and address certain Universities, say, in South America or some other overseas territories'.[63] The 'extremely reluctant' Labour members of the war cabinet were eventually prevailed upon to assent to another official effort to remove Negrín from England by friendly persuasion.[64] The cabinet agreed that Halifax and A. V. Alexander, the Labour first lord of the admiralty, should approach Negrín to remind him how awkward his presence in England was for the British government, and to seek the Spaniard's co-operation in arranging his departure for such a destination as Sinclair had proposed. Nevertheless, the Labour ministers also won one important collective declaration of principle from their war cabinet colleagues: 'If, however, Dr Negrín refused to leave this country we had no present intention of compelling him to go.'[65]

Juan Negrín was invited to the Admiralty for an appointment with A. V. Alexander at 11 a.m. on Friday 8 November 1940.[66] Negrín accepted this invitation thinking that the meeting must be related to the experiments which he had been conducting for the Royal Navy to improve safety conditions on board certain classes of warship.[67] However, on arriving at the Admiralty, the Spanish Republican found that Lord Halifax was present along with the first lord. The foreign secretary lost little time in relaying the British Government's request that Dr Negrín should agree to quit England, perhaps for South America or even New Zealand. Halifax found Negrín to be 'friendly but not very constructive'. Negrín repeated his readiness to go to North America if either the United States or Canada would grant him an entry visa, but not to South America. He explained that in the latter continent he would inevitably be drawn into an active role in the politics of the Spanish Republican Diaspora, and might even have to denounce publicly the ongoing British appeasement of Franco's Spain.[68] To make sure that the British government fully appreciated his position, Negrín took the trouble to elaborate it in a personal letter to Lord Halifax on 11 November, in which he expressed his conviction that Britain's policy of close understanding and collaboration with the Franco regime would prove counter-productive. However, Negrín also acknowledged that as a guest of the British government he did not want to obstruct the application of its official policy towards Franco's Spain, even if he doubted its wisdom. He reassured Halifax that he would strive to seek a solution to the problem of his location which would be satisfactory for all. Thus, he suggested that the government of either Canada or the United States should be approached to allow him into their territory. Nevertheless Dr Negrín categorically refused to leave for a lecture tour in New Zealand:

Or, dans les moments actuels lorsque les changements se succèdent avec cette rapidité vertigineuse dont nous sommes tous les témoins, de m'éloigner de mon pays, et de l'Europe, à une distance comme celle à laquelle se trouve la Nouvelle Zélande, se présente à mon esprit comme une véritable, désertion qui répugne à mon sentiment de l'honneur et qui me ferait apparaître à mes propres yeux, et certainement aussi aux yeux de mes concitoyens comme une véritable traître envers mon pays.[69]

In view of President Roosevelt's personal veto on Negrín's application for a United States visa the previous summer, the British government did not bother Washington again over this matter. However, to the British foreign secretary's dismay, the Canadian government proved no more accommodating when asked to admit Negrín.[70] The Canadian refusal to grant Negrín an entry visa effectively meant that the British government could only get rid of the Spanish Republican by formally expelling him, a course of action which it had just resolved not to follow – at least for the 'present'. Moreover, there occurred in November 1940 an additional event that transformed the war cabinet's self-denying ordinance towards Negrín into a virtually permanent resolution.

Negrín, probably to mobilize sympathetic British opinion in his support, had, it seems, leaked news of the latest government effort to oust him from England, to political and journalistic circles. As Halifax reported in rather injured fashion to Hoare: 'Negrín, though apparently friendly and co-operative, in fact behaved thoroughly badly and repeated the whole conversation with Alexander and me outside and it accordingly appeared almost textually correct in various publications.'[71] It was reported in the *Daily Herald* on 15 November that some members of parliament had been indignant to hear that Negrín was coming under official pressure to quit Britain in order to placate the Franco regime. While the iconoclastic newssheet, *The Week*, not only disclosed, on 20 November, details of the summer attempt to induce Negrín to abandon his British refuge, but also published a most comprehensive account of the Spaniard's 11 November meeting with Alexander and Halifax. *The Week*, which under the provocative editorship of Claud Cockburn had scourged and scandalized the British and international establishments with its political revelations and economic exposés since 1933, claimed that the official effort to eject Negrín completely contradicted the government's claim to be championing European freedom against Nazi oppression:

It would of course be absurd to suggest that the Government's policy in the Negrín case, illuminating as it is, is either illogical or . . . foolish. Despite the somewhat half-baked pleas and pretences of certain propagandists, it is ludicrous to expect that a Government of this character should deliberately go about Europe encouraging democratic or popular revolts – particularly after having spent more than 2 years co-operating in the defeat of the Spanish Republic, which was regarded as a dangerously radical affair.[72]

Other protests also focused on the incompatibility between Britain's treatment of Juan Negrín and its putative role as the protagonist of a European people's war.[73]

However, it was the reaction of party political and parliamentary opinion to the news of another official effort to pressurize Negrín into leaving Britain, that most worried the British government. Some Labour M.P.s were particularly incensed at this apparent evidence that the British cabinet was still inclined to appease 'fascist' dictators, like Franco.[74] The result was what Halifax called 'a first-class political row in Parliament'.[75] The Labour M.P. for Rotherham, William Dobbie, gave notice that he intended to ask the Foreign Office 'why an intimation has been made to Dr Negrín, the Prime Minister of Spain in the late Spanish Republican Government, at present enjoying the right of asylum in this country, in regard to his leaving the country?'[76] It devolved upon R. A. Butler, as parliamentary under-secretary of state for foreign affairs, to answer this question in the house of commons, since Halifax, as a peer, sat in the house of lords. Butler could not have relished his task since any acute parliamentary controversy over Negrín could jeopardize the wartime truce on party conflict and also embarrass Britain's relations with Spain. The under-secretary of state, indeed, appealed to Attlee to get Dobbie to withdraw his question, but the Labour leader declined to exercise his authority over the M.P. as his party chief to influence him to that end. Butler considered Attlee's attitude as 'very surprising' for 'a prominent member of the Cabinet'.[77] Butler then approached Dobbie, himself, to impress upon him that 'his question . . . would do Dr Negrín as much harm as British policy in Spain', but the Labour M.P. proved stubborn. He refused to remove his question from the order paper 'despite considerable argument' on the ground that 'if he took it off he would appear to have been "squared" '.[78]

Therefore, R. A. Butler was forced to reply to Dobbie's parliamentary question in the house of commons on Wednesday 20 November, which he did in these rather evasive terms: 'His Majesty's Government have no intention of departing from the established practice of this country in the general treatment extended to those who seek refuge here, and no steps have been taken to oblige Dr Negrín to leave.'[79] This was hardly an adequate response to the Labour man's question since, as another M.P. pointed out, Butler was being asked whether 'intimation had been given to Dr Negrín to leave the country, and the answer . . . given was that the Government had not obliged Dr Negrín to leave the country, which is quite a different matter . . .'[80] Butler also avoided answering the supplementary question put by Emanuel Shinwell, the Labour M.P., who was one of the few consistent critics of government policies during the period of wartime crisis:

Is it not true that Dr Negrín was approached by representatives of the Government in the last two months to induce him to leave the country, and that Dr Negrín declined? Is that not true? And may I further ask for an assurance that no Labour member of the Government was associated with this discreditable attempt to induce Dr Negrín to leave this country?[81]

Dobbie declared himself entirely dissatisfied with Butler's reply and gave notice that he would raise the subject again 'at the first favourable opportunity'.[82] Obviously shaken by the depth of the parliamentary feeling in favour of Negrín, Butler issued a private warning to Halifax that, while he would 'attempt to hold the situation in the House of Commons by conversations with M.P.s interested, and try to avoid any further raising of the matter', he could not guarantee that he would succeed in the endeavour.[83]

Indeed, the senior British political figures concerned in the affair, the prime minister and the foreign secretary, now realized that any further action against Negrín could do irreparable injury to the unity of the country's wartime coalition government, given the partisan passions that had been aroused by his case. Halifax informed the war cabinet on 28

November 1940 that, as both the United States and Canada were unwilling to receive Negrín, he did not intend to press further for the Spaniard's removal from England, unless Hoare expressed additional, serious objections from Madrid.[84] However, as Halifax soon informed Hoare, the case was now really closed.[85] For, the parliamentary squabble on 20 November, over Negrín's position, meant that a cabinet composed of representatives of different political parties could not 'reach unanimity about actually kicking him out', unless the Spaniard violated his 'undertaking to abstain from political activity'. All the foreign secretary could promise Hoare was that a close watch would be kept on Negrín to detect any such transgression at once.[86] Moreover, Butler had to reassure Negrín's sympathizers in the house of commons, once more, on 4 December, when the Spaniard's case was again raised there: 'I can only say ... that His Majesty's Government have taken no steps to oblige Dr Negrín to leave this country against his will, nor is any such action in contemplation.'[87]

Churchill, too, had been concerned at the harmful effects of such public political debate on Negrín and informed the war cabinet that it was 'undesirable that this matter should be discussed openly in Parliament'.[88] Such open parliamentary discussion did, indeed, damage the British government's relations with Franco's Spain. Alba told R. A. Butler on 27 November that 'it was deplorable that questions should be asked in the House of Commons since they caused the maximum of annoyance in Spain'.[89] Although the British prime minister was, doubtless, anxious about the negative diplomatic consequences of the parliamentary airing of such a sensitive topic in Anglo-Spanish relations, Churchill was more concerned about the domestic political harm that could be done by the outbreak of party or ideological dissension inside the government. He was candid enough to acknowledge that this was his priority in relation to the Negrín affair, during a luncheon conversation with the duke of Alba at the Spanish embassy in London, on 5 December 1940. Churchill declared, there and then, *inter alia*:

We are watching Negrín very closely and you can rest assured that not the least activity on his part against the Spanish Government will be tolerated. Personally I should have been very glad if he had gone to Mexico, but one could not force him, not only because of England's tradition, but also because of the heterogeneous character of my Government, a character that should enable one to understand so many other aspects of my policy.[90]

If Churchill and other Conservatives were prepared to refrain from deporting Negrín as a concession to the need for national unity, then the Labour ministers also compromised for the sake of presenting a united British front to the Axis. Among Labour's concessions was its omission to stipulate the official proclamation of a people's war in Europe as the price of its continued participation in the British government. Although a cabinet sub-committee was set up to draft war aims for Britain, its moderately progressive conclusions were ignored by Churchill.[91] For, the prime minister felt, in the terms of a compliant cabinet resolution of early 1941, that any British declaration of war aims expressing general principles 'would not strike home', while particular suggestions 'would be bound to give rise to difficulties'.[92] A social democratic programme of war aims might alienate even more anti-Nazi Europeans than it could attract.[93] Indeed, when Lord Halifax had drawn up a paper in late 1940 embodying general moral and political principles that could comprise Britain's wartime goals, the result did not please Sir Alexander Cadogan. For, Cadogan believed that to announce a British crusade for 'democracy' and 'liberty' would enable Germany to claim that Britain was intent upon restoring the 'Front Populaire' in France, and the 'Red' movement in Spain which he and, he alleged, millions of Europeans abhorred.[94]

If Britain did not enunciate a programme of progressive war aims, neither did it employ the methods of a people's war of liberation against the Nazi occupiers of continental Europe, in any substantial or sustained manner. British incitement of the European peoples to revolt against the German invaders had been one of the main planks in a series of plans drafted by the British Chiefs of Staff during 1940–1, outlining a grand strategic design for the final defeat of Nazism.[95] However, Britain did not possess the requisite resources to set Europe ablaze while it struggled alone against the Axis in 1940–1. By the time the British did have the transport aircraft, the equipment, and the weaponry to support large-scale action by the tardily formed European resistance movements, they had no need to rely upon such continental subversion as an essential condition of their victory. For, from later 1941, the big battalions of the Soviet Union and the United States were ranged alongside the British. The British-supported resistance movements in Europe were relegated then to a relatively minor role in the overall allied war effort against the Nazi 'New Order'.[96] Hitler's Germany was defeated by conventional means, in pitched battles by massed air, army and naval forces.

Moreover, the same negative inspiration that had forged the international Grand Alliance, anti-Nazism, was at the heart of the wartime domestic political consensus in Britain. It was the politics of the lowest common contaminator: Adolf Hitler. British Labour was willing to accept a governing partnership with its political rivals precisely because the danger to Britain's survival as a democratic, independent and sovereign community was so profound and proximate.[97] R. A. Butler had perceptively pointed this out to Hoare in July 1940, when reminding the latter how divided attitudes over Spain coincided with the main cleavage in domestic politics in Britain: 'But this division is appreciably less now that the menace of invasion is near.'[98] Moreover, Britain's national enemy, German fascism, was also the Labour movement's bitter ideological foe, an antipathy that imbued the British left with a patriotism that was at least as principled as it was parochial. A common enemy had engendered a vital internal political unity in Britain during later 1940, a national unanimity that Labour leaders knew they could not afford to imperil by advocating the strategy of a people's war too vigorously. Thus, Harold Laski was formally rebuked at a meeting of the National Executive Committee of the Labour Party, on 5 November 1940, for publishing his 'Open Letter' (cited above), with its call for an explicit assurance from Labour's ministers that they were 'persistently' striving within government for 'a new social order and a new international order'. Laski was upbraided for engaging in such public partisan pleading which endangered the cohesion of the coalition government.[99] However, if Labour had to moderate its international aspirations, this did not mean that it was prepared to withdraw its protection from its political friends. Juan Negrín López was allowed to remain in Britain for the duration of the Second World War, even though the Franco regime continued to complain, after 1940, about his presence there.[100]

9

Churchill and the British 'Decision' to fight on in 1940: right policy, wrong reasons

DAVID REYNOLDS

The summer of 1940 has gone down in patriotic folklore as Britain's finest hour. After France had collapsed, the British people fought on alone but united, aroused by the miracle of Dunkirk, protected by the heroic RAF, inspired above all by Churchill's bulldog spirit – 'victory at all costs', 'blood, toil, tears and sweat', 'we shall fight on the beaches . . . we shall never surrender'. It is a comforting story – one that is recalled with nostalgia in every national crisis – and its authority was enhanced by Churchill's own categorical statements in his war memoirs. There he wrote: 'Future generations may deem it noteworthy that the supreme question of whether we should fight on alone never found a place upon the War Cabinet agenda' nor was it 'even mentioned in our most private conclaves'. 'It was taken for granted', he assured his readers, that Britain would continue the struggle 'and we were much too busy to waste time upon such unreal, academic issues.'[1]

It is true that the question of fighting on was never listed explicitly as an item on the War Cabinet's agenda. In every other respect, however, Sir Winston's assurances were, to say the least, disingenuous. The question was all too real, and answers to it were certainly not taken for granted, after the world's best army had been shattered in six weeks leaving Britain isolated with only minimal defences. This essay re-examines some of the myths about 1940. First it looks at the discussions in Whitehall and Westminster about a negotiated peace and connects them with the fluid political situation during Churchill's early months as premier. Then it considers the reasons why the Government, and particularly Churchill, believed that Britain still had a chance of defeating Germany. I shall suggest that those reasons were invalid and that they rested on mistaken perceptions of Germany and the United States. To appreciate all this, we need to forget some familiar developments later in the war – unconditional surrender, the special relationship, Churchill's political pre-eminence.

And if we do so we shall also form a rather more complex picture of Churchill than that of the indomitable, single-minded, pro-American hero enshrined in the war memoirs and in national mythology.[2]

To understand the discussions in Britain about a negotiated peace, we must remember Churchill's unusual political position in the summer of 1940. For a decade from 1929 to1939 he had been in the wilderness – written off by most MPs as a spent and eccentric elder statesman, outside the Tory fold on major issues such as India, rearmament and the Abdication. In the late thirties Tory opposition to Chamberlain's foreign policy coalesced around Eden rather than Churchill, and although Churchill was brought into the War Cabinet as First Lord of the Admiralty when war broke out in September 1939 he was denied effective control over Britain's war effort. But then, in the Commons vote of confidence about the Norwegian campaign on 8 May 1940, Chamberlain's normal majority slumped from around 200 to 81. He tried in vain to draw Labour and Liberals into a national coalition, and after two days of confused politicking Churchill was asked by the King on the evening of 10 May to form a ministry. That morning the German attack on the Western Front had begun. For Churchill, this was his hour of destiny.

During the course of 1940 Churchill established a position at Westminster and in the country at large that was stronger than Chamberlain had enjoyed even at the pinnacle of his popularity after Munich. But in the early months of his premiership Churchill felt much less secure. He had not been the inside choice to replace Chamberlain. Lord Halifax, the Foreign Secretary, enjoyed the confidence of Chamberlain, the King and the Tories, and would have been supported by the Labour and Liberal parties.[3] It was Halifax's reluctance which gave Churchill his chance. Even then Churchill's position was anomalous. He was a prime minister without a party. Chamberlain remained the Conservative leader, and Tory backbenchers, somewhat chastened by the effect of their abstentions during the Norway debate, ostentatiously rallied behind him immediately after the political crisis. Churchill was keenly aware of these political realities. 'To a large extent I am in y[ou]r hands', he wrote Chamberlain after being asked to form a government,[4] and that feeling was reflected in the composition of his Cabinet. Despite the addition of the Labour and Liberal leaders, the coalition still contained many of the old guard in key positions. Chamberlain was made Lord President, with effective control over domestic policy, Halifax stayed as Foreign Secretary, together with Chamberlain intimate R. A. Butler as his Parliamentary Under Secretary, and Kingsley Wood became Chancellor of the Exchequer. After Dunkirk, when there was a vigorous press campaign to remove the 'Guilty Men' supposedly responsible for Britain's disasters, it was made very clear to Churchill that if Chamberlain was forced to resign, Simon, Kingsley Wood and several junior ministers, including Butler, would go as well. Calling on the press lords to desist, Churchill gave striking expression to his sense of insecurity:

Churchill said not to forget that a year ago last Christmas they were trying to hound him out of his constituency, and by a succession of events that astounded him he was invited by the practically unanimous vote of both Houses of Parliament to be Prime Minister. But the men who had supported Chamberlain and hounded Churchill were still M.P.s. Chamberlain had got the bigger cheer when they met the House after forming the new administration. A General Election was not possible during a war and so the present House of Commons, however unrepresentative of feeling in the country, had to be reckoned with as the ultimate source of power for the duration. If Churchill trampled on these men, as he could trample on them, they would set themselves against him, and in such internecine strife lay the Germans' best chance of victory.[5]

Churchill's fears were probably unfounded. Although Chamberlain seems initially to have entertained hopes of recovering the premiership after the war, the diagnosis of terminal cancer forced him to retire from politics in the autumn,[6] and Churchill, with the cautionary examples of Lloyd George and MacDonald before him, quickly accepted the Tory leadership when it was offered to him in October. From then on his political position was unassailable. But in the spring and summer – and this is my point – Churchill *felt* insecure, and that is what we must bear in mind as we turn to the War Cabinet discussions about a negotiated peace.

These discussions took place on 26, 27 and 28 May 1940.[7] By the 26th the bulk of the British Expeditionary Force had been trapped around Dunkirk. At this stage it was expected that only 30,000 to 50,000 could be evacuated, without their equipment – hardly the basis of a successful defence against invasion.[8] Moreover, it was feared that invasion might be imminent. For a while in late May British intelligence estimates suggested that Hitler was going to curtail operations in France to mount an immediate attack on the British Isles.[9] The outlook in short was grim as Halifax in particular was well aware. Like most of Whitehall the Foreign Secretary had been stunned by the disintegration of the French army – 'the one firm rock on which everybody had been willing to build for the last two years'[10] -- and back in December 1939 he had observed in Cabinet that, if ever the French government wanted to make peace, 'we should not be able to carry on the war by ourselves'.[11] Faced now with the inconceivable, he began to look for some way out. It is important to be clear about what Halifax was saying. He was not advocating immediate surrender or anything of the sort. He wanted to use the Italians to ascertain Hitler's likely peace terms. Halifax stressed that he would fight to the end if

Britain's integrity and independence were threatened – if, for example, Hitler demanded the fleet or the RAF. However, if terms could be secured to guarantee this independence – even if they involved surrendering part of the empire – then it was senseless, in his opinion, to permit further slaughter and destruction.[12]

Churchill's response was that no satisfactory peace could possibly be achieved until Britain had shown Hitler that she could not be conquered. Only then would a basis of equality have been reached from which negotiation might be possible. Even to inquire about German terms at this stage, Churchill insisted, would be a sign of weakness which would undermine Britain's fighting position at home and abroad.[13] The issue was thrashed out at five long meetings during which the argument became sufficiently heated for Halifax, briefly, to talk of resignation.[14] In the end Chamberlain came round to Churchill's point of view, which was also endorsed by the Labour and Liberal members of the War Cabinet and applauded at a meeting of junior ministers. Halifax was therefore isolated and the idea of approaching the Italians was rejected.[15] Moreover, by early June, the military situation seemed much better. To everyone's relief and amazement, 335,000 Allied troops had been evacuated from Dunkirk, and it also became clear that Hitler intended to finish off the French before he turned his attention to Britain. With the immediate crisis averted, a consensus now formed in the Cabinet around the Churchillian position that no question of peace terms could be raised until the Battle of Britain had been won. However, the hope was still that, by continuing the struggle, Britain would eventually secure not total victory but acceptable terms. Halifax and Butler were particularly emphatic on this point, fearing that Churchill would be carried away by emotion and bravado into prolonging the war unnecessarily.[16]

At Westminster, too, doubts were expressed about the wisdom of fighting on. A group of some thirty MPs and ten peers, loosely organised by the Labour businessman, Richard Stokes, believed it would be disastrous for Britain and Germany to continue the war. Whoever won, they argued, Europe would be ravaged and the only beneficiaries would be Russia and the United States. This was not an argument for 'peace at any price' but for serious consideration of any reasonable offer from Hitler that offered a chance of 'a just peace with disarmament'.[17] Stokes' group looked to Lloyd George as its potential leader. In fact, the former PM's attitude was broadly similar to that of the War Cabinet after Dunkirk. He did not advocate an immediate peace but believed that Britain should seek favourable terms once the Battle of Britain had been won.[18] Although we think of Lloyd George by 1940 as a spent force, that was not the opinion of contemporaries. Senility was yet to set in and he remained an influential figure at home and abroad, whom many still saw as a great leader. Churchill certainly had not written him off. On several occasions in May and June he tried to draw Lloyd George into his government, but these efforts were frustrated by Chamberlain, whose bitter hatred of Lloyd George dated back to World War I. However, Churchill persuaded Chamberlain to withdraw his opposition as the price for getting the 'Guilty Men' press campaign called off. Thereafter, Lloyd George was the main obstacle, ostensibly because he would not serve with those he called 'the architects of disaster' – Chamberlain and Halifax.[19] This was not the only reason, however. As Chamberlain and Churchill suspected, Lloyd George also saw himself as a future peacemaking prime minister, ready to take command when the battle for survival had been won and the nation appreciated the impossibility of achieving total victory. As he told his secretary in October 1940: 'I shall wait until Winston is bust.'[20]

Blessed (and burdened) as we are with hindsight, it is easy to stigmatise Halifax, Lloyd George and their like as appeasers and defeatists, out of touch with the heroic mood of the moment. Talk about a compromise peace seems a far cry from the unconditional surrender of May 1945. It is therefore important to emphasise that the idea of an eventual negotiated settlement was not aberrant and unpatriotic but was in fact the goal with which British leaders had entered the war in 1939. As Chamberlain explained to Roosevelt that October:

My own belief is that we shall win, not by a complete and spectacular victory, which is unlikely under modern conditions, but by convincing the Germans that they cannot win. Once they have arrived at that conclusion, I do not believe they can stand our relentless pressure, for they have not started this war with the enthusiasm or the confidence of 1914.[21]

Convincing the Germans that they could not win meant maintaining the pressure to cause 'a collapse of the German home front' and a coup to overthrow Hitler and the Nazi system.[22] After this it might be possible to negotiate with a new German government, perhaps involving Göring and conservative generals with whom the British Government tried to keep open tentative lines of communication during the winter of 1939–40.[23] For Chamberlain and his colleagues this seemed a balanced, realistic goal. Britain's aim was to eliminate the Nazi threat to Europe's security, not to smash the German nation, and after the horrors of 1914–18 no one could be enthusiastic about a war of attrition particularly in the absence of an Eastern Front. For some right-wingers in the Cabinet, there was a further consideration. Historically British leaders had conceived of a strong but peaceful Germany as a potential source of stability in central Europe. Eliminating the Nazi menace at the cost of exposing the Continent to the

Soviet threat was hardly a desirable prospect. Thus Sir Samuel Hoare, Chamberlain's Home Secretary and close associate, wanted an internal collapse in Germany and a moderate, peacemaking government, but not a real revolution which would lead to a Bolshevik Europe.[24]

Where did Churchill stand on this issue? On 13 May he had told the Commons that his policy was 'Victory at all costs, victory in spite of all terror, however long and hard the road may be, for without victory there is no survival.' Privately on 18 May and 1 June he spoke of his conviction that Britain would beat Germany and he rejected the idea of preparing contingency plans to evacuate the royal family and government abroad.[25] But in Cabinet during the Dunkirk crisis he was much less adamant that total victory was the only acceptable result. When asked by Halifax on 26 May 'whether, if he was satisfied that matters vital to the independence of this country were unaffected, he would be prepared to discuss terms', Churchill replied 'that he would be thankful to get out of our present difficulties on such terms, provided we retained the essentials and the elements of our vital strength, even at the cost of some territory'.[26] In Chamberlain's more colourful account of the exchange, Churchill is recorded as saying that 'if we could get out of this jam by giving up Malta and Gibraltar and some African colonies he would jump at it', although he did not see any such prospect.[27] The following day he took a similar line. According to the War Cabinet minutes he commented that 'if Herr Hitler was prepared to make peace on the terms of the restoration of German colonies and the overlordship of Central Europe, that was one thing', but he felt that such an offer was 'most unlikely'.[28] Summing up his position on 28 May, Churchill stressed that in the present crisis they could not get acceptable terms from Italy and Germany:

Signor Mussolini, if he came in as mediator, would take his whack out of us. It was impossible to imagine that Herr Hitler would be so foolish as to let us continue our rearmament. In effect, his terms would put us completely at his mercy. We should get no worse terms if we went on fighting, even if we were beaten, than were open to us now. If, however, we continued the war and Germany attacked us, no doubt we should suffer some damage, but they would also suffer severe losses. Their oil supplies might be reduced. A time might come when we felt that we had to put an end to the struggle, but the terms would not then be more mortal than those offered to us now.[29]

In each case the Prime Minister seems to have acknowledged the possibility of an eventual negotiated peace, while emphasising that this was definitely not the right moment. Certainly his language was a far cry from 'victory at all costs'.

How should we interpret these remarks? Was Churchill simply trying to maintain Cabinet unity by reassuring influential colleagues that he was not a romantic diehard. This argument is certainly plausible, especially when we remember Churchill's relatively weak political position that summer.[30] But before we dismiss his statements as a tactical ploy, we should note that he took a similar line in other, more public situations when one might have expected a pugnacious, optimistic statement to strengthen domestic opinion. For instance, on 29 May, concerned at defeatist talk in London, he issued a general injunction to ministers to maintain 'a high morale in their circles; not minimizing the gravity of events, but showing confidence in our ability and inflexible resolve to continue the war *till we have broken the will of the enemy to bring all Europe under his domination*'.[31] No mention here of total victory.

Yet one might respond that all these remarks by Churchill, like the whole War Cabinet controversy, date from the Dunkirk period, and therefore reflect the extreme but temporary crisis atmosphere before the evacuation succeeded. This interpretation, like the previous one, must be taken seriously, but it is relevant to note that Churchill made similar statements about a negotiated peace at less desperate moments. For instance, after Hitler's peace feelers in late September 1939, Churchill drafted a possible answer. Although negative, he told Chamberlain, it 'does not close the door upon any genuine offer' from Germany.[32] On 6 June 1940 Churchill told Halifax that, before admitting Lloyd George to any Cabinet post, he would put the former PM 'through an inquisition first, as to whether he had the root of the matter in him'. As the criterion, Churchill said he would adopt Halifax's formula 'that any peace terms now, as hereafter, offered must not be destructive of our independence'.[33] And in August 1940, in terms reminiscent of the previous autumn, the Prime Minister insisted that a firm reply to Hitler's current overtures was 'the only chance of extorting from Germany any offers which are not fantastic'.[34]

It seems feasible, therefore, that Churchill did not rule out the possibility of an eventual negotiated peace, even if he judged May 1940 to be an inopportune moment. Like his colleagues his object may not have been total victory, which appeared unrealistic even when France was in the war, but the elimination of Hitler and Nazism, the evacuation of Germany's conquests and a durable peace with adequate guarantees. After all, more than most Tories he feared the long-term Bolshevik threat, and in August 1941 he talked about his goal of a Germany that was 'fat but impotent'.[35] We should remember, too, that British war aims took shape slowly, and that the 'unconditional surrender' policy of January 1943 grew out of a very different phase of the war. After the Blitz Göring looked much less attractive in British eyes and during 1941 expectations about the German 'moderates' were gradually extinguished. At the same time Russia and

America became active allies. By 1943, in other words, total victory seemed both necessary and possible; this was not the case in 1940.

In the end these arguments are speculative: inferences from fragmentary and ambiguous evidence. But there can be little doubt that, contrary to the mythology he himself sedulously cultivated, Churchill succumbed at times to the doubts that plagued British leaders in the summer of 1940. In February 1946, when Churchill was reminiscing about the dark days of the war, he surprised Halifax by saying 'that he had never really believed in invasion. He had been into it all in 1913 [as First Lord of the Admiralty] and realized how difficult it was . . .'[36] But on 4 June 1940 Churchill had scribbled a hasty note to Stanley Baldwin in which his tone was more equivocal: 'We are going through v[er]y hard times & I expect worse to come: but I feel quite sure that better days will come! Though whether we shall live to see them is more doubtful.'[37] In July 1946 the American writer Robert Sherwood was discussing the same period with General Ismay, the PM's wartime military secretary. Ismay recalled a conversation he had with Churchill on 12 June 1940, after their penultimate conference with the demoralised French leaders at Briare. According to Sherwood's notes:

When Churchill went to the airport to return to England, he said to Ismay that, it seems, 'we fight alone'. Ismay said he was glad of it, that 'we'll win the Battle of Britain'. Churchill gave him a look and remarked, 'You and I will be dead in three months time.'[38]

From the evidence set out so far, it is therefore apparent that the question of a negotiated peace *was* aired in Whitehall and Westminster in the summer of 1940. It is also clear that some of those who toyed with the idea, notably Halifax and Lloyd George, were politicians whom Churchill had to take seriously, particularly in view of his sense of insecurity at this time. We have seen that Churchill probably shared some of their doubts about Britain's chances and that he spoke privately on a number of occasions about the possibility of an eventual negotiated peace. In public, however, it was obviously essential to strike the most hopeful and inspiring attitude in order to sustain domestic morale in preparation for the expected invasion. Hence Churchill's series of uplifting speeches, phrases from which have justly passed into the treasury of the English language. But rhetoric alone was insufficient. Aside from emotion, there had to be compelling *reasons* for fighting on. And those reasons have been neglected in subsequent historiography.

One of the most cogent statements of the case for an early peace came from the pen of Lloyd George in September 1940. In a long and thoughtful memorandum he laid bare the gravity of Britain's strategic position compared with World War I. Then it had taken four years of dreadful conflict, waged for the most part on two fronts in conjunction with major continental allies, before Germany had finally succumbed. This time Britain had been driven from the continent, Russia was neutral and France conquered. To defeat Germany, he argued, Britain would first have to re-establish herself on the Continent – itself no easy task – and then wage a prolonged war of attrition on the model of 1914–18. The whole process would take from five to ten years, by which time the British Isles would be devastated, depopulated and bankrupt, with most of her empire and commerce in the hands of America, Russia and Japan. Nor did Lloyd George place much hope in American intervention. 'She will no doubt help us in all ways short of War', he wrote. 'But I cannot foresee her sending another huge Army to Europe.' And even if she did decide to do so, Lloyd George reckoned from the bitter experiences of 1917–18 that the US Army 'would not be an efficient fighting machine for at least 2 years. It might then take the place of the French Army in the last war – although that is doubtful.'[39]

Lloyd George had put his finger on the two central issues at stake. Could Germany be defeated without another bloody land war across the Continent? And what were the prospects of rapid American help on a sufficiently large scale? Answers to these two questions largely determined one's assessment of Britain's chances. Lloyd George's response was negative on both counts – hence his pessimism. Churchill took a more optimistic view, which he successfully established as official policy. To appreciate this, we must look more closely at British assessments of Germany and then of the United States.

British strategists in 1940–1, and indeed for some time before and after, consistently rejected Lloyd George's first argument – that Germany could not be defeated without a war of attrition across Europe. In their view – and Churchill was outstanding here – the large scale British Expeditionary Force (BEF) of World War I had been a disastrous aberration from traditional British policy of the eighteenth and nineteenth centuries. The present war should be fought in the old way, in other words by relying on Britain's economic, financial and naval strength in conjunction with the manpower of continental allies. (Or, as the French saw it, the British would fight to the last Frenchman.) Thus, planning papers in 1939 envisaged that the French army, and a token BEF, would resist the initial German onslaught. Then the German economy and morale would be undermined by blockade, supplemented by bombing of industrial centres and intensive propaganda, until the time was ripe for the final offensive.[40] This strategy was all very well during the period of the Anglo-French alliance. But British policymakers clung to it even after the loss of the

French army. In the words of the Chiefs of Staff in September 1940: 'The wearing down of Germany by ever-increasing force of economic pressure should be the foundation of our strategy.'[41] To the triad of blockade, bombing and propaganda was added a new weapon – subversion. Britain would assist partisan movements in occupied Europe in harassing their Nazi rulers and preparing for eventual uprisings. (It was in July 1940 that Churchill created the Special Operations Executive with its mandate to 'set Europe ablaze'.) The Army would be vital for defending the British Isles and the empire, but its offensive role was still seen as limited. As the Chiefs put it:

It is not our policy to attempt to raise, and land on the continent, an army comparable in size to that of Germany. We should aim nevertheless, as soon as the action of the blockade and air offensive have secured conditions when numerically inferior forces can be employed with good chance of success, to re-establish a striking force on the Continent with which we can enter Germany and impose our terms.[42]

How could this strategy of limited liability still remain credible after June 1940? Part of the answer lies in the growing faith in strategic bombing. In their September memorandum the Chiefs of Staff still placed their principal emphasis on the blockade, but the RAF took a different line, and one that gradually became official orthodoxy thanks in large measure to the advocacy of Churchill. Now that Germany controlled Scandinavia and much of Europe, the Prime Minister observed in July 1940 that the blockade had been 'broken' as an effective weapon. In his view the only one thing that would bring Hitler down was 'an absolutely devastating, exterminating attack by very heavy bombers from this country upon the Nazi homeland'.[43] He spelled out his thinking more fully in a memorandum for the Cabinet on 3 September:

The Navy can lose us the war, but only the Air Force can win it. Therefore our supreme effort must be to gain overwhelming mastery in the Air. The Fighters are our salvation [i.e. in protecting the British Isles], but the Bombers alone provide the means of victory. We must therefore develop the power to carry an ever-increasing volume of explosives to Germany, so as to pulverise the entire industry and scientific structure on which the war effort and economic life of the enemy depend, while holding him at arm's length from our Island. In no other way at present visible can we hope to overcome the immense military power of Germany . . .[44]

Churchill continued to stress this strategy over the succeeding months. 'I consider the rapid expansion of the Bomber Force one of the greatest military objectives now before us', he wrote in December 1940. And the following July he instructed that Britain must aim at having nothing less than twice the strength of the *Luftwaffe* by the end of 1942. This was 'the very least that can be contemplated, since no other way of winning the war has yet been proposed'.[45] The RAF's idea that the Army would do little more than 'deliver the coup de grace'[46] was naturally unpopular in the War Office, where opposition mounted during 1941 to this strategy for winning the war.[47] But officially, at the top level, the three services had now come round to Churchill's view. The Chiefs of Staff review of 'General Strategy' on 31 July 1941 allowed the army only the role of an occupation force in the final stages of Germany's defeat, unless it were decided to accelerate victory by landing forces on the continent at an earlier stage. Even then, however, these would be modern armoured divisions, engaged in mobile warfare, and not the vast infantry line offensives of World War I. By contrast, the Chiefs spoke of massive bombing as the 'new weapon' on which Britain must principally rely to destroy the German economy and morale. It was to be given top priority in production and no limits would be set on the eventual size of the force required.[48]

But even this excessive faith in strategic bombing during 1940–1 is not sufficient to explain British optimism about defeating Germany at limited cost. The fundamental reason was their grave and persistent underestimation of the strength of the German war economy, a theme suggestively discussed in volume one of Hinsley's *British Intelligence*.[49] On 18 May 1940 'Chips' Channon, a junior minister at the Foreign Office, noted: 'It is now believed that the war will be over in September – the Germans will either win or be exhausted by this terrific effort.'[50] Such thinking was clearly apparent in the War Cabinet debates of 26 May. There Attlee observed, as a matter of fact, that Hitler 'had to win by the end of the year' while Chamberlain 'thought he would have to win by the beginning of the winter'. Even Halifax shared this belief in Germany's 'internal weakness': he used it to justify his contention that Hitler might not feel strong enough to insist on 'outrageous terms'.[51] The underlying assumption behind such remarks was that German shortages of food and raw materials, especially oil, would soon make themselves felt. On 25 May the Chiefs of Staff submitted their assessment of whether Britain could hope to win alone. (Significantly the exact question posed was: 'Could we ultimately bring sufficient economic pressure to bear on Germany to ensure her defeat?'.) They argued that if the blockade could be maintained, then, by the winter of 1940–1, inadequate supplies of oil and foodstuffs would weaken German rule in Europe and that by mid-1941 'Germany will have difficulty in replacing military equipments. A large part of the industrial plant of Europe will stand still, throwing upon the German administration an immense unemployment problem to handle.'[52] In a more considered verdict on 4 September the Chiefs predicted that, 'unless Germany can materially improve her position', in 1941 the deficiencies in the crucial areas of oil, food and textiles 'may prove disastrous'. They went on to draw the remarkable conclusion that although 1941 would be a year of attrition for Britain, her aim *'should be to pass to the general offensive in all spheres and all theatres with the utmost possible strength in the Spring of 1942'.*[53]

Churchill seems to have shared this assumption that the German economy was over-stretched. In fact as early as February 1939, according to an American visitor, Churchill 'felt that Hitler had now reached the peak of his military power. From now on he would grow weaker in relation to England and France.'[54] In May 1940 he was insisting that 'if only we could stick things out for another three months, the position would be entirely different.'[55] And this belief in fundamental German weakness also sheds light on a neglected part of the Prime Minister's 'finest hour' speech to the Commons on 18 June 1940. There he encouraged his countrymen, shocked at the French surrender, by a reminder that:

During the first four years of the last war the Allies experienced nothing but disaster and disappointment. . . . During that war we repeatedly asked ourselves the question, 'How are we going to win?' and no one was able ever to answer it with much precision, until, at the end, quite suddenly, quite unexpectedly, our terrible foe collapsed before us, and we were so glutted with victory that in our folly we threw it away.[56]

As we now know, the idea of a 'taut' Nazi economy, vulnerable to economic pressure and strategic bombing, was an illusion. German munitions production did not reach its peak until July 1944; bombing had only a limited impact on overall industrial output until late in that year; and civilian morale and productivity were, if anything, improved when Allied raids brought the war home to the German people.[57] So why had British policymakers been so wrong? As Hinsley emphasised the basic error was not one of information but of presuppositions. In fact, several false assumptions may be detected. First there was the conviction that Hitler's pre-eminent goal was the subjugation of Britain rather than expansion to the east. Whitehall policymakers were coming round to this view by late 1938, and from January 1939 there were recurrent scares that Germany might mount an immediate, devastating air assault on London perhaps without involving the French.[58] Indeed on 4 May 1940, less than a week before the offensive on the Western Front began, the Chiefs of Staff expressed the opinion that an attack on Britain was more likely than an attack on France,[59] and these fears recurred, as we have seen, at the time of Dunkirk. Churchill seems to have shared the conviction that Britain was Hitler's real target. On 26 May, for instance, he observed that France was 'likely to be offered decent terms by Germany, which we should not . . . There was no limit to the terms which Germany would impose upon us if she had her way.'[60] Yet, through all the historiographical debate about Hitler's war aims, it seems clear that in at least the early phases of his expansionist programme he sought and expected British acquiescence while he consolidated his grip on continental Europe. With the partial exception of the Navy, Nazi rearmament was geared to that assumption, and, when it was falsified in 1938–9, the German armed forces found themselves ill-prepared for the general European war that broke out in September 1939. Even during the summer of 1940 Hitler was still entertaining hopes of an agreement with Britain.[61]

Thus, the British wrongly assumed that Hitler intended war with Britain in 1939. They also believed that he would only have begun such a war when his economy was fully ready. By that they meant an economy completely converted from peace to wartime goals, with concomitant retooling, controls and organisation. In the German case that seemed a particularly reasonable judgement since this was a totalitarian state, supposedly under rigid regimentation. Commented the Chiefs of Staff in September 1940: 'The economic system of Greater Germany has produced spectacular results because it was based on an imposed discipline covering all activities down to individual transactions.'[62] Yet the British knew that German output and stockpiles were not impressive in absolute terms. They therefore concluded that Hitler had brought the economy to its peak performance, that this was insufficient for a sustained war and that the system was so 'taut' that it might soon collapse under continued British pressure. As the Ministry of Economic Warfare stated in September: 'the Nazi economy is much more brittle than the German economy of 1914–18 which was not so highly integrated. It is not impossible that an acute shortage of oil or a tie-up of the transport system might cause a breakdown of the closely-knit Nazi system with repercussions throughout Germany and German Europe of the utmost importance.'[63]

Two basic misapprehensions are evident here. First, the British thought in terms of an economy geared either to peace or to war: they failed to grasp the intermediate concept of *Blitzkrieg* warfare. Alan Milward has argued that this was a calculated response by Hitler to the exigencies of Germany's economic and geopolitical position – short, sharp wars against individual foes for which it was unnecessary to convert the whole economy to war production. This made it possible to avoid another two-front war for Germany and to have guns as well as butter. More recently, other historians such as Richard Overy, Williamson Murray and Wilhelm Deist have suggested that *Blitzkrieg* was not a well thought out strategy but an ad hoc response to a general war that came several years earlier than German leaders had expected. Either way, the German war economy of 1940 was characterised by rearmament in breadth rather than depth. The

Army and Air Force lacked reserves, spares and above all supplies for a sustained campaign, but they had exceptional short-term striking power, which was amply demonstrated in Poland and in France. The British appreciated this – hence their concern to survive the first few months of a German onslaught – but they believed that it marked the peak of Hitler's capacity. For, in the second place, they did not realise the uncoordinated, inefficient nature of the Nazi war economy in 1939–40. Far from being a highly regimented, totalitarian system, Germany at this time lacked a cohesive central economic administration. The three services competed indiscriminately, German industry displayed a marked reluctance to convert to war needs, and the conservative industrial structure impeded the introduction of automated, mass-production methods. Not until 1942, under Speer, were matters taken in hand, and this helps to explain why Germany did not reach its peak production until 1944. In other words, the Nazi economy, far from being 'taut' in 1940, still had a large amount of 'slack'.[64]

As Hinsley's work has shown, the crux of good intelligence is often not specific information – the product of spies, decrypts and the like, so much associated with intelligence operations in the popular imagination – but the paradigms or frameworks of assumptions into which the nuggets of information are set. British estimates of German output and stockpiles were not correct, but they were not wildly inaccurate. What mattered most was the underlying set of beliefs about Hitler's aims, the nature of war economies and the regimentation of a totalitarian state. British policy-makers in 1940 believed that the German war machine was approaching maximum efficiency and that traditional methods of economic pressure, supplemented by the 'new weapon' of the heavy bomber, would bring the struggle to a satisfactory conclusion without another major land war on the continent. These beliefs were slow to die. They help, for instance, to explain British opposition to America's 'second front' strategy in 1942–3.[65] And they constitute one part of the explanation for Britain's hopefulness in fighting on alone in 1940.

The other part, of course, was British expectations of help from the United States. In assessing Britain's chances alone, the Chiefs of Staff made it clear in May 1940 that their major assumption was that the USA was 'willing to give us full economic and financial support, *without which we do not think we could continue the war with any chance of success*'.[66] They laid particular emphasis on full co-operation from the Western Hemisphere in enforcing the blockade of Germany, on immediate US supplies of aircraft and warships and on naval assistance in the Pacific to restrain Japan. But they still did not envisage another American Expeditionary Force – and not just because that would have been utopian in the present state of American rearmament. The military planners observed in late June that although American technical personnel would be of very great value, 'we are unlikely to require troops' because Britain's own supplies of manpower should be adequate.[67] Here again is evidence of the pervasive belief that an over-stretched Germany could be broken largely by economic pressure.

Above all, British leaders in mid-1940 hoped for an early American declaration of war. Their reasons were twofold. In the long term, they believed only this would arouse the US public and permit all-out economic mobilisation. But the immediate and decisive consideration in their view was the likely impact on morale in Britain and overseas. Churchill put the point directly to Roosevelt on 15 June:

When I speak of the United States entering the war I am, of course, not thinking in terms of an expeditionary force, which I know is out of the question. What I have in mind is the tremendous moral effect that such an American decision would produce, not merely in France but also in all the democratic countries of the world, and, in the opposite sense, on the German and Italian peoples.[68]

Churchill's preoccupation there with the psychological effects of American belligerency can only be fully understood when we again remember his belief that this would not be a war of mass armies. If Britain's goal was to promote an internal collapse by destroying Germany's will to fight, then the relative morale of the belligerents would be a decisive factor. This was a point to which Churchill returned frequently. In a talk to newspaper editors on 22 August 1941:

He was very anxious that America should declare war, owing to its psychological effect. He said he would rather have America in and no American supplies for six months, than double the present level of American shipments while she maintained her present position as a neutral. He had come to the conclusion that this was a psychological war and that much depended on whether the Germans could get the inhabitants of Europe to acquiesce in their New Order before we could convince them of our ability to set them free. In this race for time, American participation in the war would be a great psychological point in our favour.[69]

The problem for Churchill in 1940, and much of 1941, was that Americans showed no apparent readiness to declare war. On the contrary their immediate response to the fall of France was a panic-stricken pre-occupation with their own defences to the detriment of even the limited material aid they were then offering to Britain. But throughout the summer of 1940 Churchill insisted that American belligerency was a matter of months at the most, and he spread his belief with such determination and skill that it became an axiom of British policy.

As with Churchill's confidence about defeating Germany, his predic-

tions about the United States depended heavily on the assumed impact of
the bomber. Essentially his thesis was that German air raids on British
cities would arouse American public opinion and lead to a declaration of
war. This was a long-standing belief, expressed for instance on several
occasions in private and in public during 1939.[70] And he used it repeatedly
in mid-1940 whenever there was talk of defeat or surrender. The precise
argument varied. Sometimes he emphasised the effect of bombing itself. In
his memoirs, de Gaulle, the Free French leader, recalled:

I can still see him at Chequers, one August day, raising his fists towards the sky as
he cried: 'So they won't come!' 'Are you in such a hurry', I said to him, 'to see your
towns smashed to bits?' 'You see', he replied, 'the bombing of Oxford, Coventry,
Canterbury, will cause such a wave of indignation in the United States that they'll
come into the war!'[71]

On other occasions Churchill stressed actual invasion, telling the anxious
Dominion prime ministers on 16 June 'that the spectacle of the fierce
struggle and carnage in our Island will draw the United States into the
war'.[72] But increasingly, after the failure in June to persuade Roosevelt to
declare war, Churchill recognised that FDR's hands were tied until the
presidential election on 5 November, and it was on this date that he pinned
his hopes. On 20 June, just after the French had asked for terms, he
addressed a crucial secret session of the House of Commons. Only his
notes survive, but they indicate clearly the burden of his remarks:

Attitude of United States.
Nothing will stir them like fighting in England.
No good suggesting to them we are down and out.
The heroic struggle of Britain best chance of bringing them in . . .
All depends upon our resolute bearing and holding out until Election issues are
    settled there.
If we can do so, I cannot doubt whole English-speaking world will be in line
    together.[73]

During the early autumn Churchill plugged away at the same theme. In a
letter about America on 15 October he told Bevin cryptically: 'I still hope
the big event may happen over there.'[74] And on 1 November Churchill said
that 'he was sure Roosevelt would win the election by a far greater
majority than was supposed, and he believed that America would come
into the war'.[75] By this stage even cautious specialists in the American
Department of the Foreign Office had come round to this view.[76] Indeed,
to Admiral Robert Ghormley, the USA's 'Special Naval Observer' in
London, it seemed 'that everybody in Great Britain expects the U.S. to
enter the war within a few days after . . . the President is re-elected'.[77]

   This expectation about the likely effect on US opinion of German
bombing helped keep Britain going during the summer of 1940. And one

can find warrant for it in the public comments of such distinguished American observers as the journalist Walter Lippmann,[78] and even in a private remark by the President himself, which was reported by King George VI to British leaders, probably including Churchill, in the summer of 1939.[79] Like the belief about an early German collapse, however, it proved to be sadly misplaced. Roosevelt's re-election did not herald a declaration of war. It was only in December 1941, and then in response to Japan and Germany, that the USA became a belligerent.

How can we explain British over-confidence? Part of the answer lies in their too sanguine estimates of the effect of bombing. The Blitz did not prove the holocaust that a generation of Britons had feared.[80] Losses of life were unexpectedly low, compared with the widespread damage to property and essential services, and although German raids did help strengthen pro-British feeling in America, they did not provide the catalyst that Churchill had predicted. Another reason was that Churchill consistently exaggerated the unity of what he called the 'English-speaking peoples'. Despite his half-American ancestry and frequent visits to the United States, Churchill had little real understanding of America's ethnic diversity or of the anglophobia that many of her European immigrants brought with them from the Old World. For him, the United States was an extension of the British family of nations – bound by ties of kin, culture and, above all, of language – so that, as he told the French leaders on 31 May 1940, an invasion of England, if it occurred, would have a profound effect, 'especially in those many towns in the New World which bore the same names as towns in the British Isles'.[81] Churchill also underestimated the political constraints still felt by Roosevelt after 5 November. Like most British policymakers he found it hard to appreciate just how far American political parties lacked the cohesion and discipline of their counterparts at Westminster. Even with large nominal majorities after the 1940 election, the President still had laboriously to build up a consensus among congressmen and the public for any foreign policy initiative, as the 1941 debates over Lend-Lease, convoying and the renewal of the draft were all to show. And, finally, it is also likely that Churchill was too optimistic about the bellicosity of the President himself. To British leaders FDR was always at his most warlike, implying that, but for public opinion, he would be in the conflict tomorrow. Yet Franklin Roosevelt was a past-master at telling his listeners what they wanted to hear.[82] The real intentions of this deeply secretive man are difficult to divine, but there is evidence to suggest that he was always hopeful of avoiding formal, total US involvement in the war if American security could be safeguarded by aid to the Allies. It is also possible that this hope was given new vitality by Hitler's move east and the successful Russian resistance in the summer of 1941.[83]

All this may serve to confirm the stereotype of Churchill as heroic but uncomplicated, even naive – someone who displayed an uncritical faith in American friendship which was inspiring yet misplaced, the man who, on 20 August 1940, likened Anglo-American co-operation to the great Mississippi, rolling on 'full flood, inexorable, irresistible, benignant, to broader lands and better days'.[84] To assess such statements properly, however, and to reach a balanced judgement on Churchill's publicly-stated confidence in the USA, we also need to bear in mind two other considerations – his deep disillusion *in private* that summer at the lack of real American help and the very tough line he adopted toward the USA in transatlantic diplomacy.

Churchill fully shared the general resentment felt in Whitehall at the isolationist panic in Washington and on 27 May 1940 he observed bitterly that the USA 'had given us practically no help in the war, and now that they saw how great was the danger, their attitude was that they wanted to keep everything which would help us for their own defence'.[85] Or, as he put it in a telegram to his old American friend, Bernard Baruch, a month later: 'Am sure we shall be alright here but your people are not doing much.'[86] In these circumstances Churchill believed that America's hand would have to be forced, and throughout the summer he therefore insisted, against the advice of the Foreign Office, that any British concession to the USA should only be made if and when some commensurate benefit was offered by Roosevelt in return. He was adamant, for example, that the USA should not be given the right to build much-needed bases on British islands in the Caribbean and western Atlantic except as part of a deal in which Britain received destroyers and other munitions. Likewise, he deprecated suggestions that the Government should throw its military secrets such as Asdic and Radar into the American lap and then wait to see what they offered in exchange. 'Generally speaking', he wrote on 17 July, 'I am not in a hurry to give our secrets until the United States is much nearer war than she is now.'[87]

Churchill even resorted to diplomatic blackmail in his efforts to prise America out of her shell. There were widespread fears in Washington that summer that the British and French fleets might be sunk or surrendered. These fears were shared by Roosevelt himself, who had received garbled and alarming reports about the Cabinet discussions of late May. At this time the USA only had a 'one-ocean navy', currently based at Pearl Harbor, two thousand miles from her *west* coast, in an effort to deter Japan, and if Hitler gained control of the Atlantic the east coast of the United States might be extremely vulnerable. Churchill played on these anxieties assiduously as the French collapsed. On 20 May he told Roosevelt that although his own government would never surrender, it might not survive a successful invasion and 'if others came in to parley amid the ruins, you must not be blind to the fact that the sole remaining bargaining counter with Germany would be the fleet, and if this country was left by the United States to its fate no one would have the right to blame those responsible if they made the best terms they could for the surviving inhabitants'.[88] This was also the burden of several other telegrams he sent to the President in May and June.

Churchill's mood was not fundamentally changed by the Destroyers Deal of September 1940, nor by Roosevelt's re-election two months later. On the contrary, the Prime Minister confessed himself 'rather chilled' on 2 December by the US attitude over the previous month,[89] and on the 20th he complained: 'We have not had anything from the United States that we have not paid for, and what we have had has not played an essential part in our resistance.'[90] The decisive change seems to have come in January 1941. Roosevelt's submission of the Lend-Lease bill to Congress and then the visit to London by his close friend and emissary, Harry Hopkins, convinced Churchill that the President was indeed Britain's 'best friend' and that he meant what he said about helping to the limits of his ability. But in mid-1940, as we have seen, Churchill was much less optimistic. Although he did tend at times to romanticise the Anglo-American relationship, his publicly-stated confidence in 1940 about American generosity and imminent belligerency was not the blind faith of an indomitable but ingenuous man. It reflected calculation as much as conviction. As with his statements about victory at all costs, Churchill forced himself to speak publicly in 1940 with an optimism that he often did not feel.

This leads us to the first of the two general conclusions in this essay – that the Churchill of myth (and of the war memoirs) is not always the Churchill of history. Scholars working on the 1930s and World War II have long been aware of this discrepancy, but it deserves to be underlined in view of the dogged rearguard action fought by popular biographers and television producers. Contrary to national folklore, Churchill did not stand in complete and heroic antithesis to his pusillanimous, small-minded political colleagues. British leaders of the 1930s and World War II all faced the same basic problem of how to protect their country's extended global interests with insufficient means at their disposal. The various policies they advanced are not to be divided into separate camps – appeasers and the rest – but rather marked on different points of a single spectrum, with no one as near either extreme as is often believed. This is true of the Chamberlain era; it is also true, as I have argued here, of 1940. In private, Churchill often acknowledged that the chances of survival, let alone victory, were slim. He also expressed acceptance, in principle, of the idea of an eventual negotiated peace, on terms guaranteeing the independence of the British Isles, even if that meant sacrificing parts of the empire and leaving Germany in command of Central Europe. And, far from already being part of an Anglo-American special relationship, his attitude to the USA in 1940 was frequently one of disillusion and suspicion, as he utilised every diplomatic weapon, including the threat of British surrender, to bludgeon a hesitant Roosevelt into providing real help. But in public, Churchill's stance on all these matters was very different. In public he maintained a mood of indefatigable optimism, insisting that Britain would settle for nothing less than total victory and arguing to sceptics at home and abroad that the USA would soon be in the war. This is not in any sense to belittle Churchill's greatness. On the contrary. My contention is that the popular stereotype of almost blind, apolitical pugnacity ignores the complexity of this remarkable man and sets him on an unreal pedestal. A not unskilful politician, handling the same issues in different ways for domestic and foreign audiences, privately wrestling with his own doubts and fears, yet transcending them to offer inspiring national and international leadership – that is surely a more impressive as well as a more accurate figure than the gutsy bulldog of popular mythology.

Equally misleading are the conventional beliefs about Britain's 'finest hour'. There was no formal 'decision' to fight on in June 1940, but it was far from being a foregone conclusion, as Churchill suggested. In Cabinet at the time of Dunkirk, and among a small group of MPs and peers, there was considerable debate about Britain's future chances and about the possibility of a satisfactory negotiated peace, immediately or when the threat of invasion had passed. Among those associated with such ideas were Halifax and Lloyd George – the former Churchill's rival for the premiership, the latter the would-be leader of a future peacemaking government. At this time Churchill was a prime minister without a party, acutely conscious of his recent years of exclusion not only from office but also from the affections of the Tory party. In the early months of his premiership he had therefore to take very seriously the possible threat posed by these senior colleagues and the policies they espoused, and it is surely significant that when the post of Ambassador to the USA fell vacant in December 1940 Churchill offered it first to Lloyd George, who refused on grounds of age, and then, successfully, to the reluctant Halifax. (It was not the first or the last time that the Washington Embassy was treated by British prime ministers as a convenient political dustbin.)[91] To counter the plausible case developed by these advocates of an early peace, Churchill and other British policymakers of like mind argued that if Britain could survive 1940 then she could win the war. They believed that the German economy was already 'taut' and vulnerable to British bombing, and that

Hitler had to defeat Britain by the winter if he was to win at all. If Britain could hang on until then it was also likely that German attempts at invasion, and particularly the merciless bombing of British cities, would have outraged opinion in the USA and brought her into the war after the November election. Churchill put the two points together in his crucial speech of 20 June to the secret session of the Commons. His notes read:

If Hitler fails to invade or destroy Britain he has lost the war.
I do not consider only the severities of the winter in Europe.
I look to superiority in Air power in the future.
Transatlantic reinforcements.
If [we] get through next 3 months [we] get through next 3 years.[92]

British expectations about Germany and about the USA were almost entirely erroneous. Their hopes of survival, let alone of victory, might also have proved too optimistic, but for Hitler himself. Their best reason for fighting on was one of which they had no knowledge at this time: namely that as early as July 1940 Hitler was already thinking of turning against Russia in 1941. Of this, no prediction can be found in the British intelligence reports and strategic assessments of 1940. Throughout that year, and for much of the next, the British still assumed that Hitler's main target was the British Isles. His Balkan campaigns in the spring of 1941 were therefore seen as part of a peripheral strategy to sever Britain's imperial lifelines as prelude to eventual invasion later in the year. And in April many British strategists accepted that Germany could create a bridgehead on the South Coast any time she was willing to make the sacrifice. A visiting US general noted: 'Dill, Beaverbrook, Freeman and Sinclair all believe that it can be done and will be tried.' Their hopes were pinned not on preventing an invasion but on stopping a German breakout from the beach-head.[93] As Hinsley has shown, it was not until early June 1941 that most of Whitehall accepted that Hitler really intended to invade the Soviet Union. Even then, such were the doubts about Russian military capabilities that when Operation 'Barbarossa' began on 22 June most British policymakers reckoned that Germany would win in three to six weeks without heavy losses.[94] Not surprisingly Churchill ordered on 25 June 1941 that anti-invasion preparations in the British Isles should be 'at concert pitch' by 1 September.[95] Had Hitler not turned east, had the Russians not survived, had Hitler not then compounded his folly by joining Japan against the United States, the outcome of the war would probably have been very different. In 1940 Churchill and his colleagues made the right decision – but they did so for the wrong reasons.

10

Britain and the Russian entry into the war

SHEILA LAWLOR

The divisions between the allies and Russia which emerged at the end of the war have often been seen in retrospect as responsible for the nature of Europe's ultimate political settlement. But these divisions can not be properly understood in the context of the last years of the war alone. They had their origins in the differences which arose when Hitler attacked Russia on 21 June 1941 and the Soviet Union became Britain's only fighting ally; and they existed not only between Britain and her new ally, but between the British leaders themselves, both civil and military. What were the true interests of Britain, and how were they to be reconciled with Russian demands?

For some weeks prior to the attack the British and the Russians had been aware that German troops had been concentrating near the Soviet frontier. But the Russians had publicly refused to concede that Hitler had any sinister intention. Maisky, the ambassador in London, had found it 'hard to believe that Germany contemplated . . . military action'.[1] He insisted that relations with Germany were 'governed by the non-aggression agreement of 1939' and that his government felt 'no anxiety about these concentrations'.[2] He 'felt sure' that Britain 'exaggerated' them, did not 'believe in the possibility of attack', and, as far as he admitted the concentrations, regarded them 'as part of a war of nerves'.[3]

It was only after the attack that the Russians conceded the position; and they accepted the military mission proposed by Eden on 13 June – when he also promised that Britain would consider Russia's economic needs.[4] But the news from the Russian front was, and continued to be, muddled and conflicting; and the Russians themselves seemed unwilling to provide any clear information.

In London, Maisky, on the one hand, professed himself as 'well satisfied with the outcome of the military operations to date'; he had not 'the slightest doubt of the ultimate issue. Russia was unconquerable.'[5] On the

168

other hand he began to issue a series of demands for assistance, which contrasted with his public confidence – even though they were couched in the language of right rather than need. His government wanted Britain to undertake an operation in the west – such as 'a landing on German occupied coasts'; and he urged that the British 'must press the Germans in the west by all means' in their power.[6] He continued to insist that Britain 'treat most seriously' their proposal of action 'on land to relieve pressure on Russia'; for this would have 'an encouraging psychological effect . . . far in excess of its actual military value'.[7] The demand was reiterated by the Russian mission (which arrived in London on 8 July): General Golikov maintained it was 'essential' that the British should do their 'utmost' to undertake operations 'which would draw some . . . weight of the German attack off Russia'.[8] He urged that combined air, naval and land operations in the north 'might also contribute to relieve the pressure'; and he hoped for 'the supply of material, particularly aircraft, anti-aircraft guns and bombs'.[9] The Russians continued to demand that 'more' should be done to help with supplies, and that action 'on land' might be staged in France – where they hoped that Britain would make an 'important diversion'.[10]

From Moscow Stalin pressed for an agreement involving 'mutual help' and 'neither country' to conclude a 'separate peace'.[11] After it had been signed he reminded Churchill that the Soviet Union and Great Britain had become 'fighting allies in a struggle against Hitlerite Germany'; and he urged that the 'military situation' of both countries would be 'considerably improved' if there were 'a front against Hitler in the west – Northern France, and in the North – the Arctic'.[12] Maisky took up the demands in London, having warned of his apprehension that though Britain gave 'generous assurances of help' she 'could not . . . give effect to them'.[13]

Reaction to these demands in London was confused by the uncertainty of the politicians and the chiefs of staff as to the prospects of Russian resistance. When Hitler invaded Russia on 21 June 1941, neither the politicians nor chiefs of staff expected that the Russians would hold out; and their doubts were exacerbated by the absence of any information from the Russians on the war. From the outset it seemed that the Russain concentrations were 'too far forward' and 'had been taken by surprise';[14] and though no 'first hand information' was available from the front, it seemed by 26 June, that the German attack north of the Pripet marshes 'aimed . . . at Leningrad and Moscow' had made some progress.[15] Some news suggested that the Germans were 'not having it *all* their own way', but it was 'impossible to say how long Russian resistance will last – three weeks or three months'.[16] Nor was it possible 'to assess the . . . situation', for according to the communiqués 'both sides were winning'.[17] But by 30 June the Russian military position appeared 'very grave' – the Germans

having broken through north and south of the Pripet marshes; and Dill
(chief of imperial general staff) was 'very gloomy' at the cabinet about
'Russian prospects'.[18] On 1 July the talk was 'pessimistic'; the Russians
were thought to be 'doing badly' and 'still being hammered'.[19] The
situation was in any case 'obscure'; and 'practically no information' had
come to London beyond that already 'published in the communiqués'.[20]
On 4 July the main German thrust was 'astride the Minsk–Smolensk
railway towards Moscow'.[21] On the 6th it seemed that Russia was 'doing
better than . . . expected', the German advance having slowed up.[22] But by
the 14th 'a serious threat to Moscow' was developing, while in the Ukraine
the Germans claimed to have 'nearly reached Kiev'; and it seemed in
London that the situation 'might well' have been 'more serious' than the
Russians were 'prepared to admit'.[23]

They refused to give any precise information, which, according to
Cripps, the ambassador in Moscow, was the result of their being 'still very
suspicious'; though he felt that nonetheless the British 'should not hold
back' on the exchange of information.[24] General Mason MacFarlane of
the British military mission in Moscow was less concerned with Russian
sensibilities, and more with their failure to tell him anything. He was 'still
waiting for evidence of the close co-operation' promised by Stalin: the
Russians, by mid July, had not let him near the front; he was 'followed by
an . . . "escort" '; he could not even go 'for a drive to pick up information';
and those whom he met had been 'confined to similar restricted
horizons'.[25] He had come to Moscow reluctantly, and believed at first that
they 'could not last three weeks'.[26] He had his doubts about Stalin's
motives in pressing for the mutual agreement with Britain, and could not
'forget that it was he who wanted [it]'.[27] Nor had he any idea what might
happen in the future. Although none of the Russian officers he met 'and
particularly Stalin' disguised 'the gravity of the situation', they were 'full of
a confidence' and without a trace of despondency, confusion or lack of
organisation'; and he could make no forecasts because he did not know
'the Russian line-up and . . . reserve situation'.[28]

Churchill's reaction to the attack on Russia was bound up with a similar
uncertainty as to whether they would hold out. Before the attack, he took
the view that he expected it and was prepared to offer help. He had, at the
outset, authorised that Maisky be told – as he was on June 13 – that if
hostilities broke out 'we should be ready to send a mission . . . to Russia'
and 'consider urgently . . . Russia's economic needs'.[29] His line – that 'all
encouragement and any help we can spare' would be given to the Russians
– rested on the 'principle' that 'Hitler is the foe we have to beat'.[30]
Although neither then, nor later, did he specify the kind of help, or indeed

its amount, he resolved to deny the Baku oil fields to the Germans lest their acquisition and that of 'wheat from the Ukraine' would 'ease' Hitler's position.[31] It was therefore, of 'paramount importance' that the soldiers and the RAF should prepare their plans to this end.[32] In general if the Russians were to fight, then 'every advantage which such a conflict offered' must be taken by Britain.[33] Moreover he affected to trust that Hitler's likely attack on the Soviet Union would not gain him the sympathies of the 'right wing' whether in America or at home. Hitler might think so; but he was wrong 'and we should go all out to help Russia'.[34] Churchill's view before the attack, therefore, was one of anticipation that the Russians might fight (to which end he offered help); of suppressed apprehension lest Hitler might gain right-wing sympathy for turning on the Bolsheviks; and of practical resolution to deny Hitler Baku oil. His position was measured, designed to encourage Russian resistance in the event of a German ultimatum and to forestall any hint of ambiguity about his position – but with no precise promise as to how far or in what way he intended to succour the Soviets.

After the attack, while his language lost this measure, his intention did not. He combined an extravagance of language in his speeches about the Russian plight, with a tone of sentimentality in his letters to Stalin; but he privately pursued a course of practical reserve in dealing with their demands; and this attitude emerged particularly when it seemed that the Russians would hold out. In his broadcast to the country on the evening of 22 June he seemed to suggest that the Nazi attack on the Soviet Union had purged it of the evils of Bolshevism and godlessness; that the past 'with its crimes, its follies and its tragedies flashes away'; and that the 'Russian [not Soviet] soldiers' now guarded their 'fields . . . their homes where mothers and wives pray' from 'the hideous Nazi war machine'. Churchill evoked the very hideousness of this machine in terms of the Germanophobic extravagance of 1914: the Russian soldiers were protecting their praying wives from the 'clanking, heel-clicking, dandified Prussian officers' and the 'dull, drilled, docile, brutish masses of the Hun soldiery'. Moreover the Russian 'cause' was now that of the western democracies: for Hitler's invasion of Russia was 'no more than a prelude to an attempted invasion of the British Isles'; and the 'cause of any Russian fighting for his hearth and home is the cause of free men and free peoples in every quarter of the globe'. Any man or people who fought against Nazidom would 'have our aid' and 'we shall give whatever help we can to the Russian people'.[35] His letters to Stalin though less extravagant commended the 'strong and spirited resistance' of the Russian armies to the 'merciless invasion of the Nazis', as they did the 'valiant fight and the many vigorous counter-attacks' with which the Russians were 'defending their native soil'; and they struck Cripps in Moscow as too 'emotional' and in danger of becoming 'somewhat sentimental'.[36]

Whether extravagant or sentimental, the language of excess seemed necessary to Churchill, partly to encourage the Russians, and partly to remove any prospect of sympathy for Hitler for turning on the Soviets. Churchill's own position as war time leader had become so publicly bound up with his denunciations of Hitler and Nazidom and his resolution to fight, that there could be no question of a peace, even at the expense of the Soviets. For as he reiterated on 22 June in his broadcast, he had but one aim 'and one . . . irrevocable purpose to destroy Hitler and every vestige of the Nazi regime'.[37] But although Churchill was neither deflected from that aim, nor from the view that Hitler was his 'sole enemy', his extravagant language towards Russia and Stalin came to conceal a more measured view – that whilst the Russians were allies (albeit essential allies) in the war against Hitler, they were not necessarily friends. But neither – and this view increasingly dominated Churchill's wartime strategy – did their interests conflict necessarily with his: the preservation of England and her empire, by virtue of keeping Egypt, Suez and the Middle East. To this end the Russians must be kept in the fight for as long as possible – in order to exhaust Hitler's forces. Churchill, although he continued to promise 'whatever help we can', nonetheless envisaged that such help would be limited – to certain naval operations, to the bombing of German cities, and to the despatch of specific supplies to the Russians; and as the Russians seemed more likely to hold out, Churchill's attitude towards them became one of increasing measure, for neither their demands nor their accusations should deflect him from securing the Middle East.

The measures which Churchill envisaged from the outset to assist Russia were designed to encourage resistance and hearten morale; to convince Stalin of his *bona fides* towards the Soviets; and to appease in some degree his new ally whose demands for every kind of help continued to escalate. Churchill urged that the bomber attacks on German cities 'must continue'; and he explained to Stalin that the 'heavy attacks' made 'by day and night' over German occupied country and 'all Germany within our reach' should 'force Hitler to bring back some of his air power to the west' and thereby 'take . . . the strain off you'.[38] He reminded Portal (chief of air staff) that the 'devastation of German cities' was needed 'urgently . . . to take the weight off the Russians by bringing back aircraft'; and he maintained that 'air attacks on the Western front must be kept up . . . for the present'.[39] He continued to remind the chiefs of staff that 'now was the time for every . . . bomber to concentrate on Germany' and he promised Stalin that 'our air attack on Germany' would continue 'with increasing strength'.[40] In addition to the air attack, Churchill intended limited naval assistance and cooperation in the north on account of the disproportionate 'value' of such a measure: its effect on the Russian navy and 'the general resistance of the Russian army'.[41] He promised Stalin on 7 July that the admiralty had prepared a 'serious operation . . . in the Arctic', after which he hoped 'contact' would be established between the two navies. In his view it was 'absolutely necessary to send a small mixed squadron of British ships' to the Arctic 'to form contact and operate with . . . Russian naval forces', and he contemplated the 'enormous value' to be derived from the arrival in the Arctic of 'a British fleet'.[42] Maisky too was to be reminded of the decision to take such action which would assist the Russian government 'in the fight they were making'.[43] He also hoped that plans would be prepared for a small naval force to operate 'with the Russians at Murmansk'; and on 21 July he informed Stalin that speedy help would be given in the north, that German shipping would be attacked, that cruisers and destroyers would be spent to Spitzbergen to raid enemy shipping 'in concert' with Stalin's forces, and that 'various supplies' would be sent to Archangel.[44] But while he did intend to press on with plans to base three squadrons at Murmansk (so that British ships could go to this port which would 'make the whole difference to our effective cooperation with the Russians in this area') this was, as he told Stalin 'the most we can do at the moment'.[45]

Churchill thought that the Russians must be kept in the fight; that rhetorical support, a sympathetic tone and limited practical support might be given to this end; that the signs of co-operation and alliance (such as the air attacks in the west or the naval action in the north) were, or had to be, as useful as more extensive military support. For this reason he had responded enthusiastically to Stalin's request for a mutual agreement involving a declaration of assistance and one to the effect that neither country would conclude a separate peace. He had favoured giving the Russians 'all they want, no haggling' and had resolved that there must be 'no hanging back with Russia'.[46] Such gestures would, in Churchill's view, help to keep Russia in the fight; for a premature surrender or defeat would be a 'terrible disappointment' to the 'great masses of people' at home.[47] But he would go no further; and despite his continued assurance to Stalin that he would give all possible aid, he became increasingly decided against anything beyond token assistance. He would not countenance raids in the west; for once it was clear that no 'large scale raid' was possible he thought a 'minor operation' useless.[48] He told Stalin that an operation in France or the low countries was out of the question; for the chiefs of staff saw no way of 'doing anything on a scale likely to be of the slightest use' while petty raids would lead to 'fiascos doing . . . more harm than good'. Nor would he agree to Stalin's request for a landing in Norway; it would be impossible to land either British or Russian troops 'on German occupied territory in perpetual daylight without . . . fighter air cover'.[49]

Churchill saw the German invasion of Russia as an opportunity to secure the Middle East. For that reason he wanted to prolong Russian resistance and had therefore proffered vocal support and limited practical aid. For the same reason he had no intention of deflecting substantial resources either to the eastern or western fronts which were unlikely to be 'of the slightest use'. Instead within three days of the attack he resolved to exploit the opportunity of the Germans being 'preoccupied elsewhere' to pass 100 cruiser tanks through the Mediterranean to Egypt, in the hope of an early offensive there.[50] At first he thought that it would be for the middle east commander, Auchinleck, to decide 'whether to renew the offensive in the Western Desert, and if so when'; though he urged him to bear in mind the situation at Tobruk, the enemy reinforcement of Libya and 'the temporary German preoccupation in their invasion of Russia'.[51] But he came to press more urgently for an early offensive and reminded Auchinleck that the western desert remained 'the decisive theatre this autumn for defence of the Nile valley'.[52] Whereas in early June there were few German reinforcements in Libya and Auchinleck would have 'decided air superiority' until September, a Russian collapse would change matters to Auchinleck's disadvantage and would 'liberate ... German air reinforcements for Africa'.[53] He continued to press for 'a strong offensive . . . in the western desert before the end of September'; for 'if we do not use the lull accorded to us by German entanglement in Russia to restore the situation in Cyrenaica' then 'the opportunity may never recur'.[54]

It had been in order to prolong such an opportunity that Churchill had wanted the Russians to remain in the fight and had been patient and indulgent of increasing Soviet demands. But when it became clearer that the Russians were in the fight for longer than he or his generals anticipated and when their demands conflicted with his own view of British interests, Churchill privately became less indulgent towards the Russians. But they must be kept nonetheless as allies: for their objects and his did not conflict; and if appeased on those issues in which he had no interest, then their support – or indifference – might be secured for that which mattered: the security of the Middle East. But he did not have the support of the Americans for such a course; Roosevelt's representative, Harry Hopkins, had made it clear that the US military authorities and 'particularly ... Marshall' were 'firmly convinced' that British strategy in the Middle East was 'governed by considerations of prestige and was fundamentally unsound'; and 'no opportunity' was lost of impressing such a view on Roosevelt. One of the short-term implications of this view was to render continued American supplies to Britain more uncertain; for the American military considered that supplies should either be sent to the UK (and not the Middle East) or else 'retained for the use of American forces'.[55] Another, and more serious implication emerged in the long term. Churchill, in pursuing a strategy of the preservation of Britain through her empire, became isolated from Roosevelt, who, on account of his own interests in the Pacific and the Far East, and his own view of how the war ought to be fought, seemed to ally more with Stalin than Churchill. But whereas Churchill imagined, with some justification, that he might ultimately deal with Stalin and Roosevelt on the basis of *realpolitik*, he could not do the same with a member of his own cabinet – his colleague, foreign minister and friend, whose pro-Soviet radicalism was as relentless in its exposition as the demands of the Soviets themselves, Anthony Eden.

Two reactions characterised Eden's attitude to the Russians immediately before and after Hitler's invasion of the Soviet Union: first he supported their claims for help, whether direct aid or air activity in the west; second he had a particular interest in collaborating with them over the Middle East – in Persia, Iraq and Turkey. The first reaction – Eden's readiness to meet Russian demands for aid – can be partly understood in the context of his view of himself as 'modern', with a dislike of the 'old Tories' and a hankering after social and political radicalism, and as being responsible for British prestige internationally. He was optimistic about Russia remaining in the fight; and he saw it as vital to British standing (especially in the USA) to fulfil her obligations to her newest (and only) fighting ally. The second reaction – to exploit the new alliance in order to collaborate over the Middle East for the purpose of maintaining the status quo in Persia, Iraq and Turkey – though less expected, was just as important. It resulted from Eden's comprehension of the Middle East and of Britain's rôle there. The attitude which Eden came to take towards Russia in the remaining years of the war depended on the merging, and to some extent confusion, of both these disparate reactions; and it cannot be understood without reference to both of them.

Even before the German attack, Eden had demonstrated his desire to meet Russian demands for help, should they be made. In the weeks preceding 22 June he had pressed Churchill and the chiefs of staff to this end. As early as 2 June he told his colleagues that he intended to tell Maisky that if Germany attacked Russia then 'we would take action elsewhere to relieve the pressure'.[56] He explained to Maisky that, given the extent to which the Middle East was now reinforced, Britain would be in position to hold her own 'in the air against any forces the Germans could bring'; or, if the Germans diverted elsewhere those forces now directed against Britain, she could 'take useful . . . action to relieve pressure against Russia'.[57] He had also begun to wonder whether 'more active air action over France and

Belgium' might be undertaken, and he put this view to Churchill on 9 June.[58] But Portal thought it would be 'better to keep this in hand' until Russia decided to fight Germany; and Eden therefore could only promise 'air action' in the west 'if Russia became involved in war with Germany'.[59] By 15 June, having consulted Churchill, he could promise Maisky that in the event of a conflict, a military mission 'representing . . . all three services' would go to Russia; and that the British government would 'consider urgently' Russia's 'economic needs'. Indeed they would even discuss 'technical details such as routing and transport'.[60]

Before the attack, therefore, Eden resolved to offer the Russians help in order to encourage their resistance; for he feared that they would make 'substantial concessions' rather than fight and would give way to Germany 'unless their skin is asked of them'.[61] Here, he may have been affected by Maisky's nonchalance and indifference to the reports of German concentrations. But Eden's resolution to help did not change after the attack. If anything it became more fervent in the face of Maisky's continued demands for more and more assistance, for operations in the west, information, supplies and naval help in the north. Eden, by contrast with Churchill or the chiefs of staff, became increasingly sympathetic to such demands and reluctant to disappoint Maisky, who liked Eden 'personally', trusted him and thought there was 'a better chance of good relations' with him than with his predecessor – while Eden himself claimed, from time to time, to hate the 'old Tories', and thought of joining the Labour Party after the war.[62] After the attack, his sympathy to Maisky's demands became manifest in the way he espoused them. He was convinced that 'this is the time for us to press the Germans in the west by any means in our power'; and he hoped it might be possible 'to have an operation on a much larger scale' in the west than the small raids proposed, which, he thought had 'nothing to recommend' them.[63] He pressed Churchill 'for more support to be given to Russia'; and he urged that not only would it harass Germany and hearten Russia, 'but it would have the best effect on neutral and American opinion'.[64] By 8 July he thought it was 'surely . . . possible that a month from now the Russians will still be in the field fighting back, though . . . very hard pressed'.[65] If Britain by then were 'still unable' to stage a land operation to relieve pressure, then 'the effect upon our position internationally will be bad'; and 'no amount of explanation' would ' convince world opinion that we have not missed a chance'.[66] Whereas Eden, like Churchill, thought a 'minor operation' in the west would be useless; he nonetheless hoped that plans would be made 'for a more important venture . . . in . . . a month's time' if not sooner.[67] On the 9th he was 'still driving and urging and pushing HMG to get on with it'; and his interventions on the 10th when aid to Russia was discussed at the defence committee, 'surprised' Brooke (commander, home command), who thought Eden's proposals seemed 'based on gross ignorance of the weakness of our defences', despite his knowing 'well what the army situation is'.[68] Eden became increasingly dissatisfied with the chiefs of staff and Churchill. He was 'worried at the lack of support of the chiefs of staff'; and the navy was particularly to blame for being 'non co-operative about operations in the north'.[69] He came to resent Churchill's refusal to grant substantial support, as well as his writing to Stalin direct. Churchill 'for all his brave words' would not agree to any but large raids and Eden (who wanted 'smash-and-grab raids' or plans for larger ones) considered Churchill was ' "dated" in military matters' and did not understand 'tank and aircraft technique'.[70] Moreover Eden's exasperation with Churchill was accentuated by Churchill's 'replying personally to Stalin' which to Eden was 'just like Neville and Musso' and left him 'very fed up' with the prime minister's 'monopolistic tendencies'.[71]

The first of Eden's reactions to the invasion of Russia, involved, therefore, his determination to concede Russian demands for more and more help. The second reaction, which will now be considered, involved the Middle East; and the way in which Eden comprehended the complicated balance of power there. In his view Syria, Iraq, Iran and Turkey were vital, and he agreed with Smuts that for this the line 'Syria–Iraq–Persian Gulf to the Indian Ocean' was 'most important'.[72] Eden wanted the Russians to resist Hitler in order to prevent Hitlerian influence or hegemony here and he also hoped to reach an agreement with the Russians to maintain the status quo. To this end he had sounded out Maisky in early June about the prospect of a joint Anglo-Soviet policy towards this area. He had told Maisky how 'given good will on both sides' there was no reason why the Germans 'should be successful in stirring up trouble between the British and Soviet governments in the Middle East', provided 'no misunderstanding' existed between the two governments 'as to their respective positions'.[73] Eden had told Maisky that Britain intended to maintain its position 'throughout the Middle East including Iran . . . and Afghanistan', while 'disclaiming any intention' to enlarge its interests 'at the expense of a third power'; and he 'assumed' the Soviet Government intended 'to pursue a similar policy', wishing to be 'assured on this point'.[74] Indeed, though he did not believe 'in a policy of appeasement towards Soviet Russia' (such as that implied by Maisky's request for a British agreement on the Baltic States) he had intimated that if the Soviets made it clear that they intended 'to pursue a policy in the Middle East' similar to that of Britain, and if they had 'no intention' of joining the

Germans in any plans – against Iran, Iraq 'and ourselves' – then the atmosphere would be 'better ... to consider what next step was possible'.[75]

To prevent the Russians joining with the Germans he had been determined to offer every possible encouragement, from assistance to the hint of appeasement distasteful to him. But collaboration with them, designed to prevent German influence here, would not be at the expense of Turkey, whose friendship, or at least neutrality, Eden had always regarded as vital in his schemes. (He had resolved in February 1941, for example, to support Greece, partly on account of its potentially beneficial effect on strengthening Turkey.) After the invasion of Russia he continued to urge that the 'present priority to Turkey' should be maintained in respect of 'both military and civil supplies'.[76] And he proposed on 30 June an exchange of notes between Turkey and Britain: Britain would reassure the Turks that it would not 'reward Russia at Turkey's expense'; that it would guarantee to respect Turkey's 'territorial integrity'; that it would reiterate that the Anglo-Turkish treaty of 1939 'remained the foundation of our policy vis-à-vis Turkey'; while the Turks might indicate that they too regarded the 1939 treaty as the 'foundation of ... foreign policy' and would 'refrain from action inimical to our interests'.[77] He was anxious that the operations – begun in early June – to secure Syria – should be 'brought to a conclusion as early as possible' on account not only of the importance of securing Syria, but also because of the beneficial effect which termination would have on both Russia and Turkey.[78] He reacted to the reports from Ankara, to the effect that the Turco-German treaty 'meant nothing', by pressing ahead with arrangements for joint staff conversations with the Turks;[79] and he seized the opportunity, presented by the reports of German infiltration in Iran, to collaborate with the Russians for their removal. Eden was 'worried about Persia and German infiltration there' and had seemed receptive to Maisky's declaration on 10 July that the Soviets were anxious 'to clear up the position in Iran' where there were five to ten thousand Germans.[80] The Soviets had been told that Britain was 'ready to act jointly with them on this matter' and he informed his colleagues at the cabinet on 17 July that 'here too we should have to apply pressure'.[81] The 'more' he examined the possibility of putting 'pressure upon Iran', 'the clearer' it became that all depended 'upon our ability to concentrate a sufficient force in Iraq to protect the Iranian oil fields'.[82] If the forces in Iraq were strengthened, then a 'reasonable chance of imposing our will on the Iranians without resort to force' existed; but it was important not to move 'diplomatically ahead of our military strength'.[83] By 31 July plans had been prepared to present demands for the expulsion of Germans to the Iranian government in mid-August, backed up by military divisions and air squadrons in Iraq and Iran.[84] Eden therefore, had through collaboration with the Russians, promoted his schemes to secure what to him seemed vital: the maintenance of the status quo from Turkey to the Persian Gulf.

Eden's peculiar interest in this region may initially have derived, as the biographies by Aster, Rees-Mogg and Carlton suggest, from his under-graduate studies in Persian and Turkish at Oxford.[85] He had initially intended to go into the foreign office and had been advised by the one-time Turkish ambassador, Sir George Clarke, to master oriental languages.[86] Although Eden was concerned with European affairs and the League of Nations between the wars, the crisis over Chanak in 1922 (which divided certain pro-Turk conservatives from Lloyd George who supported the Greeks) and the debate over India between 1929 and 1935 (which was for Baldwin as much as for Churchill about how to keep India) meant that, even when domestic or European affairs had dominated British politics, so too had considerations of empire. When Eden became secretary of state for war in Churchill's government in May 1940, his interest in Turkey and in Persia seems to have become more explicitly linked with the interests of the war office: the security of Egypt, Suez and the route to India, and the maintenance of the status quo in the Middle East – in which scheme Turkey was regarded as vital. Indeed Eden, who was in the Middle East at the time of the Italian attack on Greece on 30 October 1940, opposed, with the Middle East command, the diversion of resources to Greece, though he would have been less likely to do so for Turkey; and three months later when he changed his mind and resolved to offer succour to Greece in the event of a German attack, he did so largely on the grounds of the beneficial effect on the Turks. By June 1941, given the rumours of a possible Russo-German alliance directed against British interests in Iran, and Iraq, and given the danger of the Turks joining the axis pact, it seemed essential to Eden to secure the neutrality of the Russians, if not their friendship, and to promote their resistance to Hitler: the important oil fields in Iran and Iraq might thereby be denied to the Germans, and the status quo between the Black Sea and the Persian Gulf maintained in the interests of England and her empire.

Eden, therefore, had been resolved from the outset to promote Soviet resistance to German demands or a German attack; and to maintain, by virtue of such resistance and by political collaboration, the status quo in the Middle East. Before the attack he had already resolved on making specific promises to the Soviets, but at that stage the more measured views of Churchill and the chiefs of staff as to the nature and timing of assistance, meant that he could not do so. After the attack Eden became more persistent in his advocacy of assistance to the Soviets. Not only was he influenced by his comprehension of the nature of the balance in the Middle East, but he was affected by his view of himself as a social radical (and a 'modern' who disliked the 'old Tories' and had aspirations to joining the labour party after the war), and he also reacted to the reservations of Churchill and the chiefs of staff by becoming as thoroughly a protagonist of the claims of Russia, as the Russians themselves. At the outset, then, Eden's support for the Soviet Union had been encouraged by his view of the Middle East; but this motive began to merge with that provided by his social radicalism. And although in one sense Eden's view of the Middle East remained, it seemed to be superseded by the energy, conviction and apparent singlemindedness with which he promoted the Soviet cause as an end in itself. This involved not merely military support but political agreement. Eden hinted that some arrangement might be reached over the Baltic states, and he vigorously assisted in the discussions between Sikorski's Polish government in exile and the Russians, in the interests of their reaching a formal agreement (wanted by the Russians) even at the cost of what some Poles regarded as *their* true interests. Part of the difficulty was that 'half' the Polish government in London was 'violently anti-Russian'; that some of the Polish political prisoners whom the Poles wanted released were 'believed to have been "liquidated"' by the Russians; and that the Poles 'wanted the Russians to recognise their pre-war frontiers, both in the east and the west'.[87] Eden continued to use 'all pressure' to bring Poles and Russians together; and he resolved, with the authority of the cabinet on 24 July to write to the Poles that a treaty on the lines of the latest draft would, in the opinion of his colleagues, be 'in the interests of Poland'.[88] But neither the views of Eden nor those of his colleagues as to the 'interests of Poland' coincided with the views of the Poles themselves; and though Eden was prepared to give a private assurance to them to the effect that the British government did 'not recognise territorial changes affecting Poland, made since 1939', it became increasingly the case that (short of recognising those changes 'made by force') Eden came to look upon Poland in the context of Soviet needs.[89] For Eden the needs of the Soviet Union had become paramount. They had, at the outset, won his support, on the grounds that Russian resistance must be encouraged as a means of maintaining the status quo in the Middle East – particularly from the Black Sea to the Persian Gulf. But the means had merged with, and to some extent been confused with the end, and Eden seemed ultimately to promote the Soviet cause as an end in itself. This could not be said of the chiefs of staff.

Two factors dominated the reactions of the chiefs of staff to the invasion of Russia. On the one hand they were sceptical of Russia's willingness or ability to fight. On the other they wanted to exploit Hitler's new preoccupation in Russia, in order to promote the strategic interests of each of the respective services: Portal would extend the air war to the west when the time came and he hoped to escalate the heavy bombing of German cities; Dill (chief of imperial general staff) hoped to despatch resources to the Middle East for a fresh campaign; and Pound (chief of naval staff) disparaged those proposals which would endanger his fleet without proper return. Both factors – the scepticism about Russia's military prospects and the desire to exploit Hitler's preoccupation – tended to make the chiefs of staff cautious about undertaking any major operations. This was true in respect of military operations in the west and extensive naval operations in the north. Indeed they were sceptical about the immediate efficacy of the proposed military mission to Moscow, and they looked to it initially merely to provide intelligence of both Russian and German plans and resources.

Before the attack, the chiefs of staff doubted whether the Russians would fight; and after it, feared they would not last. Portal had refused to extend air raids to the west beforehand, but preferred 'to keep this in hand until Russia decided to fight Germany'. Only 'if' Russia were to resist, could an undertaking be given 'to draw off German air forces'.[90] Dill opposed the despatch of reinforcements out of the country 'unless' the Germans became 'embroiled in Russia', but he could not be sure that they would.[91] After the attack he continued to object to the despatch of tanks to Egypt, for there were insufficient armoured troops in Britain 'to meet a full . . . invasion' which might be the 'next item in Hitler's programme after a quick victory over Russia'; he continued to be 'v[ery] gloomy about Russian prospects'; could 'see nothing [on 4 July] to prevent the Germans from destroying utterly the armed forces of Russia . . . soon', though given the immense distances involved, the Russians might 'destroy their own property' and 'continue . . . behind the Urals'; and by 16 July, though he thought the Russians had 'done . . . better' than expected, he feared that now the Germans had reached open country 'the superiority in material training and command would tell'.[92]

Bound up with the feeling that the Russians would not last, was the view that while they did, Hitler's new preoccupation must be exploited to British advantage, or rather to the advantage of each of the services. At the outset the chiefs of staff resolved to consider how to turn 'German preoccupation in Russia to our advantage'.[93] Dill thought it would be 'a mistake' not to do so and he therefore supported plans for 'small scale raids' on the French coast – designed, not to satisfy Russian demands but to cause 'uneasiness in the German high command' and to gain information, which otherwise could not be had.[94] Portal too wanted to 'turn the

German preoccupation in Russia to our advantage'. On 23 June he 'outlined' the plans proposed by bomber, fighter and coastal commanders; he wanted to consider 'daylight raids on ports of north west Germany'; he became 'more and more convinced that, in order to take full advantage of the present disposition of the German Air Force' there must be further day bombing 'of important targets in occupied territory' and 'as heavy a weight of bombs on Germany as possible'.[95] Moreover he hoped to increase relative air strength in the Middle East up until the end of September and maintain it subsequently 'depending on the outcome of the Russian campaign'.[96]

But there would be no major operation such as the Russians demanded in the north or the west. Pound opposed operations along the coast near Murmansk, for such operations rarely produced good results and 'inevitably involved losses of ships'; he thought there would be 'difficulties' in co-operating with the Russian scheme to advance from Murmansk to Petsamo into northern Norway 'unless adequate air cover could be provided' – though he would concede a minor operation using torpedo bombers to sink German ships in the fiords near Petsamo and the despatch of two cruisers 'and a few destroyers, . . . to operate with the Russians at Murmansk'.[97] Nor could there be any substantial operation in the west. From the outset it seemed clear to the chiefs of staff that, given the limitations of shipping and landing craft and the fact that 'there were only four hours darkness at this time of year', a large raid would be 'impracticable' and a small one useless; though they continued to investigate different schemes, they nonetheless maintained that 'no possibility' existed at present of landing 'a large expedition' and that it was 'extremely unlikely that any military object would be gained'.[98]

The chiefs of staff, therefore, neither individually nor collectively, were prepared to concede any but the most superficial Russian demands, such as the despatch of specified and limited supplies, or the sending of two cruisers to the north. They looked upon Russian entry into the war as providing the opportunity, not for a new strategy based on alliance, but one to pursue their own interests, given Hitler's new preoccupation. Even when the military mission to Moscow had first been mooted, they did not consider it would have 'any immediate effect on Russia's success or failure': its object was 'to assist . . . our own effort against Germany', and its despatch could be justified 'mainly on the grounds of our need for intelligence' – that is of 'the Soviet Union and their military forces'.[99] Although the mission would provide a means through which Russian requests 'for material assistance' might be made and although it might 'act as a channel for the co-ordination of British and Russian strategy against Germany', the chiefs of staff had decided shortly after the attack that co-operation would 'not extend to military alliance', and at that stage there were no plans for the despatch 'of military forces or supply of war material'.[100] The way to meet requests for help was to 'temporise' and seek further information; and the policy, in any case was not one of direct, but rather of 'indirect' help.[101] Indeed, Mason MacFarlane might remember when the Russians in Moscow made their demands, that the 'fact' was that 'our present difficulties are largely due to Russian action in 1939', that 'we have been fighting alone' for the past twelve months, that though 'certain diversions' were being considered 'from the purely military point of view, no action beyond what we are doing now' could 'materially affect' the operations of the Red army and air force; and 'they must save themselves just as we saved ourselves in the Battle of Britain and the Atlantic'.[102]

British reaction to Soviet entry into the war was determined by the various and interacting reactions of the political and military leaders. The caution of the chiefs of staff was partly due to their doubts as to how long Russia would last and partly to their looking on the war in terms of the individual interests or strategies of each of the services – which had little in common with Russia or her war. This caution mattered particularly in that it helped Churchill resist Stalin's demands for further direct help – most notably, for an operation in the west. However, Churchill saw the opportunities provided by the German attack on Russia in terms both wider and more idiosyncratic than the chiefs of staff. On the one hand, his hatred of Hitler and Nazidom made any enemy of these, his friend; and in rhetoric at least, he was more willing than his chiefs of staff to offer friendship to Stalin. On the other hand, Hitler's engagement in Russia provided him with the opportunity to pursue what to him was paramount: the preservation of the empire and the route, by Egypt, to India. Eden too wished to use Russia's entry into the war to promote Britain's international interest. But he saw this interest in the context of approval for Britain as the defender of nations in peril (as he had also done with Greece five months earlier), and also in the context of his comprehension of Britain's rôle in the Middle East. From both points of view the prolongation of Russian resistance was vital. But the means to an end became an end in itself, and Eden became Britain's champion of Russia's fighting cause.

11

Crowning the revolution: the British, King Peter and the path to Tito's cave

MARK WHEELER

In July 1943 Fitzroy Maclean came to London for confirmation of his appointment as Churchill's 'daring Ambassador-leader' to Tito's 'hardy and hunted guerillas', as well as for successive promotion from captain to lieutenant colonel to brigadier. Maclean was advised in a brief prepared by the Foreign Office and his nominal employers, the Special Operations Executive, that British policy was now to promote, organize and support resistance by all anti-Axis forces wherever they might be in Yugoslavia. The first aim, therefore, was to seek to co-ordinate the activities of the Serb Četniks of General Draža Mihailović with those of the Partisans under the control of Britain's Middle East Command. A stiff directive had already been sent to Mihailović designed to compel him to reorient his movement's objective from fighting the Partisans in collaboration with the Axis to fighting the Axis in tandem with the Partisans; the latter, similarly, were being asked as a condition of British assistance to abjure action against the Četniks except in self-defence.

Although negotiations on the unification of all anti-Axis elements should not be rushed lest 'internal rivalries' be exacerbated, Maclean was informed that Britain's ultimate purpose was to create sufficient concord among the country's racial, religious and ideological groups as would preserve its unity and make possible a democratic settlement of its many problems. 'It is also the hope of His Majesty's Government', Maclean's brief went on, 'that King Peter will return as the constitutional monarch and it is believed that through him and with his assistance, the aims of His Majesty's Government can be realised.' To this end, British propaganda would neither ignore the new leaders and movements that had come to the fore during the occupation and resistance, nor dwell upon the failings of the old party leaders in the exile government; rather it would build up King Peter 'as the symbol of the Yugoslav ideal, as against the disintegration of the country. By this means it is hoped to pave the way for the emergence of a representative government and the acceptance of the King by all parties as the constitutional ruler.'[1]

Thus did Maclean's brief anticipate the Tito–Šubašić agreements of 1944. Even more did it point to the great expectations entertained by the British for and from the twenty-year-old King. He was, as Sir Alexander Cadogan wrote to Anthony Eden in May 1943, and as others in and outside of the Foreign Office regularly reiterated, 'the one remaining hope of a united Yugoslavia after the war'.[2] The quarrelsome politicians of the exile government had been discredited in British eyes by late 1942 and, it was assumed by the Foreign Office, counted for nothing in Yugoslavia either after their many failures to assert their relevance or to concert on a programme for post-war reconstruction. Meanwhile the forces contending for power on the ground seemed to the British to be capable only of prolonging the Yugoslavs' fratricidal agony.

The idea that the King was the key to Yugoslavia's unity and restoration was, of course, to prove as unrealistic as the concurrent aims of reconciling the Partisans and Četniks and of subordinating them both to British command. But the King's presumed authority, his formal legitimacy and Britain's responsibility for him were nonetheless to be invoked by Whitehall policy makers for very much longer. The exact content and the degree of seriousness of these invocations would vary over time until, ultimately, they resembled a mere face-saving charade. For nearly a year after Maclean arrived at Tito's headquarters, however, they formed the basis of Britain's long-term policy for Yugoslavia, and the focus of this paper.

King Peter II and the Karadjordjević dynasty were rather unlikely objects of British support and veneration. The dynasty's lineage was too recent to be glorious; and in any case the great powers had traditionally preferred to translate central European princelings onto the revived Balkan thrones. The manner of the Karadjordjević restoration in Serbia in 1903 had occasioned genuine and long-lasting horror in England. King Edward VII was in equal measure repelled and fascinated by the murder of the last Obrenović, by the exaltation of the conspirators that followed and by the behaviour of Crown Prince George towards both rodents (which he ate) and servants (whom he beat), matters on which the King's ministers reported assiduously once the British-led diplomatic strike had come to an end. British sympathy for Serbia against Austria-Hungary in the Pig War and the alliance of the First World War did much to rehabilitate Serbia's reputation, but less so that of its dynasty. King Peter I was too old and infirm to cut much of a figure. The new Crown Prince, Alexander, did better. Not only did his wartime and state-building roles appear creditable, but he later married a granddaughter of Queen Victoria. In fact it was Alexander's integral Yugoslavism, his image of strength and reliability and his martyr's death in Marseilles that did most to persuade the British that the dynasty was the vital cement holding Yugoslavia together. That he presided over a dictatorship was no particular black mark. Such was the spirit of the times; such was the prescription for far away and turbulent peoples; and such was convenient for the political and financial relations that existed between the two countries.

Britain's most intense relationship with a Karadjordjević was with the cultivated Prince Regent Paul when, following the fall of France, Yugoslavia for the first time loomed large in British calculations. That this affair turned out badly, with Yugoslavia signing the Tripartite Pact on 25 March 1941, mattered little. The real Karadjordjević spirit was shown by the anti-Hitler coup d'état carried out in the young King's name two days later. Churchill would have preferred to see King Peter stay to fight the invading Germans in his mountainous land rather than seek asylum abroad, but the Foreign Office welcomed the prospect of getting hold of a monarch in his formative years and turning him into an instrument of enlightenment and British interests.

By accounts reaching London, King Peter badly needed such solicitude. He was reported to be immature, ill-educated and tending towards an excessive admiration of things American. Residence in England, education at Cambridge, training with the RAF or a Guards battalion, and the companionship of dashing young British officers on whom he might model himself were thought likely to supply the corrective for the impressionable boy. By such means, too, Peter would be freed of his mother's apron strings; for she was regarded, particularly by Eden, as a baleful influence. Queen Marie, however, turned out to be only the first – and the least objectionable – of the three women into whose clutches King Peter was to fall during the war. The others, Princess Aspasia of Greece and her daughter, Alexandra, were eventually deemed worse.

The Prime Minister, devoted to a romantic conception of monarchy and its blessings, professed on occasion to regard the Foreign Office as a 'Republican Guard' inveterately opposed to his work on behalf of Kings George II, Peter II and Victor Emmanuel III, as well as his flirtations with the Archduke Otto von Habsburg.[3] But there is no evidence in the case of the first two that the Foreign Office yielded anything to Churchill in its commitment to seeing that they got their thrones back. In the Balkans the choice for the future seemed to lie between constitutional monarchy and bolshevism; the Foreign Office naturally preferred the former for Yugoslavia and Greece, especially as the latter bid fair to conquer in Rumania and Bulgaria. Eden was also personally fond of King Peter, albeit in an abstracted and indulgent sort of way, and shared the Prime Minister's sense of responsibility for his fate. (The horror stories spread in

London about Prince Paul's supposed ill-treatment of and ambitions to supplant his charge ensured that a feeling of guilt over having helped to precipitate the Axis invasion and dismemberment of Yugoslavia did not figure in creating this sense of obligation.)

King Peter's utter unsuitability for the great role in which the British cast him was rarely allowed to intrude. His devotion either to his studies or his kingly duties might be exiguous; his preference for driving fast motor cars or carousing with his aides-de-camp might be manifest; and his occasional intrusions into his government's affairs might be unfortunate, as his wilful dismissal of General Dušan Simović at the beginning of 1942 and his self-interested wrecking of Slobodan Jovanović's cabinet in the spring of 1943 (after forming his passion to marry Princess Alexandra) demonstrated. Yet none of this altered what the Foreign Office regarded as self-evident facts: 'that King Peter (or the dynasty) is the only real focus of Yugoslav loyalty'[4] and that Britain had no other means at its disposal with which to promote its interests.

In addition there was, in 1941 and 1942, Mihailović. King Peter might not be turning out as the British wished, but that seemed of little consequence so long as Mihailović remained the dynasty's arch-defender in the homeland and the putative victor in the civil war. It was the accumulation of information damning to Mihailović during late 1942, and his failure to extirpate the Partisans then and in early 1943, that forced the British to return to first principles; that is, to reassert the primacy of the King in their search for a non-communist or non-Russian future for Yugoslavia. To some extent this represented an act of will dictated by the absence of any perceived alternative. In the circumstances occasioned by the disrepute into which both the exiled politicians and Mihailović had fallen by late 1942, Eden was moved to write, 'I am sorry for King Peter; I wish I thought that the boy had better prospects. They seem pretty desperate to me.'[5] Yet for much of 1943 and 1944 the Foreign Secretary and his juniors were able to buck themselves up with the thought that in the person of the King, in the material assets of his government and, above all, in the fervent devotion of all Serbs to the dynasty they had been dealt a hand of considerable strength.

In the spring of 1943, when relations with the Partisans were just opening and it had yet to be demonstrated to London that Tito was presiding over a revolution as well as a resistance struggle, the Foreign Office embarked upon an examination of the ways by which King Peter might be rescued from too close an identification with his 'miserable government', the 'pan-Serb' Mihailović and his own unerring instinct for putting his foot wrong. Sir Orme Sargent, Deputy Permanent Under-Secretary, suggested the total disbandment of the exile government as a means of underlining the King's position as his country's sole hope. Cadogan and Richard Law, Parliamentary Under-Secretary of State, disagreed. Not only would such an expedient put too great a burden on Peter's slender shoulders, it would also smack of authoritarianism, so doing neither the King nor the British government any good. It would be better to leave well alone. As Law minuted, 'If the present regime continues King Peter will still be there at the end. He will be slightly shop-soiled, no doubt, but no-one will believe, in view of his youth, that he himself is responsible.'[6]

Sargent did not relent. When Sir George Rendel, Ambassador to the exile government, proposed in turn to substitute a small working administration for the immovable party coalition, and thus to give the King greater limelight while protecting him against himself,[7] Sargent rejoined that any potential government was bound to be hopeless, and hence highly dangerous to the King. He ought instead to have a three-man privy council with which he might take himself off to the Middle East, so stressing his part in the war effort. In the face of this conflicting advice, Eden noted wistfully that 'Peter is not Alexander yet and we cannot be sure that he ever will be.'[8] It was nonetheless resolved by the Foreign Office (and agreed by the War Cabinet) at the end of May to take Peter more firmly in hand and to split the difference between the Sargent and Rendel views: the King would be pressed to depart for Egypt with a bare minimum of ministers. According to Cadogan, this would achieve 'our main object of ousting the present Government from effective power without at the same time introducing any revolutionary change which might give a handle to critics both in Yugoslavia and abroad'.[9]

The fall of the Jovanović government on 19 June, the construction of a stop-gap political cabinet under the even more elderly Miloš Trifunović and the formation of Božidar Purić's government of officials on 10 August added weight to Sargent's warnings that the tendency towards ever more recklessly pan-Serbian administrations carried with it the likely ruination of Peter's reputation. But the British, despite their wish to be rid of the politicians, did not so much take an active part in these convulsions as allow them to happen by pursuing a policy of benign neglect, all the while, however, urging the attractions of Cairo upon the King. He, on the other hand, again demonstrated his capacity for doing himself injury. Already cloaked in and accustomed to exercising in the vacuum of exile the near-absolute powers of his father's 1931 constitution, he was now also threatening recourse to the 'honest sabre' of 1929, General Petar Živković.

One of the principal factors behind these ructions among the exiles was the campaign mounted by the King – but directed by Princess Aspasia – to get his ministers' and British sanction for an announcement of his betrothal to Princess Alexandra. British influence over the King, exercised through periodic heart to heart chats with Eden and supposedly reinforced by the recent appointment of a Scottish officer as one of his ADCs, counted for little beside Princess Aspasia's ambition to make her daughter a queen. The Foreign Office, which both respected the view of the Serb ministers that a wartime marriage would damage the King at home and had no very high opinion of the lady, confronted on this issue a second formidable opponent, the Prime Minister.

King Peter had sought to involve Churchill from the outset of his spring offensive;[10] but when the Foreign Office in July itself endeavoured to mobilize the Prime Minister to counsel the King against an early marriage Churchill exploded. '*Les noces de guerre*' were a 'natural' and 'becoming' dynastic tradition, as well as 'giving effect to those primary instincts to which the humblest of human beings have a right.' Neither the eighteenth-century 'refinements' of the Foreign Office nor 'the feeble trash that has been flung out of Yugoslavia' should stand in the way of the King and his Princess: 'if the King is worthy of his hazardous throne, we may leave the rest to him. . . . Are not we fighting this war for liberty and democracy? My advice to the King if you force him on me will be to go to the nearest Registry Office and take a chance. So what!' Eden was equally forthright in reply: 'My sole interest in this business is that King Peter should keep his throne for only thus can Yugoslavia continue to live as a unit, perhaps. If you think me incapable of handling even this minor Balkan domestic imbroglio the remedy is in your hands. So what!'[11] Churchill desisted.

The Foreign Office now had an additional reason for transferring King Peter to Cairo: to free him from Aspasia's grip.[12] As Douglas Howard, head of the Southern Department, summarized the position in late July,

The stock of the émigré Government is about as low as it can be, and is dragging King Peter down with it. The only hope of a united Yugoslavia lies in the King, and we should do all we can to build him up; the only way of doing so is to get him away from the political intrigue of London and of his future mother-in-law, and get him nearer the scene of action and his own country. It may even be possible to get the King into his country at some time or another, which would of course be the best thing for his own future.[13]

Since the Trifunović government appeared unlikely to survive even the suggestion of permanent relegation to the Middle East, there seemed again to be an opportunity to dissociate it from the King by allowing him to depart alone. The British might then, Sargent suggested, deal in practice only with those factors that mattered: the King in Egypt and the guerilla leaders in Yugoslavia.[14] Sargent's colleagues opposed such drastic measures. If the King's government refused to accompany him, then he too must stay put. 'This would be a defeat for us', Cadogan noted, 'but we can't save those who are determined to be damned.'[15]

Eden apparently succeeded at a meeting with the principal Yugoslav ministers on 3 August in convincing the Serbs among them that a transfer to Cairo was wise. The Croats, however, used their opposition to the move as a stick with which to beat the Serbs over their many extraneous grievances. This led Trifunović to resign and King Peter to form a small 'business cabinet' under the career diplomat Purić. The Foreign Office had self-consciously abstained from mixing in this 'dreadful muddle',[16] but was not displeased with the result. Purić was 'the most presentable' of the exiles, and was anyway less of an embarrassment than Živković would have been. A government of officials who meant nothing in themselves would allow the King, in Sargent's words, 'to stand out head and shoulders above his Government and . . . thus have a better opportunity than ever before of presenting himself to the Yugoslav people as the symbol of future liberation and unity'.[17]

Having inveigled an announcement of his engagement out of Trifunović in July and procured for himself in August a government powerless to withstand his zeal either to marry or to travel, King Peter decamped for Cairo in September. But he was wrong if he imagined that his compliance with British advice in this last respect would still their objections to an early marriage. The Foreign Office remained deaf to his entreaties during the autumn that he be allowed to return to London to claim his bride, pointing out that a royal wedding would be made to measure for anti-monarchical propaganda by the Partisans. Churchill, on the other hand, again pressed for the nuptials to go ahead, though in the Egyptian desert rather than in Mayfair. It was however the opposition of King George VI (Peter's 'Uncle Bertie') which, reinforced by the traditions of the Orthodox Church calendar, frustrated Peter's and Aspasia's plans. The King virtually ordered Peter in late November to postpone thoughts of marriage until after the Christmas season. The Prime Minister, to whom the King vouchsafed his doubts regarding Peter's haste and Alexandra's suitability, was sufficiently abashed by his sovereign's reservations to wash his hands of the problem.[18] When King Peter was finally invited to come to London in March 1944, Alexandra's hand was in effect to be used as an inducement to the King to sack Purić (and so Mihailović) and to entrust his government to a premier prepared to treat with Tito.

The Foreign Office, meanwhile, continued to maintain that Peter, with all his faults, remained his country's last best hope. Rendel, in a valedictory despatch in August, had explained what he understood to be the dynasty's position at home. The Slovenes were but 'mildly loyal'; the Croats were indifferent; and the Serbs, although the strongest supporters of the crown, were truer to the dynasty than to the monarchical principle. Their loyalty, therefore, was 'more dependent on the personal prestige of the sovereign than would be the case in a country of more advanced constitutional development'. He concluded that the King's prospects were deteriorating, especially as his own personality and character were failing to develop.[19] The Foreign Office refused to despair. As long as Peter appeared to retain the devotion of the Serbs it remained possible for officials in London to envisage circumstances in which they might effect a substitution – either corporeal or spiritual – of the pliant King for the intractable Mihailović, and thereby tame the Partisans and limit the country's civil war. The urgency of the situation was demonstrated by the first reports on the Partisans to arrive from Maclean. But in the process the role of King-Unifier, in which they had lately cast Peter, was subtly transmogrified into that of King-Pacifier. In other words, confronted as they were in the autumn of 1943 with the reality of the Partisans' power, the King appeared less the sole hope of Yugoslav unity than the only means by which a more peaceable unification under Tito might take place and Britain's influence be assured.

The new Ambassador to the exile government, Ralph Stevenson, signalled the beginning of this alteration early in October. 'Maclean's reports of the strength and good organization of Tito's forces,' he telegraphed London, 'have impressed me with the necessity for the King of Yugoslavia establishing contact of some kind with Tito as soon as possible.'[20] Happily, Maclean's proposal to come out of Yugoslavia to report in November – and to bring with him a few senior Partisan officers – offered the glimmer of an opportunity.[21]

Despite having been the prime movers in the decision to contact the Partisans in early 1943, the Foreign Office had since sought to resist conferring upon the National Liberation Movement any political stature equivalent to that which it was winning in the military sphere. This resistance was now crumbling. Michael Rose of the Southern Department minuted an SOE report in October that it showed 'what immense strides the Partisan organization has made within the past few months. It has in fact emerged from the guerilla stage and become a political movement with which we have simply got to reckon. King Peter and Mihailović are very small fry beside it.'[22] Eden agreed. Asked by Churchill for his opinion of a suggestion by Richard Casey, Minister of State in Cairo, that, given the recent decision that there could be no major landing by the Allies in the Balkans, Britain should ration carefully its support for guerillas in Greece and Yugoslavia which were 'republican at best, and communist at worst', the Foreign Secretary drew a firm distinction between the two countries. In Yugoslavia 'the communist-led army' was simply too important for

Casey's remedy to be applied. It looked like being different with ELAS; but this would soon be thrashed out in Cairo.[23]

London might accept that the Partisans were a force to be reckoned with, but that did not mean capitulation to them. The Foreign Office feared that this was what Maclean was on the verge of advocating. It was therefore with alarm that Sargent and Cadogan reacted to a passage in a telegram from him stating that it would be 'fatal' to his mission 'to raise question of King in any form'. The prospect of a delegation travelling with him to Cairo had caused the Foreign Office to conjure up a scenario for bringing the Partisans together with the King and forming a joint government or issuing a declaration of common policy. Maclean was now ordered to come out alone so that his priorities might be put right; while Stevenson, who showed signs of falling under Maclean's influence, was reminded that, 'Object of our policy is to maintain Yugoslav unity round the person of the King.' It was thus 'vital to bring together the King and the Partisans'. The Purić government had 'no importance'. Stevenson should sound out the King as to his willingness to recognize the Partisans and to include them in a reconstituted government, even at the cost of dismissing Mihailović. The King should also be prepared to take the initiative in inviting a Partisan delegation to see him, provided he could be assured beforehand that they would be ready to recognize and work with him 'both now and after liberation. On the question of the monarchy we must stand absolutely firm.'[24]

In order to reinforce this principle – and with it King Peter personally – the Foreign Office hit upon the idea of spiriting the Croat Peasant Party leader, Vladko Maček, out of internment in his native village. With Maček beside him, the King's stature would be enhanced, his unifying role emphasized and his bargaining position strengthened with the Partisans. Stevenson, who was instructed to consult with SOE about the scheme, replied that even if Maček were at liberty and susceptible to removal, which seemed not to be the case, he would be no help in dealing with the Partisans. They regarded him as a traitor.[25]

Maclean arrived in Cairo in early November bearing his eagerly awaited report. Eden was present as well and keen to settle both Greek and Yugoslav affairs. Stevenson, meanwhile, reported to London that Maclean was certain that the Partisans were well on the way to becoming the masters of Yugoslavia, and that there was no chance of railroading them into a wartime acceptance of the monarchy. On the other hand, Tito was not prejudging the issue and his propaganda machine had strict orders against attacking the King.[26]

Eden met with the Middle East Defence Committee on 7 November. They decided to try to crush EAM/ELAS, but to support Tito to the utmost. Mihailović might be ordered to carry out a 'test operation' (an idea mooted at the Moscow conference), failing which he would be denied any more British aid. Eden conveyed to the meeting Maclean's high regard for Tito and supported the plan to receive a Partisan delegation in Egypt. The Partisans ought, however, to be 'induced' to see King Peter, 'since a cardinal factor in any future policy towards Yugoslavia must be the bringing of Tito and the King together'. If Tito would not play, then a strictly military delegation would have to be entertained elsewhere than Cairo.[27]

Eden saw Peter and Purić that evening to inform them of the drift of events. The King was acquiescent; his premier angry and incredulous. The Foreign Secretary's report of his interview to London elicited the observation by Philip Nichols that Peter showed up better than did Purić, 'which is satisfactory as the King is the lynchpin of our policy, and we don't care tuppence about M Purić'.[28]

It was left to Maclean and Stevenson to acquaint Peter with the full ramifications of the Partisan movement, and to discuss with him the possibility of meeting their delegation. He was agreeable, but not inclined 'to run after them'. Maclean predicted that Tito would be even less eager to pursue him, although he undertook to raise the matter when he returned to Bosnia. It would be best, he and Stevenson informed London, to wait until British influence with the Partisans was more solidly established before attempting to exert pressure upon them. Somewhat reluctantly, the Foreign Office concurred.[29] Several days later, however, Stevenson was instructed to try to use a proposed British loan to the Partisans,[30] as well as a request by them to recruit among Italian prisoners of Slovene origin, as levers for prising Tito towards the King. The Foreign Office sought to counter Maclean's and Stevenson's inclination to avoid importuning the Partisans 'for fear of hurting their feelings'. 'If we adopt this attitude at the outset', Howard noted, 'we shall never get anything we want out of them; and what we most want, at present, is that they should get together with the King.' He concluded that the situation would be different if, as a result of Maclean's report, it were now decided to drop Mihailović altogether.[31]

Maclean's report on the Partisans[32] impressed its numerous readers, but surprised few of them. The military chiefs were enthusiastic about his assessment of the operational benefits to be derived from increasing aid to Tito, and supportive of his central recommendation that the time had come to break with Mihailović. They doubted that he was right to assume that the Četniks would fade away as a consequence, but appeared untroubled by the risk that as many Mihailović commanders would go over to the Germans as would rally to the Partisans.[33] The Foreign Office

reaction was more complicated. Eden and his officials regarded as irresolv-
able the dilemmas with which the report confronted them. To drop
Mihailović would mean handing all of Yugoslavia over to a highly
organized communist government in return for short-term military
dividends and the 'bare possibility' that Tito might be weaned away from
'the pure doctrine of communism' and induced to accept the monarchy. To
continue supporting Mihailović, on the other hand, would mean fuelling a
civil war which the Četniks appeared bound to lose – or which would end
in the break-up of the country – and with only the slight chance that
Mihailović might be persuaded to fight the Germans in the meantime. The
Foreign Office officials felt it likely that they would be compelled to go
down the trail Maclean had blazed for them, but they fought shy of doing
so immediately. It was necessary, first, to know more about Mihailović's
hold on Serbia and whether or not an agreement between Tito and the
King would bring the Serbs 'into the fold' or merely ruin Peter's standing
among them.[34]

The Maclean report thus put paid to the hopes of the British that Tito
and Mihailović might be both reconciled and subordinated to British
command. It gave new urgency to the more recent and dearer hope that
King Peter might be used to square the circle. Telegrams from Brigadier
Charles Armstrong in Serbia confirmed the Foreign Office belief that
Mihailović retained the support of the majority of Serbs for his anti-
communist crusade, so making it impossible to consider breaking with
him completely. (Ending all material support was another matter.) But no
sooner had this aspect of the Foreign Office's dilemma been resolved than
there arrived new proofs of Mihailović's collaboration with the Germans'
Serb puppet, General Milan Nedić, which, in this highly charged atmosphere, dictated the opposite. In fact, if the King were not to share in
Mihailović's obloquy, it would be necessary for him, too, publicly to
disavow his war minister. It might then be possible for him to bring into
union with the Partisans those Četnik bands which the Foreign Office
believed to be ready to defy Mihailović and collaborationism.[35]

In the aftermath of the Teheran conference, Cairo became again in early
December the venue for decisions which appeared to mark the achievement of a consensus rare in Britain's wartime relations with Yugoslavia.
The accord did not last long. What did endure was the close involvement
of the Prime Minister in the decision-making process and the basic line
then adopted: Mihailović would be dropped. The arguments in future
weeks and months – principally between Churchill and the Foreign Office,
but also involving the military and SOE – would be over the timing and
methods to be employed, and especially over whether or not a price should
be exacted first from Tito.

The Foreign Office started December keen to ditch Mihailović, but with the object of replacing him by a commander who would fight King Peter's corner without fighting the Partisans. Although Armstrong dismissed the possibility of staging a 'palace revolution' at Mihailović headquarters, and doubted that the General would obey a summons to Cairo by the King,[36] the Foreign Office drew comfort from the example of Major Radoslav Djurić, Mihailović's increasingly restive commander at Priština. London's belief in the need for haste was stimulated by the first – bowdlerized – version of the resolutions adopted at the second AVNOJ (Anti-Fascist Council of National Liberation) congress in Jajce on 29 November, but only broadcast by the Soviet-based Free Yugoslavia radio on 4 December. The officials in the Foreign Office thus deprecated from the sidelines the decision that was evolving in Cairo to clinch the case against Mihailović by ordering a 'test operation', and argued (as would Churchill later) that, 'Removal of Mihailović will be an important gesture of conciliation by the King and we want to ensure that it does not come too late to have full effect.'[37]

London knew in early December that AVNOJ had set up what amounted to a provisional government and that it had conferred the title of Marshal upon Tito. It was unaware that the congress had also attacked the King for his support of the traitor Mihailović, prohibited his return until such time as the people's will could be expressed and sought to deprive the exile government of its right to represent the country abroad. Cairo knew better: the Partisan delegation that landed at Alexandria on 5 December carried with it the complete text of the Jajce resolutions; while Lieutenant Colonel F. W. Deakin, who accompanied the delegation and was quickly embarked in Cairo upon a hectic round of debriefings by the assembled luminaries, had actually attended the congress.

Left in inexplicable ignorance of the scope of the AVNOJ decisions London chafed at the unnecessary risk and delay represented by the test scheme, while heartily embracing the necessary risk that Mihailović's dismissal would simply hand Serbia over to the Partisans. It was essential, in Rose's words, 'to effect a union between the objects of our political and military support, and to do so as soon as possible'. As Sargent further explained,

Our hand is being forced by events and these events are going to make our present position increasingly anomalous and indefensible. For one thing, we shall have to explain to the House of Commons at an early date how we stand in the light of General Tito's action in setting up what is really a rival Government to that of the King. The only way we can put ourselves right is to free ourselves at once from our commitments in connexion with Mihailović, for which we cannot possibly find any justification which we could put to the British public and House of Commons, let alone the Soviet Government.[38]

The Foreign Office was nonetheless compelled to fall in with Cairo's plan to set Mihailović a test he had to fail. The fact that Churchill outlined the case against their war minister to Peter and Purić on 10 December, and warned them that he might soon require his dismissal, was some compensation.[39]

The Foreign Office was in the last stages of preparing a paper for the Cabinet on the reasons for eliminating Mihailović when Free Yugoslavia finally broadcast, on 17 December, an ellipsis of the AVNOJ resolutions attacking the King and his government. This did not provoke Cadogan now to throw the mechanism into reverse – and so to initiate a struggle between the Foreign Office and virtually everyone else over what was dubbed the 'quid pro quo' – but it soon made converts of his colleagues. Cadogan's intervention took the form of an uncharacteristically long minute on the Cabinet brief:

It seems to me that we may be a bit rash in urging the King to throw over Mihailović until we know a bit more whether the Partisans will have anything to do with the King. If they won't, we are left with a King (and Govt.) on our hands who have no backing whatsoever in Yugoslavia. What do we do then? Acclaim Tito as Führer of Yugoslavia?

Cadogan proposed instead to find out if there had been any contacts between the King and Tito's representatives in Alexandria, or if such were in prospect. (Eden noted that it had been Stevenson's 'principal task' to promote these.) On the assumption that they had not been ruled out, it might be possible to trade Mihailović's job ('and the Marshal's baton') for Tito's acceptance of the King's 'leadership'.

What I don't quite like doing is to urge the King to throw over Mihailović while he has no other *point d'appui* in Yugoslavia (bad as M. may be). If Tito will have nothing to do with the King, we shall have to think again . . . I think we *must* try to bring Tito to some understanding with the King.

Eden, in asking for the department's comments, reminded them that it might work better the other way round: the sacking of Mihailović could pave the way for a 'rapprochement' between Tito and the King. Sargent concluded after several days' reflection that in this 'question of tactics' it would be asking 'too much of the King that he should dismiss Mihailović immediately after Tito's attack: it would look too much like yielding to threats'.[40]

The Foreign Office did not like either the suggestions from Stevenson and Maclean that, in view of Tito's bid for recognition, Yugoslav political questions should be deferred for the duration, and that the Allies concentrate solely on providing military support for the Partisans. To do so would mean according Tito recognition by degrees, while the King was left to moulder in ever-increasing irrelevance.[41] Instead Stevenson was asked to consider the possibility of packing the King up once more and despatching him to Tito's headquarters, there to sack Mihailović and to form a new government: 'It would perhaps be a gamble but as things are developing, it is doubtful whether otherwise the King has any further prospects.'[42]

Maclean's and Stevenson's response, that not only was such a scheme impracticable, but that it would serve no useful purpose even to broach the subject of the monarchy with Tito, was naturally unwelcome to London. Basing such optimism as they possessed on the supposed existence of a deep reservoir of secret monarchism among the Partisan rank and file, the Foreign Office officials considered that if only they could get Peter back home this sentiment might well up in a manner which the communist leadership would find difficult to resist. The hard part would be convincing Tito to receive the King. But even if Tito refused to swallow the whole scheme, Sargent noted, making the approach 'might lead to discussions and negotiations which might eventually produce some satisfactory result. In fact, anything would be better than the continuance of the present deadlock.'[43]

Maclean was urged to return post-haste to Tito's camp and to initiate the bargaining process. Given an opening by Tito, he might subsequently offer him the heads of Mihailović and Purić as a down payment, and the assets and legitimacy of the King and government as a final instalment.[44] London was unmoved by Stevenson's and Maclean's protest that; 'The suggestion that Partisans could improve their chances and the position of the country by adopting the King would be greeted by them with derision, and any attempt on our part to use pressure or bribes would meet with a flat refusal.' An effort to save the dynasty must be made, however great the likelihood that Britain would be forced to opt for Tito in the end.[45] The Foreign Office branded as 'appeasement' the continuing arguments from Cairo, and derided the military's reported apprehension that a political controversy might undermine the Partisans' will to fight.[46]

Churchill, laid up in Morocco with pneumonia, had already signalled to Eden his pleasure at the audacious plan to send King Peter to Tito.[47] This was convenient; for the fall-back position of the Foreign Office, in case Tito refused to entertain the current proposal, was to ask the Prime Minister to meet him. Churchill might even be able, having worked his magic on the rude guerilla chieftain, also to oversee an encounter between him and the King.[48]

Although it stemmed from near-desperation, the scheme to despatch King Peter to Partisan headquarters revealed the Foreign Office as continuing to posit a political disinterestedness which the Yugoslav monarchy had never possessed and a strength of purpose and character which Peter would never possess. In the face of categorical assurances to the contrary by Stevenson and Maclean – and Cadogan's own recent foreboding – the Foreign Office still professed to regard the Karadjordjević dynasty as a unifying factor. Tito, for his part, would by his wariness in future months seem also to exaggerate the strengths of the King and the rival attractions of the dynasty. Incredulous as the Foreign Office was at any suggestion that Tito might have a constituency of his own outraged at the notion of dealing with the King, or which might need be heeded, his reluctance to 'get together' probably served to prolong London's delusion that King Peter represented an asset as well as an obligation. Only Stalin – who would regularly urge Peter upon his Yugoslav comrades as a shortcut to power – appears to have been immune to the spell cast by kings.

The opening desired by the Foreign Office for discussions with Tito about the monarchy had meanwhile been supplied by the Marshal himself. On 22 December he sent a get well message to Churchill in Marrakech which offered the Prime Minister the opportunity to enter into a personal correspondence. At the same time Major Randolph Churchill, visiting his father prior to joining Maclean's mission, was able to convince him that Deakin, Maclean and Stevenson were right to reject the Foreign Office demand for a quid pro quo. According to a note prepared by Randolph on Christmas Day, 'the King's fortunes could be advanced' only by making a gift of Mihailović to Tito. With this view Churchill concurred.[49] For the Foreign Office, therefore, the Prime Minister's heightened interest was a mixed blessing.

On 27 December Churchill relayed to Eden the text of Tito's message and that of a letter he proposed to send in return. This, in its original form, promised Tito that Britain would 'have no further dealings with Mihailović' and informed him that the Yugoslav government had been asked 'to dismiss him from their councils'. However, it went on,

King Peter the Second . . . escaped as a boy from the treacherous clutches of the Regent Prince Paul and came to us as the representative of Yugoslavia and as a young Prince in distress. It would not be chivalrous or honourable for Great Britain to cast him aside. I hope therefore that you will understand we shall remain in official relations with him and his Government while at the same time giving you all possible military support. I hope also that there may be an end to the polemics on either side once Mihailović has been turned out as he richly deserves to be.[50]

Eden, who was growing suspicious that Cairo's long-promised evidence of Četnik collaboration with the Axis might not prove either overwhelming or quotable in Parliament, and who was as a result mindful of likely right-wing and American charges that Mihailović and the Balkans were being sold out to Stalin,[51] proposed amendments to the Prime Minister's letter designed to substitute advocacy of the King's return to Yugoslavia for the promise to break with Mihailović. It would be better tactically, he wrote, 'to keep this up our sleeves as a concession to Tito if he is prepared to discuss working with the King at all'.[52] But Churchill, who had been impressed by the military's objections to the apparent readiness of the Foreign Office 'to split the Partisan movement and undermine Tito's position' by introducing the King into the country,[53] rejected Eden's redraft. There could be no quid pro quo: 'once Mihailović is gone the King's chances will be greatly improved and we can plead his case at Tito's headquarters. I thought we were all agreed in Cairo to advise Peter to dismiss Mihailović before the end of the year.' The case against Mihailović on account of his collaboration had also seemed irrefutable then. Churchill offered Eden a choice between his original text and the loss of 'a good opportunity of my establishing a personal relationship with this important man'.[54]

The Foreign Secretary chose the former while pointing out that it was still far from certain that Peter could be prevailed upon to sack Mihailović – his 'last and only link' with Yugoslavia – without some assurance that Tito would work with him.[55] Churchill thereupon amended his text to reflect the fact that Britain had not *yet* demanded Mihailović's dismissal and added a phrase expressing reluctance to ask the King 'to cut all his existing contacts with his country'. It was nonetheless essential, he reiterated to Eden, for Peter to free himself of Mihailović. Then 'Maclean and Randolph will have a chance to work on Tito for a return of the King to his country, perhaps in a military capacity only.'[56] As he explained in a supplementary telegram, 'I have been convinced by the arguments of men I know and trust that Mihailović is a millstone tied round the neck of the little King and he has no chance till he gets rid of him.'[57] On this point Churchill remained adamant. But he was obliged to make further amendments to his letter as a result of General H. M. Wilson's observation that, since British liaison officers both should and would of necessity abide with Mihailović for some time, it was impossible to promise Tito that Britain would have no more dealings with him. Instead the Prime Minister adopted Wilson's suggestion that he pledge exclusive material support for the Partisans.[58]

Maclean and Randolph Churchill, weather-bound in Bari awaiting a flight to Bosnia, were now summoned to Morocco to collect the Prime Minister's letter. Reporting this to Eden, Churchill inveighed again against the quid pro quo:

My unchanging object is to get Tito to let the King come out and share the luck with him, and thus unite Yugoslavia and bring in the old Serbian core. I believe the dismissal of Mihailović is an essential preliminary. I wish indeed I could say that we were pressing for this. Please note that Mihailović never did anything about the test operation. I should be glad to hear your latest thoughts.[59]

These, too, remained unchanged. Eden embraced the Prime Minister's object – without commenting on the difference between sending the King to fight alongside the Partisans and despatching him to form a new government with them – but continued to dispute the means: there should be no 'sacrificial offering' of Mihailović 'before we know whether oracle is going to pronounce favourably on the question of the King's return'.[60] Nor did Eden mention the hope that sustained his officials' resistance to Churchill's instinct: that 'the association of the King with the Partisans may check such tendency as there may develop to direct the Partisan movement towards Communism'. This miracle was to be accomplished by virtue of the fact that Peter was a Serb without being a pan-Serb.[61]

Spurred by a recent Yugoslav government communiqué 'gloating' over supposed Partisan reverses, the Prime Minister sought to push matters forward by despatching to Eden on 9 January the text of a message he proposed to send to King Peter. In it he argued that only by sacking Mihailović could the King begin to close the chasm which yawned between him and his people; but he also threatened Peter that Britain would repudiate the Četnik leader whether or not he was wise enough to do so first. Churchill asked Eden either to get War Cabinet sanction for this démarche or to suggest an alternative method for making the same demand.[62] Maclean, he reported the same day, was returning to Yugoslavia with instructions to promote the King's cause, but to use his discretion in the timing of a request to Tito to meet him.[63]

Eden, who presented both his own and Churchill's cases to the War Cabinet on 11 January, was able to get his colleagues' backing for his recommendation that the assault on Peter be stayed until Tito's reaction to the Prime Minister's letter was known.[64] Yet because Churchill's letter did not ask Tito explicitly to treat with the King, and because Maclean's discretion seemed wide enough to encompass his own belief that Mihailović's dismissal remained a precondition for negotiations, it appeared unlikely that this arrangement would elicit the sort of response from Tito on which the Foreign Office counted to illuminate the way ahead. Eden resolved to tackle the Prime Minister again as soon as he returned to England.[65]

When Eden did meet Churchill on 18 January he was still unable to persuade him that forcing Peter to sack Mihailović before Tito's attitude had been clarified would be 'the end' of the King.[66] The next day Eden went so far as to seek reinforcement from Lord Selborne, the minister responsible for SOE and an unreconstructed apologist for Mihailović who had long since been cast adrift from effective policy-making. The Foreign Secretary, observing to Churchill that 'grey is a more common Balkan colour' than either black or white, proposed that they get together with

Selborne 'to hear the evidence and pronounce judgment'.[67] The Prime Minister refused to fall into this trap.

Maclean had at last been able to return to Partisan headquarters on 20 January. From there he reported Tito's gratification at receiving Churchill's letter, but also his expected disinclination to discuss the King. The Foreign Office began to mourn the death of its policy and to express increased reluctance to advise Peter to repudiate Mihailović even when Britain did so. The mood brightened, though, when another telegram arrived from Maclean recommending that he now ask Tito point blank whether or not he was prepared to work with the King.[68] The Foreign Office was uncertain only about how heavy a burden Maclean's proposed overture might bear, that is whether it should, in Eden's words, carry 'a hint that King would part with Mihailović and take up with Tito'. Churchill resolved this quandary by deciding to do the job himself: Tito's reply to his first letter had just arrived and needed an answer.[69]

The Prime Minister's telegram to Tito of 5 February was ingratiatingly candid. After explaining that his own long-held determination that Peter should sack Mihailović had been held in check by the argument that the King could not be asked to deprive himself of his only adherents, Churchill finally embraced the quid pro quo:

I should be obliged if you would let me know whether his dismissal of Mihailović could pave the way for friendly relations with you and your Movement and, later on, for his joining you in the field, it being understood that the final question of the Monarchy is reserved until Yugoslavia has been entirely liberated.

He went on to list the advantages which would accrue to Tito and to express the hope 'that you will feel able to give me the answer you can see I want'.[70]

There is no indication in the available papers that the Foreign Office objected to the tone. Perhaps the advent in Cairo in these days of an ostentatiously large and high-powered Soviet mission bound for Partisan headquarters impressed upon everyone the increased stakes of the game. In any case Churchill, having relented on the quid pro quo, was now able to force the pace of withdrawal of the British liaison officers with the Četniks. The military (including Wilson) was both keen to meet this precondition for the attachment of BLOs to the Partisan forces in or advancing on Serbia and concerned to safeguard the lives and honour of the men marooned with Mihailović. The Foreign Office, on the other hand (although not Eden himself), objected that immediate withdrawal of the BLOs from the Četniks might force Peter's hand before his prospects with Tito had been established and would certainly make more difficult either the finding of a substitute for Mihailović or the rallying of some portion of the Četnik rank and file to the Partisans – as Tito's eventual response might decree.[71]

This, when it arrived on 15 February, confirmed the contending parties in their entrenched positions. Tito demanded as his price for *sending a representative* to talk to the King about wartime co-operation the suppression of the exile government – and with it Mihailović – and the recognition of AVNOJ's National Liberation Committee in its place. The King ought also to declare himself to be at the disposal of the resistance struggle and of his people's ultimate expression of their will. These conditions were necessary, Tito explained, if Peter were to work his passage back from the treason that had been committed in his name; for although an arrangement with him would indeed do the Partisans good in Serbia, it would provoke only anxiety and suspicion in Slovenia, Croatia and Macedonia. Tito professed to see no difference in principle between his proposals and Churchill's.

Maclean was inclined to agree, and urged that Peter be induced to seize this, his 'only chance of reigning'. The atmosphere created by the Prime Minister's messages was favourable. Tito's proposals offered something for everyone. 'From what he has said to me recently', Maclean concluded, 'it seems as though Tito may be genuinely concerned to preserve the independence of Yugoslavia and would welcome our support in his efforts to do so.'[72] Among his statements creating this impression were an offer of economic concessions for Britain after the war and an assurance that he had no intention of making his country either an appendage or a replica of the USSR.[73]

Churchill accepted Maclean's assessment as 'a profound truth'. Writing to Eden on 16 February, he insisted that the order to evacuate the BLOs with the Četniks be issued and that the responsibility for advising the King to dismiss Mihailović and Purić be shouldered: 'It may be that my relations with Tito will enable us to make things go right.' The King ought to have 'the whole case laid before him' and should be brought back to England for the purpose:

If he is a man he will throw his heart over the fence, and he may well get over or through it somehow. You know how strongly I am attached to the monarchical principle and how much I would like to see this boy restored to his throne. Here is the only hope.

Churchill proposed nonetheless to appeal to Tito again for an assurance that Peter would be invited 'to join his countrymen in the field' once he had 'freed himself from Mihailović and other bad advisers'.[74]

The Foreign Office, meantime, had decided that Tito's terms were totally unacceptable. 'In order to appease Tito', Howard wrote, Britain was being asked to abandon the King and to offer up Serbia to Partisan subjugation 'in return for the nebulous bait of some future discussion on cooperation.' The BLOs should not be withdrawn from the Četniks; the King must not be pressed to repudiate Mihailović; and Tito's proposals ought not to be regarded as final.[75] Yet in the face of the reiterated demands that the BLOs be removed, Eden and his officials were compelled to give way. The evacuation order went out on 17 February.[76] Their retreat on this front seems, however, to have been a tactical one; and their counter-offensive was made the easier by Churchill's own suggestion that he try Tito once more, using the special influence which everyone was now at pains to assure him he possessed. As Eden wrote on 20 February, 'Tito's reply might have been worse', but it represented only an opening bid in a bargaining process at which Tito was doubtless 'sufficiently oriental' to be adept. He enclosed an amended version of Churchill's draft which differed from the original in making the King's dismissal of Mihailović more clearly conditional upon a better offer from Tito, in adding a paragraph which backpedalled on the promise of immediate recognition for any new Royal–AVNOJ government and in informing Tito that the King was being summoned to London for consultations.[77] The Prime Minister adopted the first and third of these alterations, but threw out the second. The British counterbid remained: Tito would be told that the BLOs had been ordered to leave Mihailović. This telegram was despatched on 26 February, four days after Churchill – against Eden's advice – reported lengthily on Tito's epic struggle – and on Mihailović's disgrace – to the House of Commons.[78]

Presentation of Churchill's 26 February message to Tito was held up while Purić and Mihailović were informed of the decision to withdraw the BLOs. This allowed Maclean the opportunity to enquire of Eden how he and the Prime Minister wished Tito to modify his demands, and specifically what fresh elements they envisaged including in a composite government capable of winning British recognition. He estimated that Tito would be willing to extend his committee to embrace uncompromised politicians abroad, mentioning General Simović and Ivan Šubašić, former Ban of Croatia, as men towards whom the Partisans were well-disposed. Eden replied with Churchill's approval on 9 March:

What we want is that Tito should agree to King going to Yugoslavia and there forming new Government which would replace present Purić Government. New Government under Tito's presidency would no doubt consist predominantly of members of National Committee of Liberation but should also contain representatives of all other Yugoslav elements opposed to the Germans. In present conditions such representatives may have to be sought for outside Yugoslavia. Simović and Šubašić seem excellent choices. We might suggest further names if asked to do so.

The composition of the government would need to be acceptable to both

Tito and the King. It would be regarded as the legitimate successor to that of Purić and would be provisional only in the sense that the country's constitution would remain for post-war settlement by free elections. King Peter could be asked to confirm this fact at the time of the government's formation.[79]

Despite this hard-won expression of an agreed strategy, the British were continuing to entertain varying and contradictory expectations of Tito, the King and the Yugoslav situation in general. It was, of course, the springtime of Churchill's enthusiasm for Tito and of his aspiration to provide that 'outstanding leader, glorious in the fight for freedom', with the means and incentive to submerge his communism and to assert his nationalism. This enthusiasm was shared by the military, to which was delegated much of the responsibility for realizing the Prime Minister's hopes, first by supporting the Partisans' resistance to the utmost, but also by beginning to build for them a modern air force which would stake Britain's claim to post-war influence. Yet Churchill would in this spring of 1944 also begin to fret morbidly and irascibly about the looming confrontation with Stalin and division of Europe. In such circumstances Tito could fall quickly from grace, and the military find itself out on a limb.

The Foreign Office, too, possessed a split personality. It was alternately beset by the urge to frustrate Tito's revolution, at least in Serbia, where schemes to supplant Mihailović in the interest of the King came again to the fore following Colonel S. W. Bailey's arrival in London from Četnik territory, and by a fatalistic inclination to accelerate it, so saving lives and face if Peter could be simultaneously and honourably disposed of. Now, when Churchill's passion for Tito was ascendant, so was the Foreign Office's scepticism. Later, when the Prime Minister despaired of co-opting Tito or of salvaging a measure of British authority in Yugoslavia, the Foreign Office would counsel forbearance. More remarkably, the two inclinations could also coexist, as Eden's message to Maclean of 9 March illustrated. In it Eden commended Simović and Šubašić as men suitable to the task of saving Peter's throne. Simović, however, was regarded by the Foreign Office as politically incompetent, and Šubašić as vain-gloriously weak. Neither of them could have been expected to prove any more of a match for Tito than could the King himself. In any case, it was accepted from the start that Tito would preside over and his nominees predominate in any united government. To imagine that the King's mere presence on Yugoslav soil would magically right the balance was ludicrous. But if these considerations indicate that by now Foreign Office officials were simply going through the motions of seeking Peter's restoration, the fight they were waging to deny Tito the King's ships and soldiers before a better offer was on the table, and the zeal with which they took up Bailey's project for a 'palace revolution' suggest otherwise. Finally, it does seem that they really believed that the King's return to Yugoslavia was far and away the most crucial factor.

King Peter and his premier reached England on 11 March, the former in happy anticipation of wedding bells, the latter in febrile calculation of enlisting Queen Marie, scattered Yugoslav emigrants, the Americans, and even the Russians in his own and in Serbia's defence. The Foreign Office, under Bailey's welcome tutelage, was indeed now resolving to oust the Purić government, albeit with the aim of freeing the King from the great-Serb incubus while keeping a revivified, non-communist Serb resistance in play. Bailey's policy prescriptions, although designed to achieve the old SOE dream of activating the anti-German potential of the Četnik movement, as well as meeting the newer danger that the Partisans would divert their efforts into a long and bloody campaign to conquer a hostile Serbia, were highly relevant politically. He recommended that Peter immediately sack Purić and denounce all Četnik collaborators with the Axis. The liaison officers still with Mihailović should meanwhile encourage his dissident lieutenants to revolt. These men, if successful in eliminating their chief, would hold Serbia for the King, fight the Germans and forswear the anti-communist struggle if Tito agreed similarly to call off his assault on Serbia. Bailey estimated that the King had 'every chance' of reigning in Serbia and a fair chance elsewhere. He rated the odds of supplanting Mihailović as even. Confronted with this relatively encouraging scenario, and with the imminent necessity of giving forceful advice to the King, the Foreign Office abandoned its own long insistence on a quid pro quo. But it also reverted to the congenial assumption that – as Cadogan wrote – the monarchy was 'the only stable element in a future Yugoslavia'.[80]

Churchill met with Eden and his senior officials, Stevenson and Bailey on 14 March to map out a strategy for manoeuvring Peter, Tito and the Serbs into accord. They agreed that the first step was for Eden to see the King the following day and to advise him to dismiss his government without worrying in the first instance about finding a replacement. If after a few days' reflection – and presumably his honeymoon – the King assented, then Churchill would inform Tito and ask him to co-operate with a new government to be composed of men sympathetic to the Partisans. Should he refuse, he would be told that although he might count on Britain's military support, 'he must recognise that we should be unable to sever our contact with King Peter and the Serbs'. (This echoed the policy of political disengagement that Stevenson had been advocating for some months.) But whatever Tito's reaction, the problem of Mihailović would not be solved by the ouster of Purić. He would remain army chief of staff and, Bailey was certain, the focus of Serbian loyalty. Invulnerable as he seemed to be to defamation or displacement from abroad, Bailey argued that he could be dislodged only by a coup from inside his movement. The meeting agreed to canvas the remaining BLOs' views about the chances of staging a 'palace revolution'.[81]

At lunch the next day Eden found the King willing to sack Purić and to replace Mihailović, but apprehensive about the difficulties he would face in constructing another government. He was also unhappy at the prospect of an interval during which he would stand alone. Finding mutually acceptable candidates for office appeared likely to be the major stumbling block.[82] The King's accommodating attitude was probably influenced by the emergence of a new threat to his marital bliss: his mother's withdrawal of her consent. In the event she was disregarded, and did not attend the wedding at the Yugoslav Embassy on 20 March. The fact that the King's political outlook had yet to be reformed was shown by the presence of another guest, Mihailović's special envoy Major Vojislav Lukačević.[83]

Tito had not been presented with Churchill's 26 February telegram until 9 March. His first reaction was to suggest to Maclean that Peter join the Partisan air force squadron being trained in Egypt. This was not to the taste of the Foreign Office, for it neither got the King home nor guaranteed Tito's co-operation with him. Having little confidence in the ardour of Maclean's advocacy or in his understanding of their requirements, the Foreign Office officials feared that Tito's formal reply would be no better. They began to repent their recent resolution to get rid of Purić. Churchill, on the other hand, forged ahead. He extracted from Peter during luncheon on Saturday, 18 March, a promise to dismiss Purić the following Tuesday.[84]

Well aware, as Cadogan noted, that 'with King Peter there's many a slip . . .', the Foreign Office doubted that he would act so quickly. It therefore held back Churchill's despatch of a message to Tito 'in which we play our big trump' – the dismissal of the Purić government. Moreover, Eden pointed out to the Prime Minister on 21 March, there were ominous signs that the Soviets, so far kept in the dark about the discussions with Peter, might use an interregnum to recognize Tito's National Committee. The King should have an alternative premier in his sights before firing Purić. Both sides of Downing Street agreed, however, that it was Tito who ought now to be subjected to maximum British pressure.[85]

He refused to provide an opportunity. His reply of 26 March to Churchill's last message ruled out a return by the King in any capacity as being contrary to AVNOJ's November resolutions. Peter's redemption could be won only by degrees, a process his own proposals had sought to facilitate. Yet the King's government remained in place and he had just seen fit to accord an honoured place at his wedding to a representative of

Mihailović. Maclean, for his part, lamented the decision to compel Tito to make his position so uncompromisingly clear.[86]

More bad news came from Armstrong. The disgruntled Četnik commanders on whom Bailey counted were too dispersed, too isolated from one another and too fearful for their own lives to topple Mihailović. Armstrong maintained his view that the King alone possessed sufficient authority to discharge Mihailović, and might do so by sending in a suitably qualified replacement. Neither SOE Cairo nor Bailey agreed. Mihailović, they felt, was certain to deny the authenticity of any orders emanating from the King, easily persuading his followers that Peter was no better than a British prisoner and his would-be successor a British stooge. He would also have no difficulty convincing himself that the King was unlikely to cavil later when he had succeeded in saving Serbia. They argued that it would be better to step up support of the Partisans, so enabling them to achieve domination over Serbia as quickly, painlessly and non-disruptively as possible.

The Foreign Office was confused. It was, of course, aghast at the suggestion that Britain actually help Tito to quash Mihailović, but was also mindful of the advantages that might lie in using the King to provoke a split in the Četnik movement which would permit Tito to extend his control over Serbia with less bloodshed and less diversion of military effort than might otherwise be the case. It therefore saw merit in Armstrong's plan.[87]

Given Tito's refusal to deal and Mihailović's refusal to fade away, the attractiveness of the Stevenson option increased. This entailed the postponement of all Yugoslav political issues until after liberation, during which time only the King's government would enjoy recognition by the Allies, and the allocation of material support according to strictly military criteria, meaning that everything would go to Tito. It remained to be seen if more could be salvaged for the King. At the end of March Eden and his officials determined that 'the best we can do for King Peter now is to try to ensure that he puts himself on as good a wicket as possible internationally'. He should be pressed, first, to make a statesmanlike declaration in which he would seek to rise above the fray and, then, to find a new government which might contrive to keep him there, 'not as part of a bargain with Tito, but in order to improve his own position generally during the next phase'. Eden recommended to Churchill that Peter be urged to form a small cabinet consisting of men like Šubašić, Simović and Mihajlo Konstantinović (a pro-British minister at the time of the 1941 coup d'état). It was, however, more important that Peter enunciate a good programme with firm British guidance than that they dilate endlessly over the selection of a government from among the 'very indifferent' persons available.[88]

Churchill impatiently agreed. The King should be provided promptly with a suitable declaration and made to dismiss Purić, repudiate Mihailović and 'form a stop-gap Government not obnoxious to Tito'. There might then be a 'forlorn hope of making a bridge' between them over the next five or six weeks. All the 'spinning out' since December had worked to the King's detriment. Military developments had meantime strengthened both Tito and the newly hostile Russians, 'and there is little doubt the Russians will drive straight ahead for a Communist-Tito governed Yugoslavia, and will denounce everything done to the contrary as "undemocratic"'. Churchill regretted especially his support of the Foreign Office line with Maclean: 'I did not visualize clearly enough the consequences of our demanding that the King should create a new Government "*in Yugoslavia*" with which Tito would be associated.'[89]

Importuning King Peter was like wrestling a tar baby. It was easy to make an impression, but impossible to make it stick – at least not without entrapment. Eden assumed that he had been successful in convincing the King during a lengthy interview on 6 April that he must move to rid himself of his government, first of all by summoning to London for talks one or two of the far-flung candidates for inclusion in a streamlined replacement. The King also promised to study the Foreign Office's draft declaration. Nothing happened.[90] Churchill took up the cudgels a week later, warning Peter that a rapid descent into the Balkans by the Red Army was now possible, and with it the danger that he might, through Mihailović, find himself at war with a principal Allied power. At the same time, a recent request by Tito for more food and armaments gave the British new leverage if he were prepared to follow their advice. Again the King appeared to acquiesce; and Churchill immediately informed the War Cabinet that Peter had promised an answer the next day. But when Stevenson called on him the following morning there was no answer to be had. Instead the King adverted repeatedly, as he had before, to the dearth of ministerial timber, despite admitting that he had not sent for any of the politicians resident abroad. He told Stevenson that he kept coming back to Jovanović as the only possible choice. The Ambassador did not point out that a third Jovanović cabinet was hardly likely to endear him to Tito, but he did press hard for Šubašić to be summoned from America.[91]

The Prime Minister's sense of urgency was acute. Eden was ill during much of April and Churchill was left in charge of the Foreign Office. Relations with the USSR were deteriorating. The assurances which he and Eden had already offered the Russians that they should 'take the lead' in Rumanian affairs were failing to forestall sullen Soviet criticism of Britain's handling of the current mutinies in the Greek forces in Egypt, and would not prevent a new row from blowing up at the end of the month over the use by the Rumanians of a captured SOE team as a channel for their peace feelers. Meanwhile a Partisan delegation was journeying to Moscow, the Yugoslav ambassador there had defected to Tito and there were indications that the Soviets might be angling to take over the training of the nascent Partisan air force. The presence of a grandiose Soviet mission at Tito's headquarters in Drvar was beginning to look sinister. And the unannounced Soviet recognition of Badoglio's government in March – although welcome in itself – was a worrying precedent. All this was more than enough to cause Churchill to lose patience with Peter.

On 14 April he sent a long message to Molotov in which he attempted to provide an account of Yugoslav developments sufficiently convincing as to cause the Russians to stay their hand.[92] The risk that the Soviets might break with the King and recognize Tito was in fact exiguous, although the sowing of doubts on this score was certainly in Moscow's interest. What was striking was that Churchill should now be prepared to seek Soviet help in a matter which he had heretofore regarded as a British preserve. He was also ready, as he hinted in a further telegram to Molotov on 23 April and spelled out to Eden in a conversation the following evening, to contemplate either recognition of Tito's government or at least use of the threat of its recognition to force King Peter to divest himself of Purić. Eden counselled caution and warned of the American reaction.[93]

Both men met again with King Peter on 26 April. There is no record available of what was said, but the upshot of their discussion was that Churchill telegraphed Roosevelt with a request to locate Šubašić and to put him on the first available aeroplane to London.[94] Peter claimed already to have invited the Ban to come, but to have received neither a response from him nor any joy from Jovanović when he suggested they work together.[95] Šubašić duly arrived on 7 May.

The manner in which Šubašić emerged as the principal candidate to replace Purić remains obscure. Šubašić had long fancied playing a unifying role, and had on several occasions sought American help in returning to Yugoslavia where he proposed to reconcile Tito and Maček.[96] His idea now was to come to England to help the Serb politicians reconcile themselves to the loss of Mihailović. He thought that only a Serb could be premier.[97] His promotion as Peter's sole champion appears to have owed much to the US Office of Strategic Services, and particularly to its head, General 'Wild Bill' Donovan. It is fairly certain that the timing of his eventual appointment came as a result of Donovan's forceful intervention with the King.[98]

The British embraced Šubašić with alacrity, both as a *deus ex machina* and as someone who shared their determination to identify the dynasty with the resistance. Šubašić's hopes to dispense sweetness and light in all directions – between Tito and Maček, the Serbs and the Partisans, the Croats and the Serbs – might be naive or out of date, but they were also in refreshing contrast to the stridency and purblindness of the other émigrés. His wrecking role in the government crisis of spring 1943 was forgotten, and with it the impression he had then made of being 'weak and muddle-headed'.[99] Once a minister he could explore the possibility of negotiating a compact with Tito. He ought certainly to succeed in the more modest task which the British had now set of improving Peter's image.[100]

Before King Peter need be compelled to accept his fate, however, the British sought to take stock of both the larger issue of the future of their alliance with Russia and the subsidiary question of the Partisans' prospects with the Serbs. Churchill, despite his inclination in April to accord de facto recognition to Tito and to let contacts with Peter 'markedly diminish', had been deeply stung by the exchange of sharp telegrams with Molotov on the Rumanian and Greek situations at the end of the month.[101] On 4 May he asked Eden to prepare a paper setting out 'the brute issues' dividing Britain and the Soviet Union, the principal one being, 'Are we going acquiesce in the Communization of the Balkans and perhaps of Italy?' He thought not; and in a second minute that day proposed the temporary recall of Ambassador Clark Kerr from Moscow. Eden and his officials, although still reluctant to follow Churchill's lead on Yugoslavia and unable to resist a collective 'we told you so' on that account ('For it is we ourselves who have built up Tito and his Partisan communist organisation'.), were also disinclined to have a showdown with the Russians. It was far too early to convict them of seeking to communize the Balkans and Italy just because communists made the best guerilla leaders.[102]

The resulting Foreign Office memorandum, 'Soviet Policy in the Balkans', was presented to the War Cabinet early in June. It attempted to distinguish between communization – which was unlikely – and the extension of Russian influence – which was unavoidable. In its recommendations it sought to steer a middle course between appeasing and provoking the Soviets. This was made easier by the Soviet agreement in mid-May (when the paper was between drafts) to the codification of the previously mooted proposal that Britain oversee Greek affairs and the Russians those of Rumania. The paper therefore urged that Britain seek to consolidate its position in Greece and Turkey while avoiding any direct challenge to the Soviets in the other Balkan states. Every opportunity should, however, be seized to spread British influence, 'inasmuch as there are elements in all these countries which will be frightened of Russian domination and anxious to reinsure with Great Britain. This indeed probably applies to General Tito himself.'

The option of offering exclusive backing to the communists, and so stealing the Soviets' thunder, was in fact tempting in the case of Yugoslavia: 'the advantage of giving full support to Tito would be that we should be backing a probable winner and make it less necessary for him to look to Russia for support'. On the other hand, the disadvantages were 'obvious'. Breaking with King Peter was not, it seems, among the worst of them, for this was judged 'possible but extremely difficult', unlike the wholly repellent notion of similarly abandoning King George for EAM. [103] Presumably these obvious disadvantages were the storms of protest that could be expected from the Commons, the Americans and the Serbs, as well as the sheer humiliation.

Churchill and Eden were feeling their way towards the spheres of influence agreement by which in October they would presume to divide South-Eastern Europe with Stalin. Then they would claim only a half share in Yugoslavia. In June, however, Churchill, perhaps beguiled by the option the Foreign Office discarded, was aiming for more. Attempting to get American sanction for a three month trial of the arrangement for Greece and Rumania, he somewhat indiscreetly provided Lord Halifax in Washington with an explication of the proposal on 8 June which added Bulgaria to the Soviet zone of control and Yugoslavia to the British one. That, in any case, was how the Americans read it. [104]

Just as Bailey's arrival in London in March had stimulated consideration of the Serb problem, so too did the return in April, after two and a half years with Mihailović, of Lieutenant Colonel D. T. Hudson. Maclean was also present, accompanied by Tito's envoy, General Vladimir Velebit. This meant that Churchill and Eden were to have the benefit of a surfeit of expert advice, given against a background of intensified military interest in Serbia as the most likely corridor for the expected German withdrawal from the Balkans.

Responding to a suggestion by the Prime Minister, who had just interviewed Hudson, Sargent called a meeting of the experts on 2 May. Bailey remained convinced that the Partisans, having failed to penetrate Serbia in force during the past nine months, would not now find it any easier to overwhelm Mihailović's 20,000 men in arms. The only way to remove the Četniks' hostility to the Partisans in time to make use of the Serbs' resistance potential was to replace Mihailović by the King. Maclean, on the other hand, had no doubt that Tito's strenuous efforts to expand his operations in (and into) Serbia would meet with success, especially as the Serb Partisans were now receiving Allied sorties. The King could get back to Yugoslavia only under the Partisans' auspices, but his chances of reigning were extremely remote. Hudson's view, which Churchill had already endorsed, was that the Serbs might be mobilized into the Partisans' ranks if Tito were both prevailed upon 'to cut out politics' – that is, to renounce any intention of imposing communism – and provided with the arms adequate to the task. Maclean felt that Tito was likely to make concessions to Serbian opinion if asked to do so by the Prime Minister. Hudson also recommended that King Peter appeal to the Serbs to rally to Tito.[105]

Churchill lunched with Bailey, Hudson, Maclean and Stevenson at Chequers on 6 May. They agreed on the need to bring the Serbs into the fight against the Germans. The Prime Minister estimated their 'importance' at twenty-five per cent, compared to the Partisans' seventy-five per cent. He also believed, according to Stevenson's record, that 'Tito would be better off with a constitutional monarch than as President of an obscure Balkan republic.' It was the consensus of the gathering that Tito should be encouraged 'to be as independent as possible of Soviet Russia' but discouraged from abetting ELAS. Churchill decided to postpone sending a telegram to Tito about the Serbs pending Peter's talks with Šubašić. He was prepared to allow a week for these to achieve a result.[106] Two days later Eden also plumped for the Hudson scheme.[107]

May was a bad month for King Peter. He was frightened of Churchill, disappointed in Roosevelt, terrified of Tito, indignant at Mihailović, intimidated by the Serb politicians, distrustful of Šubašić, bored by the nagging of Stevenson, and generally resentful of his lot. He sought to evade the crisis by absenting himself on flying exercises or, encouraged by Bailey, by dreaming of descending upon Četnik headquarters to wrest command from Mihailović. He adopted a cavalier attitude towards the dismissal of Purić and a punctilious approach to the nomination of a successor.

On 11 May, having seen Šubašić but once, he sent a message to Churchill that he intended to sack Purić the following Monday, 15 May, and would form a five-man council of advisers with whom he might carry out such acts of government as were open to him. He asked for the Prime Minister's sanction. He then went AWOL. Eden's reaction was telling: 'King Peter appears to be playing with us, but I don't know that it matters much to us, and perhaps not to him either.' When Stevenson, bearing Churchill's reply, managed to see him on the afternoon of the 15th his proposed council had become a small government in which he planned to include Šubašić. But he gave no sign of proceeding to discharge Purič that day.[108]

The following evening, however, he summoned Stevenson to tell him that he had just sacked Purić with effect from 18 May and for announcement on the 19th. He would be consulting Šubašić about the formation of a new government. The Foreign Office immediately despatched telegrams in this sense to Moscow and Washington.[109] Šubašić, still reluctant to assume the premiership, nonetheless assured Stevenson on 17 May that a government would be in place by the 22nd – in time for the Commons foreign affairs debate on the 24th.[110]

Also on 17 May, Churchill hastened to inform Tito of Purić's removal and Šubašić's imminent formation of a new government, as well as to warn him about the Serbs. Besides Mihailović and his followers, whose reaction was impossible to predict:

There is also a very large body, amounting perhaps to 200,000, of Serbian peasant proprietary who are anti-German but strongly Serbian and who naturally hold the view of a peasants' ownership community, contrary to the Karl Marx theory. My object is that these forces may be made to work with you for a united, independent Yugoslavia which will expel from the soil of Yugoslavia the filthy Hitlerite murderers and invaders till not one remains.

He asked Tito to refrain from denouncing the government changes.[111] Tito's reply was speedy and gratifying. Churchill need not worry that he would make trouble, 'the more so as the dismissal of Purić's government has a positive echo with us'.[112]

The King had not actually had the courage to sack Purić. He had instead merely requested his resignation. Purić, as head of a government of officials, saw no need to comply until a replacement, based on a new combination of the old party leaders and still tied in some way to Mihailović, was ready to take over. Consultations designed to produce such a government went on until the end of the month.[113] They were unreal. The British refused either to acknowledge that Purić remained technically in place (Churchill announced his resignation to the Commons on 24 May and again to Tito the next day) or to countenance any compromise with the Serb politicians designed to put Mihailović on an equal footing with Tito in respect to their recognition and support. The Serbs' inability to part with Mihailović and the British unwillingness to have him left the weak and duplicitous Peter with Šubašić – and with Šubašić alone. He became a one-man government on 1 June, charged with supporting 'all resistance elements in Yugoslavia'.[114]

While this drama – tragedy or farce according to taste – was playing itself out in London the Germans launched '*Rösselsprung*', a paratroop-led assault on Tito's Drvar headquarters on 25 May. The increasing ennui with which the British had been attending to Peter's performance was suddenly dissipated. Churchill urged Eden on 31 May to slow down Šubašić's appointment for a day or so,' till we see what happens to Tito, and whether he breaks out of the trap'.[115] Eden regarded the situation as 'grim', but one of his officials saw a silver lining in the shape of the massive displays of Allied air support for the Partisans over Bosnia: 'From the point of view of our standing with Tito this German attack was the best thing that could have happened.'[116]

On 3 June Tito asked that he and his staff be evacuated to the island of Vis, so putting an end to their hide and seek existence and permitting him to reestablish control over his forces. He arrived in Bari during the night in a Soviet Dakota and went on to Vis by British destroyer on 6 June. From every side the British reaction was the same: Tito would now be accessible, chastened and ready to compromise. Churchill issued stern orders to Wilson on 4 June to defend Vis at all costs and to maintain the secrecy of Tito's whereabouts, 'as the fact that Tito has been driven out of the mainland to an island protected by the British Fleet and Air Forces will soon be fatal to his influence among his supporters'. He proposed nonetheless to take quick advantage of the situation by sending the King to Vis.[117]

The next day he expanded on his thoughts to Eden. At the very least Šubašić ought to proceed to Vis to pave the way for the King. Better yet would be 'the bolder course' of sending them both to settle on the island:

They have as much right to do this as Tito, and it might well be that Tito would be strengthened by the King's presence at a time when he particularly needs support. At any rate, it seems to me that we have some good cards in our hands at last if we play them well.

The Foreign Office believed that Churchill exaggerated the direness of Tito's straits. It was unlikely, Stevenson wrote, that by dumping the King on Vis 'we could bounce Tito into being cooperative'. The Serbs, meantime, would allege that the King had been kidnapped. It would be wiser, Eden minuted to Churchill on 7 June, to send the Ban on ahead as 'John the Baptist',[118] Maclean already having reported that Tito was ready to talk to him.[119]

D Day or no, Churchill's excitement was intense. On 8 and 9 June he again pressed Eden and Wilson to rise to the occasion – 'a God-sent opportunity' and 'the last chance of safeguarding the unity of Yugoslavia and whatever hopes King Peter II may have of reigning'. 'These jangling Yugoslavian heads' should be knocked together, and Vis was the place to do it. For six months the King had 'sunk lower and lower'. Now he was rid of Purić and Mihailović and had the Ban, 'which at any rate is something'. 'Are we', he baited Eden, 'going to throw this all away by taking little mincing steps all tabulated one after the other?' They ought instead to take 'the Kingdom of Heaven by storm'. Peter and Šubašić must fly within the next two days, for 'Tito will not be long in our friendly hands at Vis'. He asked Eden to gather together the King, Šubašić and Stevenson for a meeting at 10 Downing Street: 'The danger is that Tito will flit; but if we agree upon policy, I expect it will be possible to make it very difficult for him to find an aeroplane.'[120]

The Prime Minister repeated his arguments at the meeting on 9 June, pointing out that Tito 'as mountain chieftain' and Tito as British 'guest' were 'two totally different things'. But Foreign Office caution seemed to prevail. Perhaps it was explained to him that Vis was an Anglo-Yugoslav condominium, and not under exclusive British control. It was resolved that the King, Šubašić and Stevenson would depart the next night for Malta in Churchill's York aircraft. Peter would stay on there while Šubašić and Stevenson continued to Bari and Vis. They would tell Tito that the King had come no further in order to avoid embarrassing him, but that he intended shortly to take up residence on the island. Churchill advised Šubašić to offer Tito command of the armed forces and to bear in mind the other favours he had to dispense, especially the vessels of the Yugoslav navy and the funds of the National Bank. Finally, it was agreed that Stevenson would carry a letter from the Prime Minister urging Tito to meet the King and linking the request to the problem of mobilizing and conciliating the Serbs.[121]

The strategy and itinerary of the party (augmented at the King's request by Bailey) were amended during a brief stop-over in Algiers on 11 June. There they decided, after conferring with Wilson and his political adviser, Harold Macmillan, that the former would invite Tito and Šubašić to meet him in Caserta following their talks on Vis, making use of the fact that Tito was already scheduled to come to Italy. The King would be kept close at hand touring the Italian front in case Tito should agree to meet him. It was envisaged that the Marshal, detached from the Soviet mission, would be more amenable to Wilson's influence in Italy and that Peter would be safer there than on an island full of light-triggered Partisans.[122]

HMS *Blackmore*, which a week before had carried Tito across to Vis, docked again at Komiža at 2.0 a.m. on 14 June. Šubašić, Stevenson and their party were met by Partisan Chief of Staff Arso Jovanović, various members of the National Liberation Committee and a guard of honour. Later in the morning Šubašić and Stevenson were driven eight kilometres inland, where the King's last prime minister began to climb alone the steep path to Tito's cave and the negotiations that would crown the revolution. Stevenson confined himself to encouraging Šubašić from the sidelines during the three days of talks.[123]

Šubašić, as heartened by a message from Molotov as by Stevenson's presence off-stage, and Tito and his Supreme Staff – pressed too by Moscow to reach an accord – signed an agreement on the morning of 17 June. Its basic provision was mutual recognition: by the National Liberation Movement of the Royal Government abroad and by the Šubašić government of the Partisans' army and administration in the homeland. Both sides agreed to co-ordinate their activities in such a manner as would lead rapidly to the emergence of a single 'representation' of the state. Šubašić pledged to form a 'progressive, democratic' cabinet which would devote itself to organizing assistance to the Partisan army and Yugoslav peoples. The National Liberation Movement undertook not 'to stress and to aggravate the problem of the King and the monarchy', it being understood that this was a question for post-war settlement. Lastly, both parties agreed to issue declarations: Šubašić asking all Yugoslavs to rally to the Partisans; Tito promising not to prejudice the form of the state's future organization. The acknowledgement by Šubašić of AVNOJ's principles and provisional administration did carry with it, however, acceptance of federalism.

Various practical matters were also agreed on the 17th. Tito would nominate two adherents of his movement to join Šubašić's cabinet – a Bosnian Serb and a Slovene – as well as appointing a Serb liaison officer to serve alongside it. The Yugoslav navy would be put at the service of the Partisans, but would fly its old flag. New recruits to the Partisans would be allowed to wear either royal or communist insignia. The National Liberation Committee would cease to object to the government's stewardship over National Bank funds. And Tito would succeed Mihailović as commander-in-chief.[124]

Stevenson's verdict was that both sides deserved congratulation. Tito's recognition of the King's government improved Peter's own standing and offered the Partisans the certainty of yet more Allied support. Šubašić, in recognizing the Partisans' hold on Yugoslavia, had 'accepted a situation of fact' and 'drawn all possible advantage from that acceptance'. One of these facts was that the Partisans would soon obliterate the Četniks. On the other hand, Tito had been categorical in his protestations that he had 'no intention of introducing any demoralising communist system or of imposing a "party line" on the country after the war'. Stevenson judged him to be in earnest.[125]

Churchill's first reaction to the agreement, minuted to Eden, was 'It looks to me splendid.' He asked the Foreign Office to draft a message reporting his triumph to Roosevelt, making sure to keep it short, as 'he will not read more than half a page of this stuff'.[126] The King, to whom Šubašić and Stevenson reported in Caserta on 20 June, also expressed himself 'delighted with the outcome of negotiations'.[127]

In the Foreign Office opinion was divided. Cadogan regarded the agreement as 'about as good as I expected at this stage. All depends on how it works out.' J. L. Reed thought that it exceeded their hopes. A. R. Dew, however, was downcast. Tito had won all along the line: a meeting with the King was to be 'postponed to the Greek kalends' and 'the chances of civil war are to be diminished simply by allowing the Partisans to cut all

Serbian throats'. Sargent agreed that Tito had got the best of the bargain, 'though I suppose it is a satisfactory achievement that we should have secured a bargain at all'. The deferment of Tito's acceptance of the King as the overriding and unifying authority did not bode well for him. Eden concurred, and was particularly annoyed that Tito should have escaped seeing the King. He and Churchill pressed Stevenson to try again before leaving Italy.[128]

Since it is impossible to believe that they imagined Peter capable of negotiating with Tito – let alone out-negotiating him – it must be assumed that it was the symbolism of such an encounter that loomed so large. The King would gain in prestige by identification with Tito; Tito would seem less threatening to the Serbs by virtue of his association with the King; and Britain would score over Soviet Russia by tying Tito to the dynasty. In any case – and as Churchill would attempt to persuade Tito in Naples in August – monarchy was quite simply a good thing.

The united testimony of Stevenson, Šubašić and Wilson that all was well, that Tito was willing to meet the King eventually, that Peter planned to urge the Serbs to join the Partisans, that Tito would come to Italy to discuss such issues with Wilson in two to three weeks time, and that the King approved of everything left Churchill and Eden with no alternative but to acquiesce in Šubašić's desire to return to London to begin his cabinet-making.[129]

The Foreign Office became even less happy with the provisions of the Tito–Šubašić agreement as the summer wore on. Serbia was the focus of this concern, and emollient reports from the large number of BLOs now there with the Partisans did little to alleviate it.[130] The Foreign Office also grew certain that what it had really intended to insist upon was Tito's acceptance of a totally independent Serb army. Eden pointed to this innovation in his officials' thinking as early as 26 June,[131] but it became the new orthodoxy until the disintegration of the Četnik movement in September rendered it irrelevant.

Churchill, too, made Serbia a symbol of his disenchantment with Tito following their meeting in Italy and until such time as there were more substantial bones of contention: Tito's 'levant' to the USSR in September, the new hostility of Partisan commanders towards the BLOs, the Royal Navy and the British artillery groups introduced to help stop the retreating Germans, the swagger of the country's Red Army liberators, Tito's plans for confederation with Bulgaria, the delays in the elaboration and implementation of the Tito–Šubašić accords and, above all, the race to Trieste. By then, of course, the organ grinder had replaced his monkey as the principal object of British attention.

In all this King Peter counted for nothing. It would be apparent in retrospect that June 1944 was the last point at which the British actually imagined that he might help them to pacify Yugoslavia and to save it from Soviet dominion. Thereafter he was required merely to play out the unenviable part allotted him: by appealing to the Serbs in September to rally to the Partisans, by sanctioning in early 1945 the device of a regency which would permit the formation of a united government and its recognition by the Allies and, generally, by keeping quiet. Again under the influence of Princess Aspasia – and encouraged by OSS – he would make a spirited bid to dissent and to raise a clamour. He was beaten down remorselessly by Churchill, who lectured him on the duty of a constitutional monarch to do his government's bidding, who promised him that no one would lift a finger to restore any crowned head in Europe and who ultimately threatened him with deportation.

The King had become an embarrassment, the embodiment of a failure and a reminder of what Churchill now regarded as his folly in investing his hopes in Tito. It was a long fall from the days when he alone had been seen to signify and guarantee Yugoslavia's future. Fortunately for him, he was probably incapable of comprehending very much of this. The British, on the other hand, had made their own myths – about Mihailović, the Karadjordjević dynasty, the Serbs, Tito, Stalin and their own strength. This was not discreditable. Certain of those myths had been necessary in order to sustain the war; others had been convenient helpmates in the effort to envisage a tolerable peace; at least one would prove in 1948 to have been truer than its wartime authors knew. For although the British crowned the revolution, they never really understood it.

12

Franklin Roosevelt and Unconditional Surrender

A. E. CAMPBELL

The Allied demand for the unconditional surrender of the three major Axis powers during World War II, enunciated at Casablanca in January 1943, has not found much favour with diplomatic historians. With few exceptions they have found it unnecessary and unwise. For this there are two main reasons, one general and one more particular. First, a demand so bald and absolute offends against a belief still dominant among those who are, after all, students of negotiation – that room should always be left for negotiation. In one standard account Professor Michael Howard pronounced the magisterial judgment that 'the announcement was made without any of the forethought and careful consideration which should have gone to the framing of so major an act of Allied policy'. And, after elaborating a little, he concludes, 'Had it been otherwise, the Allied leaders might have reflected a little more deeply on the question, whether total victory is necessarily the surest foundation for a lasting peace.'[1] Second, much of the formative writing on the subject was by men who had experience of trying to translate the doctrine into practical terms, whether during the war or in its immediate aftermath. They were conscious of many difficulties and ready to suppose that different policies would have lessened them. The demand, as a demand of principle, and the difficulties of civil–military and inter-Allied relations, became intimately linked.[2] Forty years on the matter may appear rather differently, and a reconsideration may be appropriate in a volume dedicated to the author of *Power and the Pursuit of Peace*.

Unconditional surrender, as Professor Howard says, became Allied policy, but there can be little doubt that, of the three great Allied leaders, it was Franklin Roosevelt who had the deepest commitment to it. The position of the United States, moreover, was then such that Roosevelt could have his way. If Roosevelt had not favoured the demand, it would not have been stated. It is therefore appropriate to concentrate on the

American side of the doctrine and on Roosevelt himself. Two preliminary points are in order. First, there is surely a certain rigidity about the kind of realism for which Professor Howard speaks. In a democracy the state of his public opinion at any time is a part of the complex of facts with which a statesman must deal. If that is unrealistic it may be impossible for him to be anything else, and therefore unrealistic of him to try. Second, as all historians would agree, the power position is a central element in that same complex of facts. The erratic brilliance of Winston Churchill's mind is part of the fascination of the man, but surely his judgment was never sounder than when he recorded his reaction to the news of Pearl Harbor: 'So we had won after all! ... All the rest was merely the proper application of overwhelming force.'[3] In other words, once the United States entered the war, there was no possibility of Allied defeat, and no doubt that the war could be fought to the unconditional surrender of the Axis powers if that is what the Allies chose to do. So far as there was a debate, it was from the start a debate among the Allies and not between them and their opponents. A moderate settlement would be a generous settlement since the Allies had it in their power to be immoderate. It is in this context that the policy must be seen.

Franklin Roosevelt established an extraordinary personal leadership over the American war effort, as did Churchill and Stalin over those of their countries. The methods by which the three leaders exercised their control, however, could hardly have been more different. Of Stalin we still know comparatively little and may never know much more. Of Churchill we know an enormous amount both from his own voluminous writings and from the accounts of those who worked for and suffered under him. Two propositions may be generally asserted. He considered that a large part of his task was to force a highly structured bureaucracy to more effective action in pursuit of British war aims. And, he had a passionate interest in military strategy which led him to bombard his commanders with exhortation and advice, not always sensible.

In both respects Roosevelt could hardly have been more different, or more differently placed. He was, constitutionally, commander-in-chief of the armed forces of the United States, a position not defined in detail by the Constitution, but certainly one of great power for a man prepared to use it. Roosevelt was prepared to use it, but his manner of doing so was his own, and derived from his handling of domestic affairs in the pre-war years. The American bureaucracy was much less structured than that of Britain, and Roosevelt himself had done much to create an administration whose weaknesses were those of informal and overlapping confusion rather than of rigidity. All knew that in the end one got one's way by first getting the ear of the President, but Roosevelt was a past-master at keeping even his closest friends guessing. He spoke freely and openly, but had a knack for concealing his real opinions. He wrote little, and comparatively rarely gave clear directives on paper. His preferred method of dealing with a policy proposal of which he disapproved – or even with one of which he was not yet ready to approve – was simply to do nothing or to return a paper without comment.[4]

Roosevelt, moreover, was perhaps the finest intuitive politician of modern times. He had learned to trust his instincts and his feelings and to rationalize from them, rather than working out problems by reasoned analysis. He knew that his own personality and power of leadership were important weights in any political balance, yet he was well aware that even the most charismatic of democratic leaders cannot long lead his people where they do not want to go. In foreign affairs Roosevelt, as Sherwood said, worked always with the shadow of Wilson at his shoulder, Wilson who had failed to carry either the Allied leaders or his own countrymen with him in his grand design.[5] Roosevelt distrusted elaborate blueprints, abroad as at home, and did so the more because administration bored him. What interested him was the immediate political situation, out of which some agreed course might come. When that course was set Roosevelt was usually content to go on his way leaving the carrying out to someone else. But the course could always be changed if necessary. Roosevelt's temperament and pre-war experience combined to ensure that he sat lightly to decisions.

Such qualities do not make a man easy to analyse, but they had different implications at different stages of the war. In the early days, before the United States was directly involved, American military men, conscious of their nation's military weakness, urged caution. Roosevelt overrode them, demanding large dramatic measures of rearmament, and trying to discourage the aggressors while encouraging resistance to them. At that point the military advisers played a traditional role, warning of American weakness and lack of readiness and trying to interpret American defence needs in restrictive terms. Roosevelt himself, aware that American opinion was deeply pacific, was always careful to cast his recommendations so far as possible in terms of hemispheric defence, to insist that his object was to keep war away from America not to take America to war, and that effective help to other nations fighting for their lives was the best way to ensure that America would not have to fight for hers. Any attack on Roosevelt's judgment here must be on his judgment of international affairs, for it can be argued that he pushed the Japanese into their attack; but he was playing the role appropriate to a domestic political leader and playing it brilliantly, while his military advisers were performing their proper function.

When the United States entered the war, the position changed. Roosevelt had to set up a working command structure. He transformed the army–navy Joint Board into the Joint Chiefs of Staff, enlarged by the addition of an airman to conform to the British pattern and so make the establishment of the Anglo-American Combined Chiefs of Staff more equitable and effective. The JCS, later enlarged by the appointment of Admiral Leahy as chairman, worked directly to the commander-in-chief, by-passing the Secretaries of War and of the Navy, the Republican elder statesmen Stimson and Knox, whom Roosevelt had brought into the administration to give it a bi-partisan colour. The command structure, with few exceptions, worked well. Roosevelt trusted his military leaders and showed himself adept at working with them. They on their side deserve no less credit for working with a commander-in-chief so ambiguous and so averse to clear-cut decisions such as military men like and, very often, need.

Perhaps the most surprising decision taken was that priority should be given to the defeat of Germany. Not only was it Japan that had attacked American forces and overrun American territory, but it had long been American military doctrine that the primary interests of the United States lay in the Far East. That position was quickly reversed and, once reversed, was never seriously reinstated. When attempts were made to reinstate it, usually under the leadership of Admiral King, it was in the context of trying to force the British to be more active, a matter on which Roosevelt was willing to overrule his military men. The threat to take their resources away to the Pacific, in a word, was used by the Americans as a weapon in a debate about different ways of defeating Germany, in which the Americans early committed themselves to a cross-Channel assault as soon as possible, while they suspected the British, rightly, of backing away from that in favour of Mediterranean operations for which military arguments concealed political purposes.

The shift in the attitude of the military is striking, if not surprising. From prudent attempts to match American commitments to American resources before the war, they became advocates, by implication, of total victory as soon as possible. The great American power which, one might suppose, would allow flexibility and calculation, in practice excluded both. That is true, of course, only on the largest scale. There were many hard-fought strategic and tactical arguments among the senior men on both sides of the Anglo-American alliance, even while the Russians were fighting their separate war on another front; but in the two great propositions, that Germany was to be defeated before Japan, and that the way to defeat Germany was by a strike in force across the Channel from Britain, the concept of unconditional surrender is surely already implicit; for even if they were reached by the Americans on military grounds, they simply set aside by neglect any secondary or limited war aims. It was not by chance that Americans constantly suspected that political purposes lay behind British military arguments, nor was it by chance that Churchill always argued the case for his Mediterranean strategy on military grounds. Britain and the United States were at one in their desire to defeat the Axis powers, and were at one in believing that Germany was the most important enemy. They differed in that Britain – like Russia – had certain definable, though secondary, war aims which might be advanced better by one strategy than by another. The United States had no such aims. Military arguments were therefore unchecked by political considerations, and Roosevelt was content that it should be so.

In this matter the historian must rely heavily on his judgment of that most elusive of political personalities, Roosevelt. One argument sometimes advanced on behalf of unconditional surrender must be rejected: that it was a device to hold together an uneasy alliance which might otherwise have fallen apart before victory had been won. It must be rejected because it stands the true argument on its head. Only *if* total victory over the Axis powers was desirable was it important that the Allies should not fall out. Any lesser victory might require that they should. In such an argument the means becomes the end. A much better argument is that even men of exceptional vitality and drive like the three great Allied war leaders have only so much time and energy to expend, so that inevitably and rightly military matters took precedence in all their minds over the more distant political future. But when all that is said, most accounts of the doctrine and of Roosevelt's part in it make him either too naive or too calculating, and sometimes both. There is a general problem of historiography here, of which this is only one example. Historians are scholars, and politicians are not. Politicians are much more like those textual critics compared by A. E. Housman to dogs hunting fleas. 'If a dog hunted for fleas on mathematical principles . . . he would never catch a flea except by accident . . . If a dog is to hunt for fleas successfully he must be quick and he must be sensitive.' Roosevelt was the supreme flea-hunter of modern politics. What he rejected – naturally without ever arguing the case – was the idea that one flea caught makes others either easier or harder to catch. Just possibly he was right.[6]

This was the Roosevelt who first publicly formulated the unconditional surrender of the Axis powers as an Allied war aim at the press conference called at the end of the Anglo-American meeting at Casablanca in January 1943. Even today there remains some mystery about the origin and the implication of Roosevelt's statement. The phrase did not appear in the communiqué of the meeting. Roosevelt later tried to claim that it was an unpremeditated phrase which came to him as he was speaking; and Churchill tried to claim that he had not been consulted but that he could not disavow the phrase once it had been used. In fact Roosevelt was speaking from well-prepared notes, which did include the phrase. He had discussed the idea with the American Joint Chiefs of Staff in Washington – or had at least told them of his purpose – before leaving for Africa. He had discussed it with Churchill at Casablanca, and Churchill had been able to consult the War Cabinet by telegram. All that has long been known, but the mystery persists. It is not clear how fully the policy was discussed at Casablanca, either between the two leaders or by their staffs. General A. C. Wedemeyer, who was present at Casablanca as a comparatively junior but influential staff officer, has recorded that the matter was raised, off the record, at a meeting of the (American) Joint Chiefs of Staff, and that he spoke vigorously against it. No other record of that discussion exists, and the likely explanation is that Marshall had already decided, after the Washington meeting, that the matter was closed, or at least could not usefully be argued further at JCS level.[7]

The discussion between the two leaders remains equally obscure, and the chief obscurity is that over Churchill's attitude. Against Elliott Roosevelt's testimony that Churchill accepted the idea readily when it was put to him there is the counter-evidence of Harriman that Churchill was in 'high dudgeon' at the announcement. 'I had seen him unhappy with Roosevelt more than once', Harriman recalled, 'but this time he was more deeply offended than before.' The fullest recent discussion is that of Professor Robert Dallek, who concludes ingeniously that the decision to have the doctrine presented as a spontaneous idea of Roosevelt's was jointly taken, as a means of papering over a difference of opinion. Dallek rightly identifies the likely point at issue as that of the treatment of Italy, but his desire to find an explanation that will do honour to both Churchill and Roosevelt probably carries him too far. In putting the proposal to the War Cabinet Churchill had tried, without success, to get their support in excluding Italy from the reference; and in that failure one may perhaps detect the anti-Italian animus of Anthony Eden. It is likely that Churchill had then succeeded in having any reference to the doctrine, which he deplored if it *did* include Italy, omitted from the communiqué and was correspondingly annoyed when Roosevelt outmanoeuvred him at the press conference. Neither man was above dubious stratagems to circumvent colleagues and allies.[8]

Such a line of explanation of the main problem, on which evidence will always, it now seems clear, be inadequate, provides the best explanation also of lesser problems. Whatever its origin, 'unconditional surrender' caught the public attention both at the time and later. The historians who dislike it also think it important. So balanced an historian as Herbert Feis can dismiss the military discussions at Casablanca as 'interim', and add, 'What has made it [the meeting] so memorable is that, at a press conference, the policy of "unconditional surrender" was announced.' This of the meeting that devoted much of its energy to trying to find some agreement among the feuding French leaders, and most of the rest to discussing the largest Anglo-American strategic disagreement of the war, that between the Mediterranean and the cross-Channel strategies. If the doctrine of unconditional surrender was important absolutely, so to say, it is hard indeed to see why it was stated only in the press conference and not in the communiqué, and why both leaders, in the immediate aftermath, tried to play down its importance. If, however, each leader had a different purpose to serve, the explanation is simpler. Having made his point in public Roosevelt could well afford to argue both that he had made it spontaneously, and that there was nothing new in it. Churchill for his part could play down the importance of the statement, and emphasize its informality, since he had lost the important issue which divided him from Roosevelt – the treatment of Italy. No devious and unrecorded agreements between principals are required (as they are by the Dallek explanation). Both men simply forgot what they preferred to forget.[9]

On one line of argument it is easy to contend that 'unconditional surrender' was of no great importance. The words had indeed not been used in public before, but phrases like fighting on till the total defeat of the enemy, and ending the power to wage aggressive war, had been common enough, and it is hard to see that they implied in practice anything less than unconditional surrender. On the other side, the phrase cannot be taken as a complete statement of Allied war aims. Long before 1943 the Atlantic Charter, and later the Declaration of the United Nations, had set out in broad general terms the sort of post-war world the western Allies at least envisioned, and that world had a place for the vanquished as for the victors. The doctrine of unconditional surrender did not stand by itself.

On such an argument, Churchill's irritation becomes no more than a storm in a teacup, for there had, after all, been no serious discussion of any *other* policy. Yet that immediately raises the question of why a new statement of a policy already well known and essentially empty of positive content was thought necessary at Casablanca, even if only by Roosevelt. As will appear, most historical discussion of the policy has focussed on its effect on the enemy powers. At the time when it was issued, however, relations among the Allies were more immediately relevant. It had just been agreed that the second front in the West must be delayed, news that had still to be broken to Stalin. And there was strain between the western Allies themselves. Even beyond the dispute about strategy in Europe, the

Americans, led in this by Admiral King, were expressing dissatisfaction with the British contribution to the Pacific war. They wanted more action in Burma at once, and they wanted assurance that Britain would contribute adequately to the war against Japan after the defeat of Germany. Roosevelt had had to intervene vigorously a few months earlier to quell the most serious revolt against the Europe-first strategy, and then to force even the Europeanists to agree to the 'diversion' of American forces to North Africa.[10]

In such a situation some scholars have seen a restatement of Anglo-American determination as a means of giving Stalin reassurance and trying to lessen his suspicion that there might be a negotiated peace at Russia's expense. They have similarly seen a restatement of British determination as a means of offering reassurance to the United States. Though both explanations have been advanced, neither is really plausible. The statement did not meet the anxieties. It is not easy to believe that so suspicious and wary a character as Stalin could be reassured by a phrase, or that Roosevelt thought he could be; but even if that point is set aside, the Russian grievance at the time was that they were doing too much of the fighting and the western Allies too little. Again, the suspicion that the British intended to let the Americans do most of the fighting against the Japanese was what divided Americans from British. These grievances could not be met by any formula but only by detailed military planning followed by performance.

The most plausible explanation for Roosevelt's statement is that it was aimed at public opinion in the United States after the complex American negotiations with the Vichy French authorities in North Africa. Although Eisenhower had entered into these reluctantly and only in order to ease the landing of his forces and the consolidation of their position, the affair left a nasty taste in the mouth, contributed to a reputation for political naiveté which was to dog Eisenhower for years, and led many people in the United States, and in Britain, to wonder whether their leaders were losing sight of the object of the war. While Stalin could hardly be placated by statements at a press conference, and while British and American military men had to hammer out their differences in many a planning session, a public announcement might well soothe an anxious public. Moreover, although the deal with Darlan had been American, and although the British public had been displeased by it, the public that Roosevelt was addressing was essentially American. During the war Roosevelt and Churchill each scrupulously avoided trying to speak directly to the people of the other nation. What Roosevelt had to deal with was American public opinion as it stood at the time; and at the time, American anxieties were that the war against the Axis might not be fully and properly waged to complete victory. Roosevelt's sense of American domestic opinion, rarely at fault, is the best explanation for his statement, and the reaction to it the best evidence that he was right.[11]

Once stated, the demand for unconditional surrender was never fully or formally abandoned. It was even extended, at the Moscow conference of October 1943, to the satellite states as well – an episode here neglected – and it survived more than one attempt to persuade Roosevelt to modify it. This was a matter on which Roosevelt proved stubborn. But what were the practical consequences of a uniform doctrine as applied to the three major enemies, enemies about whom the most obvious fact was that their circumstances, interests and characteristics were widely different?

There was something undeniably comic about the negotiations for the surrender of Italy, which our knowledge of the hard fighting and destruction to follow cannot entirely conceal. Most of the historiographical discussion of this matter has turned on the question of timing. As Stephen Ambrose put it: 'The story of the second half of 1943 in the Mediterranean is one of missed opportunities. Because the Allies were unwilling to abandon Roosevelt's unconditional-surrender formula, deal once again with a fascist like Darlan, or even move quickly, the Italian campaign was long, slow, bloody, and sterile.'[12] At Casablanca it had been agreed that the conquest of North Africa should be followed by the invasion of Sicily. Most Americans, however, including Eisenhower himself, then still believed that further operations in Italy were likely to prove a wasteful side-show, and as late as May the Combined Chiefs of Staff, while authorizing planning, were still reserving their decision. Not till 10 July was Sicily invaded. Not till 17 August was it conquered, and then the Germans, in a well-managed evacuation, got most of their men and equipment away to the mainland. Mussolini was forced to resign on 25 July, while the Allied drive was still bogged down. By then it was easy to recognize that the Italians were eager to leave the war, and the CCS had already agreed that an invasion of southern Italy should follow the conquest of Sicily. The question, then, is whether the new situation created by Mussolini's fall could have been more effectively exploited.[13]

What Eisenhower, on the spot, wanted was permission to invite an approach from the Badoglio government. That he was denied, and July dragged into August without any approach. Expecting it at any moment, however, he needed to know how to respond if it came. On that he had clear ideas of his own, and with few amendments his proposals for a military armistice, the so-called 'short terms', were approved on 1 August. It was made clear to him, however, that the 'short terms' were an interim document and that the political leaders retained the right to add further conditions which the Italians would be required to accept. In essence, the principle of unconditional surrender was to be maintained, but the Italians would be offered later concessions in the degree to which they gave the Allies active help. These, the 'long terms', took time to hammer out, and they were not sent to Eisenhower till 27 August. It is this delay on the Allied side that has given rise to the proposition that a quicker settlement should have been possible, and would have achieved less costly results. 'The bill for the delay was paid in blood at Salerno, Anzio and Cassino.'[14]

This is an argument that cannot be sustained. The important delay was not on the Allied side but on the Italian, and there was a compelling reason for it. It was not until 15 August that the Badoglio government made their first serious approach with the arrival in Madrid of General Castellano. He came in great secrecy with an elaborate cover story and the protracted negotiations which followed were to be complicated by the later appearance of another and quite independent emissary, General Zanussi. The delay was not caused by diplomatic ineptitude, by haggling over surrender terms, or even by problems of communications. It was caused by the dilemma in which the Italians found themselves. Castellano was authorized to sign the 'short terms' on 3 September, the day the Allies crossed the Straits of Messina; but it was agreed that the armistice should be kept secret until just before the later landing at Salerno on the 8th. At the last moment Badoglio tried to withdraw. It was Eisenhower who broadcast to Italy and to the world the news of the armistice and its terms, and forced Badoglio into public acceptance. At that time Eisenhower's whole attention was properly on what was bound to be a risky amphibious assault at best and one which might be even more risky if the Italians reverted to their former position. It is in this context that Ambrose writes, 'It all hinged on Badoglio.'[15]

For good or ill, nothing then hinged on Badoglio. The Allies' hopes were dupes and their fears liars. Eisenhower had hoped for substantial military benefits from a quick Italian surrender and had been willing to pay a political price to get it. His political masters were moved not so much by a desire to punish Italy as by concern for opinion in their own countries and for the wider conduct of the war. The difference was real and understandable, but both sides were arguing from the same false premise – that Badoglio presided over a real government and disposed of real forces. That was hardly true when he took office, and ceased to be true well before the Allies could have made any use of him. The Italians could not surrender, unconditionally or on any terms, until their country had actually been invaded. They were prevented from doing so not by fear of Allied severity but by fear of German severity. Their peace feelers of early August were not serious, because they were intended only to assure the Allies that the Italian–German talks then taking place were not serious either. The

Germans could see that. Anyone could have seen that. As Churchill wrote as early as 7 August, 'Badoglio admits he is going to double-cross someone . . .', and although the German leaders on their side were divided over the proper response to the fall of Mussolini, they had already long ceased to place any reliance on the Italians. Before Churchill wrote they were sending reinforcements into Italy, withdrawing divisions both from France and from the Eastern front to do so.[16]

Given this German reaction, the Allies could have brought about more rapid Italian surrender only by advancing their own invasion of Italy, not by offering softer terms. Yet military considerations ruled out any invasion before early September. What the Italians wanted was protection which the Allies could not give. The military advantages for which Eisenhower hoped were therefore illusory, and the terms of surrender quite unrealistic. The surrender to the Allies was a surrender in form only, because in fact the Italians had already surrendered to the Germans. Italy became a battleground rather than either a conquered enemy or a liberated co-belligerent. It was as much as the king and Badoglio could do to flee from Rome to Rimini; they were helpless to do more. The political settlement then became a dead letter. The Italian government protested at the 'long terms' but were forced to concede them, yet nothing in the terms required the abdication of the king or even the resignation of Badoglio. Eisenhower had won in fact what he had been denied in form, an accommodation with any Italian government, of any political colour, that would make his task easier. He won that only because any Italian government was so weak that it did not matter much what its political colour was.

The alliance between Germany and Italy had never been a natural one. It had been based solely on Italian hopes of sharing in the spoils of aggression. At most other points, as the British and the French had tried to argue during the years of appeasement, Italian and German interests conflicted. Once it became clear that there were to be no such spoils, and certainly none for Italy, the alliance lost its *raison d'être* and it was an obvious Italian interest to abandon it as soon as possible. The Italian interest was to withdraw, not to fight on the Allied side. Italy had nothing to gain by fighting on the Allied side which the Allies, fighting without Italian help, would not gain for Italy anyway. Yet how could Italy, placed as she was, safely withdraw from the war?

The situation of Italy, therefore, presented a Chinese puzzle of paradoxes. Had the Italian forces been stronger (in morale if nothing else) they might, had an Italian government so directed, have given useful support to the Allies. Had they been sufficiently stronger they might even have forced the withdrawal of the German occupying forces. It was for some measure of such support that Eisenhower initially hoped. But even a fascist state relies on popular support, and it was because Italians knew that the war was no longer their war – whichever side they took – that the Badoglio government was so ineffective. On the other side, it was only because the Anglo-American forces available for the invasion were so weak – relative to the German forces which they would oppose – that Italian policy became of major concern. If the Allies had been relatively stronger and the Germans relatively weaker, the Germans might well have pulled back whatever the Italians did or did not do. If the Italians had been relatively stronger, there would have been a real opportunity for a negotiated settlement, and it is hard to believe that, had the Italians demonstrated strength *as against the Germans*, Allied insistence on unconditional surrender would have held. As it was, every real Italian interest lay in withdrawing from the war at once, while every immediate Italian interest argued for delay. The Italians behaved as they did because they believed that Allied forces in the Mediterranean were stronger than they in fact were and because they knew their own weakness, while the Allies – or their commander – behaved as they did because they believed that Italian forces in Italy were stronger than they in fact were (and that German forces were weaker) and because they knew their own weakness.

The doctrine of unconditional surrender, then, was of no consequence to the course of events in the Mediterranean. Military arguments prevailed. American strategists had tried to argue that once north Africa was made secure and perhaps – though this they conceded with reluctance – Sicily as well, then forces should be moved to Britain for the cross-Channel assault while Italy was left to wither in the aftermath of German defeat. J. F. C. Fuller later refined the argument: 'The . . . long drawn out and exhaustive [Italian] campaign . . . may be divided into three stages: (1) The reasonable, to the capture of Naples and Foggia. (2) The political, to the occupation of Rome. (3) The daft, from the occupation of Rome onwards.' Whether in the end the Germans or the western Allies gained or lost from the mutual decision to fight in Italy is a complex matter for military experts to decide. What the political historian can say is that Italian considerations played no part in deciding it. Allied policy towards Italy, well-considered or not, was an aspect of Allied policy towards Germany and the larger post-war settlement. Harold Stein sums the immediate position up well enough: 'The Italian armistice did reflect an adequate awareness of Anglo-American political objectives, duly compromised by coalition constraints and by realistic and imminent military requirements.' It is entirely appropriate that when unconditional surrender became – briefly – a serious issue it was much later, and the troops in question were the German forces in north Italy.[17]

If the surrender of Italy was improvised, that of Germany was much more carefully considered. By general agreement Germany was the major enemy. Even Japanese and Italians of any judgment knew that Japan and Italy could not hope to win their wars unless Germany also won hers; their victories could only be subordinate and conditional. Germany alone was fighting what were two distinct wars, those against Russia and against the western Allies. Germany alone had been an enemy in both world wars, so that the mishandling of 'the German problem' after the earlier war was recognized as the major cause of the second. American planners wanted to avoid the mistakes of their predecessors. Some of those mistakes were attributed to President Wilson himself, others were those of the American people as a whole, although the failure to carry the country with him was not the least of Wilson's failures. The setting up of some kind of world organization – an improved and effective League of Nations – was an object of Anglo-American policy from the time of the Atlantic Charter, and to Roosevelt probably the most important object of policy, one for which, in an ironic echo of Wilson's attitude, lesser matters might have to be, and could be, sacrificed. The State Department formed a substantial public opinion studies staff whose purpose was to try to discover opposition to government policy in time to counter it effectively. It is in this larger context that the policy of unconditional surrender was announced for all three Axis powers – though not without hesitation for Italy – but if there was any merit in the policy at all there was merit in applying it to Germany. A large number of the foreseeable post-war problems seemed to have at least a German dimension, and the attainment of security from German ambitions was one of the largest of all.[18]

Appropriately enough, then, it is on the treatment of Germany that critics of unconditional surrender have focussed. With the advantage of hindsight it may appear that the policy made little difference to the future of Italy and Japan. It is natural to ask, however, first, whether some other policy might not have induced an earlier German surrender and so shortened the last stages of the European war; and, second, whether that same policy might not have produced better long-term results, for Germany, for eastern Europe, and for the democratic West at large. These two questions are separable, and they are linked only if it is further contended that the western Allies could have offered credible terms to a credible German government which would have offered the West substantial advantages in the Cold War whose outlines were as yet only dimly foreseen. At the time the danger that the western leaders, Roosevelt among them but only one among others, foresaw was that military advantages might be won at the cost of unacceptable political losses. The danger was that the war might be shortened only at the cost of losing it. One possibility was that the Germans might make terms which rescued something from both their opponents. Another was that they might deal with the Russians rather than with the West.

The first condition for either of these possibilities was that Hitler should be overthrown – that is, killed – before any negotiations took place. So much of a risk the Germans were expected to run for themselves. Yet that was the first sticking point. There had always been courageous Germans opposed to Hitler on principle. Before they could usefully act they had to win the support of the armed forces. By some time in 1943 all rational German generals could see that the war was lost, and that the question was how to save something from the wreck. Their efforts to answer it were feeble, and for that the political structure set up by Hitler was responsible. Anne Armstrong, one of the most vigorous historical critics of the policy of unconditional surrender, accumulated the views of surviving senior officers, all of whom indicated that they would have welcomed any reasonable peace offer. Yet they did not act, and they did not because they felt they could not. Hitler had devised a 'rather flimsy and hampered defense' for his empire, but a superb protection for himself. The German generals were inhibited by a strong tradition of loyalty to the state; it was Hitler's genius so to confuse the command structure that none was secure, but, still more important, that none could act with confident authority. The tragic plot of July 1944 was too late to be useful, and it is quite uncertain what might have followed even if Hitler had been killed. By then the generals were hopelessly divided. So key a figure as Guderian thought that his oath to Hitler prevented him from acting, though it allowed silence. At no stage was there any potential government in Germany – by definition, other than Hitler's – which could have sued for peace on realistic terms, or have responded to a peace offer of any kind. Those who want to argue that the demand for unconditional surrender placed a psychological barrier in the way of Germans who wanted to end the war are arguing, of course, from what *might* have happened in other circumstances, but the evidence they can call on is at best thin.[19]

Behind the immediate practical difficulty of finding anyone to negotiate with lay another difficulty, probably insoluble, that of bringing the ideas of the two sides as to what constituted a reasonable settlement into any sort of alignment. There were a variety of peace feelers in 1943 and 1944, as indeed there had been even before Casablanca.[20] They were not all equally serious, but they all suggest that German ideas of a reasonable settlement were still far from those of the western Allies. Much thought had been given, in the United States as in Britain, to the nature of the German problem. It could readily be agreed that the Nazi leaders were both wicked and untrustworthy, men who must be overthrown and punished. This was no realist war for limited war aims. It was an ideological struggle of good against evil, presented as such on every occasion. Such an attitude had its own logic, which pointed to unconditional surrender as a first demand.

The further implications were less clear. Perhaps three main schools of thought can be briefly identified. The first saw the leading Nazis as a powerful group of conspirators whose acts were criminal and should be dealt with under criminal law. This line – which provided the war crimes trials with their rationale – had the added advantage of giving some new weight to canons of international conduct. The second argued that, though no doubt necessary, such punishment was far from adequate. The Nazi conspiracy could never have succeeded had it not been for the support of the barons of German finance and heavy industry, who in turn had received at least tacit support from many ordinary Germans. What was needed, therefore, was a thorough programme of re-education, indeed a social revolution, which would create a class of good German social democrats to whom power could safely be transferred. No superficial imposition of the forms of democracy would do any good while the social structure of Germany remained unchanged. This was an argument which could readily be given Marxist form, but one did not need to be a Marxist to identify in Germany what would later be dubbed elsewhere the 'military–industrial complex', to identify it as the problem, and to ponder how it could be destroyed and kept from revival.

These two schools of thought had this in common, that they looked to social cures of an essentially social problem. The third school was in some ways both more pessimistic and more optimistic. It saw the problem as a national one, which would remain while the nation remained. There was room for argument as to whether the problem lay in the German national character – in racial traits, even – or in the temptations posed for Germany by her power and her geographical position, which called out the appropriate character. By either argument education could not bring about reform. What was needed was to remove the power. So clear was the evidence against Germany that the principles of the Atlantic Charter might have to yield in her case. Even here differences were possible. If Germany were to remain united then German power to wage war must be destroyed. That meant the destruction of German heavy industry at least, which in turn seemed to require a degree of continuing international interference in Germany from which many shrank. A different method to the same end was that of breaking Germany into parts, each of which, because weaker than the whole, might then be allowed to develop naturally. Much discussion turned on whether enforced partition would perpetuate German resentment or whether, properly carried out, it might be welcomed and supported at least by those Germans whom it was desired to encourage. In short, would partition advance or frustrate German democracy?[21]

We might expect such large divisions of opinion, here very broadly set out, to be fully argued to some conclusion – even if in the event it proved to be short-lived. Given the nature of American government and the degree of Roosevelt's control over it, any such conclusion would have been the President's, as indeed on a matter of such fundamental importance it should have been. All the evidence suggests, on the contrary, that policy emerged by a process of confusion if not of inadvertency. Some reasons will be suggested later, but the immediate point is that only the first and least severe of the lines of analysis and treatment listed above could make any appeal to German opponents of Hitler, military or civilian. Yet to foreclose the whole discussion in the middle of the war would have been politically impossible, either in Britain or in the United States. The time to fight a different kind of war for different ends, if it had ever existed, was long past at Casablanca.

If the western leaders remained uncertain and undecided about the future of Germany, one decision was taken as early as Teheran which virtually ruled out negotiation. Unable to offer effective resistance, Churchill and Roosevelt had accepted Stalin's demand for substantial gains at the expense of pre-war Poland, and had then thought of compensating Poland at the expense of Germany. None of the German opponents of Hitler could voluntarily have surrendered a large area of ethnic Germany. In this matter, paradoxically, it was Stalin and not the western leaders who could have made a generous deal with the Germans had he chosen to do so. Not only was he quite uninhibited by public opinion, but he had real concessions to offer. Naturally lenience was not his preference, but he warily kept his options open until the last moment. He early decided that the 'Free German Committee' should be promoted in a non-ideological fashion. 'Britain and America would not be able to monopolize the nationalist and conservative elements of the German anti-Hitler movement.'[22] All these several arguments point to the same conclusion – that if, inconceivably, negotiations between the western Allies and anti-Hitler Germans had begun, they would have come to nothing. There were no responsible Germans with whom to deal, such German ideas as were tentatively broached were still unacceptable, had they been acceptable Stalin was in a position to trump them, and, above all, negotiations would not have been understood by British or American opinion. Unconditional surrender was not a demand imposed by Roosevelt. It was the least and the most that western opinion agreed on. Had it been otherwise, and had there been a preferable policy to hand, it could have been abandoned.

One other charge against unconditional surrender deserves consideration – that it provided the Nazi propaganda machine with superb material and persuaded Germans of all political beliefs that they had no alternative but to fight to the bitter end, in the west as in the east. Different exposition of Allied purposes might have persuaded more troops, or local commanders, in the west to give in more readily, even in the absence of a negotiated settlement. This is a charge which cannot be completely refuted, but it is probably less plausible than it first appears. The morale of the German army remained astonishingly high in hopeless circumstances, but morale is a complex thing and it is hard to believe, as this argument requires, that it remained high only *because* the circumstances were hopeless, and would have been lower had concessions been offered. Certainly in the last weeks of the war German troops were well able to draw distinctions between their Russian and their western enemies, such as their leaders tried to argue after the event should have provided the basis for negotiation.

Nevertheless there is a real point here. There is plenty of evidence that when Roosevelt advanced the policy of unconditional surrender he did not intend it to represent a policy of terror. On the contrary he wanted to insist that generous treatment of a surrendered foe was in the democratic tradition, and that all but the guilty could rely on it. In practice it proved very difficult to make that point, chiefly out of the fear that making it would be seen as a sign of weakness, or as offering conditions for surrender to which the Germans might later make appeal as they had to the Fourteen Points. As D-Day approached Eisenhower suggested in mid-April a three-power statement clarifying the meaning of unconditional surrender. Characteristically Roosevelt neither accepted nor rejected the idea, but in late May he suggested a modification, that he himself should address a message to the German people just before D-Day stressing both the futility of further resistance and that the Allies sought the destruction of Nazism but not of Germany. The idea was rejected both by Churchill and by Stalin, essentially on the ground of poor timing. Any such appeal should be made after a large victory rather than before, lest it be taken as a sign of hesitation and stiffen resistance rather than weakening it. Later efforts by the State Department to revive the idea were turned down by the President himself, though not without the usual delay. Even in mid-July he felt that Allied success had not been great enough to justify an appeal.[23]

The problem posed by unconditional surrender for Allied propagandists was that it was entirely empty of content. What would follow surrender? The policy did not say. Attempts to base reassuring statements on it were almost as empty – the drafts stressed the inevitability of defeat and that the enemy was Nazism not Germany; they added no more detail. To add detail – on such matters as reparations or the treatment of war criminals – would certainly not be reassuring, yet all were agreed that the Germans must not be misled and so given grounds for new charges of treachery against the victors. On the other hand, so empty a policy presented problems for Nazi propagandists also, and they were not able to make much use of it. They were given more help by the fact that it was the western Allies rather than the Russians who were bombing German cities to destruction, and by the misguided Morgenthau plan for the pastoralization of Germany.

These two western policies, each in its different way, reveal some of the weaknesses of Roosevelt's thinking. The American commanders, largely trusted and effectively supported, were left to make their decisions on military considerations alone. The bombing of Germany was Anglo-American, not American, but it hardly occurred to anyone, and apparently not to Roosevelt, that it did not obviously suggest future leniency or an ability to distinguish between Germans and Nazis. Nor have historians done much better. The use of the atomic bomb has been much discussed. The destruction of Dresden has largely been passed in silence, not least by those concerned to criticize the policy of unconditional surrender. Yet the means by which a war is conducted speak more loudly for the intentions of the victors than any phrase can do.[24]

The Morgenthau plan, by contrast with the policy of unconditional surrender, had real content, and, for that reason, it gave real help to Nazi propagandists. It has been exhaustively analysed, and can here be passed over briefly. Whatever Morgenthau's motives may have been, surely so radical a proposal can seldom have been so lightly endorsed, and so quickly abandoned, by two great and experienced war leaders. Churchill's agreement to it, at first sight the more surprising, can be explained away. At that moment in the Quebec conference he was willing to give Roosevelt anything he wanted, and perhaps in this – though one must not make Churchill into an intriguer, a role for which, after all, some consistency is needed – because he recognized that the plan was impracticable. Roosevelt's motives are harder to follow. The difficulty is not that he was endorsing a severe policy for Germany – although the Morgenthau plan went past severity into absurdity – but that he was abandoning, however temporarily, the guiding principle which he had brought into the war from his peacetime experience – that long-term and irrevocable political decisions are to be avoided.[25]

For this brief aberration various explanations are possible. Something may be due to the fact that neither Roosevelt nor Churchill – unlike Wilson – had among their many qualities the kind of driving intellect that pursues any question to a conclusion. More may be due to the fact that Roosevelt was already failing and that, in particular, he was debilitated by illness for much of 1944; so that subordinates who needed guidance were reluctant to press for it, while those who knew what they wanted to do did it.

Morgenthau did not conjure his scheme out of thin air. He had paid a visit to London in August 1944, and had learnt that Anglo-American planning for occupation policy was already producing a *Handbook for Military Government in Germany*. From his exaggerated reaction to that, and from his influence with Roosevelt, the short-lived Quebec decision resulted.

Planning for Germany had not, obviously, been simply neglected. If Germany were to be totally defeated, the three major Allies must agree on some peace terms. If those Allies were to drive into Germany from both sides, there would be a period of occupation. Planning was put in hand at the Moscow Conference of October 1943, where the Soviet Union accepted the principle of joint three-power responsibility. At Teheran a few weeks later the European Advisory Commission was set up in London to work out the details. The EAC worked away and produced agreement on German surrender terms, on occupation zones, and on the machinery of an Allied Control Council, which were accepted by the heads of government. The State Department wanted to go further and to develop a common policy for occupied Germany. If Roosevelt had agreed there would have been no British objection. Well before Quebec Churchill was chiefly concerned to follow Roosevelt's lead. Roosevelt gave no lead. Lacking it his subordinates went ahead and did the best they could, and it was their efforts that roused Morgenthau's spleen.

Morgenthau's plan was almost stillborn. Hardly had it been accepted – 'OK. FDR. WSC' – than it was abandoned. Yet it had implications. It was an American plan, accepted by the British. When it was challenged, Roosevelt decided that any new plan should also be American. The *Handbook* which had caught Morgenthau's attention was Anglo-American and produced in London, but the JCS had been working on its own directive for policy in Germany, JCS 1067. The story of the drafting, and the re-drafting, and the non-re-drafting, of JCS 1067 has been told elsewhere and need not be recapitulated, but the work was done in Washington and without consultation with the Allies. It was done, moreover, in a way reminiscent of the New Deal years. Roosevelt formed committees of men whose views were fundamentally opposed and invited them to weave those views together. He dissolved his own committees, replaced them, and neglected their recommendations. It began to look as if he had lost the capacity for decision. Even six months earlier Stettinius had complained to Eisenhower that the President was hard to deal with 'because he changes his mind so often'.[26]

Failing health may be part of the explanation, though Roosevelt recovered somewhat in the last months of his life. More fundamentally, he was working as he had always worked. He knew that he could control his own administration, however untidy it was. He believed, rightly or wrongly, that he could reach workable agreements with Churchill and Stalin. What he distrusted was international negotiations undertaken at any lower level, particularly since he was well aware that his advisers were sharply divided among themselves. Still more, Roosevelt had not made up his own mind on the German question. Sometimes he spoke as if what he wanted was a punitive peace, but not usually. His desire that a general post-war settlement should not be restricted by wartime decisions has often been represented as a point of principle. It was even more a matter of temperament. He knew that there was no public pressure for immediate decisions (such as there had been in 1933), he disliked taking decisions before it was necessary, and he hoped that the course of events would resolve some of the differences among his advisers and among the Allies. In his thinking everything was conditional and fluid. Policy should depend 'on what we and the Allies find when we get into Germany – and we are not there yet'. Even when he wrote as if he favoured partition, he backed away. 'It may well happen that in practice we shall discover that partition, undertaken immediately after the war, may have to be abandoned.'[27]

If Roosevelt wanted drift, he got it. The State Department, opposed to partition, and fearful that too much argument would drive Roosevelt into a commitment to it, relied on the Army to hold the Treasury to short-term commitments only, and placed its hope on American–Russian agreement at Yalta. (Britain would have accepted any American–Russian agreement.) It is, of course, unlikely that State Department policy, even if backed by Roosevelt, would have succeeded over time, for it envisaged an open world trading order such as the Russians were bound to oppose, and did. But a summit conference was not the place for the sort of detailed American–Russian negotiations now for the first time needed; and Roosevelt more than anyone had frustrated the setting up of any better machinery. Even on reparations, the only question discussed in any detail, the protocol was so vague that it became a major cause of dissension.

Well before the issue arose, of course, Roosevelt was dead. What he certainly did not foresee was that partition, undertaken merely as a practical matter of military government, would become permanent because zonal cooperation broke down. Whether he, or an equally supple successor, might have identified the danger in time to forestall it, we can never know. It did not derive, however, from the demand for unconditional surrender. At only one point did that demand have lasting significance: it formed the basis for western rights in Berlin.

Since Roosevelt was already dead before the problem of Japanese surrender became imminent, that problem can here be briefly dismissed. For Japan as for Italy, once Germany was defeated there was no hope of salvaging anything much from the war. Very large western forces, chiefly

American, could now be released, in time, against her. Japanese forces, which could no longer be reinforced, could be made to give up their imperial conquests in China or Vietnam or Burma or the Dutch East Indies; and Japan itself could be invaded. None of that was in doubt. The question was what, if anything, could be done to win certain victory less expensively without rendering it less complete.

That, in a sense, had been the problem over Germany too, but there were significant differences. On VE-Day the Soviet Union was not at war with Japan, and indeed there was still a Japanese ambassador in Moscow. Even when the Soviet Union joined the war against Japan the main brunt would be borne by the Americans. The capture of Okinawa had taken nearly three months from April to June 1945, and had been won at appalling cost in spite of overwhelming Allied superiority in equipment. Okinawa was more than three hundred miles from the Japanese mainland, a short distance for the bombers that pounded Japan but a dauntingly long one if Japan itself had to be invaded. Okinawa was something of a pyrrhic victory. It proved – what had not been in doubt – that the Japanese could be driven out of their island strongholds, but it also proved – what had not been certain – just how high the cost might be. The more clear it was that the war was effectively won, the less willing Americans, and their troops, were to insist on the rigour of a formula. The American military in Europe, led in this by Eisenhower, had never liked the unconditional surrender formula; with the defeat of Germany it seemed still less appealing to those planning the last stages of the Japanese war.[28]

It is in this context that the use of the atom bomb must be assessed. It is in this context too, however, that Japanese policy and the American response to it must be assessed. The details of the timing can be omitted. There were to be found in American government those who argued that the public would not understand the abandonment of total victory when it was clearly attainable, who argued that Japanese society needed thorough reform as German society did, and who argued that the Emperor was as clearly a war criminal as any of his subordinates. Against them were ranged those whose concern was with the likely cost of victory. There was a Japanese government which could sue for peace terms – was suing for peace terms through Moscow well before Potsdam – and which could accept peace terms, however intolerable they were felt to be. That government, moreover, could lay down a single condition, the retention of the Emperor, which was not, in the event, believed by most Americans seriously to diminish their victory. A war criminal who was also a god was useful both to the Americans and to his own people. No formula could stand in the way of using him.

Two conclusions may perhaps emerge from this survey. First, the demand for unconditional surrender neither lengthened the war nor determined its outcome. It was purely negative, adding nothing to earlier statements and offering no guidance on what terms the Allies themselves should impose. The circumstances surrounding the surrender of each of the three major Axis powers were so various that the doctrine did not in fact provide any basis for treating them alike. Roosevelt's well-known disposition to postpone decisions – or, rather, not to take large decisions of principle at all – was not challenged, for reasons of their own, by either of his two great coadjutors. Second, the consequence was that the practical determination of events was worked out in a disorderly fashion by a large number of subordinate officials of varying rank, most of whom were dissatisfied in some degree with the instructions they were given, the colleagues with whom they had to work, and the results they were able to achieve. This process has little in common with the grand design for a better world order based on principle to which reference was made from time to time – a Wilsonian world order in essence, but one which would be supported this time by public opinion and protected by the vigilance of democracies in arms. It has little to do either with the moderate, prudent, realistic reconstruction of the post-war world which most historians want to advocate and which forms the basis of their criticism of absolutist thinking in politics.

Forty years after any event the historian is in some difficulty in assessing its significance. We know that the world has had the longest period of peace among the major powers, and the longest period of sustained economic advance, in modern history. It may surely be contended, then, that the post-war settlement was not a bad one. But was it a good one? It is easy to argue that the peace has been kept by the balance of terror, and that the cost of peace has been a situation unjust to many and fully satisfactory to none. Such an argument implies that a better solution was attainable as well as conceivable. Yet the failure to find any means of working towards it suggests the reverse.

Much the largest change wrought by the post-war settlement has been the division of Germany. That had been thoroughly considered, as one means of reducing German power, and had been rejected by most American experts as likely – unless separatist movements developed naturally within Germany – to cause the kind of resentment that would permanently threaten instability and war. When the division of Germany came about, it was as a result of a different process, hardly intended or even foreseen. Yet the effect has been both the reduction of German power and also the attachment of one part of Germany to each of the great power blocs, rather than a persistent competition between them for the support of a united Germany. It is at least arguable that the muddled uncertainty which set in as the war neared its end produced better results than more calculation – and more effective calculation – would have done.

Such a possibility leads to a conclusion which must be disagreeable to historians and to practising statesmen alike. It matters comparatively little what aims the statesmen announce, and whether they are reasonable or not. For the attainment of stability circumstances are almost all and intentions almost nothing. What is needed is a balance of power in one, and one only, of the several uses of that much abused term. There must be rivalry among the major powers sufficient to keep each of them applying force to the system; and there must be in the system sufficient friction – in the proper sense of that term: a force acting to oppose motion – to ensure that the system does not respond easily or greatly to changes of relative force – to ensure, in a word, that men will neither try to bring about change by force nor try to oppose it by force. The demand for unconditional surrender can of itself have done nothing to bring about such a result, but in its application it clearly did nothing to prevent it, and it may have done more than any more 'realistic' policy could have done to allow the changing power struggle among the Allies to find its own balance. If so, the charming, shifty ghost of Franklin Roosevelt – who knew that the hatred of opponents is the essence of politics – may well allow himself that familiar jaunty smile.

Part IV

13

Crimes against peace: the case of the invasion of Norway at the Nuremberg Trials

PATRICK SALMON

Few of the judgments of the International Military Tribunal at Nuremberg have aroused as much disquiet as those relating to the German invasion of Norway in April 1940.[1] The sentence on Admiral Erich Raeder, the navy chief regarded by the Tribunal, along with the Nazi ideologue Alfred Rosenberg, as one of the two leading instigators of the invasion, was described by a British critic as 'the most monstrous of all the miscarriages of justice committed as Nürnberg'.[2] In his *History of the Second World War* Sir Basil Liddell Hart wrote:

One of the most questionable parts of the Nuremberg Trials was that the planning and execution of aggression against Norway was put among the major charges against the Germans. It is hard to understand how the British and French Governments had the face to approve the inclusion of this charge, or how the official prosecutors could press for a conviction on this score. Such a course was one of the most palpable cases of hypocrisy in history.[3]

Indignation has not been confined to those who object to the Nuremberg Trials in their entirety.[4] Even among those broadly sympathetic to the Nuremberg principles the case of Norway has been regarded as a significant lapse: not as blatant as some that called in question the past record of the Soviet Union, but as serious as any involving the three western powers.[5] In the view of one of the most recent historians of the Trials, Bradley F. Smith, the Norwegian issue comes second only to the Nazi–Soviet pact in the 'awkwardness' and 'political expediency' which marked its treatment by the Tribunal.[6]

The problem which faced those involved at Nuremberg, and has troubled subsequent commentators, arose from the fact that at the same time as the Germans were planning their invasion of Norway (between the autumn of 1939 and the spring of 1940) ostensibly very similar plans were being discussed at the highest levels in Britain and France. A British violation of Norwegian neutrality – by the laying of mines in Norwegian territorial waters – actually preceded the German invasion by twenty-four hours. Although the full extent of Allied planning was known to none of the participants at Nuremberg (it began to be revealed only with the publication of the first volume of Winston Churchill's war memoirs, *The Gathering Storm*, in 1948), enough was known for the defence to make the main plank of its case the claim that Germany had taken action only in order to forestall an imminent Allied invasion of Norway.

The defendants at Nuremberg were indicted on four counts: Conspiracy, Crimes against Peace, War Crimes and Crimes against Humanity. For administrative convenience responsibility for the detailed preparation of each charge was divided among the four prosecuting powers. Count Two, defined as the 'planning, preparation, initiation, or waging of a war of aggression or a war in violation of international treaties', was allotted to Great Britain. It was a potentially embarrassing situation. Forced by American pressure to overcome their initial scepticism as to the legal validity and utility of an aggressive war charge, the British were also aware from the outset of the trouble that might arise in specific instances, first and foremost in the case of Norway. The defence, for its part, knew that Norway was a weak point in the prosecution's armour.

This paper discusses the activities of both sides at Nuremberg: the British attempts to anticipate the Norwegian danger and to deal with it when it materialised, and the German attempts to exploit that danger. Parts of the story can be found elsewhere, in the works of Eugene Davidson and Bradley F. Smith. Davidson is well informed on the activities of the defence; Smith provides a useful account of the way in which the judges arrived at their verdicts.[7] But the prosecution, as conducted by the British team at Nuremberg and managed by its rearguard in London, has not hitherto been examined. The full story of the defence, moreover, remains to be told. The transcripts of the trial proceedings, though indispensable, do not record the closed sessions where a number of exchanges over Norway took place.[8] Numerous participants at Nuremberg have recorded their impressions, and the diary of one of the defence lawyers, Viktor Freiherr von der Lippe, has been utilised by several historians.[9] However, it has a special importance in the present context owing to the fact that von der Lippe was assistant to Admiral Raeder's counsel, Dr Walter Siemers.

Liddell Hart accused the British and French governments of hypocrisy, and as we shall see, there was hypocrisy on both sides. But as usual it was more a matter of the pressure of circumstances: pressure on tired and overworked men at the end of a war whose loose ends they were trying to tie up. 'They would much rather have gone home', as Rebecca West observed.[10] The prosecution had to make the best of an unpromising brief and avoid embarrassing revelations, whilst the defence had to fight against the odds to discover and present to the court any evidence that might mitigate the overwhelming case against its clients.[11] The British side of the story may not be edifying, but it reveals the efforts made by officials, for many of whom the 'Phoney War' was distant both chronologically and psychologically, to reconstruct the bewildering outline of Allied strategic deliberations in that period of unreality and self-deception which preceded the fall of France. If there was much deliberate distortion and suppression at Nuremberg, there was also genuine ignorance and confusion.

It is a story with considerable implications for the historical interpretation of the Second World War. Even at Nuremberg the legal and moral ambiguities of the Norwegian case were implicitly recognised. Although the prosecution was largely successful in its efforts to gloss over the case, sufficient doubts were raised in the minds of the Tribunal to influence their judgment to some degree.[12] Such doubts have spread beyond the Nuremberg courtroom. Ironically, the influence of Raeder's testimony, reinforced by Churchill's revelations, has proved more long-lasting in certain quarters than that of the prosecution case. It formed the basis for the interpretations of the Norwegian campaign (the 'race for Norway') in the standard German histories of Assmann, Hubatsch and others[13] – a view which remained unchallenged until Gemzell and Loock took a fresh look at the German documentary evidence in the 1960s.[14] Raeder's testimony also provided ammunition for post-war critics of the Norwegian government's defence policies.[15] Its influence, furthermore, can be detected in more recent references to the Norwegian case. Few in number and based on limited reading, these tend to be implicitly critical of the Nuremberg verdict. The issue is treated at some length and with subtlety by Walzer.[16] Other references are briefer and more inaccurate. The use of unpublished British records has not prevented the author of a recent article from referring to 'the mining of Norwegian territorial waters which precipitated the German invasion'.[17] Even Raeder did not have the nerve to make that claim.

These misunderstandings are generally the result of ignorance and an over-readiness to ascribe cause and effect to events that followed one another closely but were not necessarily connected. There is some excuse for this tendency: the story of Allied and German interest in Scandinavia at the beginning of the war is complex, and there were points at which one side was influenced by the actions of the other. There were many more occasions when one side acted upon what it imagined the other to be doing. A fairly detailed narrative may help to clarify the chronology and the issues at stake in Scandinavia in these early months of the war, and will underpin the discussion of Nuremberg itself. It will also provide a measure of the range of knowledge on the subject possessed by the various groups at Nuremberg: prosecution, defence and Tribunal.[18]

I

Neither the British nor the German authorities, and still less the French, had shown much interest in the strategic potential of the Scandinavian peninsula before the outbreak of the Second World War. Two issues, however, did command some attention. One was Germany's heavy dependence on Sweden as her chief source of imported iron ore – a vital strategic raw material. Both sides gave consideration to the means by which this supply might be maintained or interrupted in wartime. The other issue was the role of Norway in a future naval war, a matter of concern to both the British and the German navies. The latter's interest was the more active: a school of thought associated with Admiral Wolfgang Wegener, which appears to have had some influence on Raeder and his advisers, favoured the seizure of bases on the Norwegian coast in order to improve Germany's strategic position.

In the first three months of the war both sides toyed with ideas of action in Scandinavia. On 19 September Winston Churchill, the British First Lord of the Admiralty, proposed naval action (either minelaying or patrols) in Norwegian territorial waters in order to intercept the German ore traffic from the Norwegian ice-free port of Narvik. The idea was shelved by the War Cabinet on 5 October since it was not regarded as sufficiently urgent. The possibility of obtaining U-boat bases in Norway was first discussed by the German naval command on 3 October and raised by Raeder in conference with Hitler on the 10th. Hitler merely promised to consider the matter.

It was not until December 1939 that either side took a more active interest in Scandinavia, prompted in both cases by the Soviet invasion of Finland of 30 November. By mid-December it was apparent that the Finns were holding their own; soon they were inflicting heavy defeats on the Russians – aided by winter conditions and lack of preparation on the Soviet side. The Finnish–Soviet 'Winter War' captured the attention of the world and gave rise to exaggerated hopes. The Finns might hold out until the spring, when the war itself might be over, and might even defeat the Russians and bring about the downfall of the Soviet regime. But they would need help from elsewhere. Germany would do nothing to assist them; their Scandinavian neighbours would do as much as they could afford or dared; the larger neutrals like Italy and the United States offered sympathy but little else; Finland's only hope lay with Britain and France.

Despite their previous lack of interest in Finland, the Chamberlain and Daladier governments came to believe that they might gain a number of advantages by actively supporting her. They would be assisting another victim of unprovoked aggression, and helping to tie down the Russians so that they could not make trouble elsewhere (e.g. in the Middle East or India). Military intervention, as opposed to mere material assistance, opened up still more attractive prospects: creating a new 'front of attrition' against Germany in the distant north by luring her into a retaliatory invasion of southern Scandinavia, and denying Germany the entire production of the northern Swedish ore fields, which could be occupied by an Allied force *en route* for Finland.

Such ideas, with their disregard for the formidable obstacles of climate, geography and Scandinavian neutrality, were already being debated in the highest Allied councils by the middle of December 1939. At about the same time German planning received new impetus when Rosenberg arranged for the leader of the small Norwegian National Socialist party, Vidkun Quisling, to visit Berlin. There was some German anxiety about the possibility of British–Norwegian collaboration under the pretext of assistance to Finland, on which Quisling was regarded as a reliable informant, but his visit was also a welcome opportunity for Raeder to renew his advocacy of action in Norway. Raeder was now advocating not merely the seizure of individual bases, but the occupation of the entire country either by peaceful means – a Quisling coup – or by force. Following his interview with Quisling on 14 December Hitler ordered the creation of a special planning staff within the military high command (OKW) to investigate the latter alternative.

By the beginning of January 1940 two options were competing for the approval of the Allied leadership, but one of these, Churchill's Narvik proposal, had already been relegated to the status of a 'minor scheme'. It was rejected on 12 January in favour of the emergent 'larger scheme', according to which military forces would be sent to Scandinavia ostensibly in support of Finland, but with two more immediate purposes: to occupy the nothern Swedish ore fields (this part of the operation was codenamed 'Avonmouth') and to hold a line in southern Sweden against an anticipated German counter-attack (codename 'Plymouth'). Ports on the west coast of Norway would be occupied in support of these operations and to prevent their seizure by the Germans (codename 'Stratford'). The chief problem, apart from the logistics and the patent lack of conviction with which both governments approached the enterprise, was the need to secure Scandinavian consent. A forcible violation of Scandinavian neutrality would damage the Allied cause in the eyes of the world and render the entire operation impracticable. But Scandinavian cooperation was unlikely to materialise, as became clear from the response to Allied diplomatic approaches in December and January.

The problem of obtaining Scandinavian cooperation was never satisfactorily resolved. The large-scale operation authorised by the Allied Supreme War Council on 5 February 1940 depended on an ingenious trigger mechanism. The Finns were to appeal for aid and the Allies would respond by putting moral pressure on the Norwegian and Swedish governments to let them through. As the military situation in Finland worsened in February and early March, the Finnish leadership hesitated between appealing to the Allies for an uncertain amount of aid at an unspecified date and seeking a negotiated peace. Sweden, meanwhile, was already secretly acting as an intermediary with the Soviet Union.

By 11 March, when the Finns had finally reached the decision not to appeal for aid, the British War Cabinet had painfully accepted the idea of intervening in Scandinavia with or without Scandinavian consent. The air of unreality and confusion surrounding this decision makes it doubtful whether the majority of Cabinet members fully grasped the implications of their discussions. They knew, however, that the Finns were discussing peace terms in Moscow: perhaps they took their decision knowing it was never likely to be put into effect.

One British action, incidental to these deliberations, was to have a decisive influence in bringing war closer to Scandinavia. On 16 February 1940 the German auxiliary ship *Altmark* was boarded by a British destroyer in a Norwegian fjord and the 299 British merchant seamen imprisoned on board were released. This was not the first deliberate violation of Norwegian neutrality (that had been committed by a German submarine in December 1939), but it was the most spectacular. It speeded the tempo of German planning. In late January Hitler had ordered the preliminary 'Studie Nord' to be recast under his 'direct personal guidance'. The project had also acquired at this time the codename by which the invasion was eventually to be known: 'Weserübung'. After the *Altmark* incident Hitler finally abandoned the idea of a Quisling coup, and on 21 February appointed General von Falkenhorst to lead the project and command the future expedition. The incident may have convinced Hitler that the British no longer intended to respect Norwegian neutrality; it may merely have provided an excuse for accelerating an operation on which his mind was already made up.

By the beginning of March signs of impending British action were unmistakable. Hitler decided that the security of Germany's northern flank was an essential precondition of the western offensive that remained his chief preoccupation. His directive for 'Weserübung' of 1 March 1940 stated that its objectives were to forestall British intervention, secure supplies of Swedish iron ore, and give the navy and air force advanced bases for attacking the British Isles. Given British naval superiority, the operation depended for its success on daring and surprise. All that remained undecided was the date. As the climax of the Winter War approached, it looked as though the British might reach Scandinavia first: an unusually severe winter was to keep the German Baltic ports ice-bound until 5 April.

The peace treaty signed in Moscow on the night of 12 March 'deprived England, but also ourselves, of the political justification for occupying Norway', wrote Jodl, head of the OKW (and a Nuremberg defendant), in his diary. German preparations were slowed down; the British forces were dispersed. But the Allied leaders felt unable to relapse into complete inactivity. At the Supreme War Council of 28 March they resolved to intensify the blockade and inflict a variety of token blows on Germany, mainly for their propaganda effect. One of these was Churchill's Narvik minelaying operation, now revived under the codename 'Wilfred'. The operation, originally scheduled for 5 April, was postponed after disagreement with the French until the 8th.

The Germans knew that no large-scale Allied operation was imminent but still lacked an excuse for their own. The matter was urgent: most of Germany's limited naval resources were tied up in the operation; shorter nights and clearer weather would soon make it impossible to fulfil the requirements of secrecy and surprise. Both sides were now showing increasing disregard for Norwegian neutrality at sea and in the air, and Raeder used the sinking of two German ore transports to force Hitler into a decision. Britain threatened Germany's trade with Scandinavia; Germany would have to face the necessity of carrying out 'Weserübung' sooner or later. Hitler made his decision on 1 April; the following day he designated 9 April as 'Weser-Tag'.

Thus British and German naval forces approached Norway simultaneously. The British had anticipated German retaliatory action: in accordance with plan 'R4' (the earlier 'Avonmouth' and 'Stratford' plans on a smaller scale) small bodies of troops were embarked in cruisers at Rosyth for Stavanger and Bergen and in the Clyde for Narvik and Trondheim, to be despatched 'the moment the Germans set foot on Norwegian soil, or there is clear evidence that they intend to do so'. But since no one had expected the Germans to act independently against Norway, and despite a mass of intelligence reports pointing towards such action, the German naval movements of 6 to 8 April were misinterpreted. The Admiralty believed that the Germans were trying to break out into the North Atlantic and accordingly disembarked the troops to enable the cruisers to pursue them. It was not until the early hours of the 9th that the

Admiralty was wholly convinced that Norway was the destination, and it was still some hours before they grasped the scale and audacity of the operation. By the evening of 9 April all of Norway's major ports and cities, from Oslo in the south to Narvik in the north, were in German hands.

II

British anxiety about the possibility of German counter charges over Norway was first revealed at the four-power conference on military trials held in London from June to August 1945.[19] All the participants in the conference wanted to arrive at a definition of the aggressive war charge which would prevent an extended discussion of either the origins of the Second World War, or the immediate circumstances of individual German acts of aggression. Broad political and economic issues did not lend themselves to treatment by a court of law, and the record of countries other than Germany was bound to come under scrutiny.[20] The British representative, the Attorney General Sir David Maxwell Fyfe, feared trouble of this sort in a specific instance: Norway, he said, was a clear case of German aggression:

But we have information that they are going to say that it was done in anticipation of measures which they claim we were about to take to prevent the Norwegians from assisting the Germans by the supply of iron . . . If we are going to introduce Norway – and we might want to for the atrocities in Norway – I think we are rather opening the door for trouble if there is no definition. That is a concrete point about which I am worried.[21]

What knowledge of the Norwegian question might the defence be expected to possess, and on what legal grounds might they seek to raise it? We must remember that at the time of the London conference the Allies had by no means arrived at a final list of defendants (Raeder in particular was a late addition); nor had the vast caches of enemy documents that were later to prove so crucial yet been discovered. The British would nevertheless have to assume that the defendants would be able to rely on their own recollection of the events, fortified by any captured documents to which they might be allowed access, and on any relevant published material.

The latter was actually quite extensive – far more so, it seems, than any of the British officials concerned in the preparations for Nuremberg were aware. Much, for instance, could be found in the parliamentary statements made by Chamberlain and other ministers in the debates following the Finnish defeat in March 1940 and the Allied military debacle in Norway two months later.[22] Documents on the subject had been published by the Norwegian government-in-exile and by the Royal Institute of International Affairs.[23] Potentially the most incriminating, from the British point of view, were three White Books published in Berlin by the German Foreign Office in 1940–1, which contained facsimiles of Allied documents captured by the Germans in Norway and France. White Book No. 4, *Dokumente zur englisch-französischen Kriegsausweitung* of April 1940, was devoted entirely to Norway and included evidence of British and French espionage and operational orders for 'Stratforce' (part of operation 'R4'). No. 5, *Weitere Dokumente zur Kriegsausweitungspolitik der West-mächte*, published later in 1940, contained only one document referring to Norway: the orders for 'Avonforce'. The most substantial of the three, and the one destined to play an important role at Nuremberg, was White Book No. 6, *Die Geheimakten des französischen Generalstabes* of 1941. As its title makes clear, it was drawn from the captured archives of the French General Staff. Its contents included strategic appreciations by the French military and naval chiefs Gamelin and Darlan, telegrams from Daladier to the Ambassador in London, and records of meetings of the top Allied coordinating body, the Supreme War Council. All revealed the active French interest in extending the war not only to Scandinavia, but also to the Balkans and even to the Caucasian oil fields, and were bound to shed an unfavourable light on France's ally.

There is no indication that the existence of these volumes was known to the British prosecuting team until well after the opening of the proceedings at Nuremberg.[24] It should have been. The publication of the White Books had not gone unnoticed on the Allied side: at the time, they had caused something of a stir.[25] In 1945 there was still knowledge easily available if anyone had thought to ask. E. J. Passant, the German expert in the Foreign Office Research Department, was aware of the existence of White Book No. 4, while the Foreign Office's historical adviser, E. L. Woodward, had written an official account of the diplomatic aspect of Britain's Scandinavian activities in 1939–40.[26] Woodward was later to remark in reference to White Book No. 6, 'I have always expected that they [the defence] would quote this book.'[27] As we shall see, however, the prosecution remained unalerted to the possibility of danger. The bureaucrats' lapse was almost crucial.

Despite the poverty of British information gathering, it was nevertheless possible prior to Nuremberg to anticipate certain ways in which the Germans might defend themselves in respect of Norway. They might argue, on the basis of the German memoranda handed to the governments of Denmark and Norway on 9 April 1940, that Germany had prior knowledge of Allied intentions and acted in order to forestall an imminent Allied invasion of Norway.[28] Her action was therefore the 'forcible anticipation of a breach of neutrality' sanctioned under certain circumstances by international law.[29] The German defence might alternatively rely on the more general argument of *tu quoque* by admitting German guilt but claiming in mitigation that the Allies had committed a comparable crime.[30] At the London conference and throughout the Nuremberg Trials this second argument disturbed the British much more than the first.

The first argument could be answered, for even after the White Book revelations the Germans could be asked why, if they had concrete evidence of Allied intentions, they had not published it sooner. And on the basis of the captured German documents, as they became available to the prosecution from August 1945 onwards, there was sufficient evidence to prove that the German invasion had been planned and executed independently. We shall see later how the defence tried to counteract the thrust of this evidence. The second argument could not be gainsaid so easily. Awkward questions could still be asked about Allied intentions towards Scandinavia, and it could not be denied that Britain had violated Norwegian neutrality on two occasions, with the *Altmark* incident and the minelaying episode. In 1945 the potential political embarrassment was considerable, not least for Britain's relations with Norway, one of her closest wartime allies. It was essential for the drafters of the Charter of the International Military Tribunal to avoid creating conditions in which the *tu quoque* argument could be raised.

The London conference began by trying to reach a definition of aggressive war which would apply to the actions only of the Axis powers. Realising how blatantly such a definition would contradict the principles of international law it claimed to be upholding, the conference eventually adopted the proposal of the United States representative, Justice Robert Jackson, that no definition should be attempted but that the Tribunal should be given 'jurisdiction only over those who carried out these crimes on behalf of the Axis Powers'.[31] Any attempt to employ the *tu quoque* argument could therefore be ruled irrelevant: it would be beyond the competence of the court to consider the conduct of Germany's enemies. The defence would have to fall back on the 'forcible anticipation' argument, and this would be much more difficult.

In the case of Norway, the defence would not only have to explain away apparently overwhelming evidence of German aggressive intentions, but also produce countervailing evidence pointing to firm German knowledge of impending Allied action in Scandinavia. The defence as a whole was to face immense physical and procedural obstacles in bringing evidence of any kind before the court and, as we shall see, the case of Norway was to create difficulties of its own. The usefulness to the defence of one relatively accessible class of evidence – the German White Books – was considerably diminished by the London conference's ruling. Since the documents they contained were available to the Germans only after the invasion of Norway, their main value would be in support of the *tu quoque* argument – but this line of defence was inadmissible. At best, therefore, they could only corroborate German documentary evidence of Allied aggressive intentions. Even if such material existed, the German archives where it might be found were in Allied hands.

But the defence's task was not hopeless. The London conference was unable to bind the hands of the Tribunal completely, despite the admonition of Article 18 of the Charter that it should

(a) confine the Trial strictly to an expeditious hearing of the issues raised by the charges.

(b) . . . rule out irrelevant issues and statements of any kind whatsoever.

The fact that the Tribunal was composed solely of judges from the four Allied powers naturally placed it in an ambiguous position. Both prosecution and defence were inclined to assume, from their different standpoints, that the judges would dispense 'victor's justice' – and were surprised when they did not. As we shall see, the judges were unable to free themselves entirely from prejudice or considerations of national interest, but they were also to show considerable independence. They treated defence requests for witnesses and documentary evidence with some latitude, and proved ready to overrule prosecution objections.

In the last resort, after all, the Tribunal was meant to be impartial. It might respond favourably to a strongly argued defence case or sense when the prosecution was on shaky ground. The defence placed its hopes in this unpredictability. Sufficient material might be admitted in evidence if not actually to overturn the prosecution case – for most of the defendants an extremely remote possibility – then at least to undermine its credibility at certain points. Some of the defendants, notably Goering, hoped in this way to vindicate Germany's record in the eyes of posterity. Admiral Raeder was another who showed little concern for his own fate, but was determined that on certain key issues, including Norway, the honour of the German navy should be upheld.[32] The British, meanwhile, were determined that he should not succeed.

III

Following the signature of the London Agreement and the Charter of the Tribunal on 8 August 1945, the Allied prosecuting teams began their detailed work on the indictment. The British, as we have seen, took responsibility for 'Crimes against Peace'. A number of the participants in the London conference were to play a leading role in the preparation and conduct of the prosecution case, including Maxwell Fyfe, despite his replacement as Attorney General by Sir Hartley Shawcross after the Labour election victory in July. Maxwell Fyfe was retained as deputy chief prosecutor and was in effective charge of the entire British case at Nuremberg, Shawcross being present only to deliver the opening and closing speeches. In mid-September the move to Nuremberg began. The indictment was signed on 6 October and the Trials opened on 20 November. They were to last until October 1946.

Apart from Maxwell Fyfe, the British War Crimes Executive (BWCE) at Nuremberg included five prosecuting counsel and a Foreign Office representative, Patrick Dean. There were also the two British judges, Sir Geoffrey Lawrence (elected President of the Tribunal) and Sir Norman Birkett.[33] The British team was in continuous contact with the Attorney General's Office and the Foreign Office in London. In the Foreign Office a special War Crimes Section was set up in the German Department, headed by Robert Scott Fox and supervised by Sir Basil Newton, but the Office's legal adviser, W. E. Beckett, and historical adviser, E. L. Woodward, were often consulted as well.

The Attorney General's Office on the one hand, and the Foreign Office (and ultimately also the Cabinet Office) on the other represented different departmental priorities: legal and political. These were to come into conflict at Nuremberg. Whilst the primary aim of the prosecution and of the Attorney General was to secure a conviction, the Foreign and Cabinet Offices were obliged to consider the wider interests of the State. As we shall see, the difference of opinion was especially sharp over the question of the release of secret government documents relating to Norway. The inclination of the prosecution was to reveal anything (within limits) that would strengthen its case; that of the 'political' departments was to preserve the maximum official confidentiality.[34]

As Maxwell Fyfe's remark at the London conference had suggested, the British prosecuting team was at first more worried about Norway than any other single issue in the preparation of its case, and required guidance from the Foreign Office as to how German counter charges might be met.[35] When the small intelligence section set up to advise the prosecution requested a security ruling on 'information concerning our plans to land forces in Norway', the response was reassuring.[36] The Foreign Office was confident that any plans for a British landing in Norway were entirely dependent on a prior invitation by the Norwegian government.[37] In a letter of 17 October to the Attorney General, Dean provided an authoritative statement of the Foreign Office's version and proposed that German counter charges should be met by a simple statement that 'even if such plans existed', they were entirely dependent on Norwegian consent, rather than by producing detailed evidence to refute them.[38] The latter approach would run the danger of 'placing the Prosecution in the position of defendants' as well as raising questions of confidentiality. In addition Dean took the precaution of consulting the American chief prosecutor, Jackson, who 'agreed that every step should be taken to prevent such counter-charges being made and that the Court should be urged to refuse to listen to them'.[39] The two men also agreed that every effort should be made 'to prevent the defendants being given an opportunity of demanding to see potentially embarrassing documents'.

Some anxiety probably remained. There is a passage in a letter from Maxwell Fyfe to his wife which may refer to Norway: 'Scott-Fox thinks he had better telephone the Foreign Office about some 5-year-old secrets possibly being mentioned some 6 weeks from now.'[40] But on the eve of the Trials there was apparently no fundamental uncertainty about the legal correctness of the British position.[41] The Foreign Office had clearly been negligent in failing to give the prosecution better advice. The officials concerned could have been aware only of the final, relatively modest phase of Allied planning, to which the proviso about Norwegian consent could reasonably have been applied. There is no sign that they knew anything of the earlier, much more incriminating phase associated with the Winter War.

IV

Shawcross's opening speech of 4 December 1945 and the detailed presentation of the aggressive war charge as it related to Norway and Denmark (made by Major Elwyn Jones on the 6th and 7th) contained only the briefest references to the German allegation that the Allies had been about to occupy Norway at the time of the German invasion.[42] Shawcross dismissed the allegation on the ground of irrelevance (as foreshadowed by the London conference); in Elwyn Jones' account it was submerged in a mass of highly incriminating documentary material drawn from the archives of the German navy, Rosenberg's 'Foreign Policy Office' and elsewhere.

Listening to the two speakers, Raeder's lawyers immediately identified Norway as 'probably the most awkward aspect of the indictment' against their client, not least because it associated him so closely with the unsavoury Rosenberg.[43] But they also knew that there was more to the Norwegian question than the prosecution speeches had acknowledged. An effective defence would depend on distancing Raeder from Rosenberg and, as von der Lippe put it, on 'whether we can prove or at least make it look probable that a "race" took place between England and Germany with regard to the occupation of this country'.[44] Raeder had already prepared memoranda on various subjects, including 'Attack on Norway', for his counsel, Dr Siemers, to use as the basis of his defence. The latter had also begun to assemble evidence and interview potential witnesses.[45] On 10 December he filed a request with the Tribunal for permission to use a document described as the 'White Book of the Foreign Office about Norway'.[46]

Before examining the fate of this request it is worth pausing to consider the task facing Raeder's counsel. The defence was never confronted with a clear choice of arguments along the lines indicated above ('forcible anticipation' versus 'tu quoque') because the ban on tu quoque was never made explicit. Throughout the Nuremberg proceedings, however, the defence felt the force of this 'unwritten law', as von der Lippe subsequently termed it.[47] It therefore had to operate in a kind of blurred middle ground, doing its best with the 'forcible anticipation' argument, trying to avoid incurring prosecution charges of irrelevancy, but trying also to make as much mud stick to the Allies as possible, in order to create some degree of unease about the prosecution case in the minds of the Tribunal.

In order to convey the impression that Raeder's Norway initiative of October 1939 had been essentially defensive in character, the defence would have to prove, or at least suggest, that it had been prompted by evidence of aggressive Allied intentions towards Scandinavia dating from the first weeks of the war. The White Book documents, if admitted in evidence, would push the frontier of Allied interest back to late December 1939 – but no further. How could this interest be backdated to September or early October?

This is one of the most sensitive parts of the entire story, and one where the written evidence provides only part of the explanation. To fill it out, we have to desert chronology for a moment and go forward to March 1946, when one of Raeder's key witnesses, his former adjutant Vice-Admiral Erich Schulte Mönting, was brought from his internment camp in Scotland to testify at Nuremberg.[48] Schulte Mönting's devotion to his chief was complete. At some point before the middle of May 1946, when he and Raeder were to appear in court, the two men must have reached agreement on the story they would tell.[49] This is the admission obtained by Gemzell in an interview with Schulte Mönting in 1960 which he felt unable to include in his book published five years later, even though it would have helped to buttress a then controversial thesis.[50]

What was their story? In his testimony Raeder referred to a number of intelligence reports of Allied activity in Scandinavia, allegedly received during the last week of September 1939. Some had been conveyed personally by Admiral Canaris, the head of the intelligence service.[51]

Schulte Mönting's testimony corroborated this account, providing further sources, including the German naval attaché in Oslo, and more detail: reports of 'Allied officers making surveys on Norwegian bridges, viaducts and tunnels all the way to the Swedish border', and so on.[52] By their nature such intelligence reports would be impossible to check after an interval of more than six years. Their genuineness might be in doubt but their existence could not be positively disproved. In this way the seeds of doubt about the Allied case could be sown.

As a result of Gemzell's careful research we can be fairly certain that no such reports were received by the German naval authorities in the period stated by Raeder and Schulte Mönting.[53] If they were telling less than the whole truth, they could perhaps be forgiven for doing so in the circumstances. And they may not have acted entirely in bad faith. Gemzell has shown how Raeder's version of the events leading up to the invasion of Norway had already undergone drastic modification in the course of the war, with the defensive motives, which had been entirely absent at the outset, coming to predominate by 1944.[54] Raeder may have believed much of his own reconstruction (though against this must be set the much more candid account written by Raeder in Russian captivity in July 1945).[55] But it is certainly regrettable that the Raeder–Schulte Mönting version has passed unquestioned into a number of authoritative historical works.[56]

Raeder and Rosenberg were not alone among the twenty-two Nuremberg defendants in being implicated in the invasion of Norway. Ribbentrop as Foreign Minister and the chiefs of the other branches of the armed forces, Goering (Luftwaffe), Keitel and Jodl (OKW), and Dönitz, head of the submarine section until he succeeded Raeder in 1943, were all involved to some degree. But the prosecution did not make much of the case against the others and concentrated on Raeder and Rosenberg. These were 'the most active conspirators', who had been instrumental in persuading Hitler to embark on the invasion.[57] Though the two men were regarded as equal in culpability by the prosecution, and by the Tribunal in its judgment, Raeder tended to appear more important than Rosenberg in the course of the proceedings. It became clear that Rosenberg's main function was to act as an intermediary between Quisling on the one hand and Raeder and Hitler on the other, and that he took little active part in the preparations for the invasion. Raeder alone was involved at the highest level from beginning to end.

It is therefore appropriate to concentrate on Raeder to the exclusion of the other defendants. There are two partial exceptions. One is Keitel, whose role is discussed in a moment. The other is Dönitz. Dönitz's presence at Nuremberg helped Raeder in a number of ways. He was himself unusually astute, and was represented by a naval lawyer, Otto

Kranzbühler, generally reckoned as being among the most able lawyers on either side at Nuremberg.[58] Kranzbühler acted for both Dönitz and Raeder on Count Three of the Indictment (War Crimes), where he was to score a remarkable, indeed unique success (see p. 268 below). He also helped to counteract the effect on the court of his less engaging colleague Siemers, as well as that of Raeder himself.[59] Dönitz was the focus for another unusual phenomenon: the outspoken sympathy of a number of Allied naval officers at Nuremberg, many of whom thought he should not be on trial at all.[60] Airey Neave refers to the existence of a 'Dönitz lobby': some of the sympathy extended to Raeder as well, and may have found practical expression.[61]

V

Four months were to elapse before the completion of the case for the prosecution in March 1946. It was a period in which the defence was submitting many requests for permission to use documents and witnesses, and the record of the proceedings is interspersed with exchanges, often quite bitter, between defence, prosecution and Tribunal on the admissibility of these requests. One consequence of this debate was the gradual realisation on the British side that the Norwegian question was less straightforward than the Foreign Office had assumed.

The first hint of possible complications over Norway came as the result of a request made by Keitel on 1 December 1945, that Giles Romilly, a *Daily Express* journalist and nephew of Winston Churchill who had been captured in Narvik, should be summoned by the Tribunal to give evidence.[62] The Germans naturally assumed that Romilly's presence in Narvik before the invasion was to be explained by prior knowledge of British plans. The prosecution was determined, whatever the truth of the matter, that he should not appear at Nuremberg; but it was unable to block the request completely.[63] On 2 February 1946 the Tribunal gave permission for Keitel to address twelve interrogatories to Romilly.[64] In the Foreign Office the request prompted Woodward to warn his colleagues that Norway was 'a complicated matter' and that it would be 'most impolitic to get entangled in it – not from the point of view of the Germans but from the point of view of relations with Russia' – a clear reference to the Finnish phase of Allied planning which was not picked up.[65]

A similar unconcern greeted Raeder's request of 10 December when, at the beginning of January, it finally arrived in the Foreign Office.[66] Passant of the Research Department assumed that the request referred to White Book No. 4 which, even if allowed as relevant, could do little in his view to assist Raeder's case: the 'Stratforce' orders showed that the operation was dependent on Norwegian consent; the documents as a whole could only have reached Raeder *after* the German invasion.[67] Again it was Woodward who sounded the alarm – this time to greater effect. He suggested that the book in question might be No. 6, the *Geheimakten*.[68] Woodward's colleagues, made aware of the existence of this volume for the first time, realised that it contained a number of highly compromising documents which gave 'much stronger support to a "Tu quoque" counter-charge', and did not square with the advice contained in Dean's letter to the Attorney General of 17 October.[69] Shawcross would have to be provided with an authoritative account, preferably from the Cabinet Historical Section, of 'what actually *did* happen about Norway'.[70]

An apologetic letter was duly sent to the Attorney General on 8 February;[71] the authoritative account took longer to produce. The case for such a statement was reinforced by the Tribunal's decision to grant Keitel's request. It was now realised that his twelve interrogatories were intended to produce answers from Romilly that would corroborate the version presented in the *Geheimakten*.[72] The Foreign Office fussed about whether and how it could influence Romilly.[73] In the event his answers, given in an affidavit of 14 March and presented to the court on 10 April, were suitably anodyne but failed to dispel the impression that the British had something to hide.[74]

The Raeder case was more serious. On 19 February the Attorney General responded angrily to the Foreign Office's confession.[75] The entire basis of the prosecution case had been undermined and, he went on, the Foreign Office had been guilty of serious neglect in failing to look adequately into a matter that was within the knowledge of the defendants and likely to be brought out by them in court. Now the prosecution would have to improvise a new line: '(a) that German preparations for the invasion of Norway commenced substantially earlier than and were independent of our own, and (b) that, in any event, our own plans are irrelevant to the charges before the Court'. In addition, the prosecution would have to try to demolish the 'forcible anticipation' argument.[76]

The matter was urgent, because the case for the defence was soon to begin (it opened with Goering on 8 March). The British team at Nuremberg was still largely in the dark about both the substance of the German allegations and the new official British line on Norway. It was not sent translations of the most important *Geheimakten* documents until 11 March, and it is not clear when, or whether, it received the promised statement from the Cabinet Historical Section (the picture is obscure owing to 'weeding' of the Foreign Office files).[77]

The defence was now scoring some successes with its requests for access to documents. These comprised three main categories: captured German documents, secret Allied documents and the White Books. At the beginning of February 1946 it was permitted by the Tribunal to consult the German naval war diaries at the Admiralty in London.[78] Kranzbühler's assistant, Meckel, was there from 21 February to 12 March.[79] During this period, according to Davidson, he was able to obtain material on British plans regarding Norway from 'well-disposed Americans and Britishers in London'.[80] Perhaps as a result of information from Meckel, Kranzbühler put in a request in closed session some time before 23 February for access to 'orders of the British Admiralty' (subject matter unspecified).[81] This request, which is not recorded in the available British files, seems to have caught the British prosecutors off guard. When the Americans put their weight behind Kranzbühler the British had to promise to look into the matter. On 6 March Siemers too requested access to Admiralty documents, referring specifically to 'the period of May 1939 to April 1940' and 'plans, preparations and negotiations about military intervention of the Allies in Scandinavia and Finland'.[82] The defence was 'astonished' to learn six days later that the Tribunal had approved the request, but could hardly believe that London would agree.[83]

The extent to which the German White Books would be admissible in evidence remained uncertain. The prosecution line was stated firmly by Maxwell Fyfe in an exchange with Goering's counsel, Dr Stahmer, on 23 February: these books raised the *tu quoque* argument, which was 'entirely irrelevant' and likely to cause unacceptable delays to the proceedings.[84] The President of the Tribunal, Lord Justice Lawrence, gave no clear ruling, but it appeared that he would at least allow the use of extracts from the White Book documents. From later exchanges the defence gained the impression that the Tribunal did not entirely share the prosecution's view on the matter.[85]

It was again only after considerable delay, on 29 March, that Siemers' request was transmitted to London for consideration.[86] By then the British had moved rapidly, if belatedly, to retrieve the situation. The opening of the case for the defence had been anticipated with some anxiety. Unexpectedly, however, Goering's testimony on 14 March had provided 'a little breathing space . . . to prepare our story on the Norway issue', because it had dealt with it only in general terms and without raising embarrassing questions.[87] Preparation began in earnest the following day, with an interdepartmental meeting called by the Attorney General.[88] Shawcross was now in possession of a reasonably complete picture of the British side of the story, and felt that it would now be very hard for the prosecution simply to dismiss German counter charges as irrelevant. Even if they could not claim to have anticipated a British invasion (of which they had no prior knowledge), the Germans could argue that 'their own action against

Norway ought not to be considered a matter of serious criminality, since they had merely forestalled exactly similar action by the Allies'. In other words, the *tu quoque* argument might still carry weight with the Tribunal if it could be presented effectively. Shawcross's task was to obviate this possibility.

To achieve his goal, he required from the Foreign Office 'a full argumentative brief', backed by copies of relevant documents which could be used in evidence if necessary. These documents, if they were to be of any value, would have to refer to 'actual decisions at a higher level than those indicated in the documents captured by the Germans, i.e., at a Cabinet level'. This requirement was to raise in an acute form the conflict between the demands of the prosecution and those of official secrecy.

Of the two main phases of Allied planning, the first was, in Shawcross's view, much the more embarrassing. It seemed clear that the projected operations 'did not depend at all on the friendly assent of the Norwegians': the only mitigating circumstance was that no final Cabinet decision to go ahead appeared to have been taken before the whole business was brought to a halt by the Finnish defeat in March 1940. The prosecution would have to try to persuade the Tribunal that this phase was irrelevant, and if unsuccessful use the absence of a clear-cut top-level decision to demonstrate that 'although there may have been planning, the Allies held their hands and never actually took action' – hardly a conclusive argument, but the best that could be improvised in the circumstances.

The second phase raised fewer difficulties, and this was where Shawcross required authority to deploy secret British documents in support of the prosecution case. He wanted three to be made available in order to show that in April 1940 the Allied force had simply been 'intended as a counter move to German operations against the Scandinavian countries, and was . . . clearly contingent on their assent'. One of these documents, the conclusions of a meeting of the Supreme War Council on 28 March 1940, presented few problems since it was already in the possession of the defence, having been captured and published in White Book No. 6.[89] The other two were the conclusions of a meeting of the War Cabinet on 6 April and identical telegrams sent to the Stockholm and Oslo legations on the same day in consequence of that meeting, containing an assurance formulated by Chamberlain that 'we had no intention of landing forces in Scandinavia unless the Germans forced our hands by taking such action themselves'.[90]

Neither the Foreign Office nor the Cabinet Office shared the Attorney General's 'evident keenness' to make use of these documents.[91] Both objected in principle to the release of confidential records and feared that once the process was started it might be impossible to halt.[92] They did not present a completely united front. The Foreign Office was less worried about the release of Cabinet minutes than that of diplomatic communications to foreign governments, to which the Cabinet Office retorted, not surprisingly, that the arguments against producing one category of documents must apply equally to the other.[93] But Sir Orme Sargent, the newly-appointed Permanent Under-Secretary of the Foreign Office, probably spoke for most of those concerned when he advised Ernest Bevin, the Foreign Secretary:

My personal feeling is that it is dangerous for us to communicate to the Court secret and confidential British documents, especially in a case such as our Norwegian business in 1939–1940, where there was such a lot of funny business at the time.

In any case it is surely wrong that the trial at Nuremberg should be allowed to develop in such a way that it is *we* who are forced to defend and justify *our* actions during the war![94]

However, Shawcross's request received Bevin's qualified support in a letter to the Prime Minister, Clement Attlee, on 27 March.[95] The Cabinet Office was strongly opposed to producing any documents at all. Sir Norman Brook, the Cabinet Secretary, wanted a prime ministerial ruling that 'our defence against these allegations at Nuremberg should be conducted by general arguments and reference to published statements'.[96] Leslie Rowan, Attlee's Personal Private Secretary, introduced further considerations: 'we cannot consult the P.M. whose words are to be published; we cannot tell what the immediate repercussions would be (e.g. on the person now writing Mr Chamberlain's life) – and still less what the long term repercussions would be'.[97] On 29 March Attlee wrote Bevin a characteristically terse note which is worth quoting in full:

Foreign Secretary
I am decidedly against our putting in any documents. We are not on trial and should not put ourselves on the defensive. It is most undesirable to publish Cabinet minutes. I think A.G. should be able to deal with this without putting in documents. To put in Cabinet minutes would be a most undesirable precedent.[98]

VI

On the day that the Prime Minister delivered his ruling, Maxwell Fyfe reported the Tribunal's decision of 12 March in favour of Siemers' request for access to the Admiralty files.[99] Attlee's veto on the use of British documents by the prosecution naturally applied to the defence as well.[100] The consequences were unfortunate for both sides. The prosecution would now have to rely on bluff rather than argument; the defence, for whom the request had admittedly been a long shot, would be thrown back upon oral testimony and upon any White Book documents that might be accepted by the court. From this point onwards a more determined mood could be detected among the British prosecutors.[101] It was also noticeable that Lawrence's impartiality diminished when Norway was under discussion.[102] The case for Raeder was due to be heard in the middle of May, and the defence now had to make its final preparations: rehearsing witnesses and submitting documents to the Tribunal for approval.[103] For the prosecution 'the great thing', as Maxwell Fyfe put it, was 'to refuse any more material to the defence and to deal with what they have when we have seen how they propose to develop it'.[104]

The prosecution was partially successful in its attempt to deny the defence documentary material. It objected on grounds of irrelevance to half the documents submitted by Siemers to the Tribunal on 1 May, including nearly all those relating to Norway.[105] Despite the obstructive tactics of Maxwell Fyfe (and indirectly of Lawrence as well), Siemers persuaded the Tribunal to allow forty of the seventy documents to be translated and put into Raeder's document book.[106] The Tribunal did not, however, reach a decision on their admissibility; and on 16 May, the eve of Raeder's testimony on Norway, Maxwell Fyfe launched a renewed attack on the remaining documents.[107] Supported by the French and Soviet prosecutors (the French, who had been unaware of the dangers involved in the Norwegian case, had now been alerted by the British),[108] he managed to have all documents relating to alleged Allied plans against the Balkans and the Caucasus struck out, together with a number of the less important ones relating to Norway.[109] But eight White Book documents survived, including some of the most damaging from the Allied point of view.[110] It remained to be seen what Raeder's defence would make of them.

The case for Raeder opened on 15 May 1946 and reached the subject of Norway on the 17th.[111] Much of the impact of the Norwegian revelations had been blunted by the time Maxwell Fyfe came to cross-examine Raeder on 20 May. A number of factors facilitated the prosecution's task. Raeder was unlucky in the timing of his case. When he entered the witness box the case for the defence had already been in progress for over two months, and it had slipped into a monotonous routine. Only defendants and counsel of high calibre (like Dönitz and Kranzbühler) could make much of an impression in this torpid atmosphere. Raeder and Siemers drove the Tribunal to new extremes of boredom and irritation.[112] Personality clearly played an important part. Raeder was among the most colourless of the Nuremberg defendants, arousing neither abhorrence nor sympathy among the members of the Tribunal. His loquacity in court was exceeded, in the view of the *Times* correspondent, only by that of his counsel.[113]

Siemers certainly handled Raeder's defence badly, concentrating on the wrong issues and wearying the court with his pedantic approach. Norway, as Smith points out, was an exception.[114] Here the presentation did focus on the main issue: the British preparations for a landing. Yet here too Raeder's testimony failed to impress the Tribunal. What went wrong? The defence's principal handicap appears to have been the procedure for hearing evidence adopted by the Tribunal. It is instructive to compare accounts of the proceedings from the British and German sides. Von der Lippe clearly believed that the defence had made a good impression. His account confirms, incidentally, the reconstruction of the defence's strategy proposed above (pp. 257–9):

Led circumspectly by Siemers, Raeder gives an account of the prehistory of the Norway enterprise and his own role in the affair. Raeder distances himself plainly from Rosenberg and explains his meeting with *Quisling* and Quisling's later Interior Minister *Hagelin*. Raeder and Siemers follow ... the line that Raeder received trustworthy reports of an impending Anglo-French action in Scandinavia from *Canaris*, from the naval attache *Schreiber*, from Quisling and Hagelin etc., and was of the opinion on strategic grounds that this enemy action must be forestalled. The Allied orders and other secret papers relating to Norway subsequently discovered, as published especially in the German White Books, confirmed that Raeder's subjective opinion was also objectively correct.[115]

The report sent by Dean to the Foreign Office corroborates von der Lippe's view that Raeder had borne himself well in the witness box, but gives a better picture of what actually happened:

During the course of giving evidence allegations against the Allies were gone into but very little indeed was made of them and hardly any notice taken in court. Tribunal had indicated that as they had already read all the disputed documents they did not wish them to be read aloud in Court again and this contributed largely to the matter passing almost without notice here.[116]

Siemers was unable, therefore, to do much more than list the White Book documents and give brief details of their contents.

From the British point of view the worst was now over, even though Schulte Mönting and other witnesses had still to appear in court. Although von der Lippe considered Schulte Mönting's testimony on 22 May 'a first-rate conclusion to the Raeder case', British observers again thought differently.[117] His obvious loyalty to Raeder cast doubt on his credibility as a witness, and he faltered when confronted with new evidence from German sources under cross-examination.[118] In all, Schulte Mönting 'did Raeder's case little good'.[119] Raeder had already, on 20 May, endured his 'most unpleasant day', with a six-hour cross-examination by Maxwell Fyfe and the Soviet prosecutor.[120] Maxwell Fyfe's technique was aggressive, often bordering on rudeness, and German observers thought they knew why. 'Maxwell Fyfe himself was nervous and seemed uncomfortable throughout the proceedings. The general impression was that the prosecution adopted such sharp methods because the case against Raeder rested on such weak foundations.'[121] Raeder weathered the onslaught fairly well. In Dean's view he was 'inclined to be evasive and long winded, but made a better showing that Doenitz and most of the other defendants'.[122]

Maxwell Fyfe's approach was the obvious one from the British point of view. He completely passed over Raeder's testimony on the period between September 1939 and the end of the Winter War in March 1940, concentrating instead on the period from late March to early April, where the British case was strongest. Here, Maxwell Fyfe was able to quote telling evidence from authoritative German sources that a British landing in Norway was not regarded as imminent after the end of the Winter War – evidence that Raeder was unable to explain away.

This last phase was undoubtedly the weakest point in the defence's case. As suggested above, the German invasion was in part a preventive move, the experience of the winter of 1939–40 having made it reasonable for the Germans to assume that the Allies might respond to an offensive in the west by attacking Germany's vulnerable northern flank. But none of the evidence before the court suggested that the invasion was prompted by certain knowledge of Allied aggressive intentions. The defence was unable to produce evidence to support this claim because none existed. In fact if the Germans had known the Allies were on the move, they would have called off their operation, since its success depended on confronting only minimal opposition. Only on 4 April, when the invasion forces were already at sea, did the German naval staff begin to think that 'Weserübung' might be turning into 'a "race" for Scandinavia between England and Germany'.[123]

In this respect at least, Nuremberg did not distort historical truth. Within the narrow chronological confines imposed by the prosecution, and given the prosecution's success in excluding everything irrelevant to the question of 'what was within the knowledge of the defendants before 9 April, 1940',[124] the case against Raeder was proved. It did not amount to the whole picture, but that was not Nuremberg's concern.

VII

It remained only for the defence and prosecution to deliver their concluding speeches, and the defendants to make their final speeches, before the Tribunal reached judgment. Siemers dealt with Norway on 16 July 1946.[125] Only now did he achieve an effective presentation of the 'forcible anticipation' argument (despite interruptions by Lawrence). Citing authoritative legal opinion, he insisted that Germany's action against

Norway had been justified by the 'right of self-preservation' recognised in international law. It was a preventive action exactly comparable with, for example, the British occupation of Iceland in May 1940. The claim was scornfully dismissed by Shawcross ten days later: 'All the alleged intelligence reports contain no information which comes within miles of justifying an anticipatory invasion based – you might think it is laughable – on the doctrine of self-preservation.'[126] But the judges were not to be swayed so easily. The two British members of the Tribunal, Lawrence and Birkett, found themselves in an uncomfortable position as they joined their colleagues in drafting the judgment.

The Tribunal's deliberations on the Norwegian case have been described by Smith.[127] His discussion is marred by an apparent acceptance of the defence's claim that an Allied landing in Norway was being prepared, and would have taken place but for the German attack. But Smith's reconstruction of the British judges' motives is plausible. He suggests that they probably knew more than their colleagues about the British side of the story, and for this reason tried to modify the initial American draft, which had been influenced by the defence's arguments. Birkett's alternative formula – a simple assertion that the German claims were 'unfounded' – was backed by the French, but opposed by the Soviet judges. Judge Parker of the United States proposed a compromise formula which was eventually accepted. It acknowledged the existence of definite British plans, but did not accept the German claim to prior knowledge of them.[128]

This solution seems unexceptionable, but Smith is unhappy with it. He concedes that Parker's formula both prevented a British 'whitewash' and enabled Norway to be retained as an instance of German aggressive warfare. But, he concludes, 'the legalistic tunnel vision used to reach this result must leave most members of the laity with their heads shaking in wonder'. Presumably, therefore, the Tribunal ought to have accepted, if not the 'forcible anticipation', then certainly the *tu quoque* argument in this instance. Was such a decision remotely conceivable? Surely no Allied power would have permitted its record to be equated with that of Nazi Germany on such a sensitive political issue. One may regret the mixing of politics and law, but at Nuremberg it was unavoidable.

It is true that in one case, and one only, *tu quoque* was accepted as a valid defence at Nuremberg. The Tribunal was not prepared to convict Dönitz and Raeder on the charge of waging unrestricted submarine warfare, because the evidence brought before the court by Kranzbühler had shown that the Allies had conducted such warfare in exactly the same way.[129] As suggested above, however, the Tribunal would not have been justified in reaching a similar decision in the case of Norway, whatever the political considerations involved. The Tribunal did assert its judicial independence, and implicitly registered its dissatisfaction with the aggressive war charge, by acquitting four of the sixteen defendants indicted on the charge, and condemning none to death on that charge alone.[130] Raeder received a life sentence, Dönitz ten years.

No judicial body meeting so soon after the end of the war could have been in possession of 'all the facts'. It is not clear, however, that the Nuremberg Tribunal would have been any better informed if it had met later. And it would then have failed to answer the urgent political demand that justice should be done on the perpetrators of Nazi atrocities, and the no less sincere, if more naive, desire to outlaw war once and for all. It would probably have been better if the Tribunal had confined its attention to the charges of war crimes and crimes against humanity, but this was not obvious at the time. The drafters of the Nuremberg Charter faced a dilemma. On the one hand, they had to ensure that those responsible for a 'criminal war' were brought to justice as quickly as possible. On the other, they did not want 'a result which in the light of history will fail to justify the procedures which we have taken'.[131] They knew that the Nuremberg Tribunal could not hope to establish the full background to Nazi aggression in the time available; and they did not wish it to blur the issue by getting 'into an argument over the political and economic causes of this war'.[132] In the words of Justice Jackson, 'Our definition of crime does not involve causes; it involves only actual aggressive war – the attack.'[133] The pressure to obtain a conviction, and the desire to avoid political embarrassment, overrode historical objectivity in a number of cases at Nuremberg, of which Norway was one. But in the light of what is known about the background, it would be hard to sustain the claim that the Tribunal's judgment on Norway constituted a miscarriage of justice.

Notes

3. F. H. Hinsley and the Cambridge moles: two patterns of intelligence recruitment

1 Kim Philby, *My Silent War*, paperback edn (London, 1969), p. 17. The KGB assumed its present name only 1954. It was previously known successively as the Cheka (1917–22), the GPU (1922–3), the OGPU (1923–34), the NKVD (1934–41), the NKGB (1941–6) and the MGB (1946–53). To avoid confusion I shall refer throughout to the KGB.

2 Philby, *My Silent War*, p. 15.

3 Jonathan Haslam, *Soviet Foreign Policy 1930–33* (London, 1983), ch. 10.

4 *The Granta*, 7 Feb. 1934, p. 242.

5 C. W. Guillebaud, 'Politics and the Undergraduate in Oxford and Cambridge', *The Cambridge Review*, 26 Jan. 1934.

6 R. N. Carew Hunt, 'Willi Muenzenberg' in David Footman (ed.), *St Antony's Papers*, vol. IX (1960), pp. 72–3.

7 E. H. Carr, *The Twilight of Comintern 1930–1935* (London, 1982), pp. 10, 106.

8 Richard Crossman (ed.), *The God that Failed* (London, 1950), p. 35.

9 Goronwy Rees, *A Chapter of Accidents* (London, 1972), p. 135, private information.

10 Arthur Koestler, *The Invisible Writing*, Danube edn (London, 1969), pp. 239–43.

11 *ibid.*, pp. 244–5.

12 Ernst Henry [*sic*], *Stop Terrorism* (Moscow, 1982), pp. 32–3, 195; and private information. Earlier works by the same author used the name 'Henri'.

13 Ernst Henri, *Hitler Over Russia?* (London, 1936), p. vi.

14 Interview with Henri's former secretary, Edith Cobbett, broadcast in Part 3 of the BBC Radio 4 documentary series 'The Profession of Intelligence', written and presented by Christopher Andrew (producer Peter Everett), first broadcast 16 Aug. 1981.

15 Ernst Henri, 'The Revolutionary Movement in Germany. Part 1: The Groups of Five ("Fünfergruppen")', *New Statesman and Nation*, 5 Aug. 1933; and private information. The phrase 'group' or 'ring of five' has caused some misunderstanding. It referred in the 1930s to a particular type of small secret cell rather than to a particular number of conspirators. Not all groups of five

contained five members. MI5, however, seems to have understood the phrase literally.

16 Koestler, *Invisible Writing*, p. 30.
17 *New Statesman and Nation*, 5 Aug. 1933, p. 153.
18 *Ibid.*, 7 Apr. 1934, pp. 517–18.
19 Andrew Boyle, *The Climate of Treason* (London, 1979), pp. 151, 182, 209, 222. Remarkably, Brian Howard was taken on by MI5 as, in effect, a free-lance agent for a year at the beginning of the war.
20 *New Statesman and Nation*, 7 Apr. 1934, pp. 517–18.
21 Private information.
22 On Nechaev and the first Group of Five see Philip Pomper, *Sergei Nechaev* (New Brunswick, NJ, 1979). On Burgess and Trevelyan see Boyle, *Climate of Treason*, p. 116.
23 Elizabeth Monroe, *Philby of Arabia* (London, 1973), p. 209.
24 Mrs Jenifer Hart, interviewed by Christopher Andrew on BBC2 'Timewatch', 27 July 1983 (producer Robert Marshall); and further information supplied by Mrs Hart.
25 Michael Straight, interviewed by Christopher Andrew in Part 3 of 'The Profession of Intelligence'; see also Michael Straight, *After Long Silence* (London, 1983), pp. 129–30, 134–5, 143–4, 167–8.
26 Letter from 'Nigel West' in *The Listener*, 18 Aug. 1983.
27 Philby, *My Silent War*, p. 16.
28 Interview with Edith Cobbett. See above, note 14.
29 An extract from Henri's 1942 radio talk was re-broadcast in my report for 'Timewatch' on 27 July 1983, BBC2.
30 Most of my information on Henri's career since 1951 comes from Soviet dissidents who do not wish to be identified. I am indebted to Robert Marshall for help in obtaining this information. See also Stephen Cohen (ed.), *An End to Silence* (London, 1982), pp. 179, 182, 228–34; and R. Medvedev, 'Maclean, A Dissident Abroad', *The Times*, 31 May 1983.
31 Boyle, *Climate of Treason*, p. 114.
32 FO to Phipps, 11 Mar. 1938, Churchill College Archive Centre, PHPP 2/21 (Crown copyright).
33 Footman's talk, 'Albania, a Fish and a Motor Car', was broadcast on 2 Aug. 1937. BBC Archives.
34 FO 371/16009, file E3389, Public Record Office, Kew, London.
35 Records at the Intelligence Corps Museum, Ashford, Kent.
36 Guy Burgess, 'Draft Suggestions for Talks on Russia', 15 July 1941, BBC Archives.
37 *New Statesman and Nation*, 15 June 1940, p. 748.
38 *The Journal of Careers*, vol. XVII (1938), no. 188.
39 'John Whitwell' [Leslie Nicholson], *British Agent* (London, 1966), ch. 1.
40 Hugh Trevor-Roper, *The Philby Affair* (London, 1968), p. 47.
41 Dansey to Payne Best, 15 Dec. 1945, Payne Best MSS 79/57/1, Imperial War Museum.
42 'Nigel West', *MI5* (London, 1981), pp. 43–4; and private information.
43 'Notes about Room 40 and Sir Alfred Ewing in the 1914–1918 War', Oliver MSS, OLV/8, National Maritime Museum.
44 On Room 40 see especially Patrick Beesly, *Room 40* (London, 1982).
45 A. G. Denniston, untitled 21-page history of GC & CS between the wars, 2

Dec. 1944; kindly made available to me by his son Robin Denniston and now in Churchill College Archive Centre.

46 *Ibid.*
47 E. R. P. Vincent, Unpublished Memoirs, pp. 78–9; kindly made available to me by his widow Mrs Ivy Vincent who confirms the identity of Adcock (referred to in the text simply as 'a man I knew').
48 Denniston, history of GC & CS between the wars.
49 Christopher Andrew, 'Governments and Secret Services: A Historical Perspective', *International Journal*, vol. XXXIV (1979), no. 2, p. 167.
50 Letter to the author from Peter Twinn, 29 May 1981.
51 The names of the first sixteen university 'professor types' (from a list of over fifty) to arrive at Bletchley Park are given in correspondence in FO 366/1059. Eleven had a Cambridge background, though three had moved away (Birch to the stage, Bruford to Edinburgh, Waterhouse to Belfast). Three (Boase, Campbell and Last) came from Oxford, and two (Hatto and Norman) from London. The list of 'professor types' also included four non-academics who arrived at the beginning of the war: Admiral H. W. W. Hope (a veteran of Room 40), the publisher Nigel de Grey (also from Room 40), the business-man Alan Bacon and the writer R. Gore Brown (who stayed only briefly).
52 Vincent, Unpublished Memoirs.
53 Perhaps the first wartime mathematician recruited purely for his mathemat-ical ability was J. R. F. Jeffreys from Downing College, later to die prematurely of tuberculosis.
54 Interviews with Professor Hinsley, extracts from which were broadcast in Parts 2 and 3 of my BBC Radio 4 documentaries 'The Profession of Intelligence' (9 and 16 Aug. 1981).
55 My information on Captain Tuck's Japanese courses for intelligence officers comes from extracts from his papers kindly made available by his daughter, Mrs Sylvia Crotty, and from an undergraduate dissertation prepared under my supervision by Robert Stamp for Part II of the Cambridge Historical Tripos in 1982.
56 Interview with Patrick Wilkinson, extracts from which were broadcast in Part 2 of 'The Profession of Intelligence' (9 Aug. 1981).
57 F. H. Hinsley *et al.*, *British Intelligence in the Second World War*, vol. I (London, 1979), p. 273.
58 Vincent, Unpublished Memoirs, p. 168; cf. R. Lewin, *Ultra Goes To War* (London, 1978), p. 111.
59 Peter Calvocoressi, *Top Secret Ultra* (London, 1980), p. 65.
60 Interview with Professor Hinsley broadcast in Part 2 of 'The Profession of Intelligence' (9 Aug. 1981).
61 Hinsley *et al.*, *British Intelligence*, vol. I, pp. 273–4.
62 R. Godson ed., *Intelligence Requirements for the 1980s: Analysis and Estimates* (Washington, 1980), pp. 15–16.
63 Sadly, after the war Turing could no longer remember where he had hidden the silver ingots in the woods, and discovered that his other hiding place under a bridge had been cemented over. Andrew Hodges, *Alan Turing: The Enigma* (London, 1983), pp. 193, 345, 479. Lewin, *Ultra*, pp. 53, 57.
64 Quoted by kind permission of Patrick Wilkinson. Adcock had a very pink face; F. L. Lucas, another King's classicist, always wore sky-blue jackets.

Oliver Strachey, brother of Lytton and a founder member of GC & CS, wore a broad-brimmed black hat.

65 Among that remarkable company from 1941 was Hilary Brett, now Mrs Hilary Hinsley, recruited to Bletchley by the mathematician Shaun Wylie. At a time when GC & CS, like the civil service and most of the professions, somewhat undervalued female talents and paid women at a lower rate than men, Miss Brett was a fortunate exception. The Foreign Office assumed Hilary to be a man's name and paid her at the male rate.

4. *Strategy, arms and the collapse of France, 1930–40*

1 The full body of records of the Riom trial, housed at the Archives Nationales, is not generally open to researchers, but the testimony of those on trial and the depositions of a multitude of others can be found in the Daladier MS at the Fondation Nationale des Sciences Politiques in Paris. For an overview by an historian who has had access to Riom materials at the Archives Nationales, see Henri Michel, *Le procès de Riom* (Paris, 1979). The post-war inquiry by the Assemblée Nationale gave rise to ten volumes published under the title *Les événements survenus en France de 1933 à 1945*; two volumes (most of which consist of documents) take the form of a report by Charles Serre and the other eight present testimony (with some documents included).

2 See, especially, the thoughtful presentation by Henry Chabert, 'A Possible Historical Mistake: the Causes of the Allied Military Collapse in May 1940', *Proceedings of the First Annual Meeting of the Western Society for French History*, 1 (Mar. 1974), 379–90.

3 Gen. William E. Depuy, 'Technology and Tactics in Defense of Europe', *Army*, 29 (Apr. 1979), 17–18.

4 See *ibid.*, p. 15 (Depuy is a former commander of the United States Army Training and Doctrine Command); Pétain, 'Preface', to Gen. Narcisse Chauvineau, *Une invasion est-elle encore possible?* (Paris, 1939), p. vii; and the excerpt from a British official history of the western front in the First World War quoted in Capt. B. H. Liddell Hart, 'The Ratio of Troops to Space', *Journal of the Royal United Service Institution*, 105 (May 1960), 203.

5 Liddell Hart, 'Ratio', p. 201.

6 See, for example, John J. Mearsheimer, 'Precision-guided Munitions and Conventional Deterrence', *Survival*, 21 (Mar./Apr. 1979), 68–76; Daniel Gouré and Gordon McCormick, 'PGM: No Panacea', *ibid.*, 22 (Jan./Feb. 1980), 15–19; and Neville Brown, 'The Changing Face of Non-nuclear War', *ibid.*, 24 (Sept.–Oct. 1982), 211–19.

7 Col. T. N. Dupuy, *Numbers, Predictions and War* (Indianapolis and New York, 1979), pp. 14–15. Three shortcomings limit the conclusions that can be drawn from such a table. First, manpower is a poor proxy for effective fighting strength, especially as weaponry has become much more powerful in the twentieth century. Second, the table does not distinguish between manpower ratios on a front as a whole and at the main point of attack. Third, major battles are not necessarily typical battles, though of course any rule of thumb that did not lend itself to achieving victory in a major battle would be an unsatisfactory guide for military planning.

8 Whereas the defence won in five of six cases in which the offence had a numerical superiority of more than 2:1, the defence won in only two of fifteen cases in which it enjoyed better than numerical parity. *Ibid.*

9 For a recent analysis of how surprise can undercut quantitative assessments, see Richard K. Betts, *Surprise Attack* (Washington, D.C., 1982).

10 Dupuy, *Numbers*, pp. 98–9.

11 See the table in *ibid.*, pp. 234–7, and compare Dupuy's S_x/S_y index with the outcomes (not, unfortunately, quantified in the table) of the various engagements. See also HERO staff paper, 'Significance and Effects of Surprise in Modern War', *History, Numbers, and War*, 1 (spring 1977), 4.

12 In my usage, whereas the strategic level is defined in terms of decisions on how forces are to be distributed among fronts and when the forces on a particular front are to be used, and the tactical domain centres on the methods by which units on a given battlefield seek to attain immediate objectives, the operational level is characterised, for the offence, by decisions on where and how the main attack is to be made along a selected front and, for the defence, by how those offensive moves are to be countered by shifting defensive forces from their initial disposition. On the operational level as a distinct and important domain of military action and analysis, see Edward N. Luttwak, 'The Operational Level of War', *International Security*, 5 (winter 1980/81), 61–79.

13 Carl von Clausewitz, *On War*, trans. and ed. Michael Howard and Peter Paret (Princeton, 1976), pp. 198–201.

14 The conceptual thrust behind blitzkrieg has recently been given renewed attention by analysts who view current Soviet military doctrine in light of what Germany did in 1940. The best of many articles is Luttwak, 'Operational Level'.

15 *Ibid.*, 67. It should be noted that the blitzkrieg in May 1940 differed in important respects from other German offensives in 1939–41. It should also be noted that the conceptual elegance of the campaign against France belies the twists and turns of the process by which the plan emerged. See Hans-Adolf Jacobsen, *Fall Gelb* (Wiesbaden, 1957).

16 The best example of such an effort is R. H. S. Stolfi, 'Equipment for Victory in France in 1940', *History*, 55 (Feb. 1970), 1–20.

17 The most cogent presentation is John J. Mearsheimer, 'Why the Soviets Can't Win Quickly in Central Europe', *International Security*, 7 (summer 1982), 3–39.

18 See the sources cited in *ibid.*, pp. 3–5. In actual numbers of weapons, the Warsaw Pact's advantage was 2.5:1 in tanks, somewhat higher in artillery, and somewhat less in anti-tank guided missiles and tactical aircraft. The overall index of relative force levels differs substantially from a simple comparison of numbers because of the assumptions that it embodies about relative quality and because of the way that it aggregates the value of various weapons.

19 *Ibid.*, pp. 9–30. Two assumptions in this argument are that NATO forces are initially distributed, in terms of effective fighting power, more or less evenly among corps sectors across the front and that the optimal breadth of a breakthrough attempt is the same as the width of a NATO corps sector.

20 Those four axes are the North German plain (leading to Hanover), the Fulda gap (northeast of Frankfurt), the Göttingen corridor (east of the Ruhr), and

the Hof corridor (northeast of Stuttgart). The dubious presumption is that a major thrust through the south toward Munich would not be easy because of the mountainous terrain along the Czechoslovakian border and would not be attractive because it would not result by itself in a decisive victory (though the topography beyond Munich would permit a turn toward Stuttgart and a possible envelopment of the forces in the VII American Corps Sector in the area of the Franconian Hills). It is further presumed that a major thrust through the extreme north would be hampered by urban sprawl around Hamburg and would also not be a decisive blow to NATO (though surely the loss of ports along the North Sea would be very serious and there would open up the danger of an armoured manoeuvre, after Bremen, southward behind the hilly spine of West Germany and into the core of NATO's rear).

21 Mearsheimer, 'Why', pp. 15, 24, 27.

22 Even the 1976 version of the United States Army field manual *FM100-5: Operations* had an air of pessimism about it. (The 1982 version is more optimistic.)

23 We have not only shown that the 3:1 rule of thumb rests on treacherous historical ground but have also suggested that Liddell Hart's seminal notions on force-to-space ratios are misleading. Those who are familiar with the work of Professor Hinsley and others on intelligence in the Second World War will appreciate that the gap between the collection and the accurate, timely interpretation of data can be formidable. And those who are familiar with the campaign on the western front in 1940 will look askance at confident assumptions about how terrain must limit the scope for armoured attack and operational surprise. They will also have in mind the difficulties of coalition warfare with respect to timely mobilisation and coordinated operations. And, not least, historians will realise that the character of virtually all campaigns in the early stages of major wars in the twentieth century has been at odds with the pre-war expectations of the defensive side.

24 For French fears of a German attack through Switzerland, see Service Historique de l'Armée de Terre (hereafter SHAT), 1N47, especially 'Instruction générale pour le cas d'invasion de la Suisse par nos adversaires' by Gen. Georges, 20 June 1939; and Ministère des Affaires Etrangères (hereafter MAE), série Y, vol. 79, note by Gen. Gamelin for the Comité de Guerre of 8 Sept. 1939.

25 See D. C. Watt, *Too Serious a Business* (London, 1975), pp. 90–1; the map in Gen. P. E. Tournoux, *Défense des frontières* (Paris, 1960), pp. 72–3; and the lamentation in Charles de Gaulle, *Vers l'armée de métier* (Paris, 1934), pp. 9–17.

26 Martin Van Creveld, *Supplying War* (Cambridge, 1977), pp. 144–7.

27 Malcolm W. Hoag, 'Increasing Returns in Military Production Functions', in Roland N. McKean, ed., *Issues in Defense Economics* (New York, 1967), p. 4.

28 For the best examples of 'growth accounting', see the following works by Edward F. Denison: *The Sources of Economic Growth in the United States and the Alternatives Before Us* (New York, 1962); *Why Growth Rates Differ* (Washington, D.C., 1967); *Accounting for United States Economic Growth, 1929–1969* (Washington D.C., 1974); and *Accounting for Slower Economic Growth* (Washington D.C., 1979).

29 On the consequences of one-year service, see Archives Nationales (hereafter

AN), Tardieu MS, 324AP62, report by Weygand, 28 May 1932, enclosed in a letter from Weygand to Tardieu, 30 May 1932. For a monograph that brings out well how manpower constraints weighed on the minds of French strategists, see Judith M. Hughes, *To the Maginot Line* (Cambridge, Mass., 1971).

30 The figures for manpower costs are drawn from SHAT, 1N42, annex II to a report for the Conseil Supérieur de la Guerre (hereafter CSG), n.s., n.d. (but the fall of 1934). For the cost of a light tank (at the turn of 1935–6), see SHAT, 5N582, annex to a report by Jugnet, 15 Jan. 1939.

31 For explicit statements to this effect, see AN, Tardieu MS, 324AP62, report by Weygand, 28 May 1932; SHAT, 5N579, note by Gamelin, 10 Oct. 1932; SHAT, 7N2292, General Staff note, 18 Jan. 1936; and SHAT, 7N4210, meeting of the Conseil Consultatif de l'Armement, 1 June 1938.

32 The institutional manifestation of that view was the establishment of a high-level Conseil Consultatif de l'Armement (hereafter CCA) in 1931 and, inside the General Staff, a special technical office. For the origins of the CCA, see SHAT, 1N41, Pétain to Maginot, 16 Dec. 1930.

33 A case in point is General Julien Dufieux (Inspector-General of the Infantry). See SHAT, 1N42, note by Dufieux, 13 Jan. 1934; and Dufieux to Daladier, 19 May 1938, in *Les événements survenus . . . Témoinages et documents*, vol. IV, pp. 870–1.

34 SHAT,1N22, meeting of the Conseil Supérieur de la Guerre, 24 Mar. 1934; and SHAT, 7N4209, meeting of the CCA, 28 May 1934, and 'Note concernant les engins blindés', n.s., n.d. (but Jan. 1935).

35 See *Les événements survenus . . . Rapport*, vol. II, pp. 301–3; and Lt Col Raymond E. Bell, Jr, 'Division Cuirassée 1940', *Armor* 83 (Jan.–Feb. 1974), 25–31.

36 See the data in SHAT, 1N42, note by Dufieux, 13 Jan. 1934, and 5N582, annex to a report by Jugnet, 15 Jan. 1939.

37 The General Staff had envisaged a ratio of one battalion of heavy tanks for every three battalions of light tanks, and the Inspector of Battle Tanks had wanted a ratio of one to two, but by September 1939 the ratio in battalions was one to four and in actual numbers one to six. See Lt Col Henry Dutailly, *Les problèmes de l'armée de terre française (1935–1939)* (Paris, 1980), pp. 152–3. Much of the pressure to concentrate on cheaper tanks seems to have come from budget-conscious war ministers. See SHAT, 5N581, 'Journal de Marche' of Jean Fabry, 11 Sept. 1935; and Daladier to Dufieux, 16 July 1937, *Les événements survenus . . . Témoinages et documents*, vol. IV, p. 1066.

38 The issue of how to economise on weaponry is a complex one whose key elements are imponderable. Even within the framework of forward defence, putting guns inside fortifications may not prove to be cost-effective if those fortifications do not cover the entire front: weapons fixed under concrete cannot easily be moved to other sectors where they are more urgently needed. And once the assumption of forward defence is relaxed, the issue becomes even more problematic. A defensive strategy in which firepower is concentrated in a mobile reserve may in theory economise on weaponry much more than permanent fortifications do, but in practice such a mobile defence requires a level of skill that few armies have attained.

39 I have not seen the study – Malcolm W. Hoag, *Strengthening NATO Capabilities*, Rand Corporation Report 2039 (Santa Monica, 1977) – which

is classified, but it is summarised in Lt Col Waldo D. Freeman, Jr, *NATO Central Region Forward Defense*, National Defense University, National Security Affairs Issue Paper Series 81–3 (Washington, D.C., 1981). Freeman's paper is a useful introduction to 'force multipliers'.

40 Fondation Nationale des Sciences Politiques (hereafter FNSP), Daladier MS, 1DA7, Dr3, sdr d, briefing paper for Daladier ('Audition de M. le Ministre par la Sous-Commission de Défense Nationale'), n.s., n.d. (but second half of 1936).

41 On the French fortifications and smaller works, the basic study is that of Tournoux, *Défense des frontières*.

42 Giulio Douhet, *The Command of the Air*, trans. Dino Ferrari (New York, 1942). This edition contains Douhet's original work of 1921, plus his subsequent elaborations and defences of it.

43 On the army's attitude toward the programmes of the air force, see Service Historique de la Marine (hereafter SHM), 1BB²229, Weygand to Hergault, 27 Apr. 1931, meetings of the Haut Comité Militaire, 23 May 1932 and 20 March 1933, and letter from Fabry to Denain, 10 May 1935; Service Historique de l'Armée de l'Air (hereafter SHAA), 2B 180, unsigned note on 'Question soumise au Conseil Supérieur de l'Air du 24 Novembre 1936'; SHAA, 2B1, Daladier to Cot, 4 Dec. 1936; Archives Nationales, Reynaud MS, 74AP12, letter to Reynaud from the head of the Second Bureau of the Air General Staff, 7 June 1937; and FNSP, Daladier MS, 4DA3, Dr1, sdr a, Gamelin to Daladier, 11 Feb. 1938.

44 Dupuy, *Numbers*, pp. 71–94.

45 See de Gaulle, *Vers l'armée de métier*; Paul Reynaud, *Le problème militaire français* (Paris, 1937); and the documents in the Reynaud MS, 74AP12, at the Archives Nationales. Letters from de Gaulle to Reynaud have been published in Evelyne Demey, *Paul Reynaud, mon père* (Paris, 1980).

46 See AN, Reynaud MS, 74AP12, 'Etude Relative à l'Amendement de M. Paul Reynaud', by Gamelin, n.d. (but spring of 1935), and note by the General Staff, 11 July 1936; SHAT, 5N581, 'Journal de Marche' of Jean Fabry, 6 Jan. 1936; and FNSP, Daladier MS, 4DA3, Dr 4, sdr b, note by Daladier's *cabinet*, n.d. (but late July 1936), and 'Note au sujet de l'armée de métier,' n.s., n.d. (but late July 1936), and 4DA7, Dr1, sdr a, memo by Gamelin, 27 Jan. 1937.

47 In the longest exposition that I have found of the personal views of General Maurice Gamelin (Chief of the General Staff from 1931 and prospective commander-in-chief from 1935) on how armoured divisions should be used, only two perfunctory paragraphs in twelve pages deal with the case of a breakthrough by an adversary. SHAT, 1N38, memo by Gamelin, 28 June 1938. It is worth noting that de Gaulle, far from elaborating on how an elite corps might counter a deep strategic penetration, managed to convince himself that Germany would seek only limited territorial objectives in a future war. See de Gaulle, *Vers l'armée de métier*, pp. 79–85.

48 De Gaulle to Reynaud, 8 May 1935 and 25 May 1936, in Demey, *Reynaud*, pp. 292–4, 300; and Reynaud, *Le problème*, pp. 50–7.

49 See the documents cited in note 46, plus FNSP, Daladier MS, 4DA1, Dr4, sdr b, note sent by Gamelin to Daladier, 10 July 1936, and AN, Reynaud MS, 74AP12, 'Etude sommaire sur la constitution d'un corps spécialisé', by the Secrétariat Général of the War Ministry, n.d. (but spring 1935). There were in fact difficulties with recruitment in 1936, the first of the hollow years. See

FNSP, Daladier MS, 4DA1, Dr3, two notes by the First Bureau of the General Staff, 20 June 1936.

50 For the slow process by which armoured divisions came into being, see SHAT, 1N22, meetings of the CSG, 29 Apr. 1936, 15 Dec. 1937, and 22 Dec. 1938; the materials in FNSP, Daladier MS, 4DA7, Dr1; the testimony of General Bruché (commander of the Second Armoured Division) in *Les événements survenus . . . Témoinages et documents*, vol. v, pp. 1214ff; and Gen. Maurice Gamelin, *Servir*, vol. I (Paris, 1946), pp. 266–7.

51 See the data in Organisation of European Economic Cooperation, *Industrial Statistics 1900–1959* (Paris, 1960), p. 9.

52 In addition to the sheer size of the military requirements, another reason for the doubts of the High Command about its budgetary prospects was the evident desire of the Poincaré government to expand domestic social expenditure. See SHAT, 2N6, meeting of the Conseil Supérieur de la Défense Nationale (hereafter CSDN), 4 June 1928; and MAE, Herriot MS, journal, vol. XIII, p. 128.

53 For the differing views of the generals and the politicians, see SHAT, 1N21, meetings of CSG, 17 Dec. 1926, 18 Jan. 1927, and 14 Dec. 1927, and 2N6, meeting of CSDN, 4 June 1928.

54 SHAT, 6N364, Maginot to Piétri and Flandin, 14 June 1930, 7N4207, note by the *cabinet technique* of the Chief of the General Staff, 21 Apr. 1931, and 10P155 (old classification), report by a commission established to investigate the use of military appropriations, 21 May 1935.

55 The best archival source on the budget cuts and their consequences is SHAT, 1N42, which contains the staff papers of General Maxime Weygand, Vice-President of the Conseil Supérieur de la Guerre and designated Generalissimo from 1931 to 1935. For the conflicts between Weygand and civilian leaders over the cuts, see Philip C. F. Bankwitz, *Maxime Weygand and Civil–Military Relations in Modern France* (Cambridge, Mass., 1967), ch. 3. On the state of mind among the leading generals by 1935, see Gen. André Beaufre, *1940*, trans. Desmond Flower (London, 1967), p. 44.

56 My conclusions on these financial constraints are based on the data and notes in Ministère des Finances, F^{30}/2340–2344.

57 FNSP, Daladier MS, 1DA6, Dr6, sdr b, and 1DA7, Dr4, sdr a, handwritten notes for, and typed fragments of, Daladier's unpublished memoirs; and archives of the Sénat, Commission des Finances, 29 Sept. 1936, statement by Finance Minister Vincent Auriol, pp. 209–10.

58 See the table in Robert Frankenstein, *Le prix du réarmament français (1935–1939)* (Paris, 1982), p. 307.

59 AN, Dautry MS, 307AP22, 'Etude sur la main d'oeuvre d'armement', written in Jan. 1943 by J. Toutee in the name of Raoul Dautry, who was Minister of Armament in 1939–40, and 307AP108, report by the Secrétariat Général Administratif of the Ministry of Armament, 12 Mar. 1940.

60 The decision to go so far to the northeast was the work of General Maurice Gamelin, who was Chief of Staff of National Defence and Commander-in-Chief of the Army. For his subsequent justification of the decision, see AN, Reynaud MS, 74AP22, report to Daladier, 18 May 1940, and Gamelin, *Servir*, vol. I, pp. 81–108. The decision was opposed by General Alphonse Georges, who was Commander-in-Chief of French forces on the northeastern front. See Georges's testimony in *Les événements survenus . . . Témoinages et*

documents, vol. III, pp. 684–6. The most well-informed secondary account is Jeffery A. Gunsburg, *Divided and Conquered* (Westport, Conn., 1979), pp. 119–32, 138–42.

61 The reasons for this overcommitment of forces are still obscure, but see Georges's testimony in *Les événements survenus ... Témoinages et documents*, vol. III, pp. 687–8, and also Gamelin, *Servir*, vol. I, pp. 304–5, 316.

62 See the analysis in Major Robert A. Doughty, 'French Antitank Doctrine, 1940: The Antidote That Failed', *Military Review*, 56 (May 1976), 36–48.

5. Vansittart's administration of the Foreign Office in the 1930s

I am indebted to the English Speaking Union of NSW for the award of the Ruth A. Cumming Scholarship, and to St John's College, Cambridge, for grants towards travel expenses.

1 Norman Rose, *Vansittart: study of a diplomat* (London, 1978), pp. 63–102.

2 X6175/6175/504, FO366/918; X1465/653/504, FO371/1031.

3 Stephen Roskill, *Hankey: man of secrets*, 3 vols. (London, 1970–4), III, pp. 155–64; *The memoirs of Lord Gladwyn* (London, 1972), p. 57; Lord Strang, *Home and abroad* (London, 1956), p. 310; D. C. M. Platt, *Finance, trade and politics in Britain 1815–1914* (Oxford, 1968), pp. xx–xxx.

4 Frank Ashton-Gwatkin, 'Thoughts on the Foreign Office: 1918–1939', *Contemporary Review*, CLXXXVIII (1955), pp. 374–8.

5 Fisher to a Treasury organization committee (1936), quoted in G. C. Peden, *British rearmament and the treasury* (Edinburgh, 1979), p. 35. For a full statement of Fisher's views see his memorandum and evidence to the Royal Commission on the Civil Service, 30 December 1930. Minutes of evidence, pp. 1267–94; 1929–31. Non-parl.

6 Horace P. Hamilton, 'Sir Warren Fisher and the public service', *Public Administration*, XXI (1951), pp. 3–38; Henry Roseveare, *The treasury* (London, 1969), pp. 247–8, 253.

7 Lord Vansittart, *The mist procession* (London, 1958), p. 394; Rose, *Vansittart*, pp. 66–70; David Carlton, *MacDonald versus Henderson: the foreign policy of the second Labour government* (London, 1970), pp. 15–16, 23n; Hugh Dalton, *Call back yesterday: memoirs, 1887–1931* (London, 1953), pp. 209, 215, 246; *The diaries of Sir Robert Bruce Lockhart, 1915–1938* (London, 1973), p. 351.

8 Vansittart, *The mist procession*, p. 350.

9 According to Sir Horace Hamilton 'there seemed no limit to what he would do for his friends'. *D.N.B. 1941–1950* (Oxford, 1959), p. 255. Lady O'Malley likewise gives a remarkable account of 'the generosity, kindness, even affection' which Fisher showed to her and her husband after Owen O'Malley's dismissal from the Foreign Office in 1928. Ann Bridge [Mary Lady O'Malley], *Permission to resign* (London, 1971), *passim.*, but especially pp. 127–33. Cf. Lord Avon, *The Eden memoirs. Facing the dictators* (London, 1962), pp. 319–20, 447–8, 521, and Walford Selby, *Diplomatic twilight 1930–1940* (London, 1953), pp. 1–6.

10 Edward Bridges, *The treasury* (London, 1964), pp. 171, 175.

11 *Chief of staff: the diaries of Lieutenant-General Sir Henry Pownall 1933–1940* ed. Brian Bond (London, 1972), pp. 35–6; Peden, *British rearmament*, p. 27.

12 D. G. Boadle, 'The formation of the Foreign Office Economic Relations Section, 1930–1937', *Historical Journal*, xx (1977), pp. 919–36. Wellesley himself visualized the economic department as a means of establishing FO control in areas presently managed by the Treasury and the Board of Trade. His long-term objective was 'to assert the foreign secretary's dominating influence and co-ordinating control' through the 'right of veto over any domestic measure likely to produce international friction'. 'If he is to substantiate his case he must have at his disposal the necessary independent machinery' and, provided his views seem sound, they 'should prevail over lesser considerations'. Victor Wellesley, *Diplomacy in fetters* (London, 1944), pp. 194, 196–8.

13 Note by Fisher on economic inter-departmental liaison, 25 Jan. 1934, F13701/1, T160/742.

14 L1994/51/405, FO370/471; L5309/51/405, FO370/472.

15 Minutes by Wellesley and Ashton-Gwatkin on W12966/278/50, FO371/17318; W1617/1617/50, FO371/18500.

16 DRC, 11, 19 Feb. 1934, Cab. 16/109. Fisher was unsuccessful, however, in his bid to secure appointment to the Chiefs of Staff sub-committee of the Committee of Imperial Defence: Fisher to H. J. Wilson, 15 May 1939, Fisher papers, LSE.

17 NCM (35) 3, Cab. 16/111; DRC 16, 19, Cab. 16/109.

18 DC(M) (32) 55th, 24 July 1934, Cab. 16/110; C.32(34), 25 Sept. 1934, Cab. 23/79; N. Chamberlain diary, 9 Oct. 1934; C.36(34), 24 Oct. 1934, Cab. 23/80; N. Chamberlain to his sister, 27 Oct. 1934, NC18/1/893.

19 V. H. Rothwell, 'The mission of Sir Frederick Leith-Ross to the far-east, 1935–1936', *Historical Journal*, xviii(1975), pp. 147–69.

20 Minute by Vansittart, 14 Apr. 1934, W3929/293/50, FO371/18487.

21 X1227, 1376, 2666, 3282/157/504, FO366/935.

22 Civil Service. R. Com. Rep., §§250–1; 1930–31 Cmd. 3909, X, 517; Robert T. Nightingale, 'The personnel of the British Foreign and Diplomatic Service, 1851–1929', *American Political Science Review*, xxiv (1930), pp. 310–31; Harold Nicolson MS diary, 11 July 1930; Harold Nicolson, *Curzon: the last phase, 1919–1925. A study in post-war diplomacy* (London, 1934), pp. 382–408; Harold Nicolson,'The foreign service', in William A. Robson (ed.), *The British Civil Servant* (London, 1937), pp. 47–63.

23 X3998/1602/504, FO 366/882.

24 X2039/86/504, FO 366/975.

25 X3282/157/504, FO 366/935.

26 Roseveare, *The treasury*, pp. 252–3.

27 Public accounts committee. Report, minutes of evidence; 1934–35 (93, 99), v, 1.

28 Public accounts committee. Report, minutes of evidence, QQ. 4428–30; 1935–36 (45, 144), v, 1.

29 *The Reith diaries* ed. Charles Stuart (London, 1975), pp. 210 (27 Mar. 1936), 211 (2 July 1936), 212 (20 July 1936).

30 Eden to the King, 8 Jan. 1936, *Documents on British Foreign Policy 1919–1939* [hereafter *DBFP*], ii, xv, no. 437; Eden to Baldwin, 27 Dec. 1936, Baldwin papers, 124, ff. 55–7; Vansittart to Baldwin, 30 Dec. 1936, *ibid.*, 171, ff. 326–7; Fisher to Neville Chamberlain, 15 Sept. 1936, quoted in G. C.

Peden, 'Sir Warren Fisher and British rearmament against Germany', *English Historical Review,* xciv (1979), p. 42.

31 *The diplomatic diaries of Oliver Harvey 1937–1940* ed. John Harvey (London, 1970), p. 44 (4 May 1937); Avon, *Facing the dictators,* p. 521.

32 Proposal for the establishment of a Politico-Intelligence Department in the Foreign Office, 1 Dec. 1930, W12855/12855/50, FO371/14939.

33 Boadle, 'Formation of the . . . ERS', pp. 921–7.

34 Minutes by Craigie and Wellesley, 6 Jan. 1932, W341/63/50, FO371/16384; unsigned TS., 18 Feb. 1932, and report on economic work in 1932 by Ashton-Gwatkin, 5 Jan. 1933, W278/278/50, FO371/17318.

35 Report on economic section in 1933, 5 Jan. 1934, W293/293/50, FO371/18487.

36 Minute by Vansittart, 30 Jan. 1934, *ibid.;* X4012/157/504, FO366/935.

37 *The records of the Foreign Office 1782–1939* (London, 1969), p. 15; P. J. Byrd, 'Britain and the *anschluss* 1931–8: aspects of appeasement' (Univ. of Wales [Aberystwyth] Ph.D. thesis, 1971), pp. 150–1; Valentine Lawford, *Bound for diplomacy* (London, 1963), pp. 261–2; Owen O'Malley, *The phantom caravan* (London, 1954), p. 155.

38 X4012/157/504, FO366/935; X86/86/504, FO366/975.

39 X429/86/504, *ibid.* There subsequently was a good deal of controversy over whether a separate department had been necessary: L277/89/405, FO370/521.

40 X2868/2868/504, FO366/983; X3094/43/504, FO366/975; W8502/7512/ 41, FO371/22688.

41 Vansittart outlined FO procedure in a letter to the Austrian minister, George Franckenstein, 21 May 1930, FO366/781; Civil Service. R. Com. minutes of evidence, p. 851; 1929–31. Non-parl.

42 *Bruce Lockhart diaries,* pp. 327 (6 Sept. 1935), 344 (26 May 1936); Phipps to Vansittart, 1 May 1933, Phipps papers 2/17.

43 Lawford, *Bound for diplomacy,* pp. 233, 237, 239–40, 247, 255–6, 260; Wigram to Phipps, 17 Dec. 1935, Phipps papers 2/25; Allen Leeper to his father, St Catherine's day 1931; 5 Apr., 11 May, Ascension day, 7 Sept. 1933, Leeper papers (Melbourne, Australia); Sargent to Phipps, Phipps to Sargent, 6, 8 June 1936, Phipps papers 2/10.

44 Vansittart to Phipps, 23 Aug. 1934, 12 Feb., 26 Apr. 1935, Phipps papers 2/17; Rumbold to Nicolson, 28 May 1930, Rumbold papers.

45 *D.N.B. 1941–1950,* pp. 670–1; Phipps to Simon, 4 Jan. 1934 and minute by Vansittart, 9 Jan. 1934, FO794/16.

46 Fisher to Vansittart, 8 Jan. 1934, FO794/8. This previously unpublished letter gives direct and unequivocal evidence of an attempt by Fisher to exert influence over FO appointments. Hitherto the 'weightiest evidence' against him (Rose, *Vansittart,* p. 86 n32) was provided by Eden in his memoirs (Avon, *Facing the dictators,* pp. 319–20, 521).

47 Ronald Lindsay to Vansittart, 5 Jan. 1933, FO794/17; Roskill, *Hankey,* iii, pp. 56–7; Vansittart to Simon, 13 Jan. 1934, FO794/8.

48 Fisher to Phipps, 21 Jan. 1937, Phipps papers 3/2.

49 Vansittart remained loyal to his associates. He helped pay Allen Leeper's medical bills during what proved to be his final illness (*Bruce Lockhart diaries,* p. 352), and showed great kindness to Wigram's widow (Churchill to

his wife, 7 Jan. 1937, in Martin Gilbert, *Winston S. Churchill*, Companion vol. v, pt 3 (London, 1982), p. 527). But he expected loyalty in return. Lady Vansittart recalled (conversation with D.G.B., 29 Oct. 1974) his disappointment when Churchill's Second World War memoirs offered such grudging acknowledgement of his assistance during the thirties. Cf. Rose, *Vansittart*, p. 111. Vansittart to Phipps, 5 Mar. 1935, Phipps papers 2/17.

50 Bridge, *Permission to resign* , pp. 16–17, 32–3, 69, 73, 101; O'Malley, *The phantom caravan*, pp. 107, 169, 178–9, 234–5. Draft instructions for Sir Eric Phipps, with comments by Vansittart, 28 Sept. 1933, O'Malley memoranda 1928–41 (in possession of Mrs Zara Steiner).

51 C9520/1762/3, FO371/16640; C10818/2092/3, FO371/16645; R2190/37/ 3, FO371/18351; O'Malley, *The phantom caravan*, p. 155.

52 *DBFP*, ii, xiv, no. 366 n6; W3851/79/98, FO371/20472; J5429/216/1, O'Malley memoranda; Wigram to Phipps, 28 May [1936], Phipps papers 2/25; *DBFP*, ii, xvi, no. 343 n2, 361 n4.

53 According to Lady O'Malley, Vansittart was fully aware of O'Malley's 'all-too-well-known failings'. However, as O'Malley himself observed, Vansittart was 'always friendly' and ready to assist his advancement. This is something of an understatement, since it was Vansittart who took the lead in securing O'Malley's reinstatement, after his dismissal from the Foreign Office in 1928. Bridge, *Permission to resign*, pp. 59, 62–4, 72–3.

54 Rumbold to Selby, 15 July 1927, FO794/10; Vansittart to Henderson, 18 Apr. 1935, FO800/268. Thomas Jones, *A diary with letters 1931–1950* (London, 1954), pp. 305 (15 Jan. 1937), 314 (15 Feb. 1937), makes it clear that Henderson was Vansittart's chosen candidate. Jones earlier had tried to persuade Baldwin to send either Lord Halifax or Lord Willingdon (both former viceroys of India) to Berlin. Undoubtedly the fear of a politician being appointed increased Vansittart's determination to fill the post from within the Diplomatic service at any cost. cf. Vansittart, *The mist procession*, pp. 183–4, 253, 294–5, 394, and Rose, *Vansittart*, p. 203.

55 Clifford Norton to Henderson, 9 July 1937, FO800/268. O'Malley wrote to Henderson on 10 June 1937, expressing satisfaction that he shared his views, and reminding him he could rely on backing from the highest level outside the Foreign Office. (*ibid.*)

56 Vansittart, *The mist procession*, p. 399; Martin Gilbert, *Winston S. Churchill*, V: 1922–1939 (London, 1976), pp. 630–4 *et seq.*

57 According to Vansittart, Eden wanted 'a tame and colourless civil servant with less character, less knowledge, and less persistence in arguing with politicians when he thought they were wrong'. Hugh Dalton MS diaries, vol. xix, 12 Apr. 1938.

58 Vansittart, *The mist procession*, p. 399.

59 *Ibid.*, p. 542; Nicolson MS diary, 31 June 1938; Vansittart papers 4/6; Avon, *Facing the dictators*, p. 242.

60 Vansittart minute, 8 June 1935, quoted in Gilbert, *Churchill*, v, p. 631 n1.

6. Italy's historians and the myth of Fascism

Abbreviations
A.N.I.   Associazione Nazionalista Italiana
D.C.   Democrazia Cristiana

G.U.F.   Gruppi Universitari Fascista
M.S.I.   Movimento Sociale Italiano
P.C.I.   Partito Comunista Italiano
P.L.I.   Partito Liberale Italiano
P.N.F.   Partito Nazionale Fascista
P.R.I.   Partito Repubblicano Italiano
P.S.D.I. Partito Socialista Democratico Italiano
P.S.I.   Partito Socialista Italiano
S.P.D.   Sozialdemokratische Partei Deutschlands

1 D. McKay, 'Tenth international congress of historical sciences', *American Historical Review*, LXI, 1956, pp. 504–11.
2 C. Delzell, 'Italian historical scholarship: a decade of recovery and development, 1945–1955', *Journal of Modern History*, XXVIII, 1956, pp. 374, 377–8, 388; cf. E. P. Noether, 'Italy reviews its Fascist past', *American Historical Review*, LXI, 1956, pp. 877–99.
3 E.g. see C. M. Woodhouse, *Modern Greece: a short history* (London, 1977); W. H. McNeill, *The Greek dilemma* (London, 1947); *The metamorphosis of Greece since World War II* (Oxford, 1978).
4 For a first exploration of some of these themes within a rather parochial context, see K. Adler and J. G. Paterson, 'Red Fascism – the merger of Nazi Germany and Soviet Russia in the American image of totalitarianism, 1930s–1950s', *American Historical Review*, LXXV, 1970.
5 See e.g. J. A. Moses, *The politics of illusion: the Fischer controversy in German historiography* (St Lucia, 1975); W. R. Louis (ed.), *The origins of the Second World War: A. J. P. Taylor and his critics* (New York, 1972).
6 S. Hoffman, 'Introduction' to M. Ophuls, *The Sorrow and the Pity* (St Albans, 1975).
7 See M. L. Salvadori, *Gaetano Salvemini* (Turin, 1963), pp. 32–3, for the circumstances in which Chabod helped organise and achieve this flight.
8 E.g. see C. M. De Vecchi di Val Cismon, *Bonifica fascista della cultura* (Milan, 1937).
9 For introductory studies see e.g. P. V. Cannistraro, *La Fabbrica del consenso: Fascismo e mass media* (Bari, 1975); G. Turi, *Fascismo e il consenso degli intellettuali* (Bologna, 1981); and, in English, the excellent new study of popular culture V. De Grazia, *The culture of consent: mass organisation of leisure in Fascist Italy* (Cambridge, 1981).
10 Cf. the very soft G. B. Guerri, *Giuseppe Bottai: un fascista critico* (Milan, 1976).
11 R. Bosworth, *Italy and the approach of the First World War* (London, 1983), pp. 127–8.
12 See R. Zangrandi, *Il lungo viaggio attraverso il fascismo* (Milan, 1962); cf. A. Spinosa, *I figli del Duce* (Milan, 1983), pp. 150–65 for the special role of Mussolini's eldest son, Vittorio.
13 E.g. see R. Romeo, 'Rileggendo Volpe' in *Italia moderna fra storia e storiografia* (Florence, 1977), pp. 193–7.
14 G. Turi, 'Il problema Volpe', *Studi Storici*, 19, 1978, pp. 176, 183–5.
15 R. Romano, *La storiografia italiana oggi* (Rome, 1978), p. 49; B. Vigezzi, 'Politica estera e opinione pubblica in Italia dal 1870 al 1914. Orientamenti

degli studi dopo il 1945 e prospettive della ricerca' in *Collection de l'Ecole française de Rome* (Rome, 1981), pp. 80, 82–3.

16 See especially *Studi e ricerche in onore de Gioacchino Volpe nel centenario della nascita* (Rome, 1978). The relevant publishing house is Giovanni Volpe editore.

17 E.g. see A. Casali, *Storici italiani fra le due guerre: La 'Nuova Rivista Storica' 1917–1943* (Naples, 1980), pp. xiii–xiv.

18 G. Fortunato, *Carteggio, 1865–1911*, ed. E. Gentile (Bari, 1978), pp. 122; 149.

19 G. Volpe, *Guerra dopoguerra fascismo* (Venice, 1928), p. 9.

20 *Ibid.*, pp. 259–63; B. Mussolini, *Opera omnia*, eds. E. and D. Susmel (Florence, 1951–63), vol. XVI, p. 22.

21 G. Volpe, *Guerra dopoguerra fascismo*, pp. 30, 135, 152, 180, 205.

22 G. Volpe, 'Preface' to R. Truffi (ed.), *Precursori dell'Impero Africano: lettere inedite* (Rome, 1936), p. 17.

23 See R. J. B. Bosworth, *Italy, the least of the Great Powers* (Cambridge, 1979), pp. 59–63; 89; 121–3.

24 G. Volpe, *Guerra dopoguerra fascismo*, p. 377.

25 *Ibid.*, p. 7.

26 *Ibid.*, p. 262.

27 *Ibid.*, p. 384.

28 *Ibid.*, p. 414.

29 G. Volpe, *Pacifismo e storia* (Rome, 1934), pp. 7–8, 12, 14–15, 42.

30 *Ibid.*, pp. 27, 39–40, 42.

31 G. Volpe, *Storia della Corsica italiana* (Milan, 1939).

32 *Ibid.*, p. 11 dedicated the book to 'questa Corsica italiana, che non sarà tutta la Corsica ma è il più di essa'.

33 G. Volpe, *Vittorio Emanuele III* (Milan, 1939).

34 G. Volpe, *Italia moderna*, 3 vols. (Florence, 1943–52); cf. R. Romeo, 'Rileggendo Volpe', pp. 266–8.

35 G. Volpe, *L'impresa di Tripoli 1911–12* (Rome, 1946), p. 7.

36 G. Volpe, *Gabriele D'Annunzio: L'Italiano, il Politico, il Comandante*, rev. ed; (Rome, 1981), pp. 10–11, 77, 80–1.

37 *Studi storici in onore di G. Volpe*, 2 vols. (Florence, 1958). Contributors included Federico Chabod, Franco Valsecchi, Ernesto Sestan, Ettore Rota, Walter Maturi, Mario Toscano, Augusto Torre and A. M. Ghisalberti.

38 E. R. Tannenbaum, 'Gioacchino Volpe' in H. A. Schmitt (ed.) *Historians of Modern Europe* (Baton Rouge, 1971), p. 317.

39 E.g. see G. Volpe, *Il popolo italiano tra la pace e la guerra (1914–1915)* (Milan, 1940).

40 G. Turi, 'Le istituzioni culturali del regime fascista durante la seconda guerra mondiale', *Italia contemporanea*, XXXII, 1980, pp. 17–18.

41 E. R. Tannenbaum, 'Gioacchino Volpe', p. 317; A. M. Ghisalberti, *Ricordo di uno storico allora studente in grigioverde* (Rome, 1982), p. 22; R. Moscati, 'G. Volpe', *Rassegna Storica del Risorgimento*, LIX, 1972.

42 A. M. Ghisalberti, *Ricordo*, p. xv.

43 For further details on recent historiographical debates in this area see my chapter 'Italian foreign policy and its historiography' in R. Bosworth and G. Rizzo, eds., *Altro Polo: intellectuals and their ideas in contemporary Italy* (Sydney, 1983).

44 For an English language analysis, see B. R. Clark, *Academic power in Italy: bureaucracy and oligarchy in a national university system* (Chicago, 1977).
45 A. M. Ghisalberti, *Ricordo*, pp. 7, 12, 44, 54.
46 For surveys see J. M. Cammett, 'Two recent polemics on the character of the Italian Risorgimento', *Science and Society*, XXVII, 1963; S. J. Woolf, 'Risorgimento e fascismo: il senso della continuità nella storiografia italiana', *Belfagor*, XX, 1965.
47 For an introduction, see A. Montenegro, 'Politica estera e organizzazione del consenso. Note sull' Istituto per gli studi di politica internazionale', *Studi Storici*, 19, 1978.
48 *Ibid.*, p. 801.
49 R. Zangrandi, *Il lungo viaggio attraverso il fascismo*, p. 458.
50 L. Cappuccio, *U.R.S.S.: precedenti storici, organizzazione interna, politica estera* (Milan, 1940), pp. 18–19, 148, 215–16, 289, 310, 356, 419, 439–40, 442, 445–6.
51 I. Zingarelli, *I paesi danubiani e balcanici* (Milan, 1938), p. 63; ISPI, *Albania* (Milan, 1940), pp. 88, 91.
52 M. Arrigoni, *Come gli inglesi andarono a Malta e vi restarono* (Milan, 1941).
53 A. Montenegro, 'Politica estera e organizzazione del consenso.' p. 785.
54 A. Solmi *et al.*, *Egitto moderno e antico* (Milan, 1941), pp. 10, 17, 19, 25, 55, 258, 347.
55 R. Sertoli Salis, *Italia Europa Arabia* (Milan, 1940), pp. 9–10, 78, 352.
56 C. Pettinato, *La Francia vinta* (Milan, 1941), pp. 43, 70, 76–7, 219–20.
57 A. Giannini, *I rapporti italo-inglesi* (Milan, 1940), pp. 17–19, 43, 107, 136, 140, 158. Cf. an earlier version published under the same title by the *Istituto nazionale fascista di cultura* in 1936. Giannini published *L'ultima fase della questione orientale (1913–1939)* rev. ed., 1941, and *Uomini politici del mio tempo: profili*, 1942 also with ISPI.
58 A. Pirelli, *Economia e guerra* (Milan, 1940), vol. I, pp. 19–20, 23, 72, 74, 79, 155, 297–308.
59 *Ibid.*, vol. II, pp. 8–9.
60 E.g. A. Montenegro, 'Politica estera e organizzazione del consenso', p. 785 for the role of Toscano, Sertoli Salis and R. Mosca in directing ISPI's *Rassegna di politica internazionale* from 1934.
61 E.g. P. Silva, *Italia-Francia-Inghilterra nel Mediterraneo* (Milan, 1936), p. 101, noting how Italy, after 1860, 'was driven inevitably to develop an intense policy in the Mediterranean'.
62 E.g. A. Torre, *Alla vigilia della guerra mondiale, 1914–18* (Milan, 1942).
63 See his other works for the *Istituto nazionale fascista di cultura*, F. Cataluccio, *Italia e Francia in Tunisia (1878–1939)* (Rome, 1939); *La 'Nostra' Guerra* (Rome, 1940).
64 E.g. L. Salvatorelli, *La Triplice Alleanza* (Milan, 1939).
65 F. Chabod, *Storia della politica estera italiana dal 1870 al 1896*, 2 vols. (Milan, 1951).
66 A. Torre, *Alla vigilia della guerra mondiale*, p. 10.
67 E.g. R. Sertoli Salis, *Italia Europa Arabia*, p. 9.
68 A. Montenegro, 'Politica estera e organizzazione del consenso', p. 793.
69 *Dizionario di politica* (Rome, 1940), vol. IV, pp. 345–7.
70 *Ibid.*, vol. I, p. 646.
71 *Ibid.*, p. 1.

72 *Ibid.*, vol. I, pp. 166–7; vol. IV, p. 330.
73 For a somewhat equivocal example of Jemolo's disavowal of 'the sins of youth' see E. R. Papa, *Fascismo e cultura: il prefascismo* (Venice, 1978), pp. 207–10.
74 *Dizionario di politica*, vol. I, pp. 448, 462–9, 691; vol. II, pp. 705–10.
75 *Ibid.*, vol. III, p. 236.
76 E.g. *ibid.*, vol. I, pp. 191–4, 426–34; vol. III, p. 279; vol. IV, p. 77.
77 *Ibid.*, vol. IV, p. 494.
78 *Ibid.*, vol. II, pp. 366–8.
79 *Ibid.*, vol. II, p. 57.
80 *Ibid.*, vol. III, p. 474.
81 *Ibid.*, vol. I, pp. 779–80; vol. II, pp. 252–72; vol. III, pp. 250–62.
82 M. Isnenghi, *Intellettuali militanti e intellettuali funzionari: appunti sulla cultura fascista* (Turin, 1979), p. 197.
83 A. Montenegro, 'Politica estera e organizzazione del consenso', p. 816.
84 For the commencement of this debate, see R. De Felice, *Mussolini il duce: gli anni del consenso, 1929–1936* (Turin, 1974).
85 E. Ragionieri cited by A. Montenegro, 'Politica estera e organizzazione del consenso', p. 789.
86 M. Isnenghi, *Intellettuali*, p. 54.
87 E.g. see R. Ciasca, *Storia coloniale dell'Italia contemporanea* (Milan, 1938).
88 Cf. generally the comments of K. D. Bracher, *The German dilemma* (London, 1974).
89 A. Moravia, *Intervista sullo scrittore scomodo* (Bari, 1978), p. 30.
90 See e.g. L. Villari, *The Liberation of Italy, 1943–1947* (Appleton, Wisc., 1959); A. Tamaro, *La condanna dell'Italia nel trattato di pace* (Rocca San Casciano, 1952.)
91 D. Mack Smith, 'Benedetto Croce: history and politics', *Journal of Contemporary History*, 8, 1973, pp. 41–61.
92 Cited from K. Marx, *The revolutions of 1848*, ed. D. Fernbach (Harmondsworth, 1973), p. 77.
93 Cited by V. R. Berghahn, *Modern Germany* (Cambridge, 1982), p. 243.

7. The political uses of military intelligence: evaluating the threat of a Jewish revolt against Britain during the Second World War

The research for this article was completed while the author was a Junior Fellow in Modern History at the Oxford Centre for Postgraduate Hebrew Studies. I would like to record my gratitude to the Centre and its Fellows for the assistance and the facilities which they so generously provided.

All documents, unless otherwise stated, are located in the Public Record Office, Kew, London.

1 Downie minute, 11 July 1939, CO 733/408/75872/18(1939).
2 Haining to Shuckburgh, 13 Aug. 1939, CO 733/395/75113/2/1(1939).
3 For a discussion of the attempts to implement the constitutional provisions of the White Paper, cf. R. Zweig, *Britain and Palestine During the Second World War* (Royal Historical Society, forthcoming), chs. 1 and 2.
4 MacMichael to CO No.1021, Most Secret and Personal, 13 July 1941, CO 733/444(1)/75872/115(1941).

5 MacMichael to Moyne, Despatch, 1 Sept. 1941, CO 733/444/ 75872/115(1941).
6 MacMichael to Moyne, Private and Personal [letter], 14 Dec. 1941, *ibid.*
7 Anthony de Rothschild to Eden, 29 Oct. 1941, FO 371/27129 E7072. de Rothschild was a leading figure in British non-Zionist Jewish circles. His letter was supported by Rabbi Lazaron, a leading American anti-Zionist.
8 The documents had been taken by Censorship from Ben Gurion's luggage when he left the United Kingdom for America in Nov. 1941, and copied. (Boyd to Baxter, 24 Dec. 1941, FO 371/27129 E8556). Amongst the documents were protocols of a meeting held in September between leading British non-Zionist Jews (including de Rothschild, Lord Bearsted and Sir Robert Waley-Cohen) and Weizmann, Ben Gurion and members of the London offices of the Jewish Agency. The meeting was convened in an attempt to find common ground between the Zionists and the non-Zionists in dealing with post-war Jewish problems. Weizmann put forward his argument that there would be 2½ to 3 million Jewish refugees who could not be resettled in Europe after the war, and that that fact would require the creation of a Jewish state in Palestine. While the non-Zionists demurred from this conclusion, they supported the argument that Palestine would have to support large numbers of refugees after the war. It would not be unreasonable to presume that Ben Gurion wanted these protocols brought to H.M.G.'s attention, and that a good way of ensuring this would be to carry the documents where they would be copied by Censorship when he left the U.K.
9 Y. Bauer, *From Diplomacy to Resistance* (New York 1973), pp. 231–2.
10 Chaim Weizmann, 'Palestine's Role in the Solution of the Jewish Problem', *Foreign Affairs*, vol. xx, Jan. 1942, p. 337.
11 Halifax informed the Foreign Office of the Conference's deliberations by Saving (i.e. surface mail) telegram. (Halifax to FO. No. 155 Saving, 21 May 1942, FO 371/31378 E3184). In the Colonial Office the minuted reaction was that 'There is nothing new in this.' Clark minute, 29 May 1942, CO 733/ 443/75872/14(1942).
12 Caccia minute, 29 Dec. 1941, FO 371/27129 E8556. The reaction of the Colonial Office is on closed files, but it was in any case already familiar with Ben Gurion's views on the political objectives of Zionism.
13 The *Hagana* was formed in 1920 in order to defend isolated Jewish settlements from Arab attack. It was controlled by a body representing various sections of the *Yishuv*, but was primarily an organization of the left-wing *Histadrut* (Trades Union Federation). The *Irgun Zvai Leumi* was formed in 1931 as a breakaway group from the *Hagana*, and pursued a more aggressive military policy. Following a split in its ranks in 1973 it became a purely Revisionist (i.e. right-wing) organization.
14 The question was discussed by the 1938–39 Cabinet Committee on Palestine during April 1939 (cf. minutes on FO 371/23234 E2995).
15 Some circles within the *Hagana* and the official Zionist leadership in Palestine did discuss the possibility of the use of force to prevent the implementation of the new policy. Y. Slutzky, *Toldot Hahagana*, vol. II part 1, Tel. Aviv 1976, pp. 19ff. However as Bauer states, opposition was envisaged 'not in order to deny the British the right to stay in Palestine, but in order to prove that Jewish nuisance value was no less dangerous than the Arab variety and that capitulation to Arab demands contained in the White Paper would not bring

peace to Palestine'. Y. Bauer, 'From Cooperation to Resistance: The Hagana 1938–1946', *Middle Eastern Studies*, vol. ii no. 2, 1966, p. 188. Indeed, given the small size of the armed forces which the *Yishuv* had at its disposal (illegal as well as authorized) any opposition against the large number of British troops in the country (and the Arab majority of the population) could only have been of 'nuisance value'. With the outbreak of war only a few months after the release of the White Paper, the Zionist movement as a whole hoped that the strategic worth of Jewish Palestine's industries, and the recruiting potential both of the *Yishuv* and of world Jewry, would impress upon Britain that much more was to be gained by encouraging the continued growth of the *Yishuv* than was to be gained by appeasing Arab opinion over Palestine. However H.M.G. had discounted this possibility in the deliberations which led up to the White Paper policy, and the outbreak of war, rather than re-opening the debate on Palestine only heightened Britain's anxieties about her position in the Middle East and increased her willingness to meet Arab demands. The Jewish world was seen as a 'captive ally' of Britain, regardless of official policy in Palestine, and the only question which remained was whether the *Yishuv*'s military capabilities presented any sort of threat to Britain's ability to impose the policy which it had adopted.

16 For a full discussion of the *Yishuv*'s contribution to Britain's military efforts in the Middle East and elsewhere, cf. Y. Gelber, *Hahitnadvut ve'Mekoma be'Mediniut Hazionit ve'Hayishuvit, 1939–1942* [The Role of Volunteering In Zionist Policy, 1939–1942] (Jerusalem 1980).

17 G.O.C. Conference 20 Nov. 1939, WO 169/148.

18 Barker to WO 2 Nov. 1939 HP 1589, WO 169/146. The relevant Colonial Office file for 1939 on the disarming of the *Yishuv* (75998(1939)) remains closed to research.

19 Barker to MacMichael 10 Nov. 1939, CO 733/398/75156/141(39). The estimates by Palestine Military Intelligence in 1939–40 of the number of arms held illegally by the Jews were fairly accurate. Furthermore, in 1940 there appears to have been a well-founded degree of scepticism concerning the Jewish illegal arsenal. As the Middle East Department noted: 'The trouble is that we do not know how many Jewish arms there are in Palestine; some estimates are large, while other authorities such as General Haining think that the Jews like us to have the impression that the stocks are much larger than they are in fact. (Luke minute, 12 June 1940, CO 733/422/75241(1940)) According to Bauer (conversation with author), Hainings observation was correct. The Jewish authorities adopted a policy of intentional exaggeration of the *Yishuv*'s self-defence capabilities during the Arab revolt as a deterrent against the Arabs. Subsequently, as will be discussed below, it was the British authorities in the Middle East who themselves substantially inflated the estimates of the *Yishuv*'s armed strength.

20 Barker to MacMichael 10 Nov. 1939, CO 733/398/75156/141(39).

21 HCr to CO No. 1354, 3 Nov. 1939, FO 371/23251 E7479; and Wavell to WO No. 6077, 4 Nov. 1939, WO 169/146. Wavell argued that Barker's policy was unlikely to produce results, could not be enforced and (as Barker admitted) would cause serious repercussions in Palestine.

22 WP(G)(40)17 'Illegal Jewish Military Organisations', Cab 67/4.

23 WM 39(40)14, Cab 65/5.

24 Slutzky, *Toldot Hahagana*, p. 130.

25 'Appreciation to Determine the Extent to Which Troops May be Made Available From Palestine For Use Elsewhere.' 7 May 1940, CR/PAL/15956, WO 201/168.
26 Protocols of meeting of 30 May 1940, CO 733/428/75998 (1940).
27 Bauer, *From Diplomacy to Resistance*, pp. 104–5.
28 Protocols of meeting of 14 June, CO 733/428/75998(1940).
29 *Ibid.*
30 G.O.C. Conference, 9 July 1940, WO 169/147.
31 Lloyd to MacMichael, Despatch, 22 July 1940, CO 733/428/75998(1940).
32 Neame succeeded Godwin-Austin on 5 Aug. 1940 and new operational instructions were issued shortly afterwards. ('Searches – Illegal Arms Held In Jewish Settlements', 2 Sept. 1940, CR/PAL/16009/G, WO 169/147.)
33 Following an arms search at the Jewish village of Ein Harod in Aug. 1941, the Middle East Department pointed out that the policy of arms searches as a whole had been adopted by the previous Government and had not been endorsed by Churchill's Cabinet, and that therefore the matter should be put before the Cabinet once again. (Luke and Boyd minutes, 6 and 8 Oct. 1941, CO 733/445/75998(1941).) However Shuckburgh wanted to avoid this, and suggested that the Colonial Office resolve that the 'doctrine of continuity' justified them in permitting the Palestine Government to continue with the searches. (Shuckburgh minute 11 Oct. 1941, *ibid.*) As Churchill had made clear on all matters relating to Palestine, and especially on the arms question, that he did not endorse the policy of the preceding Government, Shuckburgh's advice was quite unjustified. Nevertheless Lord Moyne endorsed the tactic (Moyne minute 15 Oct., *ibid.*). It was, however, decided to obtain the concurrence of the War and Foreign Offices first. Once this had been received, MacMichael was instructed to continue with the arms searches. (Moyne to MacMichael, 20 Nov. 1941, *ibid.*)
34 Shuckburgh minute, 11 Oct. 1941, CO 733/445/75998(1941).
35 The question has been discussed in detail by Gelber, *The Role of Volunteering, passim.*
36 Cf. WO 201/2669 and CO 968/39/13117/15F, *passim*. For a full statement of the political objections to meeting the Jewish demands, cf. memo by Luke, 17 March 1942 on CO 733/443/75872/14(1942); and Hopkinson to Hoyar Millar, 9 Dec. 1942, *ibid.*
37 Colonial Office and Minister of State, Cairo files contain frequent verbatim accounts of the Agency's debates, and it is clear that the political institutions of the *Yishuv* were well infiltrated.
38 MilPal Weekly Intelligence Summary No. 15, 22–8 Sept. 1941, WO 169/1040.
39 MilPal Weekly Intelligence Summary No. 1, 16–22 June 1941, WO 169/1037. In November S.I.M.E. announced: 'A reliable report states that at a recent meeting of the *Hagana* [it was announced that] the buying of arms and ammunition in Syria had been very successful and that their distribution throughout Palestine was practically complete.' (Appendix to Survey No. 655, 10 Nov. 1941, WO 169/1560.)
40 FO 371/31375 E2026.
41 MacMichael to Moyne, 16 Oct. 1941, introductory letter to 'Note', *ibid.*
42 Cf. also HCr to CO Most Secret, Private and Personal, 4 Nov. 1941, CO 968/39/13117/15 Part 2.

43 Cf. Security Summary Middle East No. 2, S.I.M.E., Dec. 1941 WO 208/1560.

44 Cf. note 21 above.

45 In June 1942 S.I.M.E. gave a far more accurate account of the size and arms of the *Hagana*: 'Reports agree in placing the strength of the *Hagana* at 30,000 men, of whom 50–70 per cent are armed, and possibly 4,000 additional sympathisers and members of Revisionist bodies who would cooperate with the *Irgun* if it were mobilised . . . The following estimate of Jewish secret arms is stated to come from a reliable source:

	1st class condition	2nd class	total
Machine guns	162	—	162
L.M.G.s & automatic rifles	2,245	2,300	4,545
Rifles	10,000	8,000	18,000
Pistols	12,000	4,000	16,000

(Security Survey, Middle East No. 51, 4 June 1942, WO 208/1561.)

46 According to Bauer (who cites *Hagana* Archives), the actual strength of the *Hagana* in 1944 – i.e. after two years of growth and significant increases in its armoury as a result of arms thefts from British forces, purchases and gleanings from the battlefields of the Western Desert – was: '36,871 members, of whom 1517 were in the Palmach, 4609 in the Field Force, . . . a moderately well-trained unit – and the balance in the militia only 4372 of whose members had received adequate training. The force had 10,338 rifles (or one rifle per three men), 437 sub-machine guns, 132 machine guns and 3933 revolvers. Two-inch and three-inch mortars were being produced, but on a small scale.' (Bauer, 'From Cooperation to Resistance', p. 202) Perhaps the most reliable source of all for the actual strength of the *Hagana* alone in this period is the report of the *Hagana*'s own armaments division dated Oct. 1945. According to a published version of this report the *Hagana* was even weaker in Oct. 1945 than Bauer estimated for one year earlier. (Slutzky, *Toldot Hahagana*, p. 290.) The discrepancy between the figures given by Slutzky and those given by Bauer might be explained by the impact of British arms searches in the last years of the war.

47 The immediate reactions of the Colonial Office are on a closed file ('C(10)K'). Apparently the Colonial Office maintained a separate series of highly sensitive files, which remain unrecorded in the holdings of the Public Record Office, Kew.

48 Luke Memorandum 'The Jewish War Effort', March 1942, CO 733/448/76147/A(1942).

49 The twenty-six page report listed very many coded sources of information, and concluded: 'About 40,000 Palestine Arabs with small arms for all could be mobilised for a future revolt. But this quasi-military organisation is far more decentralised, informal and spontaneous than that of the Zionists, who are perhaps overorganised . . . Zionists with military training number 45–50,000, with arms for about 65%. Moreover the Palestine Jews have better technicians than the Arabs.' O.S.S. Research and Analysis Branch. *Illicit Arming by Jews and Arabs in Palestine* No. 1014, 30 Sept. 1943. (National Archives, Washington D.C.)

50 WP(42)108, 4 March 1942, Cab 66/22.

51 Lyttelton's paper was eventually circulated as WP(43)265, Cab 66/38, in June 1943.
52 Lyttelton sent the draft paper to Churchill with the note: 'I enclose a draft, and would not in any circumstances propose to release it until you say that I may or should.' (Lyttelton to Churchill, 11 April 1942, Prem 4/52/5.)
53 Entitled 'Memorandum on Internal Security in Palestine, December 1942' it covered both Arab and Jewish military capabilities, with the emphasis on the latter. (CO 733/439/75156/75(1943)) Whereas his 'Note' of 1941 had mentioned a total Jewish force of 108,000, by late 1942 he argued that the Jews could mobilize 135,000 people in order to oppose British policy and to impose a solution of their own. For a discussion of the origins of this document, cf. R. Zweig, 'British Plans for the Evacuation of Palestine, 1941–42', *Studies in Zionism*, No. 8, 1983.
54 The strident references to the Jews were matched by increasingly favourable references to the Arabs in an effort to counter the impression created by the record of Anglo-Arab relations during the years of fighting in the Middle East. Thus during 1943 the Foreign Office went to some lengths to encourage the circulation of a lengthy memorandum prepared by a member of its Research Department, entitled 'Arab Nationalism and Great Britain'. When discussing Iraq, the memorandum argued that the pro-Nazi Raschid Ali revolt should not be seen as a revolt against Britain but rather 'as a gesture of defiance against the universe' and a release of pent-up emotional tension. The Foreign Office ensured that a summary of the memorandum was also published as a feature article in *The Times*.(CO 732/87/79031.)
55 Butler minute 11 April 1943, FO 371/34956 E2039.
56 In Jan. 1943 Nuri Said approached Casey in Cairo with a series of proposals on the future of the Arab world, including Palestine, calling on both Britain and the United States to make a declaration of their intentions. This demand embarrassed the Foreign Office, and it attempted to dissuade Nuri from raising these questions at that stage. (Minutes on FO 371/34955 E1196.)
57 As Eden minuted on 29 Nov. 1942: 'I had always hoped that we could take a firm line at the Peace Conference that the bulk of the Jews should stay where they were in Europe. One hopes that the post-war Europe will not be a home of recurrent persecution, and there is anyway no room for these people in Palestine, even if every Arab were sent packing.' (FO 371/31380 E6946.) When, in 1943, the Middle East War Council forwarded to London a series of proposals on the future of the Middle East, one of which called for a reaffirmation of the White Paper, a senior Foreign Office official noted: 'Mr. Casey seems to be flying in the face of a hint which, unless I am mistaken, was conveyed to him by the Secretary of State not very long ago, after consultation with Colonel Stanley.' (Sir Maurice Peterson minute, 7 June 1943, FO 371/34975 E3234.)
58 Halifax to Foreign Office, Despatch No. 77, 8 Feb. 1943, FO 371/35032 E1027.
59 Eyres minuted: 'We are not allowed to reaffirm the White Paper, which is what we must do if we are to make a statement.' (21 Feb. 1943, *ibid*.)
60 FO to Halifax No. 1523 8 March 1943, *ibid*.
61 Halifax to FO No. 66 2 Feb. 1943, FO 371/35031 E826, & No. 52, FO 371 35031 E815.
62 Eden to Churchill PM/43/44, 3 March 1943, FO 371/35031 E826.

63 Churchill to Eden M139/3, 9 March 1943, Prem 4/52/3.
64 Peterson minute 17 March 1943, FO 371/35033 E2342.
65 Grey minute 2 April 1943, *ibid.*
66 Butler minute 19 March 1943, *ibid.*
67 Caccia minute 13 April 1943, FO 371/35033 E2341.
68 Peterson minute 16 April 1943, *ibid.*
69 Weizmann to Churchill 2 April 1943, Prem 4/52/3.
70 Churchill to Cranborne and Stanley, M291/3 18 April 1943, *ibid.*
71 Stanley to Churchill 19 April 1943, *ibid.*
72 WP(43)178 28 April 1943, Cab 66/36.
73 'With the exception of Ibn Saud and the Emir Abdullah, both of whom have been good and faithful followers, the Arabs have been virtually of no use to us in the present war. They have taken no part in the fighting, except in so far as they were involved in the Iraq rebellion against us. They have created no new claims upon the Allies, should we be victorious.' *Ibid.*
74 Churchill to Stanley and Cranborne, M319/3 27 April 1943, Prem 4/52/1.
75 WP(43)192 'Palestine: Memorandum by the Secretary of State for the Colonies', 4 May 1943, Cab 66/36.
76 WP(43)200 'Palestine: Memorandum by the Secretary of State for Foreign Affairs', 10 May 1943, Cab 66/36.
77 WP(43)265 'Palestine: Memorandum by the Minister of Production', 23 June 1943, Cab 66/38: 'I do not think that a Jewish National State can be founded and maintained except by the force of arms, that is by the force of our arms.'
78 WP(43)246 'Palestine: Memorandum by the Minister of State', 17 June 1943, Cab 66/37.
79 WP(43)247 'Resolutions of the Middle East War Council on the Political Situation in the Middle East.' Cab 66/37.
80 The Middle East War Council resolution had been adopted despite Moyne's warning (he was then Deputy-Minister of State in Cairo) that to do so would 'give members of the Cabinet at home the opportunity of re-opening the issue. In short he was against any mentioning of the White Paper at all.' (*Lampson Diaries* at St Anthony's College, Oxford, entry for 10 May 1943.) Casey repeated the warning two days later: 'Casey said that he had an indication from home (Anthony Eden) that we must exercise great care how we handled this matter or our good Prime Minister would fly off the handle and tear everything up including the White Paper itself. (*Ibid.*, entry for 12 May 1943.) Nevertheless, despite Moyne's and Casey's arguments, Lampson and Kinahan Cornwallis (British Ambassador to Iraq) insisted that the reaffirmation of the White Paper be one of the recommendations forwarded to London, and they won their point.
81 In May 1943 the Commander-in-Chief, Middle East Forces (Alexander) informed the War Office that 'Internal political situation in Palestine [is] dangerous and there is probability of anti-British revolt by Jews before or immediately after the end of the war. This would inevitably be followed by Arab insurrection. Jews mean business and are now armed and trained.' (C.-i.-C., M.E.F. to WO 0/49079 12 May 1943, FO 371/35030 E2902.) In his paper to the Cabinet Casey warned that 'the explosion is timed to go off as soon as the War ends in Europe, or possibly a few months earlier. Opinions differ as to the form the outbreak will take, whether civil disobedience, revolt, civil war, or an attempted coup d'état, and as to how and by which side the

actual shooting will be started.' (WP(43)246, 'Palestine: memorandum'.) The resolution of the Middle East War Council, which Casey circulated together with his own paper was more direct in identifying the likely source of trouble: 'The principal danger lies in an endeavour on the part of the Jews, who are rapidly producing a highly organised military machine on Nazi lines, to seize the moment which is most favourable to themselves for the prosecution by force of their policy of establishing an exclusively Jewish state in Palestine.' (WP(43)247, 'Resolutions of the Middle East War Council'.)

82 Churchill's last expression of support for Jewish statehood had been in 1941, but while the various Cabinet papers were being circulated in May–June 1943, he confirmed that he still adhered to his earlier views during a talk with Major-General Edward Spears. As Spears subsequently recorded: 'On the previous evening the Prime Minister had laid down his Zionist policy in the most emphatic terms. He said he had formed an opinion which nothing could change. He intended to see to it that there was a Jewish state. He told me not to argue with him as this would merely make him angry and would change nothing . . . There is simply no arguing with him on this subject. He was strongly anti-Arab and would always be turning to the Raschid Ali rebellion as a proof of Arab worthlessness.' (*Spears Papers*, Box 2 File 7, St Anthony's College, Oxford.)

83 The Cabinet Conclusions record two separate accounts of the deliberations on 2 July: on WM 92(43)2 (Cab 65/39) and on WM 92(43)3 (Cab 65/35).

84 Amery had first raised the idea of partition in a letter to Churchill over one month earlier. (Amery to Churchill 29 April 1943, Prem 4/52/1.) In his letter Amery pointed out that it would not be possible to go back on the White Paper entirely by resolving that all of Palestine be opened to unlimited Jewish immigration, but that partition was an acceptable compromise. The Cabinet Conclusions do not record who raised the proposal in Cabinet, but Amery, in his diary entry for 2 July 1943, claims that he raised it and that Churchill ('to my delight') supported him (*Amery Diaries*, in private possession of the Rt Hon Mr Julian Amery.)

85 WM 92(43)2, Cab 65/39.

86 WP(43)563 'Report of the Committee on Palestine', 20 Dec. 1943, Cab 66/44. The work of this Committee has been considered in detail by M. Cohen, 'The British White Paper on Palestine, May 1939, Part 2: The Testing of a Policy, 1942–1945'. *The Historical Journal*, vol. XIX, 1976, 727–58.

87 WM 11(44)4, 25 Jan. 1945, Cab 65/45.

8. The politics of asylum, Juan Negrín and the British Government in 1940

1 CAB 65/10, W.M. 281(40)6, Public Record Office, London. Quotations from Crown copyright material appear by permission of the Controller of Her Majesty's Stationery Office.

2 Halifax Diary, 1 November 1940, Hickleton papers: A7.8.6. (made available to the author in York Public Library by kind permission of the Earl of Halifax).

3 David Dilks (ed.) *The Diaries of Sir Alexander Cadogan, 1938–1945* (London, 1971), p. 334.

4 CAB 65/10, W.M. 281(40)6.

5 CAB 65/8, W.M. 191(40)7; CAB 65/10, W.M. 281(40)6.

6 An English translation of the Spanish decree of non-belligerency is contained in *Foreign Relations of the United States* 1940, vol. II (Washington, D.C., Department of State, 1957), p. 797. Franco defined non-belligerency as 'a state of more definite sympathy towards Italy and a wide awake attitude'. (*Ibid.*, p. 888.)

7 FO 371/24516, C8045/113/41, P.R.O.

8 Halifax to Hoare, 30 July 1940, Templewood papers (the papers of Sir Samuel Hoare), the University Library, Cambridge, XIII, 20 (permission to quote from the Templewood papers has been kindly granted by P. E. Paget, Esq.).

9 CAB 79/6, C.O.S. (40) 251st Meeting, Minute 5; FO 371/24516, C8045/113/41.

10 Hoare to Halifax, 15 August 1940, Templewood papers, XIII, 20; CAB 66/11, W.P. (40)362, appendix 1, para. 22.

11 This question is dealt with in detail in the author's forthcoming book, *Diplomacy and Strategy of Survival: British Policy and Franco's Spain, 1940–41* (Cambridge University Press). However, see also, for example, *Documents on German Foreign Policy*, Series D, vol. IX (London, H.M.S.O., 1956), pp. 620–1; vol. XI (London, H.M.S.O., 1961), pp. 38–40, 83–91, 93–102, 106–8, 153–5, 166–74, 183–4, 199–204, 214–19, 259–60, 283, 371–80, 383, 392–3, 402, 452, 598–606, 619–23, 705–6, 816–17 and Ramón Serrano Suñer, *Entre el silencio y la propaganda, la Historia como fue: Memorias* (Barcelona, 1977), pp. 283–348.

12 CAB 65/8, W.M. 191(40)7; Dilks (ed.), *Cadogan Diaries*, p. 309.

13 CAB 65/8, W.M. 191(40)7.

14 Hoare to Halifax, 5 July 1940, FO 800/323, Halifax papers, P.R.O.

15 Halifax to Hoare, 17 July and 30 July 1940, Templewood papers, XIII, 20.

16 FO 371/24527, C7501/7501/41.

17 Ivan Maisky, *Memoirs of a Soviet Ambassador: The War, 1939–43* (London, 1967), pp. 117–18, 155–6, 180.

18 FO 371/24527, C7501/7501/41.

19 Diary 23, 26.7.40, Dalton papers, British Library of Political and Economic Science.

20 Halifax to Hoare, 30 July 1940, Templewood papers, XIII, 20.

21 FO 371/24527, C7501/7501/41.

22 Halifax to Hoare, 30 July 1940, Templewood papers, XIII, 20.

23 Attlee to Halifax, 27 July 1940, FO 371/24527, C7501/7501/41.

24 CAB 65/8, W.M. 215(40)4.

25 See, e.g., Kim Philby, *My Silent War* (London, 1968), 1969 edn, pp. 60–1, 91.

26 Rafael Rodríguez-Moñino Soriano, *La Misión Diplomática del XVII Duque de Alba en la Embajada de España en Londres (1937–1945)* (Valencia, 1971), pp. 127–31.

27 Alba to Colonel Juan Beigbeder Atienza, 15 October 1940, legajo R. 985, expediente 6, General archive of the Spanish Ministry of Foreign Affairs (hereinafter cited as M.A.E.), Palacio de Santa Cruz, Madrid.

28 Alba's dispatch no. 807, 5 August 1940, M.A.E.: legajo R.985, E.12.

29 Alba to Beigbeder, 27 August 1940, M.A.E.: legajo R.985, E.12; Alba to Beigbeder, 15 October 1940, M.A.E.: legajo R.985, E.6.

30 Caja 1ª, no. 6, Alba papers, Palacio de Liria, Madrid. (The author is grateful

to His Excellency, the Duke of Alba, for permission to consult, and cite, the papers of the seventeenth Duke of Alba.)

31 Alba to Halifax, 12 August 1940, FO 371/24511, C8570/75/41.

32 Halifax to Alba, 28 August 1940, Alba's dispatch no. 884, anejo no. 1, 2 September 1940, M.A.E.: legajo R. 985, E.8.

33 Alba to Beigbeder, 15 October 1940, enclosing copy of Halifax to Alba, 8 October 1940, M.A.E.: legajo R. 985, E.6. See also the minute by Cadogan, of 30 October 1940, in FO 371/24512, C 11725/75/41.

34 Alba to Beigbeder, 15 October 1940, M.A.E.: legajo R.985, E.6.

35 Hoare to Halifax, received 10 September 1940, FO 800/323.

36 FO 371/24511, C 10117/75/41.

37 *Ibid.*

38 FO 371/24511, C9159/75/41.

39 Attlee to Halifax, 30 October 1940, FO 800/323.

40 Stephen Spender, *The Thirties and After: Poetry, Politics, People (1933–75)* (London, 1978), Fontana edn, p. 82.

41 Butler to Hoare, 20 July 1940, Templewood papers, XIII, 17.

42 Halifax to Hoare, 24 September 1940, FO 371/24510, C6473/75/41.

43 Nigel Nicolson (ed.), *Harold Nicolson: Diaries and Letters, 1939–45* (London, 1967), 1970 edn, p. 96.

44 Sonia Orwell and Ian Angus (eds.), *The Collected Essays, Journalism and Letters of George Orwell,* vol. II, *My Country Right or Left, 1940–1943* (London, 1968), 1970 edn, p. 402.

45 J. B. Priestley, *All England Listened: The Wartime Broadcasts of J. B. Priestley* (New York, 1967), p. 54.

46 *Ibid.,* p. 132. Priestley returned to the air waves for a further period in the earlier part of 1941.

47 Quoted by Paul Addison, *The Road to 1945: British Politics and the Second World War* (London, 1975), 1977 edn, p. 119.

48 Priestley, *All England Listened,* pp. 55–7.

49 *Ibid.,* p. 127.

50 This particular phrase is Oliver Harvey's description of the people's war in his diary entry for 27 October 1940 (John Harvey (ed.) *The War Diaries of Oliver Harvey, 1941–1945* (London, 1978), p. 9). See, also, the Diaries and papers of Lord Harvey of Tasburgh, 27 October 1940, Add. Mss. 56397, British Library. Oliver Harvey was working at the Ministry of Information at the time of the diary entry specified above, but he returned to the Foreign Office, in June 1941, as private secretary to the then foreign secretary, Anthony Eden.

51 FO 371/24511, C10117/75/41; Victor Gollancz published a book entitled *100,000,000 Allies – If We Choose* in the summer of 1940. It had been written by Crossman and Kingsley Martin, editor of the left-wing weekly, the *New Statesman,* under the *nom de plume,* 'Scipio'. This book called on Britain to arouse Europe's oppressed: 'One hundred million peoples *(sic)* suffer under the tyranny of the Nazi War Lords. We can make them, or at least the bravest of them, our allies if we pledge this country to the cause of European revolution and build here in Britain an organisation through which that revolution can be brought about.' p. 34.

52 Charles Duff, *A Key to Victory: Spain* (London, 1940) pp. 114–15.

53 Attlee to Halifax, 30 October 1940, FO 800/323.
54 Smyth, *British Policy and Franco's Spain* (forthcoming).
55 FO 371/24508, C11460/40/41.
56 *Ibid.*; Hoare to Halifax, 29 October 1940, enclosing a message from Beigbeder to Hoare, FO 800/323; Hoare to Halifax, 30 October 1940, enclosing a message from Beigbeder to Hoare, FO 800/323, Hoare to Halifax, 4 November 1940, FO 800/323; FO 371/24517, C12295/113/41; Hoare to Churchill, 22 October 1940, Templewood papers, XIII, 16.
57 FO 371/24508, C11460/40/41.
58 CAB 69/1, D.O. (40) 37th Mtg., Min. 4; Halifax to Dalton and Alfred Duff Cooper, Minister of Information, 31 October 1940, FO 371/24508, C11460/40/41.
59 CAB 65/10, W.M. 281(40)6.
60 *Ibid.*
61 Churchill to Ernest Bevin, Minister of Labour, 25 November 1940, PREM 4/83/1A, P.R.O.
62 CAB 65/10, W.M. 281(40)6.
63 *Ibid.*
64 Halifax to Hoare, 21 December 1940, Templewood papers, XIII, 20.
65 CAB 65/10, W.M. 281(40)6.
66 FO 371/24512, C11725/75/41.
67 *The Week*, no. 393, 20 November 1940.
68 *Ibid.*; CAB 65/10, W.M. 285(40)8; FO 371/24512, C11725/75/41.
69 Negrín to Halifax, 11 November 1940, FO 371/24512, C11725/75/41.
70 FO 371/24512, C11725/75/41.
71 Halifax to Hoare, 21 December 1940, Templewood papers, XIII, 20.
72 *The Week*, no. 393, 20 November 1940.
73 See, e.g. W. Alexander (secretary of the British International Brigade Association) to Halifax, 18 November 1940, FO 371/24513, C12472/75/41.
74 *Daily Herald*, 15 November 1940.
75 Halifax to Hoare, 21 December 1940, Templewood papers, XIII, 20.
76 365 House of Commons Debates, 5th series, Column 1954.
77 FO 371/24513, C12589/75/41; FO 371/24512, C11725/75/41.
78 FO 371/24512, C11725/75/41.
79 365 H.C. DEB 5.s., Col. 1954.
80 *Ibid.*, Col. 1955.
81 *Ibid.*, Col. 1954.
82 *Ibid.*, Col. 1955.
83 FO 371/24512, C11725/75/41.
84 CAB 65/10, W.M. 298(40)3.
85 FO 371/24512, C11725/75/41.
86 Halifax to Hoare, 21 December 1940, Templewood papers, XIII, 20.
87 367 H.C. DEB. 5.s., Col. 510.
88 CAB 65/10, W.M. 295(40)7.
89 FO 371/24512, C11725/75/41.
90 Alba's dispatch No. 1126, 9 December 1940, Alba papers, caja1ª, no. 5; M.A.E.: legajo R. 985, E.8.
91 Addison, *Road to 1945*, pp. 121–6.
92 Quoted by Joseph P. Lash, *Roosevelt and Churchill, 1939–1941: The Partnership that saved the West* (London, 1977), pp. 280–1.

93 John Lawrence argued in this vein in an article, 'The Strategy of Propaganda', published in the *News Chronicle* on 16 October 1940. He maintained that, if Britain championed a set of revolutionary war aims, it would inevitably alienate many Europeans from its cause. He argued that Britain's appeal to Europe should be based upon its ability to feed the continent's hungry inhabitants, and on British respect for the principle of national independence so brutally violated by Hitler.

94 Dilks (ed.), *Cadogan Diaries*, p. 338.

95 CAB 66/7, W.P. (40) 168; CAB 66/11, W.P. (40)362; CAB 80/59, C.O.S. (41) 144(0); CAB 80/30, C.O.S. (R)14.

96 David Stafford, 'The Detonator Concept: British Strategy, SOE and European Resistance After the Fall of France', *Journal of Contemporary History*, x (1975), 191–2, 200, 203.

97 T. D. Burridge, *British Labour and Hitler's War* (London, 1976), pp. 42–5, 50, 53, 58, 164.

98 Butler to Hoare, 20 July 1940, Templewood papers, xiii, 17.

99 Burridge, *British Labour*, pp. 50, 54–5; *Daily Herald*, 21 October 1940.

100 See, e.g., Harvey Diaries, 25, 28 November 1942, Add. 56399.

9. *Churchill and the British 'Decision' to fight on in 1940: right policy, wrong reasons*

Earlier versions of this essay have been given to the Cambridge Historical Society and to the University of London Seminar in 20th Century British History. I am grateful to Sir Owen Chadwick, Mr A. J. P. Taylor and members of these two seminars, especially Dr David Carlton, for their helpful comments and criticisms.

Quotations from manuscript collections appear by kind permission of The Controller, H.M. Stationery Office; Birmingham University Library; the Borthwick Institute, University of York; the British Library of Political and Economic Science, London; Houghton Library, Harvard University; A. J. P. Taylor and the Beaverbrook Foundation.

1 Winston S. Churchill, *The Second World War* (6 vols., London, 1948–54), ii, pp. 157, 159.

2 For a broader discussion of British foreign policy and of Anglo-American relations, on which this essay draws, see David Reynolds, *The Creation of the Anglo-American Alliance, 1937–1941: A Study in Competitive Co-operation* (London, 1981).

3 I remain unconvinced by David Carlton's ingenious argument that Chamberlain may have preferred Churchill to Halifax, and stand by the more traditional accounts. See David Carlton, *Anthony Eden: A Biography* (London, 1981), pp. 161–2.

4 Churchill to Chamberlain, 10 May 1940, Neville Chamberlain papers, NC 7/9/80 (Birmingham University Library).

5 Cecil H. King, *With Malice toward None: A war diary*, ed. William Armstrong (London, 1970), p. 50, entry for 7 June 1940 (quotation by kind permission of Messrs Sidgwick and Jackson, Ltd). Or, as R. A. Butler put it picturesquely in July: 'If intrigue or attacks on the Government grow to any great extent all we have to do is to pull the string of the toy dog of the 1922 Committee and make it bark. After a few staccato utterances it becomes clear

that the Government depends upon the Tory squires for its majority.' Butler to Hoare, 20 July 1940, Templewood papers, T/xiii/17 (Cambridge University Library).

6 After being operated on for cancer Chamberlain wrote in his diary on 9 Sept. 1940 of the need 'to adjust myself to the new life of a partially crippled man which is what I am. Any ideas of another Premiership after the war have gone. I know that is out of the question.' Chamberlain papers, NC 2/24A.

7 They have been discussed at some length by several historians, esp. Sir Llewellyn Woodward, *British Foreign Policy in the Second World War* (London, 1970), i, pp. 197–208; P. M. H. Bell, *A Certain Eventuality: Britain and the Fall of France* (Farnborough, Hants, 1974), pp. 38–48; Elisabeth Barker, *Churchill and Eden at War* (London, 1978), pp. 140–6; Eleanor M. Gates, *The End of the Affair: The Collapse of the Anglo-French Alliance, 1939–1940* (London, 1981), pp. 143–52; Martin Gilbert, *Winston S. Churchill* (London, 1983), vi, pp. 402–22. The records are in CAB 65/13, Confidential annexes, WM (40) 139/1, 140, 141/1, 142, 145/1 (Public Record Office, London – henceforth PRO).

8 Churchill told junior ministers on 28 May that 'we should certainly be able to get 50,000 away. If we could only get 100,000 away, that would be a magnificent performance.' Hugh Dalton, diary, vol. xxii, p. 93 (British Library of Political and Economic Science, London).

9 F. H. Hinsley, *British Intelligence in the Second World War: Its Influence on Strategy and Operations* (London, 1979), i, pp. 165–6.

10 Halifax, diary, 25 May 1940, Hickleton papers, A 7.8.4 (Borthwick Institute, York).

11 War Cabinet minutes, WM 107 (40) 2, 7 Dec. 1939, CAB 65/2.

12 See e.g. CAB 65/13, pp. 149, 151, 179–80.

13 See e.g. CAB 65/13, pp. 150, 187, and Chamberlain diary, 26 May 1940, NC 2/24A.

14 Halifax, diary, 27 May 1940, Hickleton papers, A 7.8.4.

15 It is interesting to see how Churchill handled the episode in his war memoirs. There it is discussed almost entirely in the context of Anglo-Italian relations – could Mussolini be bought off and prevented from entering the war? – without any reference to its wider implications *Second World War*, ii, pp. 108–11.

16 Cf. Woodward, *British Foreign Policy*, i, p. 204, note.

17 E.g. Stokes to Lloyd George and enclosed memo, 17 July 1940, Lloyd George papers, G/19/3 (House of Lords Record Office, London). The basis of Stokes' organisation was the 'Parliamentary Peace Aims Group' formed by dissident Labour MPs the previous autumn. For background see Richard R. Stokes papers, files 73 and 76 (Bodleian Library, Oxford).

18 As stated in e.g. Lloyd George to the Duke of Bedford, 14 Sept. 1940, Lloyd George papers, G/3/4.

19 Lloyd George to Churchill, 29 May 1940, and drafts, Lloyd George papers, G/4/5. See also Chamberlain, diary, 31 May, 4–7, 10–11 June 1940, NC 2/24A, and *Life with Lloyd George: The Diary of A. J. Sylvester, 1931–45*, ed. Colin Cross (London, 1975), pp. 360–70.

20 Sylvester, diary, 3 Oct. 1940, in *Life with Lloyd George*, p. 281. See also the interesting discussion in Paul Addison, 'Lloyd George and Compromise Peace in the Second World War' in *Lloyd George: Twelve Essays*, ed. A. J. P. Taylor

(London, 1971), pp. 361–84. On the larger question of German peace feelers in the summer of 1940 and the British and American responses, see Bernd Martin, *Friedensinitiativen und Machtpolitik im Zweiten Weltkrieg, 1939– 1942* (Düsseldorf, 1974), pp. 234–336. Although tendentious in its view of Roosevelt (as bent on world domination), this rightly notes the disingenuousness of official British accounts, such as those by Churchill and Woodward, on the peace issue (e.g. pp. 298–9).

21 Chamberlain to Roosevelt, 4 Oct. 1939, PREM 1/366 (PRO).

22 Neville Chamberlain to Ida Chamberlain, 10 Sept. 1939, Chamberlain papers, NC 18/1/1116.

23 See Callum A. MacDonald, 'The Venlo Affair', *European Studies Review*, VIII (1978), 443–64 (but cf. Hinsley, *British Intelligence*, I, 56–7); Peter Ludlow, 'Papst Pius XII, die britische Regierung und die deutsche Opposition im Winter 1939/40', *Vierteljahrshefte für Zeitgeschichte*, XXII (1974), 299–341.

24 Notes of interview with Hoare, 22 Sept. and 15 Oct. 1939, Kingsley Martin papers, box 30, file 6 (Sussex University Library, Brighton).

25 House of Commons, *Debates*, 5th series, vol. 360, col. 1502; Gilbert, *Churchill*, VI, pp. 358, 449.

26 CAB 65/13, pp. 179–80, WM 142 (40) CA, 27 May 1940. Halifax was reminding the PM of a discussion on the previous day, but Churchill made no demurrer to this paraphrase of his comments.

27 Chamberlain, diary, 26 May 1940, NC 2/24A.

28 CAB 65/13, p. 180.

29 CAB 65/13, p. 187, WM 145 (40) 1, CA.

30 For this argument see J. A. S. Grenville, 'Contemporary trends in the study of the British "appeasement" policies of the 1930s', *Internationales Jahrbuch für Geschichts- und Geographie-Unterricht*, 17 (1976), 245–7; also Jonathan Knight, 'Churchill and the approach to Mussolini and Hitler in May 1940: a note', *British Journal of International Studies*, III (1977), 92–6.

31 Churchill, memo, 29 May 1940, copy in Beaverbrook papers, D 414/3 (House of Lords Record Office, London). Emphasis added.

32 Churchill to Chamberlain, 9 Oct. 1939, PREM 1/395 (PRO).

33 Halifax, diary, 6 June 1940, Hickleton papers, A 7.8.4.

34 Churchill, note, 3 Aug. 1940, PREM 4/100/3, p. 131.

35 Dalton, diary, vol. xxv, p. 57, 26 Aug. 1941.

36 Churchill added that 'although he didn't entirely appreciate it at the time he had no doubt that the Germans had made an overwhelming error in frittering away their fleet on all the Norwegian business'. Halifax, diary, 10 Feb. 1946, Hickleton papers, A 7.8.18. Cf. Churchill, *Second World War*, II, p. 144: 'I was always sure we should win'.

37 Churchill to Baldwin, 4 June 1940, Stanley Baldwin papers, vol. 174, p. 264 (Cambridge University Library).

38 'Ismay said, "Quite possibly, but we'll have a hell of a good time those last seven days." Churchill seemed to feel that this point was well taken.' Robert E. Sherwood, notes of interview with Ismay on 11 July 1946, Sherwood papers, folder 1891 (Houghton Library, Harvard University).

39 Lloyd George, memo, 12 Sept. 1940, Lloyd George papers, G/81.

40 E.g. Chiefs of Staff sub-committee, 'European Appreciation', 20 Feb. 1939, CAB 16/183A, DP (P) 44, esp. paragraphs 27–37, 267–8.

41 Paper on 'Future Strategy', 4 Sept. 1940, CAB 80/17, COS (40) 683, para. 211.

42 *Ibid.*, para. 214.

43 Churchill to Beaverbrook, 8 July 1940, Beaverbrook papers, D 414/36.

44 Memo, 'The Munitions Situation', 3 Sept. 1940, WP (40) 352, CAB 66/11. In deference to the Chiefs of Staff Churchill was here a little less pessimistic about the blockade, speaking only of it as having been 'blunted' by the German victories.

45 Minutes M 485 and M 740/1, 30 Dec. 1940 and 12 July 1941, Ministry of Aircraft Production papers, AVIA 9/5 (PRO).

46 The phrase used by Sir Cyril Newall, Chief of the Air Staff, on 31 Aug. 1940, SA (J) 3rd mtg, pp. 5–6, CAB 122/59.

47 Cf. *Chief of Staff: The Diaries of Lieutenant-General Sir Henry Pownall*, ed. Brian Bond (2 vols, London, 1972–1974), II, pp. 38–9, entry for 20 Aug. 1941.

48 CAB 99/18, COS (R) 14, esp. paragraphs 28–9, 36–8. This extreme faith in strategic bombing was confined (except for Bomber Command) to 1940–1. Thereafter it declined, partly because of growing evidence of bombing's inaccuracy but mainly because the advent of new allies in 1942 revolutionised the strategic situation. As Churchill remarked in July 1942: 'In the days when we were fighting alone, we answered the question, "How are you going to win the war?" by saying, "We will shatter Germany by bombing." Since then the enormous injuries inflicted on the German Army and man-power by the Russians, and the accession of the man-power and munitions of the United States, have rendered other possibilities open. We look forward to mass invasion of the Continent by liberating armies, and general revolt of the populations against the Hitler tyranny.' ('A review of the War Position', 21 July 1942, CAB 66/26, WP (42) 311.) Churchill went on, however, to note that bombing could prepare the way for the final onslaught, and it was in this 'complementary' role that it was henceforth to figure in Allied strategy. See also Sir Charles Webster and Noble Frankland, *The Strategic Air Offensive against Germany, 1939–1945* (4 vols, London, 1961), I, pp. 184, 319, 342–9; R. J. Overy, *The Air War, 1939–1945* (London, 1980), ch. 5.

49 Hinsley, *British Intelligence*, I, pp. 63–73, 232–48, 500–4.

50 *'Chips': The Diaries of Sir Henry Channon*, ed. Robert Rhodes James (London, 1967), p. 253.

51 CAB 65/13, pp. 148–9. Cf. Halifax, secret diary, 16 March 1941, A 7.8.19: 'I remember last May and June everybody was saying "if we can hold out till the autumn we shall be all right." '

52 CAB 66/7, WP(40) 168, para. 18.

53 CAB 80/17, COS (40) 683, paras 50, 47 and 218. Emphasis in original.

54 William S. Wasserman, 'Interview with Mr Winston Churchill', 10 Feb. 1939, p. 3, President's Secretary's File (PSF) 73: 'Agriculture Department' (Franklin D. Roosevelt Library, Hyde Park, New York).

55 CAB 65/13, p. 147, WM 140 (40) CA, 26 May 1940.

56 House of Commons, *Debates*, 5th series, vol. 362, cols 59–60.

57 Burton H. Klein, *Germany's Economic Preparations for War* (Cambridge, Massachusetts, 1959), pp. 225–35; see also Overy, *The Air War*, pp. 122–5.

58 Cf. Hinsley, *British Intelligence*, I, p. 80.

59 CAB 66/7, WP (40) 145.

60 CAB 65/13, p. 148.
61 See Klaus Hildebrand, *The Foreign Policy of the Third Reich* (Berkeley, 1973); Andreas Hillgruber, 'England's place in Hitler's plans for world dominion', *Journal of Contemporary History*, IX (1974), 5–22; Wilhelm Deist, *The* Wehrmacht *and German Rearmament* (London, 1981).
62 CAB 80/17, COS (40) 683, 4 Sept. 1940, para. 44. For earlier examples of this assumption see Wesley K. Wark, 'British Intelligence on the German Air Force and Aircraft Industry, 1933–1939', *The Historical Journal*, XXV (1982), 644, 646–7.
63 Ministry of Economic Warfare, note, appendix to CAB 79/6, COS 295 (40) 2, 5 Sept. 1940. From late 1940, however, British oil experts became progressively less sanguine about Germany's position.
64 Alan S. Milward, *The German Economy at War* (London, 1965), esp. chs. 1–2. Cf. R. J. Overy, 'Hitler's war and the German economy: A reinterpretation', *Economic History Review*, 2nd series, XXXV (1982), 272–91; see also Deist, *Wehrmacht*, esp. pp. 102–12; Williamson Murray, 'The Luft-. waffe before the Second World War: A Mission, A Strategy?', *Journal of Strategic Studies*, IV (1981), 261–70, and 'Force Strategy, Blitzkrieg Strategy and the Economic Difficulties: Nazi Grand Strategy in the 1930s', *Journal of the Royal United Services Institute*, 128/1 (March 1983), 39–43.
65 After discussing strategy for the attack on continental Europe with Churchill on 22 May 1943, Henry Wallace, the US Vice-President, noted: 'Churchill and Cherwell [F. A. Lindemann, the PM's scientific adviser] still think that the job can be done from the air and sea without the help of the land.' *The Price of Vision: The Diary of Henry A. Wallace, 1942–1946*, ed. John M. Blum (Boston, 1973), p. 210.
66 Chiefs of Staff, 'British strategy in a certain eventuality', 25 May 1940, WP (40) 168, para. 1, CAB 66/7. Emphasis in original.
67 Chiefs of Staff, Joint Planning Sub-Commt., draft aide mémoire, 27 June 1940, COS (40) 496, para. 29, CAB 80/13.
68 Churchill to Roosevelt, telegram, 15 June 1940, PREM 3/468, pp. 126–7.
69 King, *With Malice toward None*, p. 139, diary entry for 23 Aug. 1941.
70 In Feb. 1939 Churchill told an American visitor that if war broke out with Germany and Italy, the main fighting would be in the Mediterranean while the Maginot Line kept Germany out of France. 'In the meanwhile there would be much unpleasantness in the air. London would be bombed. The spectacle of 50,000 English women and children being killed might readily bring the United States into the conflict – especially in view of Mr. Roosevelt's present attitude.' (Wasserman, 'Interview with Mr. Winston Churchill', 10 Feb. 1939, p. 5, cited in note 54). In September he told the British Ambassador in Washington that Hitler might shrink from making a decisive air attack on British factories. 'If however he tried and succeeded, the United States would come into the front line.' (Churchill to Lothian, 24 Sept. 1939, Ge/39/2, FO 800/397.) For similar, if more veiled predictions in print, see his articles 'Bombs don't scare us now', *Colliers*, 17 June 1939, reprinted in *The Collected Essays of Sir Winston Churchill*, ed. Michael Wolff (London, 1976), I, p. 453; and in *News of the World*, 18 June 1939, quoted in Martin Gilbert, *Winston S. Churchill* (London, 1976), V, p. 1075.
71 Charles de Gaulle, *War Memoirs*, trans. Jonathan Griffin (London, 1955), I, p. 108.

72 Churchill to Dominion PMs, 16 June 1940, PREM 4/43B/1, p. 278.
73 Winston S. Churchill, *Secret Session Speeches*, compiled by Charles Eade (London, 1946), p. 15.
74 Churchill to Bevin, 15 Oct. 1940, Ernest Bevin papers, 3/1, p. 58 (Churchill College, Cambridge).
75 Sir John Colville, *Footprints in Time* (London, 1976), pp. 144–5, quoting diary entry for 1 Nov. 1940.
76 Reynolds, *The Creation of the Anglo-American Alliance*, pp. 108, 149.
77 Admiral Robert L. Ghormley to Admiral Harold L. Stark, 11 Oct. 1940, US Navy Strategic Plans Division, Box 117: 'Naval Attaché, London' (Naval Historical Division Archives, Washington Navy Yard, Washington, D.C.).
78 Lippmann, 'Today and Tomorrow' column, *Washington Post*, 23 March 1939. This was taken seriously by the Foreign Office – see FO 371/22829, A 2439/1292/45.
79 After talking with Roosevelt on 10–11 June 1939 the King recorded in his notes of their conversations: 'If London was bombed U.S.A. would come in.' Back in London, according to his biographer, the King 'communicated the essence of his talks with the President to the proper quarters'. See John W. Wheeler-Bennett, *King George VI: His Life and Reign* (London, 1958), pp. 391–2. Churchill was definitely told by the King about the naval aspects of his talks with Roosevelt (Churchill to Pound, 7 Sept. 1939, Admiralty papers, ADM 116/3922, p. 255, PD 07892/39) and it is likely that George VI would also have given him the gist of Roosevelt's other remarks at the same time. If so, Churchill's conviction about the effect of bombing must have been greatly strengthened.
80 A particularly vivid indication of this fear comes in a letter by the historian Arnold Toynbee to an American international lawyer just after Munich: 'It is probably impossible to convey what the imminent expectation of being intensively bombed feels like in a small and densely populated country like this. I couldn't have conveyed it to myself if I hadn't experienced it in London the week before last (we were expecting 30,000 casualties a night in London, and on the Wednesday morning we believed ourselves, I believe correctly, to be within three hours of the zero hour). It was just like facing the end of the world. In a few minutes the clock was going to stop, and life, as we had known it, was coming to an end. This prospect of the horrible destruction of all that is meant to one by "England" and "Europe" was much worse than the mere personal prospect that one's family and oneself would be blown to bits. Seven or eight million people in London went through it.' (Arnold Toynbee to Quincy Wright, 14 Oct. 1938, in Roger S. Greene papers, folder 747, Houghton Library, Harvard University.)
81 Supreme War Council (39/40) 13th mtg., p. 12, 31 May 1940, CAB 99/3. Cf. this report by the US Ambassador in London: 'Churchill said quite definitely to me he expects the United States will be in right after the election; that when the people in the United States see the towns and cities of England, after which so many American cities and towns have been named, bombed and destroyed they will line up and want war.' (Joseph P. Kennedy to Cordell Hull, tel. 1603, 12 June 1940, State Dept. decimal file, 740.0011 EW 1939/3487 6/10, National Archives, Washington, D.C.)
82 It is quite likely, for instance, that the King was handled in this fashion in June 1939 (see above, note 79). More experienced Roosevelt-watchers in the

Foreign Office took such utterances with the necessary grain of salt. For further discussion see David Reynolds, 'FDR's foreign policy and the British royal visit to the USA in 1939', *The Historian*, XLV (1983), pp. 468–9.

83 For elaboration of this argument see Reynolds, *The Creation of the Anglo-American Alliance*, ch. 8, esp. pp. 211–12, 217–19.

84 House of Commons, *Debates*, 5th series, vol. 364, col. 1171. Cf. Correlli Barnett, *The Collapse of British Power* (London, 1972), pp. 588–9.

85 Cabinet minutes, WM 141 (40) 9, CAB 65/7.

86 Churchill to Baruch, telegram, 28 June 1940, Selected Correspondence, vol. 47, Bernard M. Baruch papers (Seeley G. Mudd Library, Princeton University).

87 Churchill to Ismay, 17 July 1940, PREM 3/475/1. For fuller discussion of material in this and the next two paragraphs see Reynolds, *The Creation of the Anglo-American Alliance*, esp. pp. 113–32, 158–60, 167–8.

88 Churchill to Roosevelt, tel., 20 May 1940, FO 371/24192, A3261/1/51.

89 Cabinet minutes, CAB 65/10, WM 299 (40) 4.

90 Churchill to Foreign Secretary, 20 Dec. 1940, PREM 4/25/8, p. 502.

91 In May 1923 Stanley Baldwin had urged his predecessor as Tory leader, Austen Chamberlain, to take the post. See Keith Middlemas and John Barnes, *Baldwin: A Biography* (London, 1969), pp. 175–6; Sir Charles Petrie, *The Life and Letters of the Right Hon. Sir Austen Chamberlain* (London, 1940), II, pp. 221–2. In May 1979 Margaret Thatcher offered the Washington Embassy to the former Conservative leader, Edward Heath.

92 Churchill, *Secret Session Speeches*, p. 14. A few days later Churchill recalled: 'I was strongly pressed in the House of Commons in the Secret Session to give assurances that the present Government and all its Members were resolved to fight on to the death, and I did so, taking personal responsibility for the resolve of all.' (Churchill to Halifax, 26 June 1940, FO 800/322, p. 277.)

93 General Henry H. Arnold, diary of visit to England, 24 April 1941, p. 20, Arnold papers, box 271 (Library of Congress, Washington, D.C.). Beaverbrook was often prone to defeatist moods, but the same cannot be said of the others. (Sir John Dill was Chief of the Imperial General Staff, Sir Wilfred Freeman was Vice-Chief of the Air Staff and Sir Archibald Sinclair was Secretary of State for Air.) Similar views had been expressed to Arnold a few days before by, among others, the First Lord of the Admiralty, A. V. Alexander (*ibid.*, p. 14, 21 April).

94 Hinsley, *British Intelligence*, I, chs. 8, 11, 13, 14, esp. pp. 248–9, 347, 355, 429, 470–83.

95 As he put it in a telegram to Roosevelt on 1 July (PREM 3/469, p. 212).

10. Britain and the Russian entry into the war

The following abbreviations are used to designate repositories and collections:

CAB: Cabinet papers in the Public Record Office.
WO: War Office papers in the Public Record Office.
Avon: Avon papers in Birmingham University Library.
Dalton diary, in the library, London School of Economics.
Cadogan diary, in the Churchill College Cambridge archives.
Harvey diary, in the British Library.
Portal: Portal papers, Christ Church, Oxford.

Auchinleck: Auchinleck papers in Manchester University Library.
BBK: Beaverbrook papers, in the House of Lords Record Office.
Brooke diary, in the archives centre, King's College, London.
Dep. Monckton Trustees: Monckton papers in the Bodleian Library, Oxford.

1 Foreign Office to Moscow, 2 June 1941, appended to WM(41)56, CAB 65/18.
2 Eden to Baggallay, 10 June 1941, Avon SU/41/16.
3 Eden to Baggallay, 13 June 1941, Avon SU/41/16.
4 *Ibid.*
5 Eden to Baggallay, 24 June 1941, Avon SU/41/19.
6 Eden to Churchill, 24 June 1941, Avon SU/41/18; Eden to Baggallay, 24 June 1941, Avon SU/41/19; Eden to Cripps, 30 June 1941, Avon SU/41/24.
7 Eden to Cripps, 7 July 1941, Avon SU/41/32.
8 Eden to Cripps, 9 July 1941, Avon SU/41/33.
9 *Ibid.*
10 Eden to Cripps 16 and 21 July, Avon SU/41/37 and SU/41/43.
11 Cabinet, 9 July 1941, WM(41)67, CAB 65/19; Mason MacFarlane to Dill, 14 July 1941, WO 216/124
12 Stalin to Churchill, 18 July 1941 in Foreign Office to Moscow of 20 July 1941, SU/41/41
13 Eden to Cripps, 18 July 1941, Avon SU/41/38.
14 Cabinet, 23 and 30 June 1941, WM(41) 62 and WM(41)64, CAB 65/18.
15 Cabinet, 26 June 1941, WM(41)63, CAB 65/18.
16 Cadogan diary, 28 June 1941; Pownall diary 29 June 1941.
17 Kennedy note for 29 June, in J. Kennedy, *The Business of War*, ed. B. Ferguson, (London, 1957), p. 148.
18 Cabinet, 30 June 1941, WM(41)64, CAB 65/18; Cadogan diary, 30 June 1941.
19 Dalton diary, 1 July 1941; Cadogan diary, 2 July 1941.
20 Cadogan diary, 3 July 1941; Cabinet, 4 July 1941, WM(41)65, CAB 65/19.
21 Cabinet 4 July 1941, WM(41)65, CAB 65/19.
22 Harvey diary, 6 July 1941; Cadogan diary, 8 July 1941.
23 Cabinet, 14 July 1941, WM(41)69, CAB 65/19.
24 Cripps to Eden, 29 June 1941, Avon SU/41/21; Cripps to Eden, 2 July 1941, Avon SU/41/26.
25 Mason MacFarlane to Dill, 14 July 1941, WO 216/124.
26 Dalton diary, 1 July 1941; Kennedy note for 22 June, Kennedy, *Business of War*, p. 147.
27 Mason MacFarlane to Dill, 14 July 1941, WO 216/124.
28 *Ibid.*
29 Eden to Baggallay, 13 June 1941, Avon SU/41/17.
30 Churchill to Roosevelt, 15 June 1941, W. Churchill, *The Second World War*, III; *The Grand Alliance* (London, 1950), p. 330.
31 Defence committee, 17 June 1941, DO(41)42, CAB 69/2.
32 Defence committee, 16 June 1941, DO(41)41, CAB 69/2.
33 Defence committee, 17 June 1941, DO(41)42, CAB 69/2.
34 Colville note in Churchill, *Second World War*, p. 331.
35 Broadcast, 22 June 1941, in *The Unrelenting Struggle. War Speeches by the Rt. Hon. W. S. Churchill*, ed. C. Eade (London, 1942), pp. 176–80.

36 Churchill to Stalin, 7 and 21 July 1941, Avon SU/41/31 and SU/41/42; Cripps to Eden, 26 July 1941, Avon SU/41/48.
37 Broadcast, 22 June 1941.
38 Cabinet, 30 June 1941, WM(41)64, CAB 65/18; Churchill to Stalin 7 July 1941, Avon SU/41/31.
39 Churchill to Portal, 7 July 1941, Portal:2:7, Cabinet, 10 July 1941, WM(41)68 CAB 65/19.
40 Defence committee, 21 July 1941, DO(41)52, CAB 69/2; Churchill to Stalin, 25 July 1941, Avon SU/41/46.
41 Churchill to first lord and first sea lord, 10 July 1941, in Churchill, *Second World War*, pp. 341–2.
42 *Ibid*; also Churchill to Stalin, 7 July 1941, Avon SU/41/31.
43 Eden to Cripps, 7 July 1941, Avon SU/41/32.
44 Churchill to Stalin, 21 July 1941, Avon SU/41/42.
45 *Ibid*; also cabinet 24 July 1941, WM(41)73, CAB 65/19.
46 Cadogan diary, 9 July 1941; Harvey diary, 9 July 1941.
47 Churchill to first lord and first sea lord, 10 July 1941, Churchill, *Second World War*, pp. 341–2.
48 Defence committee, 7 July 1941, DO(41)47, CAB 69/2; Eden to Churchill, c. 8 July 1941, BBK D/338.
49 Churchill to Stalin, 21 July 1941, Avon SU/41/42.
50 Defence committee, 25 June 1941, DO(41)44, CAB 69/2.
51 Churchill to Auchinleck, 1 July 1941, WO 216/13.
52 Churchill to Auchinleck, 6 July 1941, circulated to defence committee on 25 July 1941, CAB 69/3.
53 *Ibid*.
54 Defence committee, 17 July 1941, DO(41)51, CAB 69/2; also Churchill to Auchinleck, 20 July 1941, Auchinleck 288.
55 Chiefs of staff, 21 July 1941, COS(41)254, CAB 79/13.
56 Cabinet, 2 June 1941, WM(41)56, CAB 65/18.
57 Foreign Office to Moscow, appended to WM(41)56, CAB 65/18.
58 Cabinet, 9 June 1941, WM(41)58, CAB 65/18 and CAB 65/22.
59 *Ibid*; also Eden to Churchill, 9 June 1941, Avon SU/41/15.
60 Eden to Baggallay, 13 June 1941, Avon SU/41/17.
61 Eden diary, 5 June 1941; cabinet, 5 June 1941, WM(41)57, CAB 65/18.
62 Memorandum of conversation between Monckton and Maisky, 6 June 1941, Dep. Monckton Trustees:5:96; Harvey diary, 11 August 1941.
63 Eden to Churchill, 24 June 1941, Avon SU/41/18; defence committee, 4 July 1941, DO(41)46, CAB 69/2.
64 Harvey diary, 8 July 1941.
65 Eden to Churchill, c. 8 July 1941, BBK D338.
66 *Ibid*.
67 *Ibid*.
68 Harvey diary, 9 July 1941; Brooke diary, 10 July 1941.
69 Harvey diary, 9 and 16 July 1941.
70 Harvey diary, 16 July 1941.
71 Harvey diary, 10 July 1941.
72 Smuts to Eden, with Eden notes, 3 June 1941, Avon, Dom 41/7.
73 Eden to Cripps, 2 June 1941, appended to WM(41)56, CAB 65/18.
74 *Ibid*.

75 *Ibid.*
76 Defence committee, 25 June 1941, DO(41)44, CAB 69/2.
77 Cabinet, 30 June 1941, WM(41)64, CAB 65/18.
78 *Ibid*; also Harvey diary, 6 July 1941.
79 Cabinet, 24 July 1941, WM(41)73, CAB 65/19.
80 Cabinet, 10 July 1941, WM(41)68, CAB 65/19, Harvey diary, 16 July 1941.
81 Cabinet, 17 July 1941, WM(41)71, CAB 65/19.
82 Eden to Churchill, 22 July 1941, in Churchill, *Second World War* pp. 424–5.
83 *Ibid*; cabinet 28 and 31 July 1941, WM(41)75 and WM(41)76, CAB 65/19.
84 Cabinet and confidential annex, 31 July 1941, WM(41)76, CAB 65/19 and CAB 65/23.
85 S. Aster, *Anthony Eden* (London, 1976), pp. 8–9; W. Rees Mogg, *Sir Anthony Eden* (London, 1956), p. 24; D. Carlton, *Anthony Eden* (London, 1981), p. 13.
86 Rees Mogg, *ibid.*
87 Cadogan diary, 5 July 1941; Harvey diary 12 July 1941; Cabinet, 17 July 1941, WM(41)71, CAB 65/19.
88 Harvey diary, 12 July 1941; cabinet, 24 July 1941, WM(41)74, CAB 65/19.
89 Cabinet, 24 July 1941, WM(41)74, CAB 65/19.
90 Cabinet, 9 June 1941, WM(41)58, CAB 65/18 and CAB 65/22.
91 Chiefs of staff, 21 June 1941, COS(41)220, CAB 79/12, Brooke diary, 17 June 1941.
92 Defence committee, 25 June 1941, DO(41)44, CAB 69/2; Kennedy note for 25 June 1941, Kennedy, *Business of War*, pp. 141–2;Cadogan diary, 30 June 1941; Dill to Montgomery Massinberd, 4 July 1941, MM 160/18; Dill to Auchinleck, 16 July 1941, Auchinleck 283.
93 Chiefs of staff, 23 June 1941, COS(41)221, CAB 79/12.
94 Chiefs of staff, 7 July 1941, COS(41)235, CAB 79/12; Defence committee, 7 July 1941, DO(41)47, CAB 69/2.
95 Chiefs of staff, 23 June 1941, COS(41)221, CAB 79/12; Portal to Peirse, 7 July 1941, Portal:9:1941:33A; Portal to Churchill, 7 July 1941, Portal:2:7A.
96 Defence committee, 17 July 1941, DO(41)51, CAB 79/12.
97 Defence committee, 3 and 10 July 1941, DO(41)45 and DO(41)50, CAB 69/2; cabinet, 24 July 1941, WM(41)73, CAB 65/19, CAB 65/23; chiefs of staff, 10 and 24 July 1941, COS(41)239 and COS(41)260, CAB 79/12 and CAB 79/13.
98 Chiefs of staff 24 and 26 June 1941, COS(41)222 and COS(41)225, CAB 79/12; chiefs of staff 1, 7 and 9 July 1941, COS(41)230, COS(41)235, COS(41)238, CAB 79/12; defence committee 3 and 7 July 1941, DO(41)45 and DO(41)47, CAB 69/2.
99 Chiefs of staff, 20 June 1941, COS(41)218, CAB 79/12.
100 Draft directive, annex to chiefs of staff, 24 June 1941, COS(41)223, CAB 79/12; chiefs of staff to commanders in chief, Far East, appended to chiefs of staff, 26 June 1941, COS(41)225, CAB 79/12.
101 Chiefs of staff, 26 and 30 June 1941, COS(41)225 and COS(41)229, CAB 79/12; chiefs of staff, 2 July 1941, COS(41)231, CAB 79/12.
102 Chiefs of staff, 14 July 1941, COS(41)244, CAB 79/12.

11. *Crowning the revolution: the British, King Peter and the path to Tito's cave*

A longer version of this paper was presented to the Third Anglo-Yugoslav Colloquium on the History of the Second World War at the Imperial War Museum in December 1982. I am grateful to Sir William Deakin for having invited me to participate.

Abbreviations and acronyms
SOE   Special Operations Executive.
ELAS   National Popular Liberation Army (Ellinikos Laikos Apeleftherotikos Stratos) – the military arm of EAM
EAM   National Liberation Front (Ethnikon Apeleftherotikon Metopon)
AVNOJ   Antifascist Council of National Liberation of Yugoslavia (Antifašističko veće narodnog oslobodjenja Jugoslavije)
BLOs   British liaison officers
AWOL   Absent without leave
OSS   Office of Strategic Services
MI3b   Military Intelligence (European Country Section).

1 FO 371/37610, R6619/143/92, Brief of 20/7/43.
2 FO 371/37593, R4802/17/92, Memorandum of 28/5/43 by the Permanent Under-Secretary of State. For an account of how and why Yugoslavia's restoration became a British war aim, see my *Britain and the War for Yugoslavia, 1940–1943* (New York and Boulder, 1980), ch. 4.
3 See Elisabeth Barker, *Churchill and Eden at War* (London 1978), ch. 22.
4 FO 371/33454, R2384/151/92, Minute by P. Dixon, 12/4/42.
5 FO 371/33433, R6810/12/92, Minute of 14/11/42.
6 FO 371/37639, R2580/2578/92, Minutes by Sargent, Cadogan and Law, 25–26/3/43.
7 FO 371/37639, R3280/2578/92. Letter of 9/4/43.
8 FO 371/37625, R4538/198/92, Minutes of 23–25/5/43.
9 FO 371/37593, R4802/17/92, Memoranda by Cadogan of 28 and 31/5/43.
10 FO 371/37624, R3617/198/92. Letter to Churchill, 31/3/43; FO 371/37593, R5270/17/92, Exchange of minutes between Churchill and Eden, 11–14/6/43.
11 FO 371/37625, R6005/198/92, Minutes of 11/7/43. Churchill censored the version of his minute published in his war history. Winston S. Churchill, *The Second World War*, vol. v (London, 1952), pp. 571–2.
12 FO 371/37595, *passim*.
13 FO 371/37596, R6745/17/92, Minute of 26/7/43.
14 FO 371/37596, R7001/17/92, Minute of 29/7/43.
15 FO 371/37596, R7157/17/92, Minutes of 3–4/8/43.
16 FO 371/37596, R7245/17/92, Minute by Howard of 9/8/43.
17 FO 371/37596, R7463/17/92, Minutes by Howard and Sargent of 11/8/43.
18 FO 371/37626, *passim*.
19 FO 371/37611, R7276/143/92, Despatch of 4/8/43.
20 FO 371/37612, R9579/143/92, Telegram and minutes of 3–4/10/43.
21 FO 371/37613, R10072/143/92, Telegrams of 10 and 17/10/43.
22 FO 371/37613, R10152/143/92, Minute of 15/10/43.
23 PREM 3; 66/2, Telegrams and minutes 3–9/10/43.

24 FO 371/37614, R10940/143/92, Telegrams and minutes 30/10–3/11/43. Eden was absent in Moscow for the big three foreign ministers' conference. He had taken with him a briefing paper by Stevenson which affirmed the old faith in the dynasty as the sole unifying element in Yugoslavia and ruled out any break with Mihailović. FO 371/37613, R10562/143/92, Paper of 9/10/43.

25 FO 371/37615, R11458/143/92, Minute of 2/11/43, Telegram of 4/11/43; R11735/143/92, Telegrams of 11 and 19/11/43.

26 FO 371/37614, R11248/143/92, Telegram of 5/11/43.

27 FO 371/37184, R11941/6780/67, Minutes of meeting, 7/11/43.

28 FO 371/37591, R11411/2/92, Telegram and minutes of 8–9/11/43.

29 FO 371/37615, R11528/143/92, Telegram and minutes, 11–15/11/43.

30 FO 371/37615, R11639/143/92, Telegrams and minutes, 11–17/11/43.

31 FO 371/37616, R11783/143/92, Telegrams and minutes, 14–21/11/43.

32 FO 371/37615, R11589/143/92, Maclean report of 6/11/43, printed and distributed as a War Cabinet paper.

33 *Ibid.* for Chiefs' of Staff views (Minute of 16/11/43 by V. Cavendish-Bentinck); FO 371/37617, R12759/143/92, Telegram of 26/11/43 for reactions of Joint Intelligence Committee and Vice-Chiefs of Staff.

34 FO 371/37615, R11589/143/92, Minutes by Rose, Howard, Sargent, Cadogan and Eden, 16–20/11/43.

35 FO 371/37616, R11921/143/92, R11922/143/92, R12012/143/92, R12036/143/92 (Telegrams from Stevenson relaying reports by Armstrong and Cope), R12204/143/92 (Minute by Howard of 22/11/43 summarizing the about face).

36 FO 371/37591, R13299/2/92, Telegram SE/27. Another message from Armstrong was even more insistent that Mihailović, his movement and the Serbs of Serbia could not be dissociated. FO 371/37591, R13154/2/92, Telegram of 3/12/43.

37 FO 371/37617, R12701/143/92, Telegrams from and to Stevenson of 3 and 6/12/43, Telegram to Washington of 7/12/43.

38 FO 371/37591, R12862/2/92, Minutes of 10–11/12/43.

39 FO 371/37618, R13053/143/92. Telegram from Stevenson of 11/12/43, minutes by Howard, Sargent and Eden of 12–14/12/43. It is uncertain whether Mihailović was meant actually to blow up the two specified railway bridges by the deadline of 29 December, or merely to signify his agreement to do so by that date. It was the impossibility of citing to the Yugoslav King and government (or to Parliament) a chapter and verse account of Mihailović's transgressions based on intercepts of German radio signals that formed a large part of the rationale behind the 'test operation'.

40 FO 371/37591, R13954/2/92, Minutes of 17–20/12/43 by Cadogan, Eden and Sargent.

41 FO 371/37619, R13467/143/92, R13469/143/92, Telegrams from Stevenson of 20/12/43, Minutes by A. R. Dew and Sargent of 21 and 22/12/43.

42 FO 371/37619, R13493/143/92, Telegram of 20/12/43. See Elisabeth Barker's explanation of the misapprehension which probably encouraged this fantastic idea in Phyllis Auty and Richard Clogg, eds., *British Policy towards Wartime Resistance in Yugoslavia and Greece* (London, 1975), p. 42. The Soviets also encouraged such hopes, presumably because of their anger at the 'stab in the back' which Tito had supposedly administered to the Teheran decisions by his unannounced AVNOJ resolutions. Ambassador

F. T. Gusev's helpful note of 20/12/43 in which Yugoslav unity was commended is contained in FO 371/37619, R13613/143/92.
43 FO 371/37619, R13491/143/92, Telegram from Stevenson of 21/12/43, Minutes by Dew and Sargent of 21/12/43.
44 *Ibid.*, Telegram to Stevenson of 23/12/43.
45 FO 371/37619, R13688/143/92, Telegrams from and to Stevenson of 24 and 25/12/43.
46 FO 371/37620, R13715/143/92, Telegrams from and to Stevenson of 25/12/43, minutes by Dew, Sargent and Eden of 26–28/12/43.
47 PREM 3; 511/2, Telegram of 26/12/43 to Eden.
48 FO 371/44242, R138/8/92, Minutes of 22/12/43 by Dew, Cadogan and Eden, telegram to Stevenson of 23/12/43.
49 PREM 3; 511/2, Telegram from Churchill to Eden, 29/12/43.
50 PREM 3; 511/2, Telegram to Eden of 27/12/43.
51 FO 371/37620, R13731/143/92 (Telegram to Stevenson of 28/12/43) and R13913/143/92 (Especially the minute by Sargent of 31/12/43).
52 PREM 3; 511/2, Telegram to Churchill of 29/12/43.
53 PREM 3; 511/2, Telegrams from Churchill to Eden and from Jacob to Hollis of 1/1/44.
54 PREM 3; 511/2, Telegram to Eden of 30/12/43.
55 PREM 3; 511/2, Telegram to Eden of 2/1/44, Frozen 1057.
56 PREM 3; 511/2, Telegram to Eden of 2/1/44, Frozen 1058.
57 PREM 3; 511/2, Telegram to Eden of 2/1/44, Frozen 1058.
58 PREM 3; 511/2, Telegrams Grand 1049 of 4/1/44 and Frozen 1112 of 5/1/44. The final version of Churchill's first letter to Tito (dated 8/1/44) is printed in *The Second World War*, vol. v, pp. 416–17.
59 PREM 3; 511/2, Telegram Frozen 1132 of 6/1/44.
60 PREM 3; 511/2, Telegram Grand 1217 of 7/1/44.
61 FO 371/44242, R22/8/92, Minute by Dew of 2/1/44 on an intelligence report suggesting that the Partisans were not so much communists as nationalists and democrats.
62 PREM 3; 511/2, Telegram Frozen 1184 of 9/1/44.
63 PREM 3; 511/2, Telegram Frozen 1187 of 9/1/44.
64 FO 371/44244, R739/8/92, (Memorandum for the War Cabinet of 10/1/44) and R700/8/92 (Cabinet minutes of 11/1/44).
65 FO 371/44244, R740/8/92, Minutes by Dew, Eden and Dixon, 10–13/1/44.
66 FO 371/44245, R840/8/92 and R1114/8/92, Minutes by Howard of 18 and 19/1/44.
67 PREM 3; 511/2, Memorandum of 19/1/44. The resistance of the Foreign Office was weakened in these days by the arrival of Cairo's long-promised and very damning dossier on Četnik collaboration with the Axis – a summary of which was sent to the Prime Minister (see FO 371/44244, R656/8/92) – as well as by several reports from Bailey and Armstrong suggesting that Četnik misdeeds were continuing (see FO 371/44246, *passim*). In addition, an MI3b appreciation of the military situation requested by the Foreign Office concluded on 26/1/44 that none of the twenty-three Axis divisions in Yugoslavia 'would be freed for employment elsewhere by the disintegration of the forces under General Mihailović's control'. FO 371/44246, R1396/8/92.
68 FO 371/44246, R1419/8/92, R1422/8/92, R1423/8/92, R1501/8/92, Telegrams from Stevenson of 25–28/1/44 and minutes by Howard, Sargent and Eden of 27–29/1/44.

69 FO 371/44246, R1508/8/92, Telegrams, minutes and memoranda 28/1–4/2/44. Tito's reply arrived on 3 February.
70 FO 371/44247, R2146/8/92.
71 PREM 3; 511/9, Churchill's minutes to Eden of 11, 12 and 19/2/44; FO 371/44247, R2197/8/92 (Minutes by Rose, Howard, Cadogan and Eden of 11–12/2/44) and R2204/8/92 (Prime Minister's minute to General Ismay of 11/2/44).
72 FO 371/44247, R2435/8/92 (Tito's telegram to Churchill of 9/2/44, held up in Cairo until 15/2/44 for clarification of corrupt passages) and R2409/8/92 (Maclean's exegesis of 10/2/44, also held up until 15/2/44).
73 FO 371/44247, R2349/8/92, Record of a conversation on 6/2/44.
74 FO 371/44247, R2571/8/92.
75 FO 371/44247, R2435/8/92, Minutes by Howard and Sargent of 15 and 16/2/44.
76 FO 371/44247, R2411/8/92.
77 FO 371/44247, R2571/8/92.
78 FO 371/44248, Minute PM/44/87 of 19/2/44. Eden, who as Leader of the House was sensitive to backbench opinion, protested at the gift of so large a 'bouquet' to Tito and so galling a potion to Mihailović's parliamentary supporters. For the texts of both the telegram to Tito and the speech to the Commons see *The Second World War*, vol. v, pp. 420–21.
79 FO 371/44249, R3494/8/92. In the first draft of this telegram the names of eight other exiled politicians were mentioned as possibilities. The hope was expressed that dissatisfied Serbs from Mihailović's movement might also be considered.
80 FO 371/44250, R4147/8/92 (Minutes by Rose, Howard, Cadogan and Eden of 11–14/3/44) and R4148/8/92 (Bailey's report of 14/3/44).
81 FO 371/44290, R4550/44/92 (Minutes of meeting by Howard) and R4149/8/92 (Bailey's telegram of 16/3/44 to Cairo for Armstrong).
82 FO 371/44290, R4550/44/92, Minute from Eden to Churchill of 16/3/44.
83 FO 371/44304, R4368/439/92, Letter from Peter to Churchill of 13/3/44. The Prime Minister was outraged at the hostile reaction which the marriage provoked among Serbs, and particularly at the suggestions from Cairo that Peter ought to abdicate in favour of his younger brother Tomislav: 'If Peter goes', Churchill thundered, 'we shall back Tito whole-heartedly.' The Serbs' odd views about wartime marriages were of a piece with their abysmal failure to manage their own affairs. FO 371/44305, R5605/439/92, Despatch from Broad to Eden of 29/3/44; FO 371/44254, R6639/8/92, Telegram from Churchill to Broad of 19/4/44.
84 FO 371/44250, R4249/8/92 (Telegram from Maclean to Churchill of 9/3/44) and R4250/8/92 (Telegram from Maclean to Churchill of 13/3/44, minutes by Howard and Sargent of 18 and 19/3/44, minute from Churchill to Eden of 18/3/44.)
85 FO 371/44250, R4533/8/92, Minutes by Howard, Sargent and Cadogan of 20/3/44, Memoranda from and to Churchill of 19 and 21/3/44.
86 FO 371/44251, R5021/8/92 (Tito's telegram which reached London on 29/3/44) and R4963/8/92 (Maclean's telegram to Churchill of 27/3/44).
87 FO 371/44269, R4937/11/92, Telegram from Armstrong and SOE Cairo of 23/3/44, minutes by Bailey, Howard and Sargent of 2/4/44. W/T sets were to be left with various Četnik commanders just in case.

88 FO 371/44251, R4963/8/92, Minute from Eden to Churchill of 31/3/44.
89 FO 371/44309, R5728/658/92, Minute from Churchill to Eden of 1/4/44.
90 FO 371/44309, R5730/658/92, Minute from Eden to Churchill of 6/4/44.
91 FO 371/44309, R6007/658/92, Record of conversations on 13 and 14/4/44;
    PREM 3; 511/9, War Cabinet minutes, Confidential Annex to 48th Conclu-
    sions, 13/4/44.
92 FO 371/44309, R6088/658/92, Telegram from Churchill to Molotov of
    14/4/44.
93 FO 371/44331, R6673/1270/92, Telegrams from and to Molotov of 22 and
    23/4/44; FO 371/44310, R6713/658/92, Minutes of a conversation between
    Churchill and Eden on 24/4/44 by Dixon for Sargent.
94 FO 371/44294, R6760/195/92, Telegram of 26/4/44.
95 FO 371/44309, R6688/658/92, Minutes by Stevenson of 20/4/44 and
    Howard of 27/4/44. The King denied in his ghosted memoirs ever having
    asked the Ban to come to London. *A King's Heritage* (London, 1955), pp.
    147–8.
96 FO 371/44294, R195/195/92 and R1816/195/92.
97 FO 371/44294, R7671/195/92.
98 The most circumstantial account can be found in Ilija Jukić, *The Fall of
    Yugoslavia* (New York, 1974), pp. 232–4, although Jukić was not in London
    at the time. Maclean seems to have regarded Šubašić as an OSS protégé. FO
    371/44270, R6399/11/92. It need be no cause for wonder that the Roosevelt
    administration was capable of speaking with many voices at this or any other
    time. Nonetheless it is remarkable that both the President (who rebuffed in
    May Peter's pathetic plea of 17 April to save him, a fatherless child, from
    British pressure) and Donovan should act as helpmates to Churchill in a
    campaign deprecated by the State Department and contradicted by the pro-
    Četnik activities of the lower echelons of OSS.
99 FO 371/37611, R7276/2/92, Despatch by Rendal of 4/8/43.
100 FO 371/44325, R7110/850/92, Minutes by Rose, Howard and Sargent of
    4–7/5/44; FO 371/44305, R6806/439/92, Memorandum by Stevenson of 28/
    4/44.
101 Barker, *Churchill and Eden at War*, pp. 276–8.
102 FO 371/43636, R7380/68/67, Minutes from Churchill to Eden of 4/5/44 and
    from Eden to Churchill of 9/5/44.
103 FO 371/43646, R9092/349/67, Memorandum of 4/6/44 by Sargent and
    Howard considered by the War Cabinet on 7/6/44.
104 Churchill, *The Second World War*, vol. VI, p. 65; Herbert Feis, *Churchill–
    Roosevelt–Stalin* (Princeton, 1967), pp. 340–1. Churchill's wording was
    ambiguous. He may have been flying a kite.
105 FO 371/44290, R7213/44/92. Bailey regularly reiterated his belief that the
    choice lay between the extremes of reforming the Četniks under the King and
    affording Tito every encouragement to overrun Serbia as quickly as possible.
    FO 371/44290, R7680/44/92. Nor was Hudson's proposal entirely novel. He
    had recommended a similar solution in September 1942. The Foreign Office
    had then been unable to conceive of how the raggle-taggle Partisans could be
    impressed by assurances of post-war political freedom. See my *Britain and the
    War for Yugoslavia*, pp. 180–1.
106 FO 371/44290, R7679/44/92.
107 FO 371/44290, R7340/44/92.

108 FO 371/44310, R7560/658/92, R7833/658/92, R7834/658/92.
109 FO 371/44310, R7835/658/92.
110 FO 371/44310, R7946/658/92.
111 FO 371/44290, R7947/44/92.
112 FO 371/44290, R8118/44/92, Telegram from Broad of 21/5/44.
113 Kosta St Pavlović, 'Pad Purićeve vlade' ('The Fall of Purić's Government'), *Glasnik srpskog istorisko-kulturnog društvo 'Njegoš'*, no. 7 (June 1961), pp. 20–5.
114 FO 371/44310 and FO 371/44311, *passim*. Churchill's message to Tito of 25/5/44 is on FO 371/44365, R8322/6132/92.
115 FO 371/44311, R8816/658/92.
116 FO 371/44257, R8628/8/92 (Minute by Rose of 2/6/44) and R8899/8/92 (Minute by Eden of 30/5/44).
117 PREM 3; 514, Telegram to Wilson of 4/6/44.
118 FO 371/44291, R9323/44/92, Minutes by the Prime Minister, Stevenson, Cadogan and Eden of 5–7/6/44.
119 FO 371/44258, R8992/8/92, Telegram from Maclean to Wilson and Churchill of 6/6/44.
120 PREM 3; 512/7, Telegram to Wilson of 9/6/44 and minute to Eden of 8/6/44 here partially conflated.
121 FO 371/44290, R9247/44/92 (Record of meeting on 9/6/44 by Stevenson); Churchill sent a telegram to Wilson the next day in which he made it plain that *he* still hoped that Peter would proceed with Šubašić to Vis (R9247/44/92). He also had delivered to the King, just prior to departure, a message invoking 'the blessings of Providence' on 'Your Majesty's spirited adventure'. PREM 3; 512/7, Note of 10/6/44; FO 371/44291, R9423/44/92, Letter to Tito of 10/6/44.
122 FO 371/44290, R9249/44/92, Telegram from Macmillan to Eden of 11/6/44.
123 Milovan Djilas, *Wartime* (London, 1977), p. 395; Stevenson's amusing account of the Vis discussions – including the texts of the agreements – is on FO 371/44259, R10457/8/92.
124 FO 371/44259, R10457/8/92. Actually as chief of staff to the King, the supreme commander.
125 FO 371/44312, R9591/658/92, R9649/658/92.
126 PREM 3; 512/5, Minute to Eden of 19/6/44.
127 FO 371/44291, R9809/44/92.
128 FO 371/44312, R9591/658/92 (Minutes by Reed, Dew, Sargent, Cadogan and Eden of 19/6/44) and R9675/658/92 (Minute by Dew of 20/6/44 and telegram to Stevenson of 21/6/44).
129 FO 371/44291, R9809/44/92, Telegram from Stevenson of 21/6/44.
130 Elisabeth Barker, 'Serbia 1944' (an unpublished paper presented to the Anglo-Yugoslav Colloquium, Imperial War Museum, London, 1978).
131 FO 371/44291, R9921/44/92, Minutes by Dew of 24/6/44 and Eden of 26/6/44.

12. *Franklin Roosevelt and Unconditional Surrender*

1 M. E. Howard, *Grand Strategy*. Vol. IV. *August 1942–September 1943* (London, 1972), pp. 284–5. The most vehement attack remains that of Anne Armstrong, *Unconditional Surrender* (New Brunswick, N.J., 1961). Without

attempting a full list, one may remark that military historians are at least as critical of the doctrine as diplomatic historians; and that those who write more kindly of it are usually Americans with a broad general sympathy for Roosevelt's politics. See, for example, R. G. O'Connor, *Diplomacy for Victory. FDR and Unconditional Surrender* (New York, 1971) and Robert Dallek, *Franklin D. Roosevelt and American Foreign Policy, 1932–1945* (New York, 1979), pp. 373–6.

2 See, for examples, Philip E. Mosely, 'Dismemberment of Germany. The Allied Negotiations from Yalta to Potsdam' in *Foreign Affairs*, 28:3, April 1950, pp. 487–98, and 'The Occupation of Germany. New Light on How the Zones Were Drawn', *ibid.*, 28:4, July 1950, pp. 580–603; Carl J. Friedrich and associates, *American Experiences in Military Government in World War II* (New York, 1948); and Walter L. Dorn, 'The Debate over American Occupation Policy in Germany in 1944–1945' in the *Political Science Quarterly*, 72:4, December 1957, pp. 481–501.

3 Winston S. Churchill, *The Second World War*. Vol. III. *The Grand Alliance* (London, 1950), p. 539.

4 Maurice Matloff, 'Franklin Delano Roosevelt as War Leader' in Harry L. Coles (ed.), *Total War and Cold War. Problems in Civilian Control of the Military* (Columbus, Ohio, 1962), pp. 42–65.

5 Robert E. Sherwood, *Roosevelt and Hopkins. An Intimate History* (New York, 1948), pp. 227, 360, 697, 756, 855.

6 A. E. Housman, 'The Application of Thought to Textual Criticism' in *Selected Prose* (ed. John Carter, Cambridge, 1962), pp. 132–3.

7 *Foreign Relations of the United States. The Conferences at Washington, 1941–1942, and Casablanca, 1943* (Washington, D.C., 1968), pp. 506, 635, 727, 833–7, 847–9; Winston S. Churchill, *The Second World War*. Vol. IV. *The Hinge of Fate* (London, 1951), pp. 612–16; Sherwood, *Roosevelt and Hopkins*, pp. 695–7; Albert C. Wedemeyer, *Wedemeyer Reports!* (New York, 1958), p. 186; Forrest C. Pogue, *George C. Marshall: Organizer of Victory* (New York, 1973), pp. 32–5.

8 Elliott Roosevelt, *As He Saw It* (New York, 1946), pp. 117–19; W. Averell Harriman and Elie Abel, *Special Envoy to Churchill and Stalin 1941–1946* (New York, 1975), pp. 188, 190; Dallek, *Roosevelt and American Foreign Policy*, pp. 375–6.

9 Herbert Feis, *Churchill, Roosevelt, Stalin. The War They Waged and the Peace They Sought* (Princeton, N. J., 1957), p. 108.

10 Feis, *Churchill, Roosevelt, Stalin*, chs. 5, 6; Christopher Thorne, *Allies of a Kind. The United States, Britain and the war against Japan, 1941–1945* (London, 1978), ch. 10; Dallek, *Roosevelt and American Foreign Policy*, pp. 347–72; Pogue, *Marshall*, chs. 1, 2; Matloff, 'Roosevelt as War Leader', pp. 44–54.

11 Roosevelt may, of course, have had more than one purpose in mind; he often had. But in this matter the verdict of Sherwood, *Roosevelt and Hopkins*, p. 697, is persuasive. See also Harley A. Notter, *Postwar Foreign Policy Preparation 1939–1945* (Washington, D.C., 1950), p. 163, and Dallek, *Roosevelt and American Foreign Policy*, p. 374. For Eisenhower see Stephen E. Ambrose, *The Supreme Commander: The War Years of General Dwight D. Eisenhower* (Garden City, N.Y., 1970), pp. 125–36.

12 Ambrose, *The Supreme Commander*, p. 235.

13 The fullest critical account known to me is Robert J. Quinlan, 'The Italian Armistice' in Harold Stein (ed.), *American Civil–Military Decisions. A Book of Case Studies* (Birmingham, Ala., 1963), pp. 203–310, to which I am much indebted.

14 Ambrose, *The Supreme Commander*, p. 253

15 *Ibid.*, p. 266.

16 Winston S. Churchill, *The Second World War*. Vol. v. *Closing the Ring* (London, 1952), p. 91; Ambrose, *The Supreme Commander*, pp. 239, 243.

17 Major-General J. F. C. Fuller, *The Second World War 1939–45. A Strategical and Tactical History* (London, 1948), p. 268; Stein (ed.), *American Civil-Military Decisions*, p. 310.

18 On attempts to measure and influence public opinion, as on other aspects of the State Department's work, the indispensable guide through archives even now poorly arranged remains Notter, *Postwar Foreign Policy Preparation*. See also Wallace Carroll, *Persuade or Perish* (Boston, 1948).

19 Armstrong, *Unconditional Surrender*, pp. 127, 137–47, 187, and more generally chs. 3, 4.

20 John P. Glennon, ' "This Time Germany is a Defeated Nation" ': The Doctrine of Unconditional Surrender and Some Unsuccessful Attempts To Alter It, 1943–1944' in Gerald N. Grob (ed.), *Statesmen and Statecraft of the Modern West* (Barre, Mass., 1967) discusses many of these with full references.

21 Notter, *Postwar Foreign Policy Preparation*, passim; Dorn, 'The Debate Over American Occupation Policy', pp. 482–5; Jacob Viner, 'The Treatment of Germany' in *Foreign Affairs*, 23:4, July 1945, pp. 567–81.

22 Adam B. Ulam, *Expansion and Coexistence. The History of Soviet Foreign Policy, 1917–67* (London, 1968), p. 349. See also Vojtech Mastny, *Russia's Road to the Cold War. Diplomacy, Warfare, and the Politics of Communism, 1941–1945* (New York, 1979), chs. 4, 5.

23 Ambrose, *The Supreme Commander*, pp. 390–1; Glennon, 'This Time Germany Is a Defeated Nation', pp. 130–4.

24 John L. Chase, 'Unconditional Surrender Reconsidered', in the *Political Science Quarterly*, 70:2, June 1955, pp. 258–79, citing (p. 267) Allen W. Dulles, *Germany's Underground* (New York, 1947). I have not found a later reference making the point.

25 *Foreign Relations of the United States. The Conference at Quebec, 1944* (Washington, D.C., 1972), pp. 360–2, 466–7; Dallek, *Roosevelt and American Foreign Policy*, pp. 472–5. On the Morgenthau plan in general see John M. Blum, *From the Morgenthau Diaries*, Vol. III, *Years of War, 1941–1945* (Boston, 1967) chs. 7, 8.

26 Cit. Ambrose, *The Supreme Commander*, p. 390. A full discussion of the debate may be found in Paul Y. Hammond, 'Directives for the Occupation of Germany: The Washington Controversy' in Stein (ed.), *American Civil-Military Decisions*, pp. 311–464. See also the references in note 2 above.

27 Cit. Bruce Kuklick, *American Policy and the Division of Germany. The Clash with Russia over Reparations* (Ithaca, N.Y., 1972), pp. 27, 59. See also Tony Sharp, *The Wartime Alliance and the Zonal Division of Germany* (Oxford, 1975).

28 Brian L. Villa, 'The U. S. Army, Unconditional Surrender and the Potsdam Proclamation' in the *Journal of American History*, 63:1, June 1976, pp. 66–92, sets out the debate, including that within the State Department, and the

problem well. The description in Thorne, *Allies of a Kind*, of Iwo Jima as 'only 750 miles from Tokyo' and of the landing on Okinawa as 'an even greater blow' (p. 520) reads ironically.

13. Crimes against peace: the case of the invasion of Norway at the Nuremberg Trials

I am grateful to Professor Carl-Axel Gemzell and my colleague Dr David Saunders for their comments on earlier versions of this paper.

1 The invasion of Denmark, a subsidiary operation which took place at the same time, is not discussed in this paper because it was not a source of controversy at Nuremberg.

2 F. J. P. Veale, *Advance to Barbarism* (Appleton, Wisconsin, 1953), p. 169.

3 Liddell Hart, *History of the Second World War* (London, 1970), pp. 58–9.

4 E.g. Lord Hankey, *Politics, Trials and Errors* (Oxford, 1950), pp. 60–5, 70–9. Hankey was a member of the British War Cabinet when the plans for action in Scandinavia were under discussion.

5 C. A. Pompe, *Aggressive War an International Crime* (The Hague, 1953), pp. 246–8; Michael Walzer, *Just and Unjust Wars* (London, 1978), p. 249; Michael Biddiss, 'The Nuremberg Trial: Two Exercises in Judgment', *Journal of Contemporary History*, xvi (1981), 597–615 (p. 610).

6 Smith, *Reaching Judgment at Nuremberg* (London, 1977), pp. 148–51.

7 Eugene Davidson, *The Trial of the Germans* (New York, 1966), pp. 374–9 (see also note 80 below); Smith, *Reaching Judgment*, pp. 148–51, 241–7. Davidson's book contains many inaccuracies and displays a rather naive acceptance of the defence's viewpoint on a number of contentious issues, including Norway.

8 *Trial of the Major War Criminals before the International Military Tribunal* (42 Vols., Nuremberg, 1947–9) (hereafter cited as IMT. Proceedings (cited from the edition published in London, 1946–50): vols. 1–22; documents in evidence: vols. 23–42).

9 V. F. von der Lippe, *Nürnberger Tagebuchnotizen* (Frankfurt am Main, 1951).

10 R. West, *A Train of Powder* (London, 1955), p. 23.

11 For numerous illustrations of the obstacles facing the defence see von der Lippe, *passim*, and Davidson, *Trial of the Germans*, pp. 30–6.

12 Smith, *Reaching Judgment*, pp. 148–51, 241–7. See also p. 268 below.

13 Kurt Assmann, *Deutsche Schicksalsjahre* (Wiesbaden, 1950); *Deutsche Seestrategie in zwei Weltkriegen* (Heidelberg, 1957); Walther Hubatsch, *Die deutsche Besetzung von Dänemark und Norwegen* (Göttingen, 1952); 2nd, revised edition: *Weserübung* (Göttingen, 1960). For a similar 'western' interpretation see Alfred Vagts, *Defense and Diplomacy* (New York, 1956), pp. 315–17, 327–8.

14 Carl–Axel Gemzell, *Raeder, Hitler und Skandinavien* (Lund, 1965); Hans-Dietrich Loock, *Quisling, Rosenberg und Terboven* (Stuttgart, 1970). See also Loock's earlier polemical essay, 'Die deutsch-skandinavischen Beziehungen während des Zweiten Weltkrieges im Spiegel der deutschen Literatur', *Internationales Jahrbuch für Geschichtsunterricht*, 8 (1961/62), 260–76.

15 Johan Scharffenberg, *Norske aktstykker til okkupasjonens forhistorie* (Oslo, 1950).

16 Walzer, *Just and Unjust Wars*, pp. 242–50. But Walzer too (p. 249) falls into the trap of referring to the German invasion as a 'response' to the British mining of Norwegian waters.

17 Joan Beaumont, 'Great Britain and the Rights of Neutral Countries: The Case of Iran, 1941', *Journal of Contemporary History*, XVI (1981), 213–28 (p. 223).

18 Recent studies on this subject include, for the German side, Gemzell and Loock (note 14 above); for the Allied side, Patrick Salmon, 'Churchill, the Admiralty and the Narvik Traffic, September–November 1939', *Scandinavian Journal of History*, IV (1979), 305–26; 'British Plans for Economic Warfare against Germany 1937–1939: The Problem of Swedish Iron Ore', in Walter Laqueur (ed.), *The Second World War: Essays in Military and Political History* (London and Beverly Hills, 1982), pp. 31–49; Thomas Munch-Petersen, *The Strategy of Phoney War: Britain, Sweden and the Iron Ore Question 1939–1940* (Stockholm, 1981).

19 *Report of Robert H. Jackson, United States Representative to the International Conference on Military Trials, London, 1945* (Department of State Publication No. 3080, Washington, D.C.,1949).

20 *Jackson Report*, pp. 305–7.

21 *Ibid.*, pp. 303–4.

22 358 H.C. Deb. 5s, cols. 1833–1952; 360 H.C. Deb. 5s, cols. 906–13, 1073–1196, 1251–1366.

23 *Ny norsk kvitbok* (London, 1940); Monica Curtis (ed.), *Norway and the War September 1939 – December 1940* (London, 1941).

24 See pp. 257, 262 below.

25 Ribbentrop's speech of 27 April 1940 unveiling the documents published in White Book No. 4 (printed as an introduction to the volume and, in translation, in Curtis (ed.), *Norway and the War*, pp. 80–9) caused a flurry in British official circles: see the speech by Sir Samuel Hoare of 27 April (*Norway and the War*, pp. 89–90), and the curious attempt at a refutation by Ronald Scarfe ('With the collaboration of Military and Naval experts'), *In the Norwegian Trap* (London, 1940). The Germans also published foreign-language editions of the White Books, e.g. No. 4 as *Britain's Designs on Norway* (New York, 1940).

26 Minutes by Passant, 11 January 1946, and Woodward, 16 January 1946, Public Record Office (PRO), Foreign Office (FO) 371/57528, U212/120/73. All official documents cited subsequently are held in the PRO, unless otherwise stated.

27 Woodward minute, 29 January 1946, FO 371/57528, U212/120/73.

28 Text of German memoranda printed in *Documents on German Foreign Policy*, series D, vol. 9 pp. 88–92.

29 Opposing views on this doctrine are expressed in August von Knieriem, *The Nuremberg Trials* (Chicago, 1959), pp. 301–8, and Ian Brownlie, *International Law and the Use of Force by States* (Oxford, 1963), pp. 309–16.

30 For discussions of *tu quoque* at Nuremberg see von Knieriem, *The Nuremberg Trials*, pp. 309–15, and Robert K. Woetzel, *The Nuremberg Trials in International Law* (London, 1962), pp. 119–21.

31 *Jackson Report*, p. 361.

32 Von der Lippe, *Nürnberger Tagebuchnotizen*, p. 14; Raeder's final statement to the Court, IMT, 22, p. 397. Raeder was himself a historian, having written a two-volume contribution to the German official history, *Der Krieg zur See 1914–18* in 1920–22: Gemzell, *Raeder*, p. 150.

33 Maxwell Fyfe's memoirs, *Political Adventure: The Memoirs of the Earl of Kilmuir* (London, 1964), contain a lengthy account of Nuremberg, pp. 78–135, and Appendix: 'Nuremberg: the Legal Controversy', pp. 329–39. Extensive diary extracts are published in H. Montgomery Hyde, *Norman Birkett* (London, 1964), pp. 494–531. Another British participant, Airey Neave, the Secretary General of the Tribunal, published his recollections in *Nuremberg* (London, 1978). See also an account by an unofficial observer close to the British team: Sir John Wheeler-Bennett, *Friends, Enemies and Sovereigns* (London, 1976), pp. 25–57.

34 The distinction is perhaps overstated. It is worth nothing that there was also a body of opinion within the Foreign Office (including Beckett and the head of the German Department, J. M. Troutbeck) which felt that it would be unjust to deny the defence any reasonable opportunity to strengthen its case. Minutes of 12, 14 and 26 January 1946, FO371/57528, U212/120/73.

35 This may be deduced from the absence of other requests for guidance in the FO files. See also minute by R. A. Beaumont (War Crimes Section), 12 February 1946, FO 371/57538, U1662/120/73: 'The Norwegian issue is a separate and exceptional one. Here we fear counter-charges of a sort unlikely to be brought in any other connexion . . .'

36 Director of Military Intelligence to Joint Intelligence Committee (JIC), no date (*c.* 13 October 1945), FO 371/51036, U6864/29/73. For the origins of the intelligence section (headed by Wing Commander Peter Calvocoressi) see Shawcross to Ernest Bevin (Foreign Secretary), 5 September 1945, *ibid.*, and Cabinet Office to JIC, 3 October 1945, FO 371/51073, U7938/7535/73.

37 Statement by Roger Allen (FO) at JIC meeting, 16 October 1945, FO 371/51036, U6864/29/73.

38 FO 371/51036, U6864/29/73.

39 Dean, 'Note on Interview with Justice Jackson on 24th October', FO 371/50992, U8625/16/73 (also quoted in Smith, *Reaching Judgment*, pp. 87, 101).

40 1 November 1945: printed in Kilmuir, *Political Adventure*, pp. 104–5.

41 An FO brief of 11 November 1945 (reference FO 371/50992, U8660/16/73), apparently along the same lines as Dean's letter of 17 October, is now missing from the files: see the references in FO 371/50992, U8659/16/73, and Newton to Shawcross, 8 February 1946, FO 371/57528, U212/120/73.

42 IMT, 2, pp. 73–5, 176–98.

43 Von der Lippe, *Nürnberger Tagebuchnotizen*, pp. 58–9.

44 *Ibid.*

45 *Ibid.*, pp. 15, 21.

46 BWCE to FO, 4 January 1946, FO 371/57528, U212/120/73.

47 *Nürnberger Tagebuchnotizen*, p. 9.

48 *Ibid.*, p. 179.

49 It is not clear whether they were permitted actually to meet at Nuremberg, or whether the defence lawyers acted as intermediaries.

50 I am indebted to Professor Gemzell for this information, and for his permission to publish it. His own reconstruction of the background to

Raeder's Nuremberg testimony (*Raeder*, pp. 312–26) is essentially the same, in greater detail, as the one attempted here, minus this one crucial point.

51 IMT, 14, pp. 145–8.
52 *Ibid.*, pp. 289–90. Raeder and Schulte Mönting were of course unaware of the actual British interest in Scandinavia at this time.
53 Gemzell, *Raeder*, pp. 213–15.
54 *Ibid.*, pp. 294–307.
55 *Ibid.*, pp. 308–12.
56 *Ibid.*, pp. 337–9. See also note 13 above.
57 IMT, 2, p. 179.
58 Smith, *Reaching Judgment*, p. 249; Neave, *Nuremberg*, p. 206.
59 Smith, *Reaching Judgment*, p. 246; Hyde, *Birkett*, p. 518. The *Times* correspondent at Nuremberg described Siemers and Kranzbühler as the two most skilful defence lawyers at Nuremberg: a view of the former at variance with his report cited below, note 113: R. W. Cooper, *The Nuremberg Trial* (London, 1947), p. 247.
60 Described sceptically in Neave, *Nuremberg*, pp. 200–13.
61 *Ibid.*, p. 204. See p. 262 below.
62 BWCE to FO, 1 December 1945, FO 371/50999, U9568/16/73.
63 Dean minute, 10 December 1945, *ibid.* Romilly's own account of his capture (in Giles Romilly and Michael Alexander, *The Privileged Nightmare* (London, 1954), pp. 3–23), states only that he was sent by his paper from Stockholm to Narvik at the beginning of April 1940. His affidavit (note 74 below) provides little further detail. The *Express* may have had inside knowledge; however, rumours of impending action in Norwegian waters (many officially-inspired) were rife at this time.
64 BWCE to FO, 2 February 1946, FO 371/57537, U1312/120/73.
65 Woodward minute, 6 December 1946, FO 371/50999, U9568/15/73.
66 BWCE to FO, 4 January 1946, FO 371/57528, U212/120/73. The delay, excessive by Nuremberg standards, is inexplicable. It was not caused by the prosecution, which received the request only on 3 January. Perhaps it was due to the Christmas break. All minutes cited in this paragraph are from this file.
67 Passant minute, 11 January 1946.
68 Woodward minute, 16 January 1946.
69 Passant minute, 26 January 1946.
70 Minutes by Woodward, 29 January 1946, and others, 1–7 February 1946.
71 Newton to Shawcross, 8 February 1946, FO 371/57528, U212/120/73.
72 FO minutes, 5–19 February 1946. FO 371/57527, U1312/120/73.
73 Beaumont (FO) to Dean (Nuremberg), 19 February 1946, FO 371/57539, U1770/120/73; Beaumont minute, 7 March 1946, FO 371/57541, U2508/120/73.
74 Interrogatories and replies printed in IMT, 40, pp. 396–8; von der Lippe, *Nürnberger Tagebuchnotizen*, p. 216.
75 Shawcross to Newton, 19 February 1946, FO 371/57540, U2127/120/73.
76 *Ibid.*
77 FO correspondence on *Geheimakten* documents, FO 371/57541, U2440/120/73. The FO was told that it would be sent the Cabinet Office memorandum on 23 February: Beaumont minute, 23 February 1946, FO 371/57540, U2127/120/73. The next two items in this file, U2242 and U2245, have been 'retained in department'. The former appears to have been

a memorandum (?) by Beckett: see reference in FO 371/57543, U3038/120/73. The latter may therefore be the Cabinet Office memorandum.

78 Maxwell Fyfe to First Lord of the Admiralty, 5 February 1946, FO 371/57537, U1478/120/73.

79 Von der Lippe, *Nürnberger Tagebuchnotizen*, pp. 141, 176.

80 Davidson, *Trial of the Germans*, p. 390. Davidson consulted Kranzbühler, Siemers and von der Lippe, among others, when preparing his book. It is conceivable that they gave him this story in order to cover up the deception discussed above p. 258.

81 Von der Lippe, *Nürnberger Tagebuchnotizen*, p. 147.

82 *Ibid.*, pp. 162–3.

83 *Ibid.*, p. 170. The ruling was given in closed session.

84 IMT, 7, pp. 257–8.

85 Von der Lippe, *Nürnberger Tagebuchnotizen*, pp. 207–8, 249–51.

86 Maxwell Fyfe to Shawcross, 29 March 1946, FO 371/57544, U3419/120/73.

87 BWCE to FO, 14 March 1946; Beaumont minute, 16 March 1946, FO 371/57542, U2578/120/73.

88 Shawcross memorandum, 15 March 1946, FO 371/57543, U2995/120/73. All quotations in the next three paragraphs are from this memorandum, unless otherwise stated. Its substance was communicated by the FO to BWCE on 16 March 1946, and a detailed brief followed on 23 March, *ibid*. The file also contains an unsigned and undated narrative, 'Events leading up to the German invasion of Norway in April 1940' (this may be the Cabinet Office survey mentioned above, note 77), and 'Notes on Operations Stratford, Plan R.4 and Avonmouth', compiled by the War Office.

89 CAB 99/3, SWC(40)2; White Book No. 6, pp. 255–7.

90 CAB 65/6, WM (40)83; FO 371/24815, N3979/N3989/2/63.

91 Sargent minute, 20 March 1946, FO 371/57543, U2995/120/73.

92 Newton brief for Bevin, 20 March 1946, *ibid.*; Brook (Cabinet Office) to Sargent, 16 March 1946, FO 371/57544, U3269/120/73.

93 Bevin to Attlee, 27 March 1946, FO 371/57545, U3539/120/73; Brook minute, 29 March 1946, Prime Minister's files (PREM) 8/393.

94 Sargent minute, 20 March 1946, FO 371/57543, U2995/120/73. Sargent's remarks may have been given extra force by the fact that in 1939–40 he had been one of the strongest FO advocates of military intervention in Scandinavia.

95 FO 371/57545, U3539/120/73. Bevin appears to have been persuaded by Shawcross at a meeting with him on 22 March: see Bevin to Shawcross, 8 April 1946, FO 371/57544, U3419/120/73.

96 Minute of 29 March 1946, PREM 8/393.

97 Minute of 29 March 1946, *ibid.*; Keith Feiling's *Life of Neville Chamberlain* was published in 1946.

98 PREM 8/393 and FO 371/57545, U3539/120/73.

99 Maxwell Fyfe to Shawcross, 29 March 1946, FO 371/57544, U3419/120/73. Unless von der Lippe's diary entry (note 83 above) is erroneous, the delay in transmitting the request is again inexplicable. There is no indication as to when it was received by the prosecution.

100 FO to BWCE, 6 April 1946; Bevin to Shawcross, 8 April 1946, FO 371/57544, U3419/120/73; Neave to Siemers, 12 April 1946, IMT, 41, Document Raeder–130; von der Lippe, *Nürnberger Tagebuchnotizen*, p. 226.

101 Ibid., pp. 248–51, 264.
102 Ibid., pp. 248–51, 357–9, 385–6.
103 Ibid., pp. 258–60.
104 Maxwell Fyfe to Shawcross, 29 March 1946, FO 371/57544, U3419/120/73.
105 IMT, 12, pp. 423–32; von der Lippe, Nürnberger Tagebuchnotizen, pp. 248–51.
106 IMT, 13, pp. 1–2.
107 IMT, 14, pp. 120–9; von der Lippe, Nürnberger Tagebuchnotizen, p. 276.
108 Scott Fox (Paris) to FO and BWCE, 23 March 1946, FO 371/57544, U3182/120/73; FO to BWCE, 4 April 1940, FO 371/57545, U3804/120/73.
109 BWCE to FO, 17 May 1946, FO 371/57547, U5354/120/73.
110 IMT 41, Documents Raeder–41, 59, 77, 79, 82, 83, 85 (all from White Book No. 6) and 88 (from No. 5).
111 IMT, 14, pp. 145–56; von der Lippe, Nürnberger Tagebuchnotizen, pp. 277–8.
112 Smith, Reaching Judgment, p. 246.
113 'Raeder's Defence at Nuremberg', The Times, 17 May 1946, p. 3.
114 Reaching Judgment, p. 246.
115 Nürnberger Tagebuchnotizen, pp. 277–8.
116 BWCE to FO, 17 May 1946, FO 371/57547, U5354/120/73.
117 IMT, 14, pp. 283–316; von der Lippe, Nürnberger Tagebuchnotizen, pp. 185–6.
118 'The German Navy's "Clean War"', The Times, 23 May 1946, p. 3.
119 R. W. Cooper, The Nuremberg Trial, p. 253.
120 IMT, 14, pp. 183–235; von der Lippe, Nürnberger Tagebuchnotizen, pp. 280–1.
121 Ibid., p. 281.
122 BWCE to FO, 20 May 1946, FO 371/57548, U5415/120/73.
123 Naval war diary, quoted in Loock, Quisling, Rosenberg und Terboven, p. 259.
124 IMT, 12, p. 424.
125 IMT, 19, pp. 54–64; von der Lippe, Nürnberger Tagebuchnotizen, pp. 385–6.
126 IMT, 19, p. 424.
127 Reaching Judgment, pp. 148–51.
128 IMT, 22, pp. 434–7.
129 Ibid., pp. 507–12. In A Train of Powder, pp. 52–3, Rebecca West wrote: 'That submarine warfare cannot be carried on without inhumanity, and that we have found ourselves able to be inhumane . . . This nostra culpa of the conquerors might well be considered the most important thing that happened at Nuremberg. But it evoked no response at the time, and it has been forgotten.'
130 Pompe, Aggressive War, p. 221; Smith, Reaching Judgment, p. 17.
131 Jackson Report, p. 113.
132 Ibid., pp. 305–6.
133 Ibid., p. 84.

Bibliography of the writings of F. H. Hinsley

Command of the Sea, British Naval History, 1918–45, Christopher, 1950.

Hitler's Strategy, Cambridge University Press, 1951.

New Cambridge Modern History, volume xi (editor), Cambridge University Press, 1962.

Power and the Pursuit of Peace, Cambridge University Press, 1963.

Sovereignty, Watts, 1966.

Nationalism and the International System, Hodder and Stoughton, 1973.

British Foreign Policy under Sir Edward Grey (editor), Cambridge University Press, 1977.

British Intelligence in the Second World War, vol. 1 (with E. E. Thomas, C. F. G. Ransom and R. C. Knight), H.M.S.O., 1979.

British Intelligence in the Second World War, vol. 2 (with E. E. Thomas, C. F. G. Ransom and R. C. Knight), H.M.S.O., 1981.

British Intelligence in the Second World War, vol. 3 (with E. E. Thomas, C. F. G. Ransom and the late R. C. Knight), H.M.S.O., 1984.

Lectures and articles

'The Development of the European States System since the Eighteenth Century', *Transactions of the Royal Historical Society*, Fifth Series, vol. xi, 1961.

'Soviet Russia and International Law', *Disarmament and Arms Control*, vol. ii, no. 2, 1964.

The Causes of the First World War, St John's College Lecture, University of Hull, 1964.

'Reflections on the History of International Relations', in *A Century of Conflict, Essays for A. J. P. Taylor*, ed. Martin Gilbert, Hamish Hamilton, 1966.

'The Concept of Sovereignty and the Relations between States', *International Affairs*, xxi, 1967.

'The Causes of War: the Two World Wars Considered', *New Zealand Journal of History*, vol. i, no. 1, 1967.

'Nationalism and International Relations', in *Aberystwyth Papers, International Politics, 1919–1969*, ed. Brian Porter, Oxford University Press, 1972.

'The Modern Pattern of Peace and War', *Grotian Society Papers*, Studies in the history of the law of nations, ed. C. H. Alexandrowicz, Martinus Nijhoff, 1972.

'Immanuel Kant and the pattern of peace and war', in *Vom Staat des Ancien Regime zum modernen Parteienstaat*, Festschrift für Theodor Schieder, ed. Helmut Berding, Kurt Düwell, Lothar Gall, Wolfgang J. Mommsen, Hans-Ulrich Wehler, Oldenbourg, 1978.

The Fall and Rise of the Modern International System, the Arthur Yencken Memorial Lecture, Australian National University, 1980.

'The Rise and Fall of the Modern International System', the Martin Wight Memorial Lecture, *Review of International Studies*, vol. 8, no. 1, 1982.

'Reflections on the Debate about Nuclear Weapons', in *Unholy Warfare, The Church and the Bomb*, ed. David Martin and Peter Mullen, Blackwell, 1983.

Index

Printed in the United Kingdom
by Lightning Source UK Ltd.
98787UKS00001B/167-200